Collins
BIG ROAD ATLAS
BRITAIN

Contents

KU-043-333

Published by Collins
An imprint of HarperCollins Publishers
Westerhill Road, Bishopbriggs, Glasgow G64 2QT

www.harpercollins.co.uk

Copyright © HarperCollins Publishers Ltd 2011

Collins® is a registered trademark of HarperCollins Publishers Limited

Mapping generated from Collins Bartholomew digital databases

The grid on this map is the National Grid taken from the Ordnance Survey map with the permission of the Controller of Her Majesty's Stationery Office.

Please note that roads and other facilities which are under construction at the time of going to press, and are due to open before the end of 2011, are shown in this atlas as open. Roads due to open during 2012 or begin construction before the end of June 2012 are shown as 'proposed or under construction'.

Printed in China

Paperback ISBN 978 0 00 742737 6 Imp 001
Spiral ISBN 978 0 00 742736 9 Imp 001

e-mail: roadcheck@harpercollins.co.uk

Information on fixed speed camera locations provided by PocketGPSWorld.Com Ltd.

With thanks to the Wine Guild of the United Kingdom for help with researching vineyards.

Information regarding blue flag beach awards is current as of summer 2009. For latest information please visit www.blueflag.org.uk

CASTLE COVER
The 50+ Insurance Specialists

Europcar

See back pages for money-off vouchers and Castle Cover Insurance

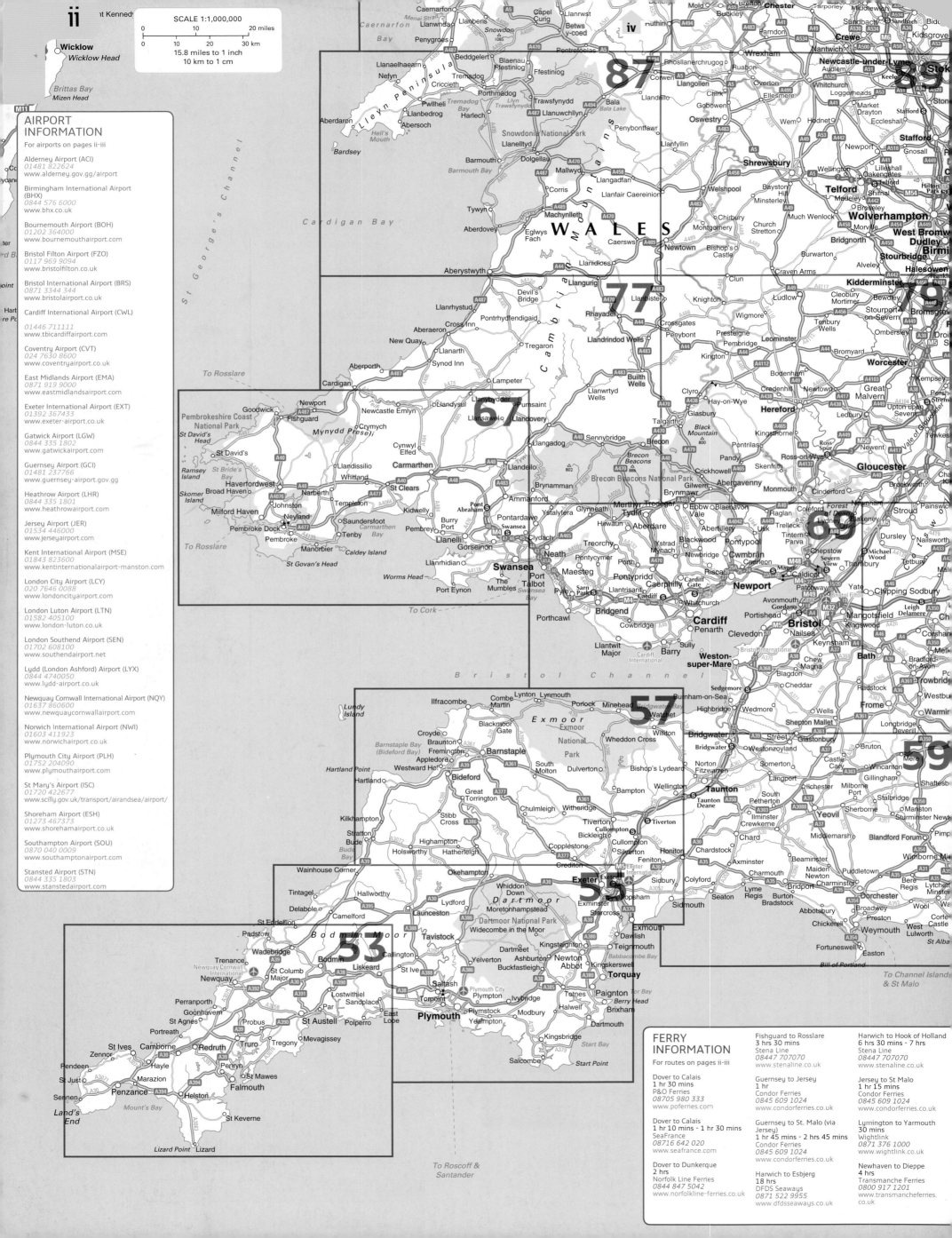

SCALE 1:1,000,000

0   10   20 miles
0   10   20   30 km

15.8 miles to 1 inch
10 km to 1 cm

AIRPORT INFORMATION
For airports on pages ii–iii

Alderney Airport (ACI)
01481 822624
www.alderney.gov.gg/airport

Birmingham International Airport (BHX)
0844 576 6000
www.bhx.co.uk

Bournemouth Airport (BOH)
01202 364000
www.bournemouthairport.com

Bristol Filton Airport (FZO)
0117 969 9094
www.bristolfilton.co.uk

Bristol International Airport (BRS)
0871 3344 344
www.bristolairport.co.uk

Cardiff International Airport (CWL)
01446 711111
www.tbicardiffairport.com

Coventry Airport (CVT)
024 7630 8600
www.coventryairport.co.uk

East Midlands Airport (EMA)
0871 919 9000
www.eastmidlandsairport.com

Exeter International Airport (EXT)
01392 367433
www.exeter-airport.co.uk

Gatwick Airport (LGW)
0844 335 1802
www.gatwickairport.com

Guernsey Airport (GCI)
01481 237766
www.guernsey-airport.gov.gg

Heathrow Airport (LHR)
0844 335 1801
www.heathrowairport.com

Jersey Airport (JER)
01534 446000
www.jerseyairport.com

Kent International Airport (MSE)
01843 823600
www.kentinternationalairport-manston.com

London City Airport (LCY)
020 7646 0088
www.londoncityairport.com

London Luton Airport (LTN)
01582 405100
www.london-luton.co.uk

London Southend Airport (SEN)
01702 608100
www.southendairport.net

Lydd (London Ashford) Airport (LYX)
0844 4740050
www.lydd-airport.co.uk

Newquay Cornwall International Airport (NQY)
01637 860600
www.newquaycornwallairport.com

Norwich International Airport (NWI)
01603 411923
www.norwichairport.co.uk

Plymouth City Airport (PLH)
01752 204090
www.plymouthairport.com

St Mary's Airport (ISC)
01720 422677
www.scilly.gov.uk/transport/airandsea/airport/

Shoreham Airport (ESH)
01273 467373
www.shorehamairport.co.uk

Southampton Airport (SOU)
0870 040 0009
www.southamptonairport.com

Stansted Airport (STN)
0844 335 1803
www.stanstedairport.com

FERRY INFORMATION
For routes on pages ii–iii

Dover to Calais
1 hr 30 mins
P&O Ferries
08705 980 333
www.poferries.com

Dover to Calais
1 hr 10 mins - 1 hr 30 mins
SeaFrance
08716 642 020
www.seafrance.com

Dover to Dunkerque
2 hrs
Norfolk Line Ferries
0844 847 5042
www.norfolkline-ferries.co.uk

Fishguard to Rosslare
3 hrs 30 mins
Stena Line
08447 707070
www.stenaline.co.uk

Guernsey to Jersey
1 hr
Condor Ferries
0845 609 1024
www.condorferries.co.uk

Guernsey to St. Malo (via Jersey)
1 hr 45 mins - 2 hrs 45 mins
Condor Ferries
0845 609 1024
www.condorferries.co.uk

Harwich to Esbjerg
18 hrs
DFDS Seaways
0871 522 9955
www.dfdsseaways.co.uk

Harwich to Hook of Holland
6 hrs 30 mins - 7 hrs
Stena Line
08447 707070
www.stenaline.co.uk

Jersey to St Malo
1 hr 15 mins
Condor Ferries
0845 609 1024
www.condorferries.co.uk

Lymington to Yarmouth
30 mins
Wightlink
0871 376 1000
www.wightlink.co.uk

Newhaven to Dieppe
4 hrs
Transmanche Ferries
0800 917 1201
www.transmancheferries.co.uk

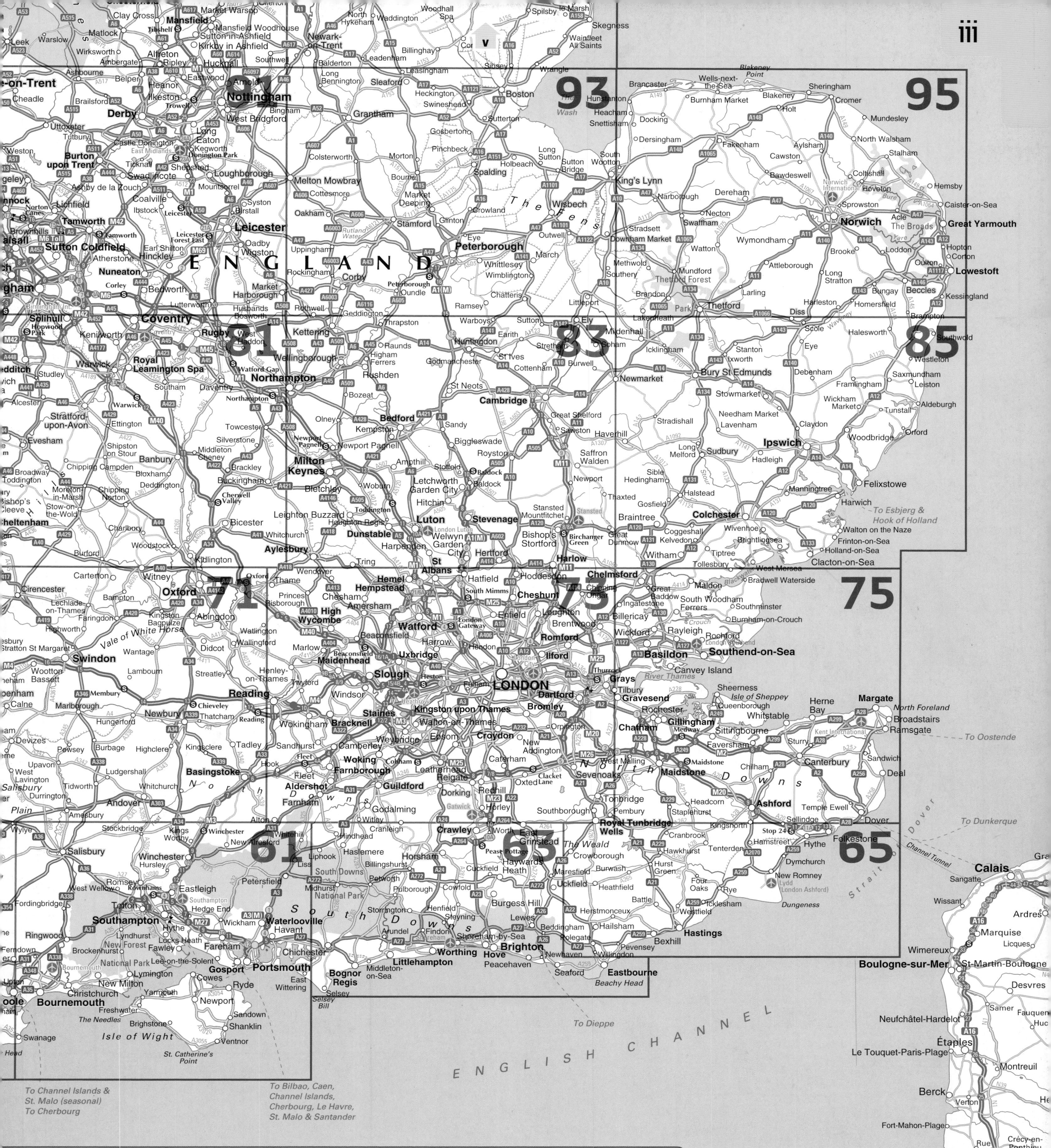

ENGLAND

ENGLISH CHANNEL

Pembroke to Rosslare
4 hrs
Irish Ferries
08717 300400
www.irishferries.co.uk

Plymouth to Roscoff
6 hrs - 8 hrs
Brittany Ferries
0871 244 0744
www.brittany-ferries.co.uk

Plymouth to Santander
20 hrs
Seasonal
Brittany Ferries
0871 244 0744
www.brittany-ferries.co.uk

Poole to Cherbourg
2 hrs 15 mins - 6 hrs 30
Brittany Ferries
0871 244 0744

Poole to Guernsey
2 hrs 30 mins
Seasonal
Condor Ferries
0845 609 1024
www.condorferries.co.uk

Poole to Jersey (via
Guernsey)
3 hrs 45 mins - 3 hrs 45 mins
Seasonal
Condor Ferries
0845 609 1024
www.condorferries.co.uk

Poole to St Malo
(via Guernsey & Jersey)
4 hrs 35 mins
Seasonal
Condor Ferries
0845 609 1024

Portsmouth to Bilbao
34 hrs
Brittany Ferries
0871 244 0744
www.brittany-ferries.co.uk

Portsmouth to Caen
3 hrs 45 mins - 7 hrs
Brittany Ferries
0871 244 0744
www.brittany-ferries.co.uk

Portsmouth to Cherbourg
3 hrs
Brittany Ferries
0871 244 0744
www.brittany-ferries.co.uk

Portsmouth to Cherbourg
5 hrs 30 mins
Condor Ferries
0845 609 1024
www.condorferries.co.uk

Portsmouth to Fishbourne
40 mins
Wightlink
0871 376 1000
www.wightlink.co.uk

Portsmouth to Guernsey
7 hrs
Condor Ferries
0845 609 1024
www.condorferries.co.uk

Portsmouth to Jersey (via
Guernsey)
10 hrs 30 mins
Condor Ferries
0845 609 1024
www.condorferries.co.uk

Portsmouth to Le Havre
3 hrs 15 mins - 8 hrs
LD Lines
0844 576 8836
www.ldlines.co.uk

Portsmouth to St. Malo
9 hrs - 10 hrs 45 mins
Brittany Ferries
0871 244 0744
www.brittany-ferries.co.uk

Portsmouth to Santander
24 hrs
Brittany Ferries
0871 244 0744
www.brittany-ferries.co.uk

Ramsgate to Oostende
4 hrs
Transeuropa Ferries
01843 595522
www.transeuropaferries.
co.uk

Southampton to East Cowes
55 mins
Red Funnel Ferries
0844 844 9988
www.redfunnel.co.uk

Swansea to Cork
10 hrs
Seasonal
Fastnet Line
0844 576 8831
www.fastnetline.com

Weymouth to Guernsey
2 hrs 10 mins
Condor Ferries
0845 609 1024
www.condorferries.co.uk

Weymouth to Jersey
(via Guernsey)
3 hrs 25 mins
Condor Ferries
0845 609 1024
www.condorferries.co.uk

Weymouth to St. Malo
(via Guernsey & Jersey)
5 hrs 15 mins
Condor Ferries
0845 609 1024
www.condorferries.co.uk

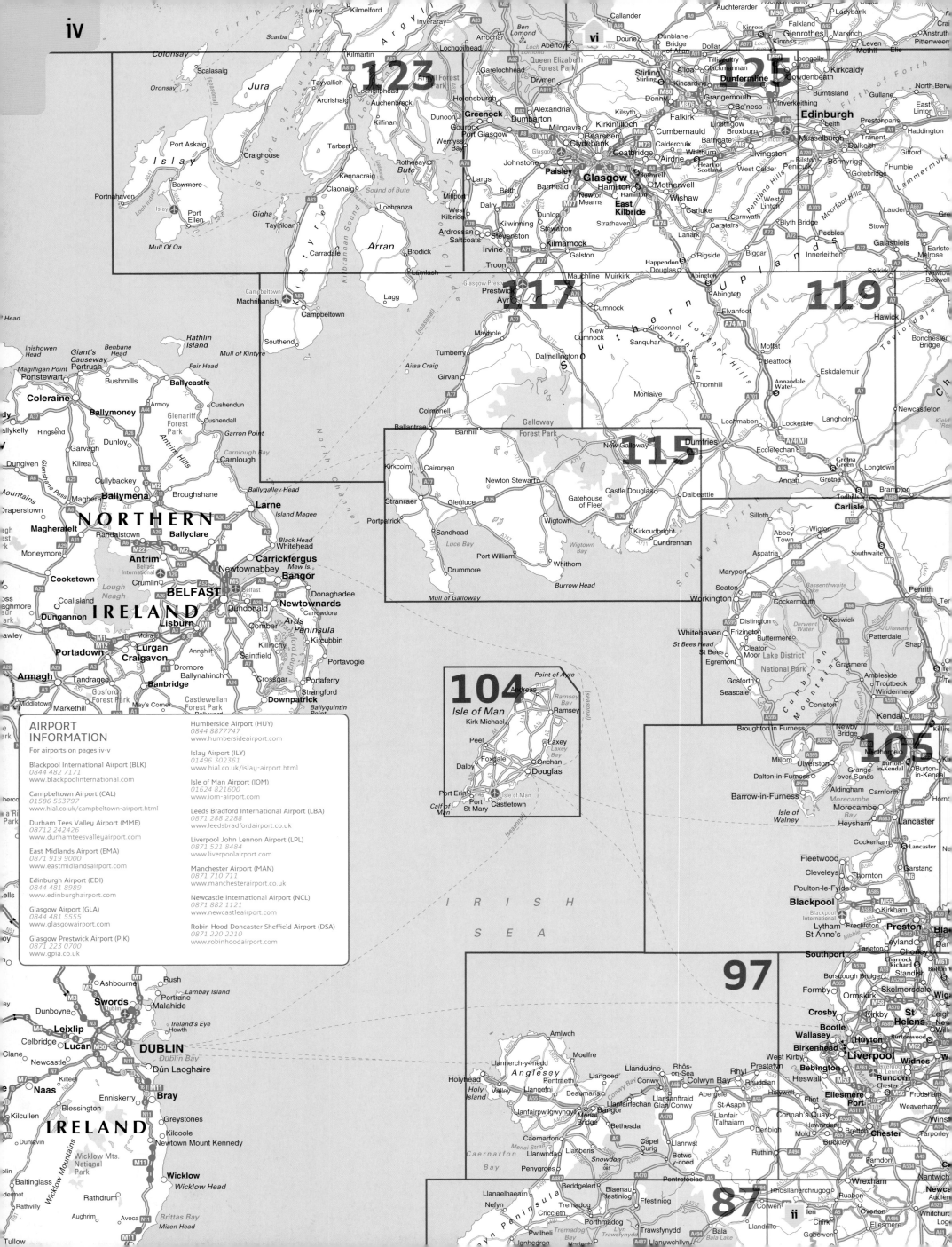

AIRPORT INFORMATION

For airports on pages iv-v

Blackpool International Airport (BLK)
0844 482 7171
www.blackpoolinternational.com

Campbeltown Airport (CAL)
01586 553797
www.hial.co.uk/campbeltown-airport.html

Durham Tees Valley Airport (MME)
08712 242426
www.durhamteesvalleyairport.com

East Midlands Airport (EMA)
0871 919 9000
www.eastmidlandsairport.com

Edinburgh Airport (EDI)
0844 481 8989
www.edinburghairport.com

Glasgow Airport (GLA)
0844 481 5555
www.glasgowairport.com

Glasgow Prestwick Airport (PIK)
0871 223 0700
www.gpia.co.uk

Humberside Airport (HUY)
0844 8877747
www.humbersideairport.com

Islay Airport (ILY)
01496 302361
www.hial.co.uk/islay-airport.html

Isle of Man Airport (IOM)
01624 821600
www.iom-airport.com

Leeds Bradford International Airport (LBA)
0871 288 2288
www.leedsbradfordairport.co.uk

Liverpool John Lennon Airport (LPL)
0871 521 8484
www.liverpoolairport.com

Manchester Airport (MAN)
0871 710 711
www.manchesterairport.co.uk

Newcastle International Airport (NCL)
0871 882 1121
www.newcastleairport.com

Robin Hood Doncaster Sheffield Airport (DSA)
0871 220 2210
www.robinhoodairport.com

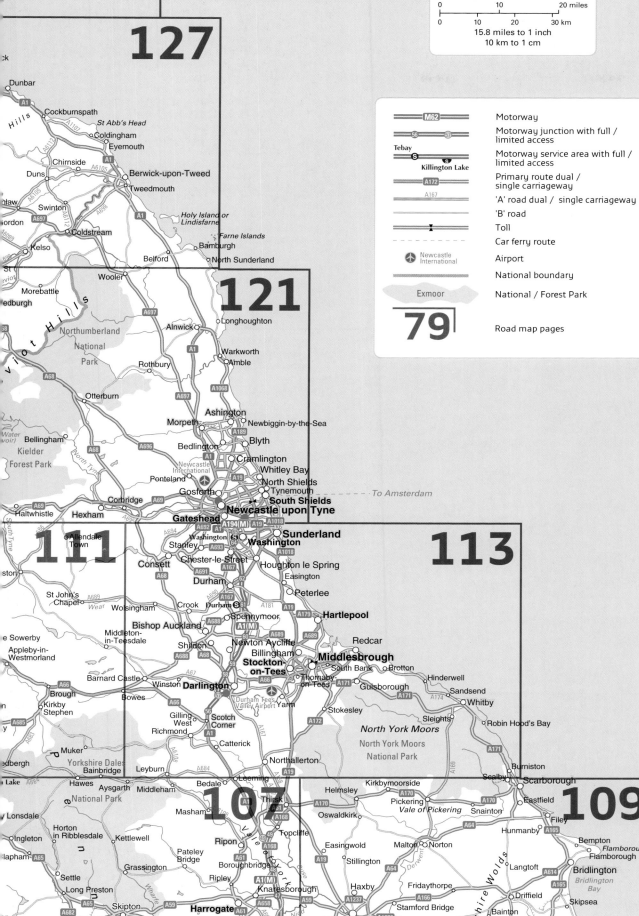
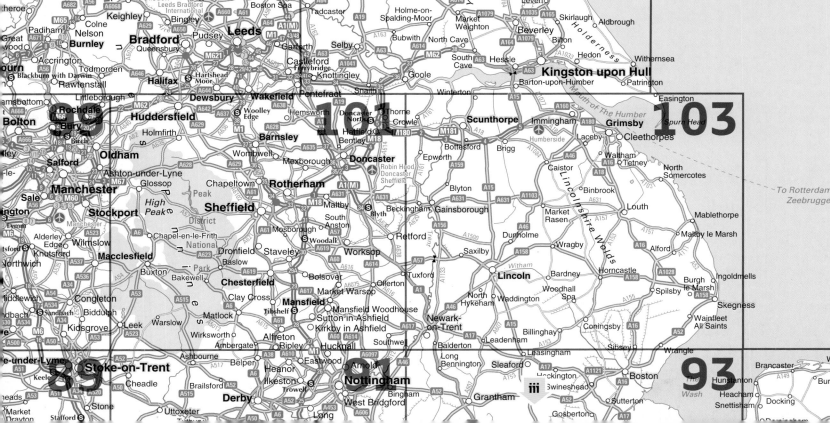

SCALE 1:1,000,000

0 — 10 — 20 miles
0 — 10 — 20 — 30 km
15.8 miles to 1 inch
10 km to 1 cm

M62	Motorway
Tebay / Killington Lake	Motorway junction with full / limited access
	Motorway service area with full / limited access
A172	Primary route dual / single carriageway
A167	'A' road dual / single carriageway
	'B' road
	Toll
Newcastle International	Car ferry route
	Airport
	National boundary
Exmoor	National / Forest Park
79	Road map pages

FERRY INFORMATION

For routes on pages iv-v

Ardrossan to Brodick
55 mins
All Year
Caledonian MacBrayne
08000 66 5000

Birkenhead to Belfast
8 hrs
All Year
Stena Line
0844 70 7070
www.stenaline.co.uk

Birkenhead to Douglas
4 hrs 15 mins
All Year
Isle of Man Steam Packet Co
08722 992 992

Cairnryan to Larne
1 hr - 1hr 45 mins
All Year
P&O Irish Sea
08716 64 2121
www.poirishsea.com

Claonaig to Lochranza
30 mins
Seasonal
Caledonian MacBrayne
08000 66 5000
www.calmac.co.uk

Colintraive to Rhubodach
5 mins
All Year
Caledonian MacBrayne
08000 66 5000
www.calmac.co.uk

Colonsay to Port Askaig
1 hr 20 mins
Seasonal
Caledonian MacBrayne
08000 66 5000
www.calmac.co.uk

Douglas to Belfast
2 hrs 55 mins
Seasonal
Isle of Man Steam Packet Co
08722 992 992

Douglas to Dublin
2 hrs 55 mins
Seasonal
Isle of Man Steam Packet Co
08722 992 992

Feolin to Port Askaig
5 mins
All Year
Argyll & Bute Council
01496 840681

Gourock to Dunoon
20 mins
All Year
Caledonian MacBrayne
08000 66 5000
www.calmac.co.uk

Gourock to Dunoon
20 mins
All Year
Western Ferries
01369 704452
www.western-ferries.co.uk

Heysham to Douglas
3 hrs 15 mins - 3 hrs 45 mins
All Year
Isle of Man Steam Packet Co
08722 992 992
www.steam-packet.com

Holyhead to Dublin
1 hr 50 mins - 3 hrs 15 mins
All Year
Irish Ferries
08717 300 400
www.irishferries.com

Holyhead to Dublin
2 hrs - 3 hrs 15 mins
All Year
Stena Line
08447 707070
www.stenaline.co.uk

Holyhead to Dún Laoghaire
2 hrs - 3 hrs 15 mins
All Year
Stena Line
08447 707070
www.stenaline.co.uk

Kennacraig to Port Askaig
2 hrs 5 mins
All Year
Caledonian MacBrayne
08000 66 5000
www.calmac.co.uk

Kennacraig to Port Ellen
2 hrs 20 mins
All Year
Caledonian MacBrayne
08000 66 5000
www.calmac.co.uk

Kingston upon Hull to Rotterdam
10 hrs - 11 hrs 15 mins
All Year
P&O Ferries
08716 64 2020
www.poferries.com

Kingston upon Hull to Zeebrugge
12 hrs 45 mins - 13 hrs 45 mins
All Year
P&O Ferries
08716 64 2020
www.poferries.com

Liverpool to Douglas
2 hrs 30 mins - 4 hrs 15 mins
All Year
Isle of Man Steam Packet Co
08722 992 992
www.steam-packet.com

Liverpool to Dublin
8 hrs
All Year
P&O Irish Sea
08716 64 2020
www.poirishsea.com

Newcastle to Amsterdam (Ijmuiden)
15 hrs
All Year
DFDS Seaways
0871 522 9955
www.dfdsseaways.co.uk

Stranraer to Belfast
2 hrs - 2 hrs 50 mins
All Year
Stena Line
08447 707070
www.stenaline.co.uk

Tarbert to Portavadie
25 mins
All Year
Caledonian MacBrayne
08000 66 5000
www.calmac.co.uk

Tayinloan to Gigha
20 mins
All Year
Caledonian MacBrayne
08000 66 5000
www.calmac.co.uk

Troon to Larne
1 hr 49 mins
Seasonal
P&O Ferries
08716 64 2121
www.poferries.com

Wemyss Bay to Rothesay
35 mins
All Year
Caledonian MacBrayne
08000 66 5000
www.calmac.co.uk

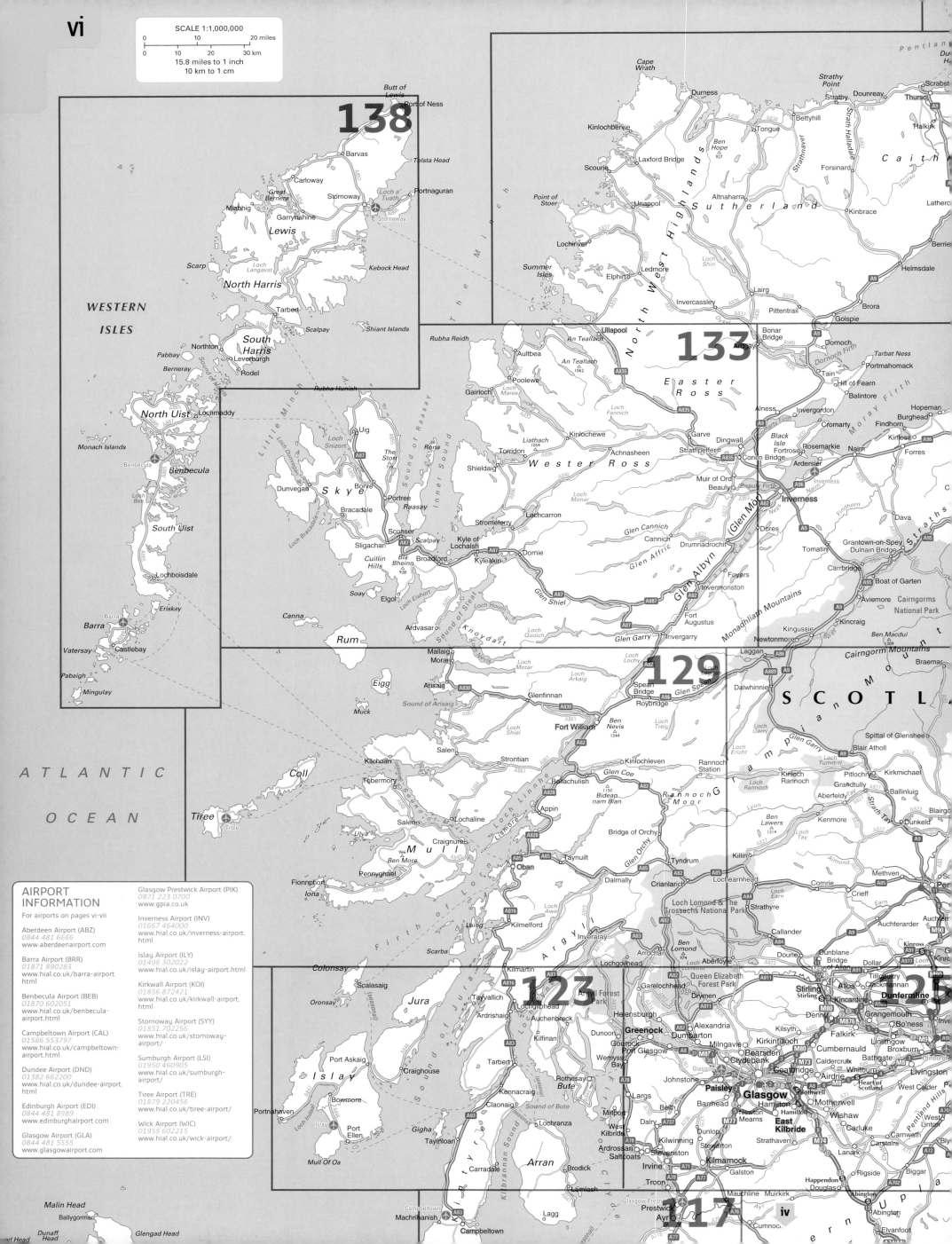

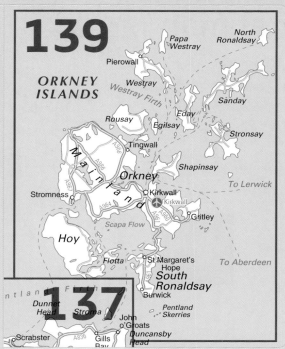

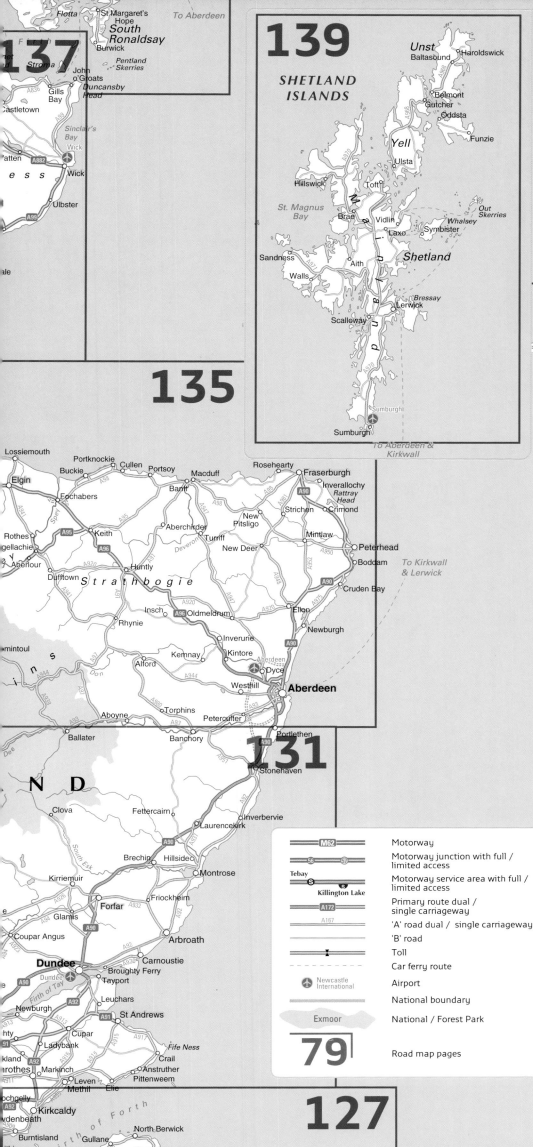

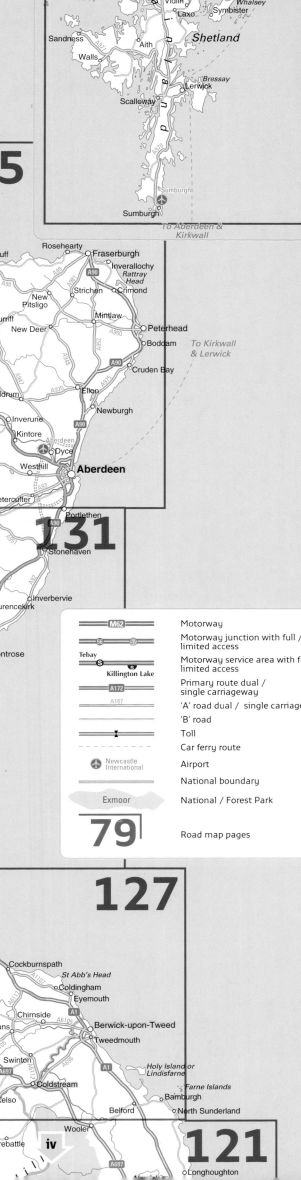

137

139
SHETLAND ISLANDS

139
ORKNEY ISLANDS

137

135

131

127

119

121

iv

Map legend

M62	Motorway
	Motorway junction with full / limited access
Tebay	Motorway service area with full / limited access
Killington Lake	
A1	Primary route dual / single carriageway
A167	'A' road dual / single carriageway
	'B' road
	Toll
	Car ferry route
Newcastle International	Airport
	National boundary
Exmoor	National / Forest Park
79	Road map pages

FERRY INFORMATION

For routes on pages vi-vii

Aberdeen to Kirkwall
6 hrs - 7 hrs 15 mins
All Year
North Link Ferries
0845 6000 449
www.northlinkferries.co.uk

Aberdeen to Lerwick
12 hrs 30 mins
All Year
North Link Ferries
0845 6000 449

Ardrossan to Brodick
55 mins
All Year
Caledonian MacBrayne
08000 66 5000
www.calmac.co.uk

Barra to Eriskay
40 mins
All Year
Caledonian MacBrayne
08000 66 5000
www.calmac.co.uk

Belmont to Gutcher
10 mins
All Year
Shetland Islands Council
01957 722259
www.shetland.gov.uk/ferries/

Belmont to Oddsta
30 mins
All Year
Shetland Islands Council
01957 722259
www.shetland.gov.uk/ferries/

Castlebay to Lochboisdale
1 hr 50 mins
All Year
Caledonian MacBrayne
08000 66 5000
www.calmac.co.uk

Claonaig to Lochranza
30 mins
Seasonal
Caledonian MacBrayne
08000 66 5000
www.calmac.co.uk

Coll to Tiree
55 mins - 1 hr
All Year
Caledonian MacBrayne
08000 66 5000
www.calmac.co.uk

Colonsay to Port Askaig
1 hr 20 mins
Seasonal
Caledonian MacBrayne
08000 66 5000
www.calmac.co.uk

Cromarty to Nigg
5 mins
Seasonal
Cromarty Ferry Company
01381 610269
www.cromarty-ferry.co.uk

Eday to Sanday
20 mins
All Year
Orkney Ferries
01856 872044
www.orkneyferries.co.uk

Eday to Stronsay
35 mins
All Year
Orkney Ferries
01856 872044
www.orkneyferries.co.uk

Egilsay to Rousay
20 mins
All Year
Orkney Ferries
01856 872044
www.orkneyferries.co.uk

Egilsay to Wyre
20 mins
All Year
Orkney Ferries
01856 872044
www.orkneyferries.co.uk

Gill's Bay to St. Margaret's Hope
1 hr
All Year
Pentland Ferries
01856 831226
www.pentlandferries.co.uk

Glenelg to Kylerhea
5 mins
Seasonal
Skye Ferry
01599 522273
www.skyeferry.co.uk

Gourock to Dunoon
20 mins
All Year
Caledonian MacBrayne
08000 66 5000
www.northlinkferries.co.uk

Gourock to Dunoon
20 mins
All Year
Western Ferries
01369 704452
www.western-ferries.co.uk

Gutcher to Oddsta
25 mins
All Year
Shetland Islands Council
01957 722259
www.shetland.gov.uk/ferries/

Houton to Flotta
30 mins
All Year
Orkney Ferries
01856 872044
www.orkneyferries.co.uk

Houton to Lyness
35 mins
All Year
Orkney Ferries
01856 872044
www.orkneyferries.co.uk

Kennacraig to Port Askaig
2 hrs 5 mins
All Year
Caledonian MacBrayne
08000 66 5000
www.calmac.co.uk

Kennacraig to Port Ellen
2 hrs 20 mins
All Year
Caledonian MacBrayne
08000 66 5000
www.calmac.co.uk

Kirkwall to Eday
1 hr 15 mins
All Year
Orkney Ferries
01856 872044
www.orkneyferries.co.uk

Kirkwall to North Ronaldsay
3 hrs
All Year
Orkney Ferries
01856 872044

Kirkwall to Papa Westray
1 hr 50 mins
All Year
Orkney Ferries
01856 872044

Kirkwall to Sanday
1 hr 25 mins
All Year
Orkney Ferries
01856 872044

Kirkwall to Shapinsay
25 mins
All Year
Orkney Ferries
01856 872044

Kirkwall to Stronsay
1 hr 35 mins
All Year
Orkney Ferries
01856 872044

Kirkwall to Westray
1 hr 25 mins
All Year
Orkney Ferries
01856 872044

Largs to Cumbrae Slip
10 mins
All Year
Caledonian MacBrayne
08000 66 5000
www.calmac.co.uk

Laxo to Symbister
30 mins
All Year
Shetland Islands Council
01806 566259
www.shetland.gov.uk/ferries/

Lerwick to Bressay
5 mins
All Year
Shetland Islands Council
01595 743974
www.shetland.gov.uk/ferries/

Lerwick to Kirkwall
7 hrs 15 mins - 7 hrs 45 mins
All Year
North Link Ferries
0845 6000 449
www.northlinkferries.co.uk

Lerwick to Skerries
2 hrs 30 mins
All Year
Shetland Islands Council
01806 515226
www.shetland.gov.uk/ferries/

Leverburgh to Berneray
1 hr
All Year
Caledonian MacBrayne
08000 66 5000
www.calmac.co.uk

Lochaline to Fishnish
15 mins
All Year
Caledonian MacBrayne
08000 66 5000
www.calmac.co.uk

Longhope to Flotta
30 mins
All Year
Orkney Ferries
01856 872044
www.orkneyferries.co.uk

Longhope to Lyness
30 mins
All Year
Orkney Ferries
01856 872044
www.orkneyferries.co.uk

Luing to Seil
5 mins
All Year
Oban Tourist Information Centre
01631 563122

Lyness to Flotta
30 mins
All Year
Orkney Ferries
01856 872044
www.orkneyferries.co.uk

Mallaig to Armadale
30 mins
All Year
Caledonian MacBrayne
08000 66 5000
www.calmac.co.uk

Oban to Castlebay
4 hrs 50 mins
All Year
Caledonian MacBrayne
08000 66 5000
www.calmac.co.uk

Oban to Coll
2 hrs 45 mins
All Year
Caledonian MacBrayne
08000 66 5000
www.calmac.co.uk

Oban to Colonsay
2 hrs 20 mins
All Year
Caledonian MacBrayne
08000 66 5000
www.calmac.co.uk

Oban to Craignure
45 mins
All Year
Caledonian MacBrayne
08000 66 5000
www.calmac.co.uk

Oban to Lismore
50 mins
All Year
Caledonian MacBrayne
08000 66 5000
www.calmac.co.uk

Oban to Lochboisdale
5 hrs 20 mins
All Year
Caledonian MacBrayne
08000 66 5000
www.calmac.co.uk

Oban to Tiree
3 hrs 30 mins - 4 hrs 15 mins
All Year
Caledonian MacBrayne
08000 66 5000
www.calmac.co.uk

Rousay to Wyre
5 mins
All Year
Orkney Ferries
01856 872044
www.orkneyferries.co.uk

Sconser to Raasay
15 mins
All Year
Caledonian MacBrayne
08000 66 5000

Scrabster to Stromness
1 hr 30 mins
All Year
North Link Ferries
0845 6000 449
www.northlinkferries.co.uk

Tarbert to Lochranza
1 hr 25 mins
Winter Only
Caledonian MacBrayne
08000 66 5000
www.calmac.co.uk

Tarbert to Portavadie
25 mins
All Year
Caledonian MacBrayne
08000 66 5000
www.calmac.co.uk

Tayinloan to Gigha
20 mins
All Year
Caledonian MacBrayne
08000 66 5000
www.calmac.co.uk

Tingwall to Rousay
25 mins
All Year
Orkney Ferries
01856 872044
www.orkneyferries.co.uk

Tobermory to Kilchoan
35 mins
Seasonal
Caledonian MacBrayne
08000 66 5000

Toft to Ulsta
20 mins
All Year
Shetland Islands Council
01957 722259
www.shetland.gov.uk/ferries/

Troon to Larne
1 hr 49 mins
Seasonal
P&O Ferries
08716 64 2121
www.poferries.com

Uig to Lochmaddy
1 hr 45 mins
All Year
Caledonian MacBrayne
08000 66 5000
www.calmac.co.uk

Uig to Tarbert
1 hr 40 mins
All Year
Caledonian MacBrayne
08000 66 5000

Ullapool to Stornoway
2 hrs 45 mins
All Year
Caledonian MacBrayne
08000 66 5000
www.calmac.co.uk

Vidlin to Skerries
1 hr 30 mins
All Year
Shetland Islands Council
01806 515226
www.shetland.gov.uk/ferries/

Vidlin to Symbister
40 mins
All Year
Shetland Islands Council
01806 566259
www.shetland.gov.uk/ferries/

Wemyss Bay to Rothesay
35 mins
All Year
Caledonian MacBrayne
08000 66 5000

Westray to Papa Westray
40 mins - 1 hr 45 mins
All Year
Orkney Ferries
01856 872044

Wyre to Tingwall
25 mins
All Year
Orkney Ferries
01856 872044
www.orkneyferries.co.uk

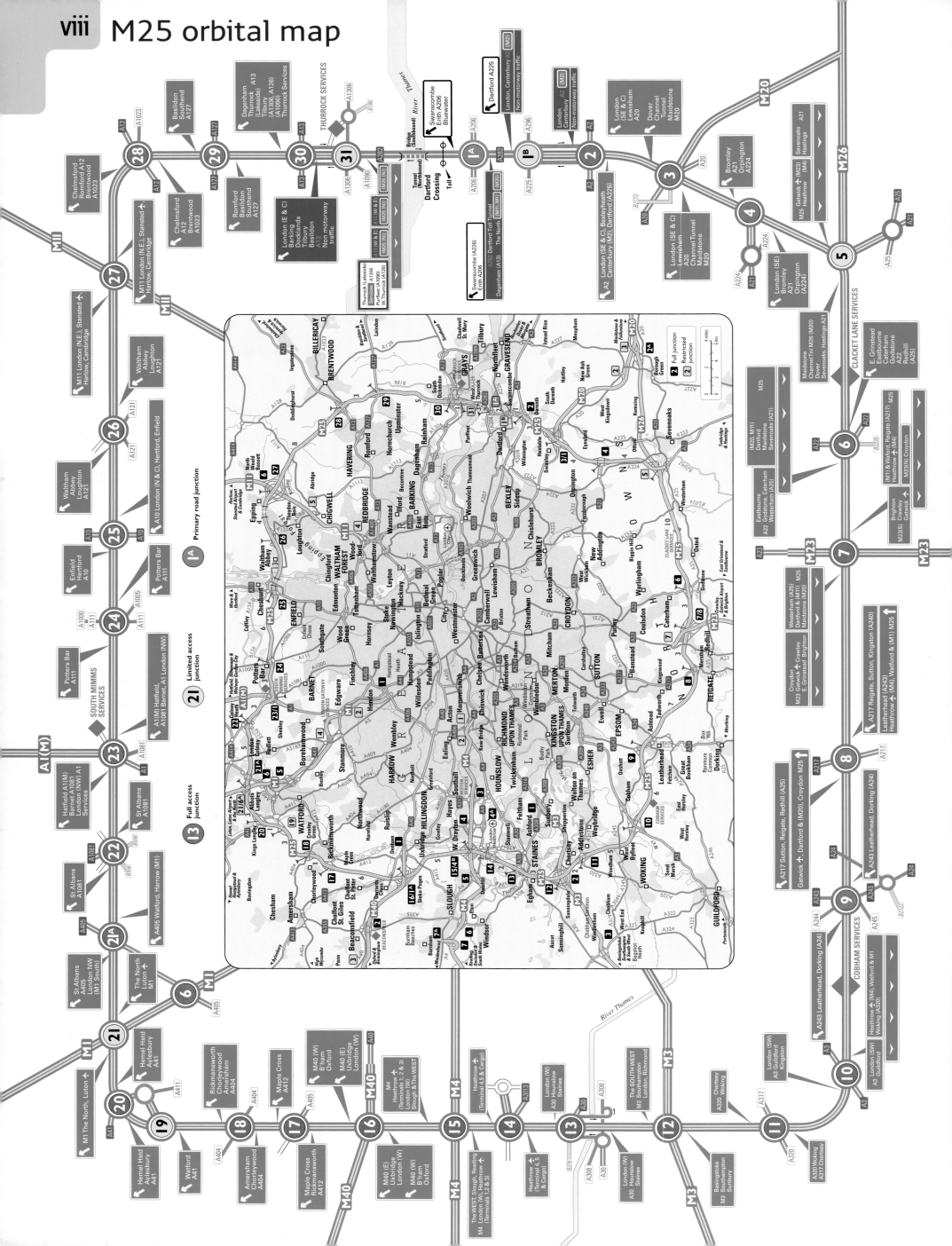

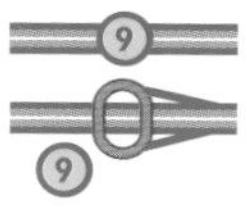

Restricted motorway junctions are shown on the maps as

Restricted motorway junctions

A1(M) LONDON TO NEWCASTLE
2
Northbound : No access
Southbound : No exit
3
Southbound : No access
5
Northbound : No exit
Southbound : No access
: No exit
41
Northbound : No exit to M62 Eastbound
43
Northbound : No exit to M1 Westbound
Dishforth
Southbound : No access from A168 Eastbound
57
Northbound : No access
: Exit only to A66(M) Northbound
Southbound : Access only from A66(M) Southbound
: No exit
65
Northbound : No access from A1
Southbound : No exit to A1

A3(M) PORTSMOUTH
1
Northbound : No exit
Southbound : No access
4
Northbound : No access
Southbound : No exit

A38(M) BIRMINGHAM
Victoria Road
Northbound : No exit
Southbound : No access

A48(M) CARDIFF
Junction with M4
Westbound : No access from M4 29 Eastbound
Eastbound : No exit to M4 29 Westbound
29A
Westbound : No exit to A48 Eastbound
Eastbound : No access from A48 Westbound

A57(M) MANCHESTER
Brook Street
Westbound : No exit
Eastbound : No access

A58(M) LEEDS
Westgate
Southbound : No access
Woodhouse Lane
Westbound : No exit

A64(M) LEEDS
Claypit Lane
Eastbound : No access

A66(M) DARLINGTON
Junction with A1(M)
Northbound : No access from A1(M) Southbound
: No exit
Southbound : No access
: No exit to A1(M) Northbound

A74(M) LOCKERBIE
18
Northbound : No access
Southbound : No exit

A167(M) NEWCASTLE
Campden Street
Northbound : No exit
Southbound : No access
: No exit

M1 LONDON TO LEEDS
2
Northbound : No exit
Southbound : No access
4
Northbound : No exit
Southbound : No access
6A
Northbound : Access only from M25 21
: No exit
Southbound : No access
: Exit only to M25 21
7
Northbound : Access only from A414
: No exit
Southbound : No access
: Exit only to A414
17
Northbound : No access
: Exit only to M45
Southbound : Access only from M45
: No exit
19
Northbound : Exit only to M6
Southbound : Access only from M6
21A
Northbound : No access
Southbound : No exit
23A
Northbound : No access from A453
Southbound : No exit to A453
24A
Northbound : No exit
Southbound : No access
35A
Northbound : No access
Southbound : No exit
43
Northbound : No access
: Exit only to M621
Southbound : No exit
: Access only from M621
48
Northbound : No exit to A1(M) Southbound
: Access only from A1(M) Northbound
Southbound : Exit only to A1(M) Southbound
: No access

M2 ROCHESTER TO CANTERBURY
1
Westbound : No exit to A2 Eastbound
Eastbound : No access from A2 Westbound

M3 LONDON TO WINCHESTER
8
Westbound : No access
Eastbound : No exit
10
Northbound : No access
Southbound : No exit
13
Southbound : No exit to A335 Eastbound
: No access
14
Westbound : No access
Eastbound : No exit

M4 LONDON TO SWANSEA
1
Westbound : No access from A4 Eastbound
Eastbound : No exit to A4 Westbound
2
Westbound : No access from A4 Eastbound
: No exit to A4 Eastbound
Eastbound : No access from A4 Westbound
: No exit to A4 Westbound
21
Westbound : No access from M48 Eastbound
Eastbound : No exit to M48 Westbound
23
Westbound : No exit to M48 Eastbound
Eastbound : No access from M48 Westbound
25
Westbound : No access
Eastbound : No exit
25A
Westbound : No access
Eastbound : No exit
29
Westbound : No access
: Exit only to A48(M)
Eastbound : Access only from A48(M) Eastbound
: No exit
38
Westbound : No access
39
Westbound : No exit
Eastbound : No access
: No exit
41
Westbound : No exit
Eastbound : No access
42
Westbound : No exit to A48
Eastbound : No access from A48

M5 BIRMINGHAM TO EXETER
10
Northbound : No exit
Southbound : No access
11A
Northbound : No access from A417 Eastbound
Southbound : No exit to A417 Westbound

M6 COVENTRY TO CARLISLE
Junction with M1
Northbound : No access from M1 19 Southbound
Southbound : No exit to M1 19 Northbound
3A
Northbound : No access from M6 Toll
Southbound : No exit to M6 Toll
4
Northbound : No exit to M42 Northbound
: No access from M42 Southbound
Southbound : No exit to M42
: No access from M42 Southbound
4A
Northbound : No access from M42 8 Northbound
: No exit
Southbound : No access
: Exit only to M42 8
5
Northbound : No access
Southbound : No exit
10A
Northbound : No access
: Exit only to M54
Southbound : Access only from M54
: No exit
11A
Northbound : No exit to M6 Toll
Southbound : No access from M6 Toll
24
Northbound : No exit
Southbound : No access
25
Northbound : No access
Southbound : No exit
30
Northbound : Access only from M61 Northbound
: No exit
Southbound : No access
: Exit only to M61 Southbound
31A
Northbound : No access
Southbound : No exit

M6 Toll BIRMINGHAM
T1
Northbound : Exit only to M42
: Access only from A4097
Southbound : No exit
: Access only from M42 Southbound
T2
Northbound : No exit
: No access
Southbound : No access
T5
Northbound : No exit
Southbound : No access
T7
Northbound : No access
Southbound : No exit
T8
Northbound : No access
Southbound : No exit

M8 EDINBURGH TO GLASGOW
8
Westbound : No access from M73 2 Southbound
: No access from A8 Eastbound
: No access from A89 Eastbound
Eastbound : No access from A89 Westbound
: No exit to M73 2 Northbound
9
Westbound : No exit
Eastbound : No access
13
Westbound : Access only from M80
Eastbound : Exit only to M80
14
Westbound : No exit
Eastbound : No access
16
Westbound : No access
Eastbound : No exit
17
Eastbound : Access only from A82, not central Glasgow
: Exit only to A82, not central Glasgow
18
Westbound : No access
Eastbound : No access
19
Westbound : Access only from A814 Eastbound
Eastbound : Exit only to A814 Westbound, not central Glasgow
20
Westbound : No access
Eastbound : No exit
21
Westbound : No exit
Eastbound : No access
22
Westbound : No access
: Exit only to M77 Southbound
Eastbound : Access only from M77 Northbound
: No exit
23
Westbound : No access
Eastbound : No exit
25A
Eastbound : No exit
Westbound : No access
28
Westbound : No access
Eastbound : No exit
28A
Westbound : No access
Eastbound : No exit

M9 EDINBURGH TO STIRLING
1A
Westbound : No access
Eastbound : No exit
2
Westbound : No exit
Eastbound : No access
3
Westbound : No access
Eastbound : No exit
6
Westbound : No exit
Eastbound : No access
8
Westbound : No access
Eastbound : No exit

M11 LONDON TO CAMBRIDGE
4
Northbound : No access from A1400 Westbound
: No exit
Southbound : No access
: No exit to A1400 Eastbound
5
Northbound : No access
Southbound : No exit
8A
Northbound : No access
Southbound : No exit
9
Northbound : No access
Southbound : No exit
13
Northbound : No access
Southbound : No exit
14
Northbound : No access from A428 Eastbound
: No exit to A428 Westbound
: No exit to A1307
Southbound : No access from A428 Eastbound
: No access from A1307
: No exit

M20 LONDON TO FOLKESTONE
2
Westbound : No exit
Eastbound : No access
3
Westbound : No access
: Exit only to M26 Westbound
Eastbound : Access only from M26 Eastbound
: No exit
11A
Westbound : No exit
Eastbound : No access

M23 LONDON TO CRAWLEY
7
Northbound : No exit to A23 Southbound
Southbound : No access from A23 Northbound
10A
Southbound : No access from B2036
Northbound : No exit to B2036

M25 LONDON ORBITAL MOTORWAY
1B
Clockwise : No access
Anticlockwise : No exit
5
Clockwise : No exit to M26 Eastbound
Anticlockwise : No access from M26 Westbound
Spur of M25 5
Clockwise : No access from M26 Westbound
Anticlockwise : No exit to M26 Eastbound
19
Clockwise : No access
Anticlockwise : No exit
21
Clockwise : No access from M1 6A Northbound
: No exit to M1 6A Southbound
Anticlockwise : No access from M1 6A Northbound
: No exit to M1 6A Southbound
31
Clockwise : No exit
Anticlockwise : No access

M26 SEVENOAKS
Junction with M25 5
Westbound : No exit to M25 Anticlockwise
: No exit to M25 spur
Eastbound : No access from M25 Clockwise
: No access from M25 spur
Junction with M20
Westbound : No access from M20 3 Eastbound
Eastbound : No exit to M20 3 Westbound

M27 SOUTHAMPTON TO PORTSMOUTH
4 West
Westbound : No exit
Eastbound : No access
4 East
Westbound : No access
Eastbound : No exit
10
Westbound : No access
Eastbound : No exit
12 West
Westbound : No exit
Eastbound : No access
12 East
Westbound : No access from A3
Eastbound : No exit

M40 LONDON TO BIRMINGHAM
3
Westbound : No access
Eastbound : No exit
7
Eastbound : No exit
8
Northbound : No access
Southbound : No exit
13
Northbound : No access
Southbound : No exit
14
Northbound : No exit
Southbound : No access
16
Northbound : No exit
Southbound : No access

M42 BIRMINGHAM
1
Northbound : No exit
Southbound : No access
7
Northbound : No access
: Exit only to M6 Northbound
Southbound : Access only from M6 Northbound
: No exit
7A
Northbound : No access
: Exit only to M6 Eastbound
Southbound : No access
: No exit
8
Northbound : Access only from M6 Southbound
: No exit
Southbound : Access only from M6 Southbound
: Exit only to M6 Northbound

M45 COVENTRY
Junction with M1
Westbound : No access from M1 17 Southbound
Eastbound : No exit to M1 17 Northbound
Junction with A45
Westbound : No exit
Eastbound : No access

M48 CHEPSTOW
M4
Westbound : No exit to M4 Eastbound
Eastbound : No access from M4 Westbound

M49 BRISTOL
18A
Northbound : No access from M5 Southbound
Southbound : No access from M5 Northbound

M53 BIRKENHEAD TO CHESTER
11
Northbound : No access from M56 15 Eastbound
: No exit to M56 15 Westbound
Southbound : No access from M56 15 Eastbound
: No exit to M56 15 Westbound

M54 WOLVERHAMPTON TO TELFORD
Junction with M6
Westbound : No access from M6 10A Southbound
Eastbound : No exit to M6 10A Northbound

M56 STOCKPORT TO CHESTER
1
Westbound : No access from M60 Eastbound
: No access from A34 Northbound
Eastbound : No exit to M60 Westbound
: No exit to A34 Southbound
2
Westbound : No access
Eastbound : No exit
3
Westbound : No exit
Eastbound : No access
4
Westbound : No access
Eastbound : No exit
7
Westbound : No access
Eastbound : No exit
8
Westbound : No exit
Eastbound : No access
9
Westbound : No exit to M6 Southbound
Eastbound : No access from M6 Northbound
15
Westbound : No access
: No access from M53 11
Eastbound : No exit
: No exit to M53 11

M57 LIVERPOOL
3
Northbound : No exit
Southbound : No access
5
Northbound : Access only from A580 Westbound
: No exit
Southbound : No access
: Exit only to A580 Eastbound

M58 LIVERPOOL TO WIGAN
1
Westbound : No access
Eastbound : No exit

M60 MANCHESTER
2
Westbound : No exit
Eastbound : No access
3
Westbound : No access from M56 1
: No access from A34 Southbound
: No exit to A34 Northbound
Eastbound : No access from A34 Southbound
: No exit to M56 1
: No exit to A34 Northbound
4
Westbound : No access
Eastbound : No exit to M56
5
Westbound : No access from A5103 Southbound
: No exit to A5103 Southbound
Eastbound : No access from A5103 Northbound
: No exit to A5103 Northbound
14
Westbound : No access from A580
: No exit to A580 Eastbound
Eastbound : No access from A580 Westbound
: No exit to A580
16
Westbound : No access
Eastbound : No exit
20
Westbound : No access
Eastbound : No exit
22
Westbound : No access
25
Westbound : No access
26
Eastbound : No access
: No exit
27
Westbound : No exit
Eastbound : No access

M61 MANCHESTER TO PRESTON
2
Northbound : No access from A580 Eastbound
: No access from A666
Southbound : No exit to A580 Westbound
3
Northbound : No access from A580 Eastbound
: No access from A666
Southbound : No exit to A580 Westbound
Junction with M6
Northbound : No exit to M6 30 Southbound
Southbound : No access from M6 30 Northbound

M62 LIVERPOOL TO HULL
23
Westbound : No exit
Eastbound : No access
32A
Westbound : No exit to A1(M) Southbound

M65 BURNLEY
9
Westbound : No exit
Eastbound : No access
11
Westbound : No access
Eastbound : No exit

M66 MANCHESTER TO EDENFIELD
1
Northbound : No access
Southbound : No exit
Junction with A56
Northbound : Exit only to A56 Northbound
Southbound : Access only from A56 Southbound

M67 MANCHESTER
1
Westbound : No exit
Eastbound : No access
2
Westbound : No access
Eastbound : No exit

M69 COVENTRY TO LEICESTER
2
Northbound : No exit
Southbound : No access

M73 GLASGOW
1
Northbound : No access from A721 Eastbound
Southbound : No exit to A721 Eastbound
2
Northbound : No access from M8 8 Eastbound
Southbound : No exit to M8 8 Westbound
3
Northbound : No exit to A80 Southbound
Southbound : No access from A80 Northbound

M74 GLASGOW
2
Westbound : No access
Eastbound : No exit
3
Westbound : No exit
Eastbound : No access
7
Northbound : No exit
Southbound : No access
9
Northbound : No access
: No exit
Southbound : No access
10
Southbound : No exit
11
Northbound : No exit
Southbound : No access
12
Northbound : Access only from A70 Northbound
Southbound : Exit only to A70 Southbound

M77 GLASGOW
Junction with M8
Northbound : No exit to M8 22 Westbound
Southbound : No access from M8 22 Eastbound
4
Northbound : No exit
Southbound : No access
6
Northbound : No exit to A77
Southbound : No access from A77
7
Northbound : No access
: No exit
8
Northbound : No access
Southbound : No access

M80 STIRLING
3
Southbound : No access
5
Northbound : No access
: No access from M876
Southbound : No exit
: No exit to M876

M90 EDINBURGH TO PERTH
2A
Northbound : No access
Southbound : No exit
7
Northbound : No exit
Southbound : No access
8
Northbound : No access
Southbound : No exit
10
Northbound : No access from A912
: No exit to A912 Southbound
Southbound : No access from A912 Northbound
: No exit to A912

M180 SCUNTHORPE
1
Westbound : No exit
Eastbound : No access

M606 BRADFORD
Straithgate Lane
Northbound : No access

M621 LEEDS
2A
Northbound : No exit
Southbound : No access
5
Northbound : No access
Southbound : No exit
6
Northbound : No exit
Southbound : No access

M876 FALKIRK
Junction with M80
Westbound : No exit to M80 5 Northbound
Eastbound : No access from M80 5 Southbound
Junction with M9
Westbound : No access
Eastbound : No exit
2
Northbound : No access
Southbound : No exit

Motorway services information

All motorway service areas have fuel, food, toilets, disabled facilities and free short-term parking

For further information on motorway services providers:
Moto www.moto-way.com   RoadChef www.roadchef.com   Welcome Break www.welcomebreak.co.uk
Extra www.extraservices.co.uk   Westmorland www.westmorland.com

Motorway	Junction	Service provider	Service name	Fuel supplier	Information	Accommodation	Conference facilities	Showers	M&S Simply Food	Costa Coffee	Starbucks	Burger King	KFC	McDonalds	Wimpy
A1(M)	1	Welcome Break	South Mimms	BP	●	●	●	●				●	●	●	
	10	Extra	Baldock	Shell	●	●		●	●			●	●		
	17	Extra	Peterborough	Shell	●	●		●	●				●	●	
	34	Moto	Blyth	Esso	●	●		●		●			●		
	46	Moto	Wetherby	BP	●	●		●	●	●			●		
	61	RoadChef	Durham	Total	●	●	●		●						
	64	Moto	Washington	BP	●	●			●						
A74(M)	16	RoadChef	Annandale Water	BP	●	●			●						
	22	Welcome Break	Gretna Green	BP	●	●		●				●	●	●	
M1	2-4	Welcome Break	London Gateway	Shell	●	●	●	●				●	●	●	
	11-12	Moto	Toddington	BP	●	●		●	●	●			●		
	14-15	Welcome Break	Newport Pagnell	Shell	●	●	●	●				●	●	●	
	15A	RoadChef	Northampton	BP	●			●							
	16-17	RoadChef	Watford Gap	BP	●	●		●						●	
	21-21A	Welcome Break	Leicester Forest East	BP	●	●	●	●		●	●		●		
	22	Moto	Leicester	BP	●	●		●		●			●		
	23A	Moto	Donington Park	BP	●	●	●	●		●			●		
	25-26	Moto	Trowell	BP	●	●		●		●			●		
	28-29	RoadChef	Tibshelf	Shell	●	●	●		●						
	30-31	Welcome Break	Woodall	Shell	●	●			●	●	●	●	●		
	38-39	Moto	Woolley Edge	Esso	●	●		●	●	●			●		
M2	4-5	Moto	Medway	BP	●		●	●	●	●					
M3	4A-5	Welcome Break	Fleet	Shell	●	●	●	●		●	●		●	●	
	8-9	Moto	Winchester	Shell	●			●		●					
M4	3	Moto	Heston	BP	●	●	●	●		●					
	11-12	Moto	Reading	BP	●	●	●	●	●	●			●		
	13	Moto	Chieveley	BP	●	●		●	●	●					
	14-15	Welcome Break	Membury	BP	●	●		●			●	●	●		
	17-18	Moto	Leigh Delamere	Esso	●	●	●	●	●	●			●		
	23A	First	Magor	Esso	●	●		●							
	30	Welcome Break	Cardiff Gate	Total	●		●			●	●				
	33	Moto	Cardiff West	Esso	●	●		●							
	36	Welcome Break	Sarn Park	Shell	●	●		●					●		
	47	Moto	Swansea	BP	●	●		●		●					
	49	RoadChef	Pont Abraham	Texaco	●			●							
M5	3-4	Moto	Frankley	Esso		●		●	●	●					
	8	RoadChef	Strensham (South)	BP		●			●			●			
	8	RoadChef	Strensham (North)	BP		●	●	●		●			●		
	13-14	Welcome Break	Michaelwood	BP		●		●		●	●		●		
	19	Welcome Break	Gordano	Shell		●		●		●	●		●		
	21-22	RoadChef	Sedgemoor (South)	Total		●		●					●		
	21-22	Welcome Break	Sedgemoor (North)	Shell		●	●	●		●	●		●		
	24	Moto	Bridgwater	BP		●		●	●	●			●		
	25-26	RoadChef	Taunton Deane	Shell		●			●						
	27	Moto	Tiverton	Shell		●		●							
	28	Extra	Cullompton	Shell					●				●		
	29-30	Moto	Exeter	BP		●	●	●	●	●			●		

Motorway	Junction	Service provider	Service name	Fuel supplier	Information	Accommodation	Conference facilities	Showers	M&S Simply Food	Costa Coffee	Starbucks	Burger King	KFC	McDonalds	Wimpy
M6	3-4	Welcome Break	Corley	Shell	●	●	●	●				●	●	●	
	10-11	Moto	Hilton Park	BP	●	●	●	●	●	●			●		
	14-15	RoadChef	Stafford (South)	Esso	●	●	●	●		●					
	14-15	Moto	Stafford (North)	BP	●	●		●	●	●			●		
	15-16	Welcome Break	Keele	Shell	●	●		●		●	●		●		
	16-17	RoadChef	Sandbach	Esso	●			●		●					
	18-19	Moto	Knutsford	BP	●	●		●	●	●			●		
	20	Moto	Lymm	Total	●	●		●		●				●	
	27-28	Welcome Break	Charnock Richard	Shell	●	●		●		●	●		●		
	32-33	Moto	Lancaster	BP	●	●		●	●	●					
	35A-36	Moto	Burton-in-Kendal (N)	BP	●	●		●		●					
	36-37	RoadChef	Killington Lake (S)	BP	●	●		●		●					
	38-39	Westmorland	Tebay	Total	●	●	●	●							
	41-42	Moto	Southwaite	Esso	●	●		●	●	●					
	44-45	Moto	Todhills	BP/Shell	●			●							
M6 Toll	T6-T7	RoadChef	Norton Canes	BP	●	●		●		●					
M8	4-5	BP	Heart of Scotland	BP				●	●	●					
M9	9	Moto	Stirling	BP	●			●							
M11	8	Welcome Break	Birchanger Green	Shell	●	●	●	●				●	●		
M18	5	Moto	Doncaster North	BP	●	●		●							
M20	8	RoadChef	Maidstone	Esso	●	●		●		●				●	
	11	Stop 24	Stop 24	Shell	●			●		●			●		
M23	11	Moto	Pease Pottage	Shell	●			●		●	●				
M25	5-6	RoadChef	Clacket Lane	Total	●	●		●		●			●		
	9-10	Extra	Cobham (opening 2012)	Shell		●					●	●		●	
	23	Welcome Break	South Mimms	BP	●	●	●			●			●		
	30	Moto	Thurrock	Esso	●	●		●	●	●			●		
M27	3-4	RoadChef	Rownhams	Esso	●	●			●						●
M40	2	Extra	Beaconsfield	Shell		●			●			●	●	●	
	8	Welcome Break	Oxford	BP		●	●			●	●		●		
	10	Moto	Cherwell Valley	Esso	●	●		●		●			●		
	12-13	Welcome Break	Warwick	BP/Shell	●	●	●	●		●	●		●		
M42	2	Welcome Break	Hopwood Park	Shell	●	●		●		●	●		●		
	10	Moto	Tamworth	Esso	●	●		●	●	●			●		
M48	1	Moto	Severn View	BP		●		●							
M54	4	Welcome Break	Telford	Shell	●	●		●					●		
M56	14	RoadChef	Chester	Shell	●	●		●		●					
M61	6-7	Euro Garages	Bolton West	BP		●	●	●					●		
M62	7-9	Welcome Break	Burtonwood	Shell	●	●		●					●		
	18-19	Moto	Birch	Esso	●	●		●	●	●			●		
	25-26	Welcome Break	Hartshead Moor	Shell	●	●		●					●		
	33	Moto	Ferrybridge	Esso	●	●		●							
M65	4	Extra	Blackburn with Darwen	Shell	●	●	●	●					●	●	
M74	4-5	RoadChef	Bothwell (South)	BP	●	●		●		●					
	5-6	RoadChef	Hamilton (North)	BP	●	●		●		●					
	11-12	Cairn Lodge	Happendon	Shell	●			●							
	12-13	Welcome Break	Abington	Shell	●	●		●		●	●				
M90	6	Moto	Kinross	BP	●	●		●							

There are a number of operators of motorway service areas in Britain; RoadChef, Welcome Break and Moto being the biggest three. All motorway service areas are required by law to provide fuel, free toilets and free short term parking 24 hours a day. Details of other facilities provided at each service area are shown opposite, although most of these will not be open 24 hours a day.

As part of its *Think, don't drive tired* road safety campaign the Government has the following tips for drivers:

- If you are feeling tired, opening the window or turning up the radio does not work, instead find a safe place to stop.

- On long journeys take a 15 minute break every 2 hours.

- If feeling tired, a 15 minute nap will help as will drinking 2 cups of coffee or other high caffeine drink. The most effective solution is to have some caffeine and then take a short sleep which gives the caffeine time to kick in.

- Avoid making long trips between midnight and 6am when you are most susceptible to sleepiness.

- Don't begin a journey if you are already feeling tired.

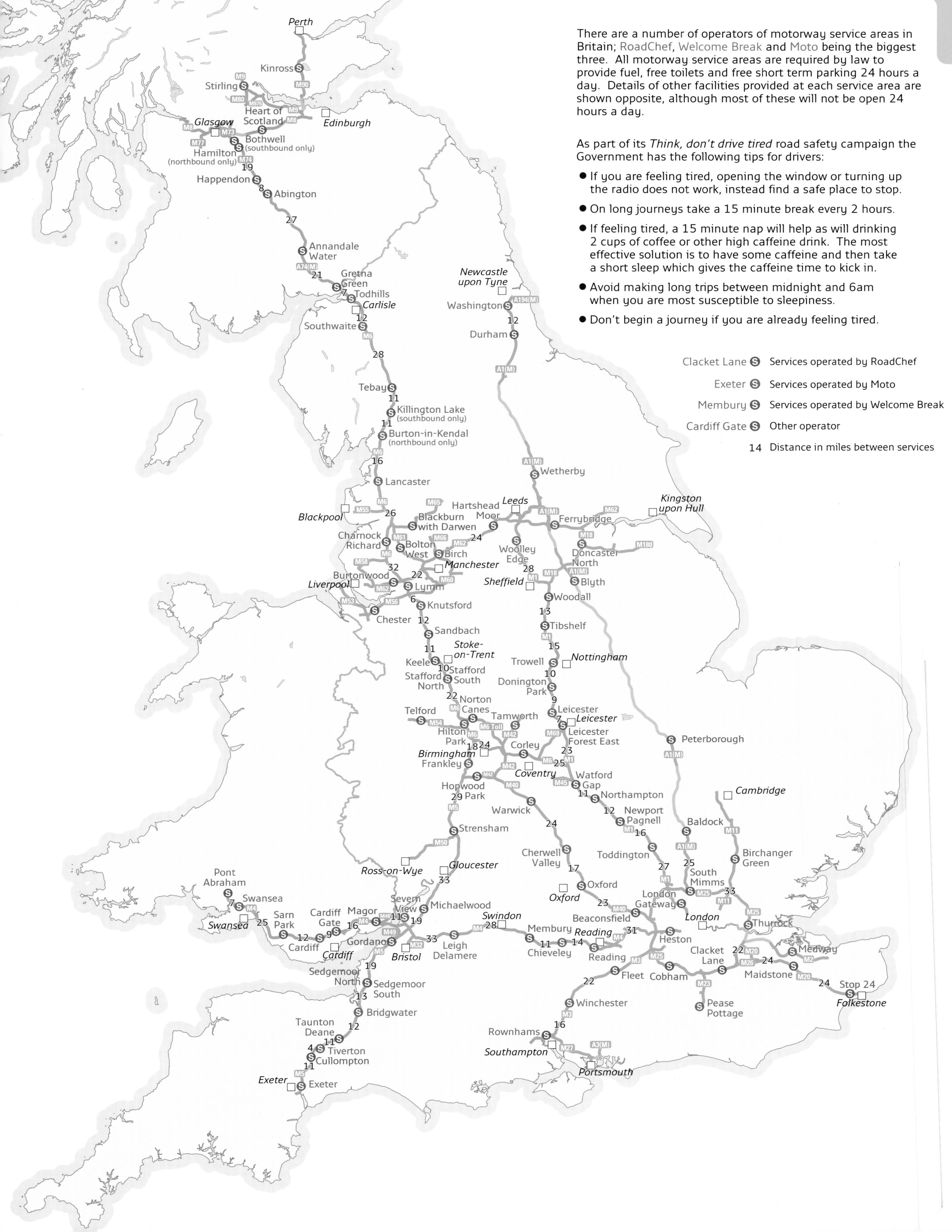

Clacket Lane Ⓢ	Services operated by RoadChef
Exeter Ⓢ	Services operated by Moto
Membury Ⓢ	Services operated by Welcome Break
Cardiff Gate Ⓢ	Other operator
14	Distance in miles between services

Perth
Kinross Ⓢ
Stirling Ⓢ M9 M90
M80 M876
Heart of Scotland Ⓢ M8 Edinburgh
Glasgow
Bothwell Ⓢ (southbound only)
Hamilton (northbound only) M74
19
Happendon Ⓢ
8 Abington Ⓢ
27
Annandale Water Ⓢ
A74(M) 21
Gretna Green Ⓢ
7 Todhills Ⓢ
Carlisle
12
Southwaite Ⓢ
M6
28
Newcastle upon Tyne
Washington Ⓢ A194(M) 12
Durham Ⓢ
A1(M)
Tebay Ⓢ
11
Killington Lake Ⓢ (southbound only)
11
Burton-in-Kendal Ⓢ (northbound only)
M6
16
Lancaster Ⓢ
Wetherby Ⓢ A1(M)
M65 Hartshead Moor Ⓢ Leeds
Blackpool M55 26 Blackburn with Darwen Ⓢ
Charnock Richard Ⓢ M61 Bolton West Ⓢ Birch Ⓢ M62 Woolley Edge Ⓢ
M58 32 22 Manchester M60
Burtonwood Ⓢ Lymm Ⓢ Sheffield
Liverpool M62 M56 6 Knutsford Ⓢ
Chester Ⓢ 12 Sandbach Ⓢ
11 Stoke-on-Trent
Keele Ⓢ 10 Stafford South Ⓢ
Stafford North Ⓢ
22 Norton Canes Ⓢ M6
Telford Ⓢ M54 Tamworth Ⓢ M6 Toll
Hilton Park Ⓢ M6
18 24 Corley Ⓢ M42
Birmingham Frankley Ⓢ
M42 Coventry
Hopwood Park Ⓢ M40
29 Warwick
M5
Strensham Ⓢ
M50
Cherwell Valley Ⓢ
33 Gloucester
Ross-on-Wye
Oxford Ⓢ
Oxford
23
Beaconsfield Ⓢ
Pont Abraham Ⓢ
7 Swansea
Sarn Park Ⓢ Cardiff Gate Ⓢ Magor Ⓢ Severn View Ⓢ Michaelwood Ⓢ Swindon
Swansea 25 16 M6 11 19 Membury Ⓢ Reading
12 9 Gordano Ⓢ M5 28 M4 11 Ⓢ 14
Cardiff Ⓢ M49 33 Leigh Delamere Ⓢ Chieveley Reading
Cardiff Bristol
Sedgemoor North Ⓢ 19
Sedgemoor South Ⓢ 13
Bridgwater Ⓢ
Taunton Deane Ⓢ 12
11
4 Tiverton Ⓢ Cullompton
11
Exeter Ⓢ M5 Exeter

A1(M) Wetherby
M62 Kingston upon Hull
Ferrybridge Ⓢ
M18
Doncaster North Ⓢ M180
A1(M) Blyth Ⓢ
M1 Woodall Ⓢ
13
Tibshelf Ⓢ
M1 15
Trowell Ⓢ Nottingham
10
Donington Park Ⓢ
9 Leicester Ⓢ
7 Leicester
M69 Leicester Forest East Ⓢ
Peterborough Ⓢ A1(M)
23
25 Watford Gap Ⓢ
11 Northampton
12 Newport Pagnell Ⓢ Cambridge
16 Baldock Ⓢ M11
Toddington Ⓢ 27 25 South Mimms Ⓢ Birchanger Green Ⓢ
A1(M) M11 33
London Gateway Ⓢ
31 London
Heston Ⓢ M25 Thurrock Ⓢ
M4 Medway Ⓢ M20 M2
Clacket Lane Ⓢ 22 M20 24
M3 Fleet Ⓢ Cobham Ⓢ Maidstone M20 24 Stop 24 Ⓢ
22 M23 Folkestone
Winchester Ⓢ Pease Pottage Ⓢ
Rownhams Ⓢ M27 A3(M) 16
Southampton
Portsmouth

Risk rating of Britain's motorways and A roads

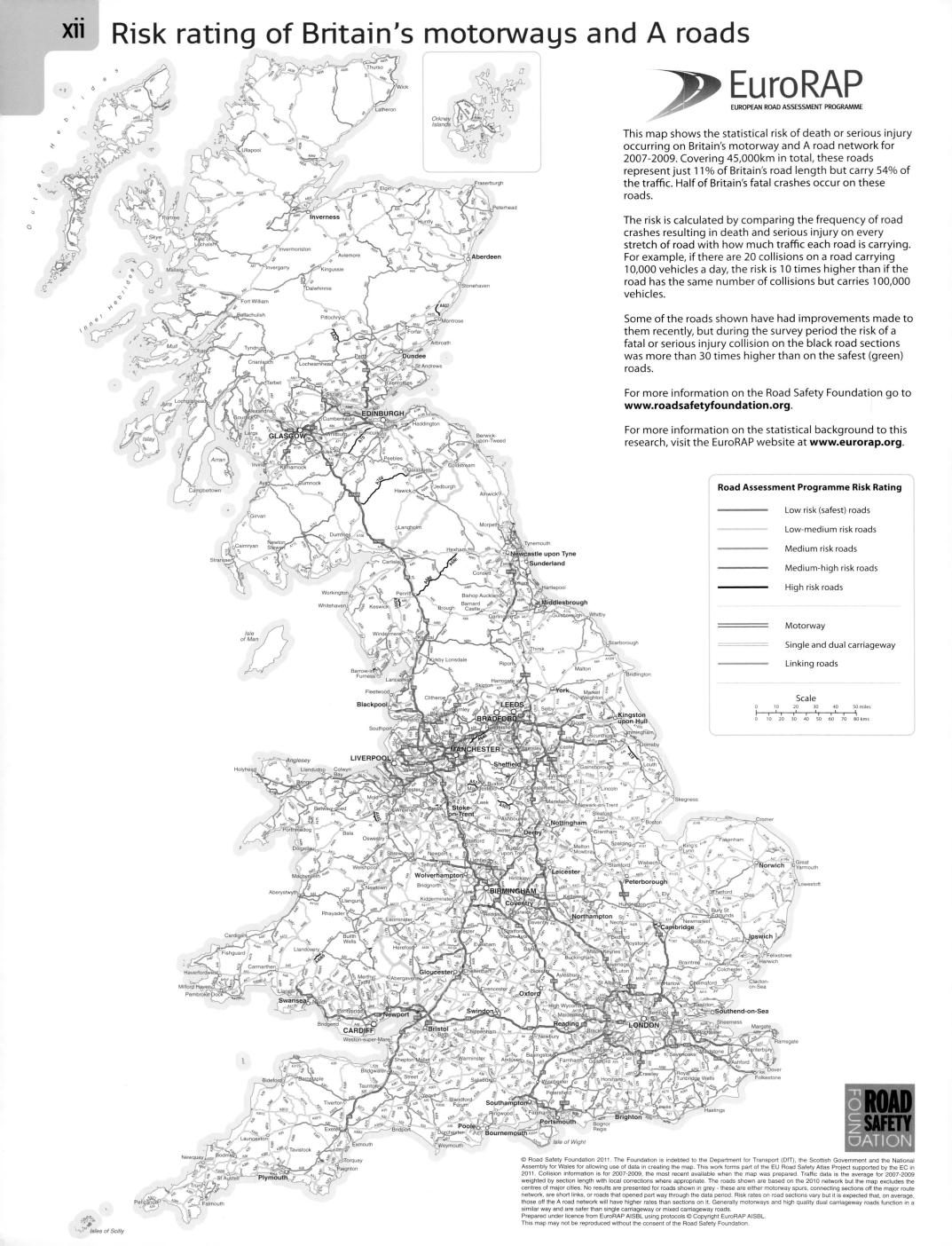

EuroRAP
EUROPEAN ROAD ASSESSMENT PROGRAMME

This map shows the statistical risk of death or serious injury occurring on Britain's motorway and A road network for 2007-2009. Covering 45,000km in total, these roads represent just 11% of Britain's road length but carry 54% of the traffic. Half of Britain's fatal crashes occur on these roads.

The risk is calculated by comparing the frequency of road crashes resulting in death and serious injury on every stretch of road with how much traffic each road is carrying. For example, if there are 20 collisions on a road carrying 10,000 vehicles a day, the risk is 10 times higher than if the road has the same number of collisions but carries 100,000 vehicles.

Some of the roads shown have had improvements made to them recently, but during the survey period the risk of a fatal or serious injury collision on the black road sections was more than 30 times higher than on the safest (green) roads.

For more information on the Road Safety Foundation go to **www.roadsafetyfoundation.org**.

For more information on the statistical background to this research, visit the EuroRAP website at **www.eurorap.org**.

Road Assessment Programme Risk Rating

———	Low risk (safest) roads
———	Low-medium risk roads
———	Medium risk roads
———	Medium-high risk roads
———	High risk roads
═══	Motorway
———	Single and dual carriageway
———	Linking roads

Scale

0 10 20 30 40 50 miles
0 10 20 30 40 50 60 70 80 kms

ROAD SAFETY FOUNDATION

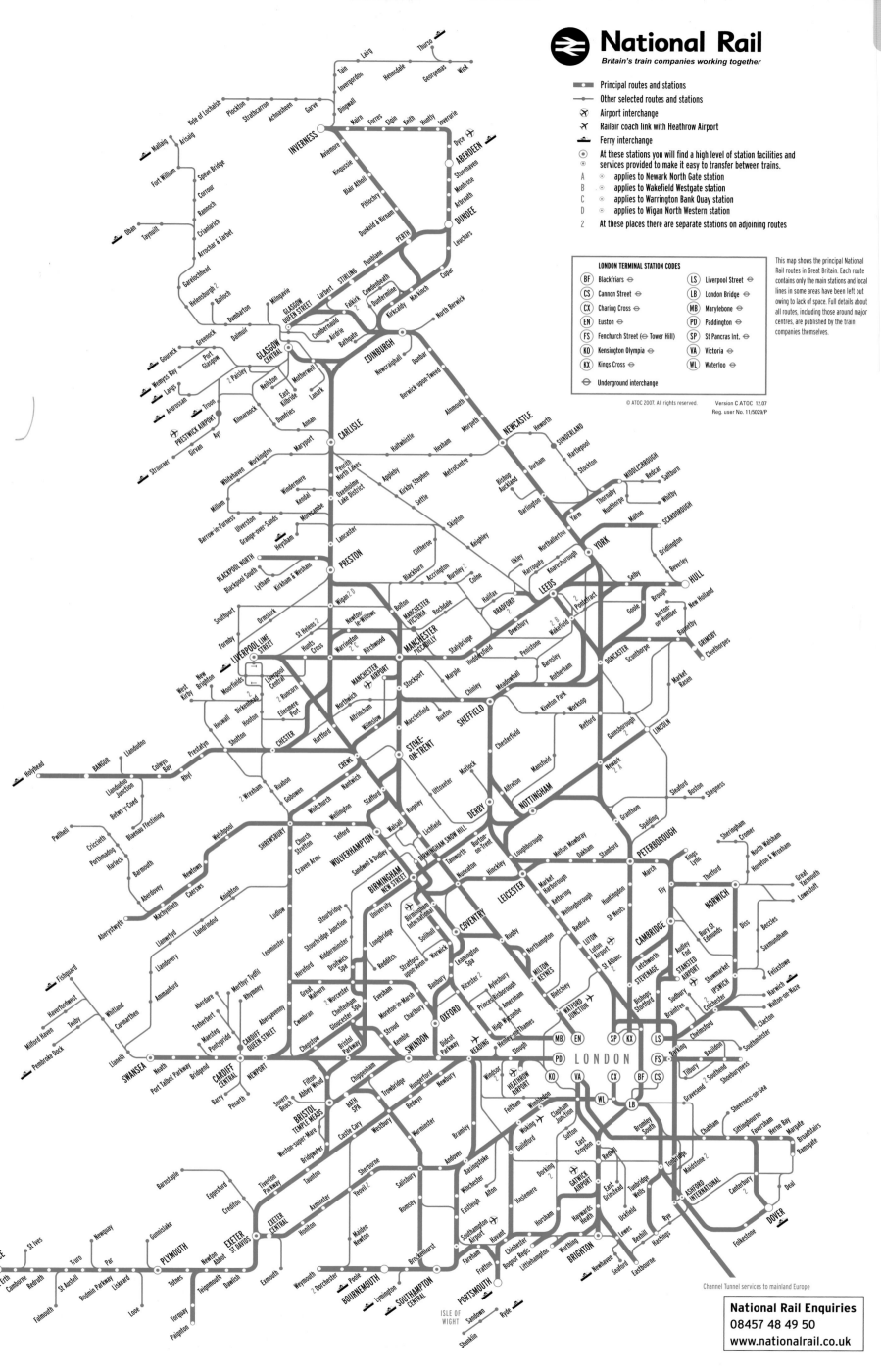

National Rail
Britain's train companies working together

Symbols used on the map

Blue place of interest symbols e.g ★ are listed on page 51

Motorway junction with full / limited access

Motorway service area

LEICESTER SERVICES

M6 Toll — Toll motorway

A316 — Primary route dual / single carriageway / junction / service area

A4054 — 'A' road dual / single carriageway

B7078 — 'B' road dual / single carriageway

Minor road dual / single carriageway

Restricted access road

Road proposed or under construction

Road tunnel

Roundabout

Toll / One way street

Level crossing

Hadrian's Path — National Trail / Long Distance Route

Fixed safety camera / fixed average-speed safety camera. Speed shown by number within camera, a V indicates a variable limit.

P&R   P&R — Park and Ride site operated by bus / rail (runs at least 5 days a week)

Dublin 8hrs — Car ferry with destination

West Cowes ¾hr — Foot ferry with destination

Airport

Railway line / Railway tunnel / Light railway line

Railway station / Light rail station

London Underground / London Overground / Glasgow Subway station

H — Hospital

Extent of London congestion charging zone

Notable building

362 ▲ — Spot height (in metres) / Lighthouse

Built up area

Woodland / Park

National Park

Heritage Coast

BRISTOL — County / Unitary Authority boundary and name

SEE PAGE 35 — Area covered by street map

Locator map

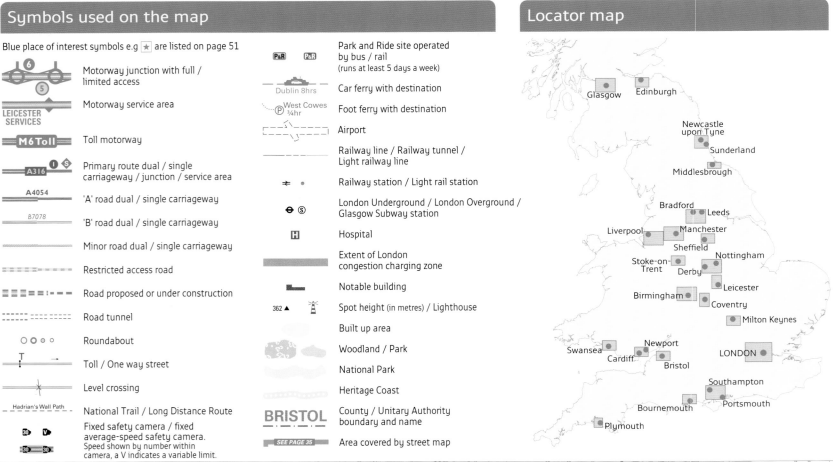

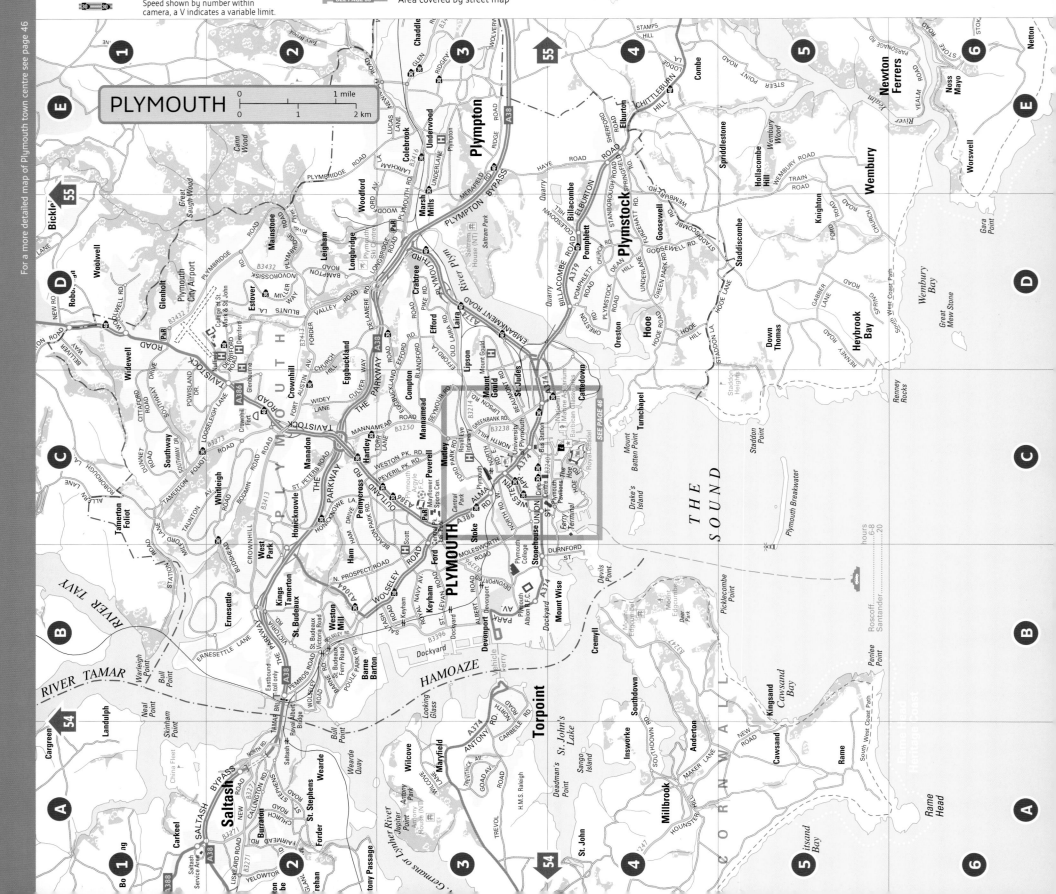

PLYMOUTH

For a more detailed map of Plymouth town centre see page 46

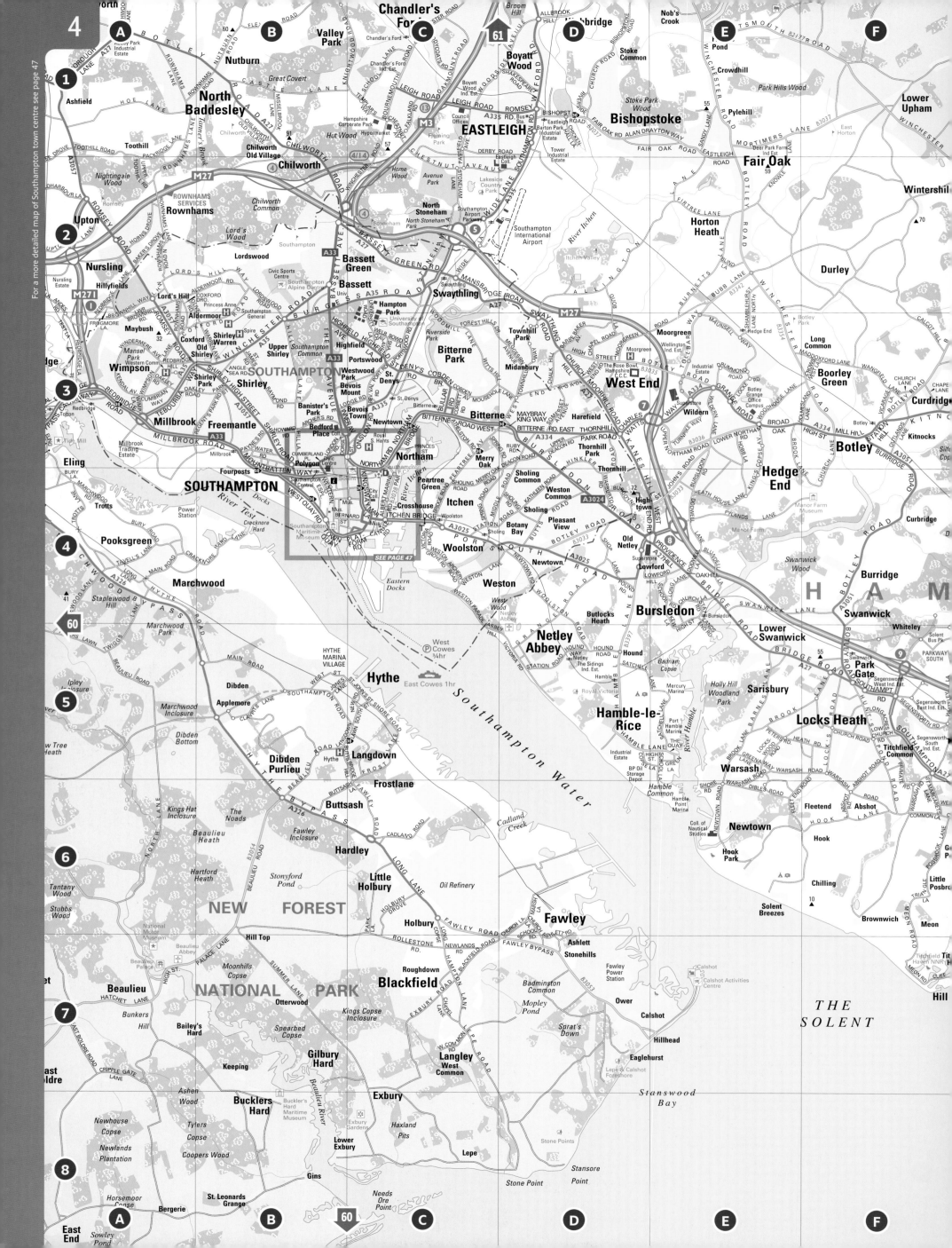

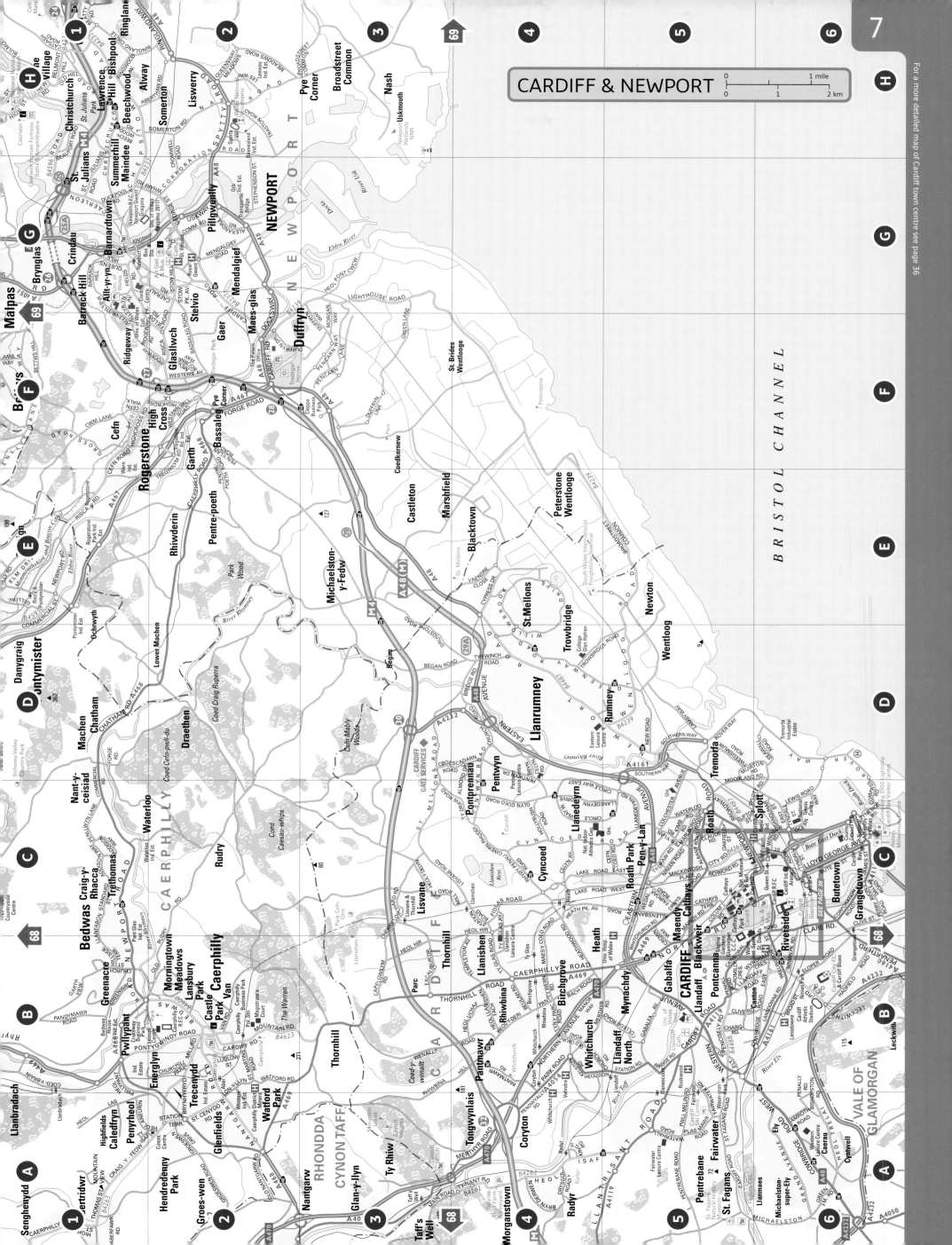

For a more detailed map of Cardiff town centre see page 36

CARDIFF & NEWPORT

NEWPORT

CAERPHILLY

CARDIFF

RHONDDA CYNON TAFF

VALE OF GLAMORGAN

BRISTOL CHANNEL

For a more detailed map of Bristol town centre see page 35

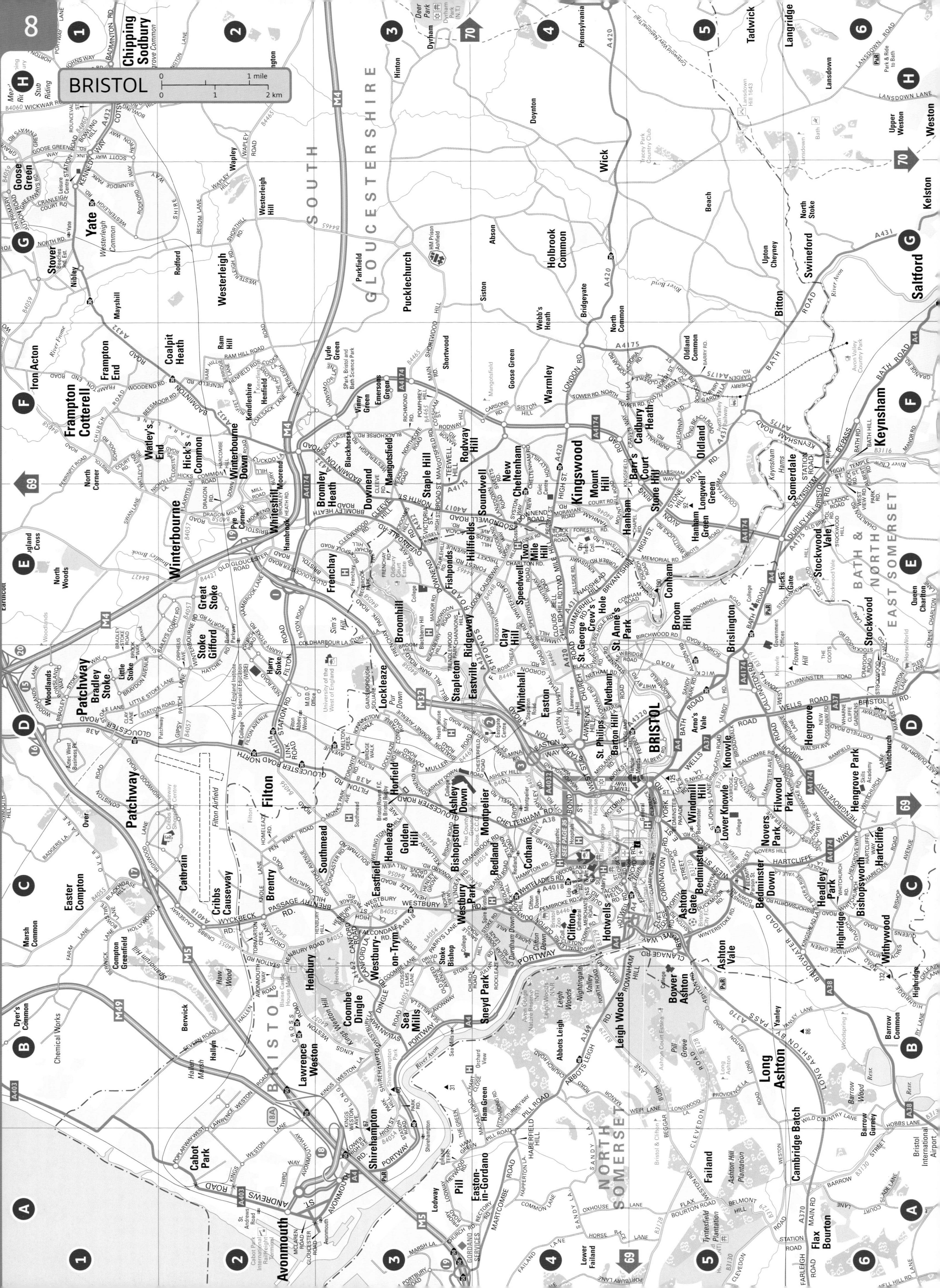

BRISTOL

0 — 1 mile
0 — 1 — 2 km

SOUTH GLOUCESTERSHIRE

BATH & NORTH EAST SOMERSET

NORTH SOMERSET

Chipping Sodbury
Goose Green
Stover
Yate
Westerleigh
Iron Acton
Frampton Cotterell
Frampton End
Coalpit Heath
Ram Hill
Watley's End
Hick's Common
Winterbourne Down
Winterbourne
Whiteshill
Bromley Heath
Downend
Mangotsfield
Staple Hill
Rodway Hill
New Cheltenham
Kingswood
Oldland
Keynsham
Saltford
Swineford
Bitton
Upton Cheyney
North Stoke
Pennsylvania
Tadwick
Langridge
Lansdown
Upper Weston
Weston
Wick
Beach
North Common
Warmley
Holbrook Common
Pucklechurch
Shortwood
Siston
Webb's Heath
Bridgeyate
Hanham
Hanham Green
Longwell Green
Barr's Court
Stone Hill
Mount Hill
Soundwell
Hillfields
Fishponds
Speedwell
Two Mile Hill
St George
Crew's Hole
St Anne's Park
Brislington
Stockwood
Stockwood Vale
Somerdale
Queen Charlton
Conham
Broom Hill
Whitehall
Easton
Netham
St Philips
Barton Hill
Bristol
Arno's Vale
Knowle
Hengrove
Hengrove Park
Whitchurch
Hartcliffe
Withywood
Bishopsworth
Headley Park
Bedminster Down
Novers Park
Filwood Park
Lower Knowle
Windmill Hill
Bedminster
Ashton Gate
Ashton Vale
Hotwells
Clifton
Cotham
Redland
Montpelier
Bishopston
Golden Hill
Henleaze
Ashley Down
Horfield
Lockleaze
Eastville
Stapleton
Ridgeway
Clay Hill
Frenchay
Broomhill
Hambrook
Bradley Stoke
Little Stoke
Stoke Gifford
Great Stoke
Harry Stoke
Filton
Patchway
Pathway
Catbrain
Cribbs Causeway
Brentry
Southmead
Eastfield
Westbury Park
Westbury-on-Trym
Stoke Bishop
Sneyd Park
Sea Mills
Shirehampton
Lawrence Weston
Avonmouth
Cabot Park
Dyer's Common
Berwick
Easter Compton
Compton Greenfield
Marsh Common
Henbury
Coombe Dingle
Pill
Easton-in-Gordano
Lower Failand
Failand
Long Ashton
Leigh Woods
Abbots Leigh
Bower Ashton
Cambridge Batch
Barrow Common
Barrow Gurney
Flax Bourton
Bristol International Airport
Eglland Cross
North Woods
Nibley
Mayshill
Rodford
Westerleigh Common
Shorthill
Besom Lane
Parkfield
Hinton
Dyrham
Doynton

GLOUCESTERSHIRE

EAST SOMERSET

University of the West of England
Filton Airfield
HM Prison Ashfield

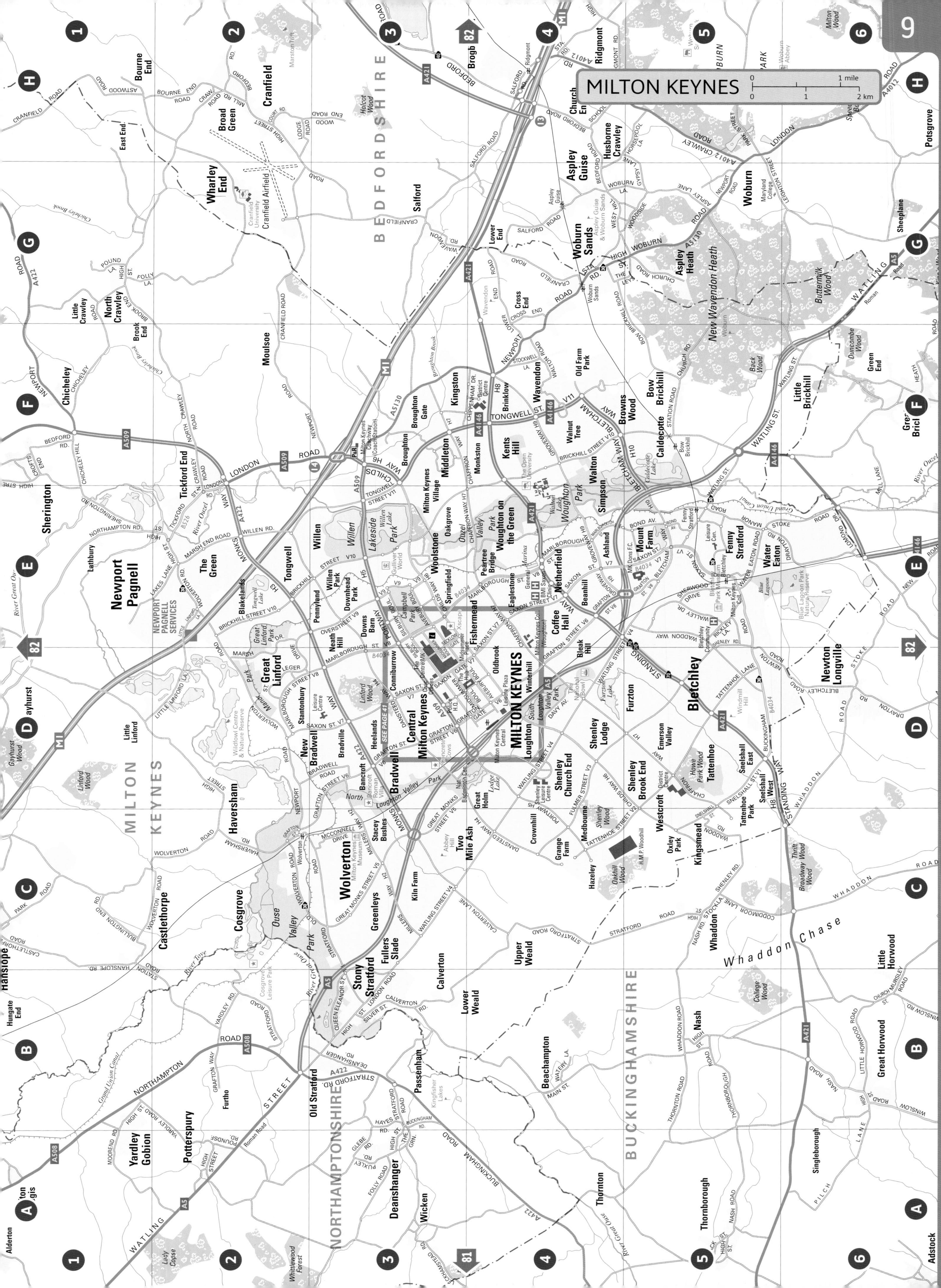

For a more detailed map of Milton Keynes town centre see page 41

MILTON KEYNES

0 — 1 mile
0 — 1 — 2 km

BEDFORDSHIRE

BUCKINGHAMSHIRE

NORTHAMPTONSHIRE

MILTON KEYNES

Bourne End
East End
Cranfield
Broad Green
Wharley End
Cranfield University
Cranfield Airfield
Salford
Moulsoe
Lower End
Cross End
Woburn Sands
Aspley Guise
Husborne Crawley
Aspley Heath
Woburn
New Wavendon Heath
Buttermilk Wood
Sheeplane
Potsgrove

Little Crawley
North Crawley
Brook End
Chicheley
Sherington
Lathbury
Tickford End
Newport Pagnell
Newport Pagnell Services
The Green
Tongwell
Blakelands
Kingston
Broughton Gate
Broughton
Middleton
Milton Keynes Village
Wavendon
Old Farm Park
Tongwell
Browns Wood
Bow Brickhill
Little Brickhill
Green End

Willen
Willen Lake
Willen Park
Woolstone
Oakgrove
Pennyland
Downhead Park
Springfield
Peartree Bridge
Eaglestone
Netherfield
Kents Hill
Walnut Tree
Walton
Simpson
Ashland
Coffee Hall
Beanhill
Caldecotte
Fenny Stratford
Water Eaton
Water Eaton

Great Linford
Little Linford
New Bradwell
Bradville
Heelands
Stantonbury
Neath Hill
Downs Barn
Conniburrow
Central Milton Keynes
Fishermead
Oldbrook
Bleak Hill
Winterhill
Loughton
Bletchley
Newton Longville

Gayhurst
Haversham
Wolverton
Greenleys
Stony Stratford
Fullers Slade
Two Mile Ash
Kiln Farm
Calverton
Crownhill
Grange Farm
Shenley Church End
Shenley Lodge
Shenley Brook End
Emerson Valley
Furzton
Medbourne
Hazeley
Oxley Park
Kingsmead
Westcroft
Tattenhoe
Snelshall East
Snelshall West
Tattenhoe Park

Castlethorpe
Cosgrove
Hanslope
Hungate End
Yardley Gobion
Pottespury
Furtho
Old Stratford
Passenham
Deanshanger
Wicken
Lower Weald
Upper Weald
Beachampton
Thornton
Nash
Thornborough
Whaddon
Whaddon Chase
Little Horwood
Great Horwood
Singleborough
Adstock

Cranfield University
The Open University
MK Dons F.C.
Milton Keynes Coachway Coach Station
Gulliver's World
Milton Keynes Central
Milton Keynes Museum

GREATER LONDON - WEST

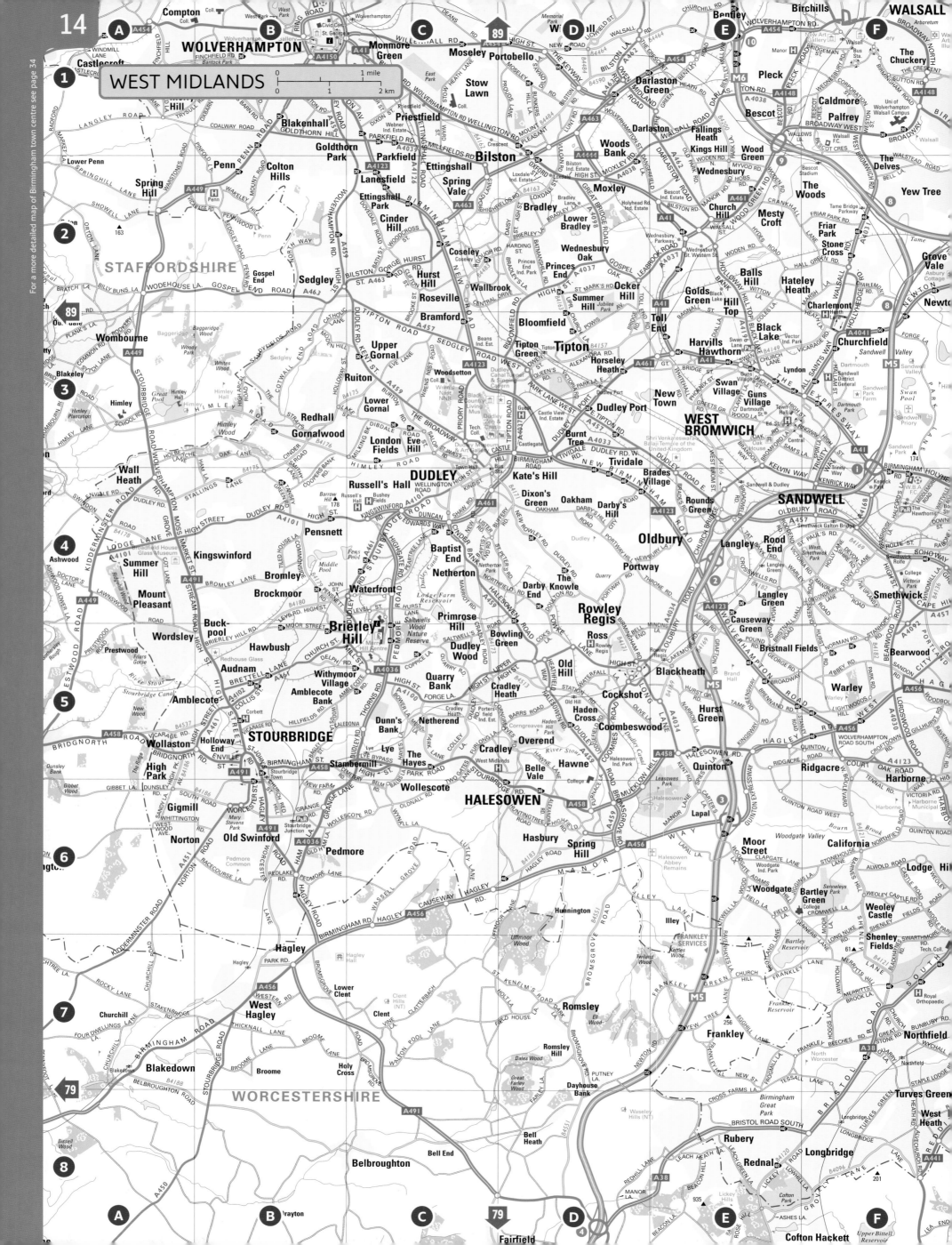

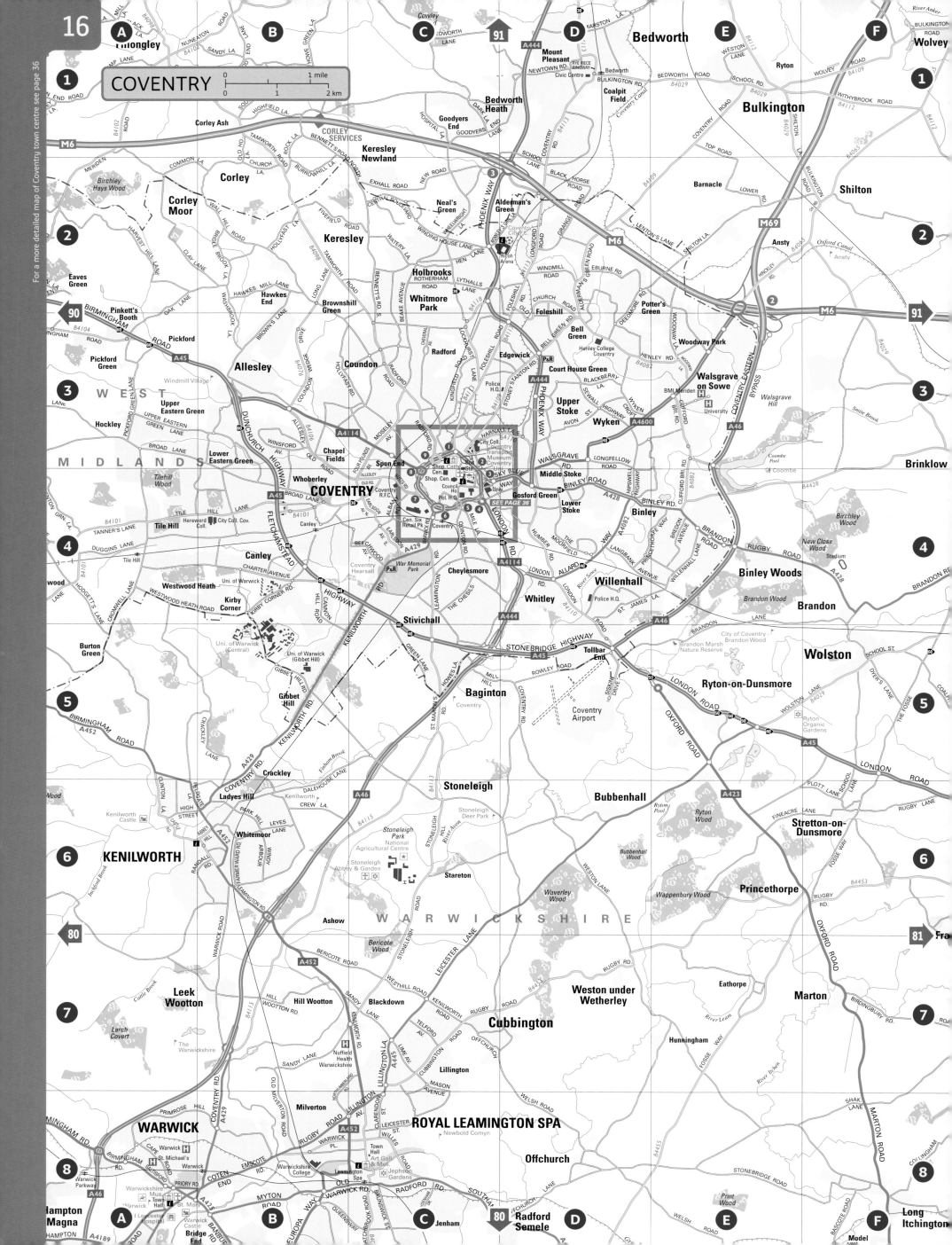

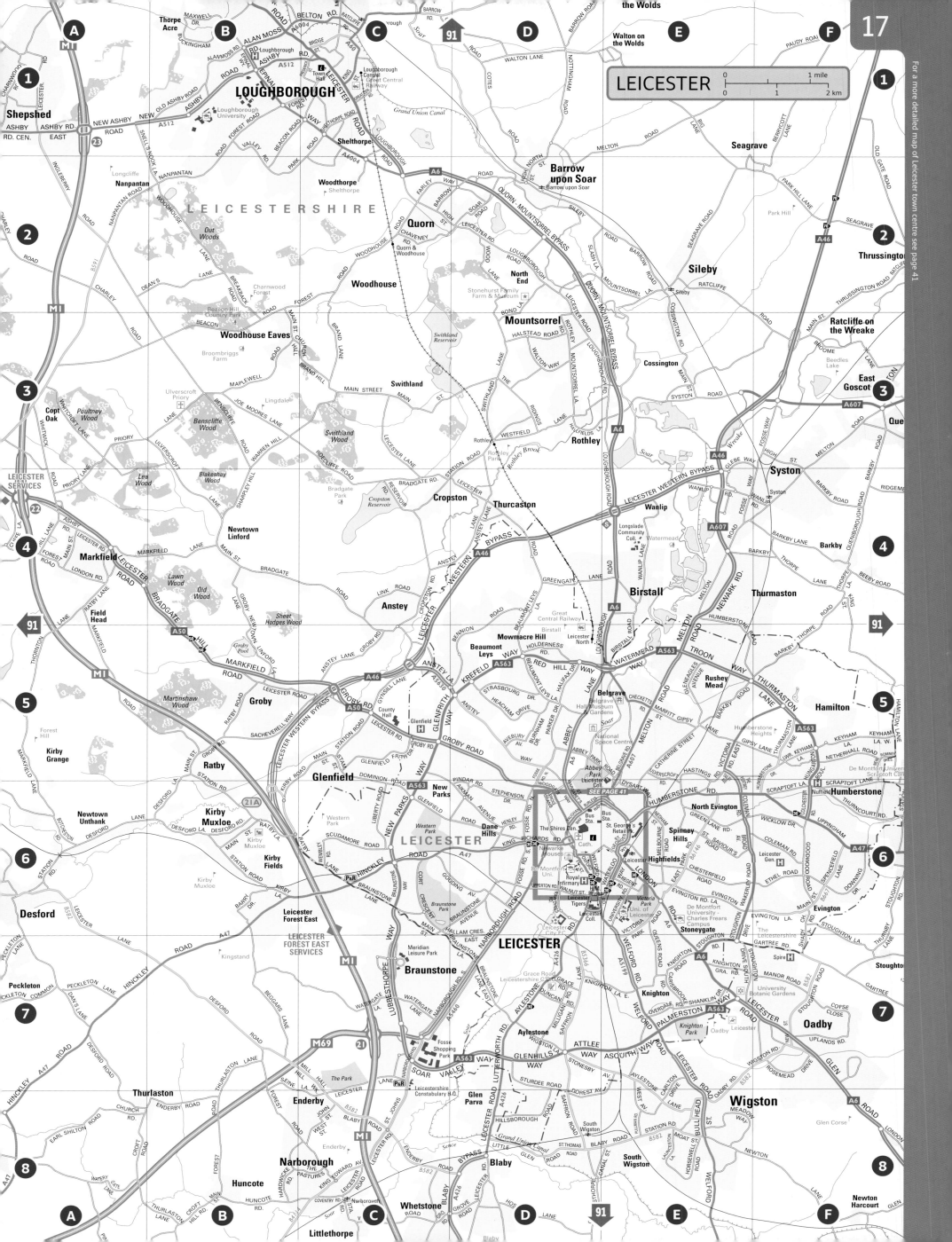

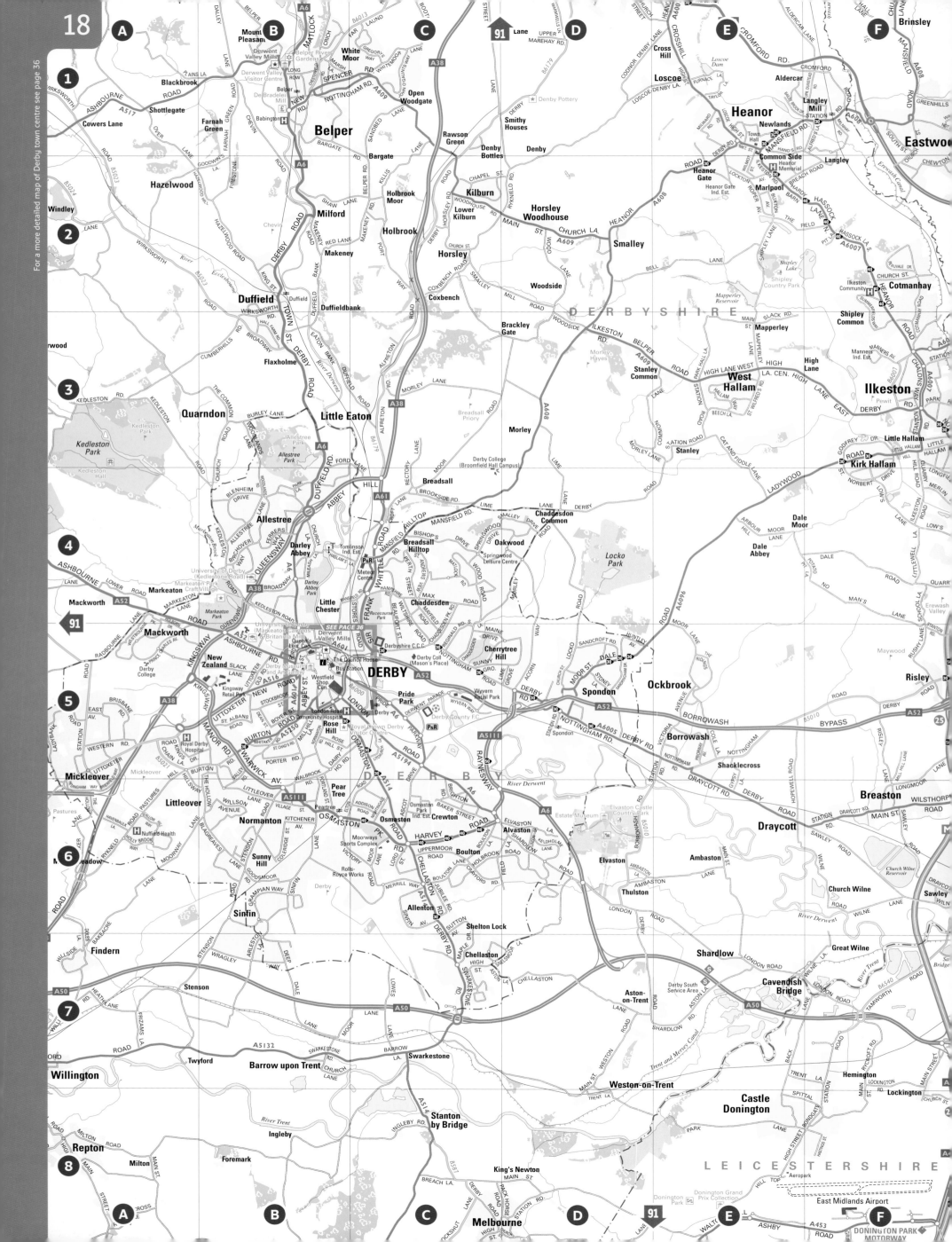

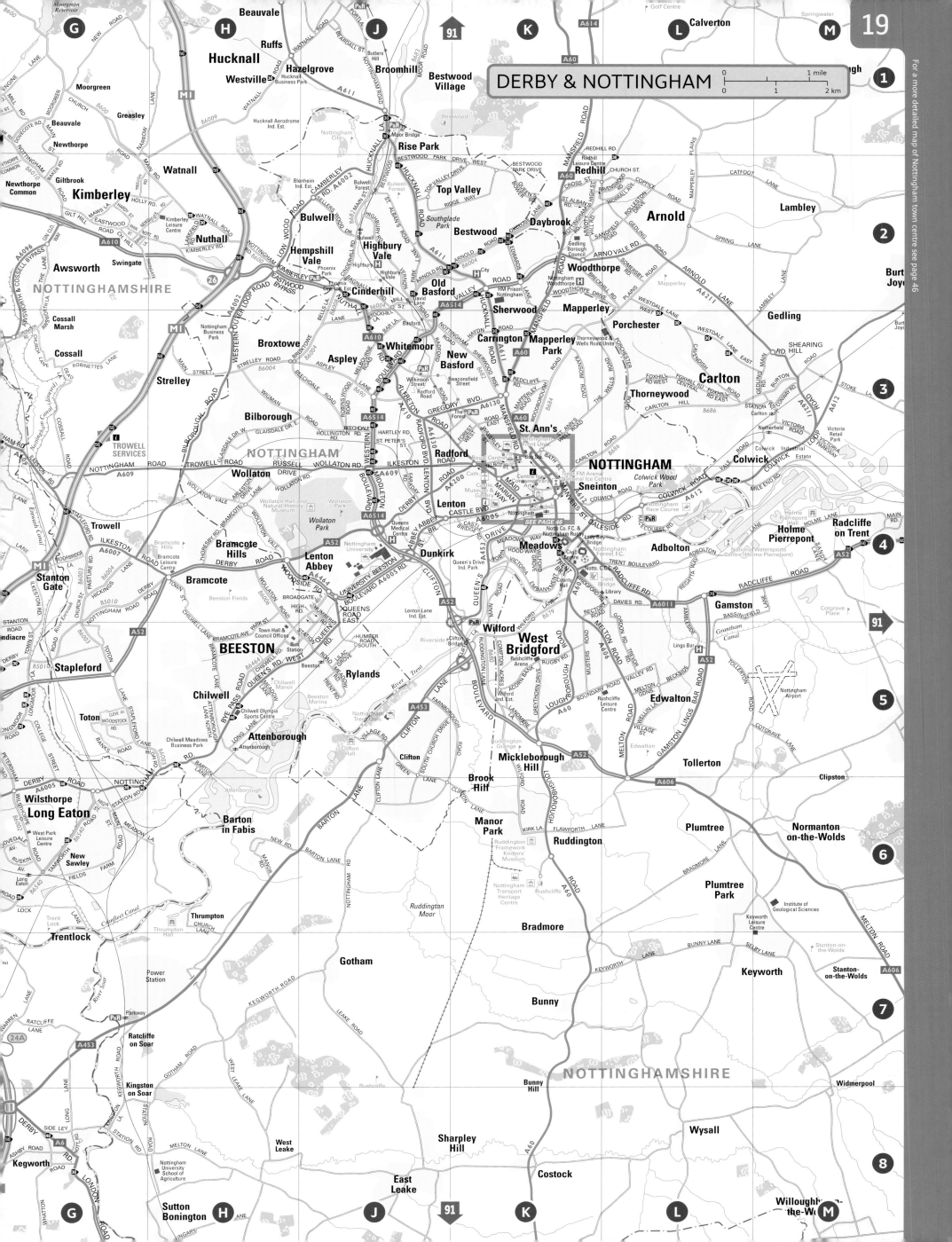

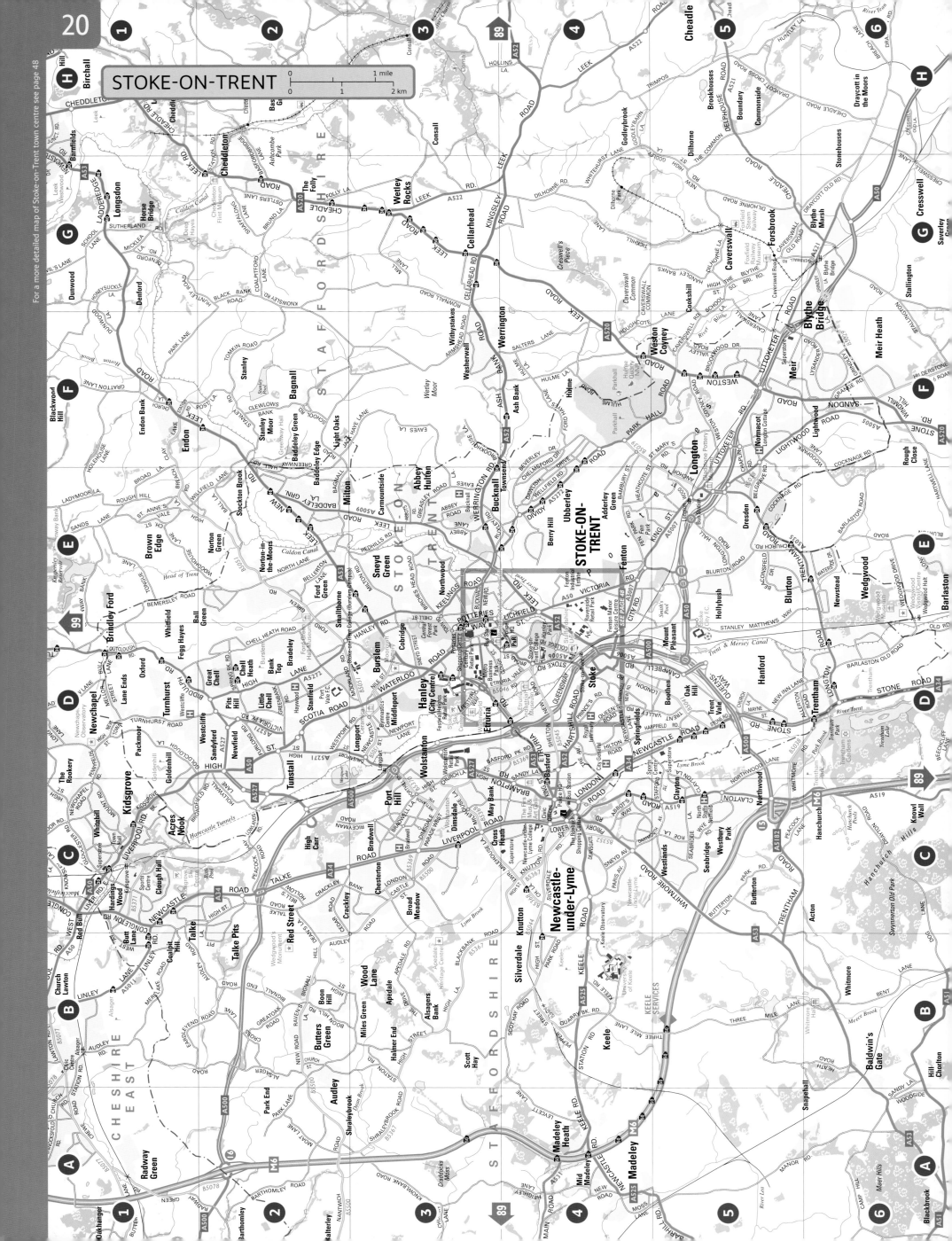

For a more detailed map of Stoke-on-Trent town centre see page 48

STOKE-ON-TRENT

0   1 mile
0   1   2 km

SEE PAGE 48

SHEFFIELD

For a more detailed map of Sheffield town centre see page 47

SOUTH YORKSHIRE

DERBYSHIRE

Maltby
Braithwell
Micklebring
Hooton Levitt
Hellaby
Bramley
North Anston
South Anston
Dinnington
Laughton Common
Brookhouse
Thurcroft
Carr
Springvale
Morthen
Brampton en le Morthen
Wales
Wales Bar
Aston
Todwick
Kiveton Park
Harthill
Woodall Services
Norwood
Killamarsh

Ravenfield
Thrybergh
Sunnyside
Wickersley
Listerdale
Dalton Magna
Upper Whiston
Whiston
Ulley
Aughton
Swallownest
Beighton
Halfway
Holbrook
Eckington

Greasbrough
Parkgate
Aldwarke
Dalton
Dalton Parva
East Dene
Herringthorpe
Broom
Moorgate
Canklow
Brinsworth
Catcliffe
Treeton
Orgreave
Woodhouse Mill
Woodhouse
Crystal Peaks
Mosborough
Marsh

Wingfield
ROTHERHAM
Bradgate
New Wortley
Kimberworth
Kimberworth Park
Richmond Park
Masbrough
Ickles
Handsworth
Richmond
Stradbroke
Normanton Spring
Frecheville
Ridgeway

Scholes
Dropping Well
Hill Top
Blackburn
Meadow Hall
Tinsley
Darnall
Greenland
Handsworth Hill
Woodthorpe
Intake
Hollins End
Gleadless Townend
Charnock Hall
Troway

Ecclesfield
Wincobank
Brightside
Grimesthorpe
Attercliffe
Manor Park
Manor Estate
Gleadless
Hemsworth
Jordanthorpe
Coal Aston
Dronfield

Thorpe Common
Shiregreen
Pismire Hill
Pitsmoor
Burngreave
Park Hill
SHEFFIELD
Highfield
Meersbrook Bank
Norton
Batemoor
Greenhill

Grenoside
Parson Cross
Southey Green
Longley
Sheffield Lane Top
Norwood
Crabtree
Heeley
Lowfield
Norton Woodseats
Meadow Head
Lowedges

Birley Carr
Wadsley Bridge
Shirecliffe
Owlerton
Parkwood Springs
Walkley
Crookesmoor
Sharrow
Nether Edge
Millhouses
Beauchief

Worrall
Wadsley
Hillsborough
Malin Bridge
Crookes
Lydgate
Broomhill
Ranmoor
Greystones
Brincliffe
Ecclesall
Bents Green
Beauchief
Abbeydale Park
Totley Rise

Wharncliffe Side
Oughtibridge
Loxley
Knowle Top
Den Bank
Sandygate
Fulwood
Whirlow
Parkhead
Abbeydale
Dore
Totley
Townhead
New Totley

Whitley
Stannington
Hallam Head
Carsick
Bradway

Worrall
Middlewood

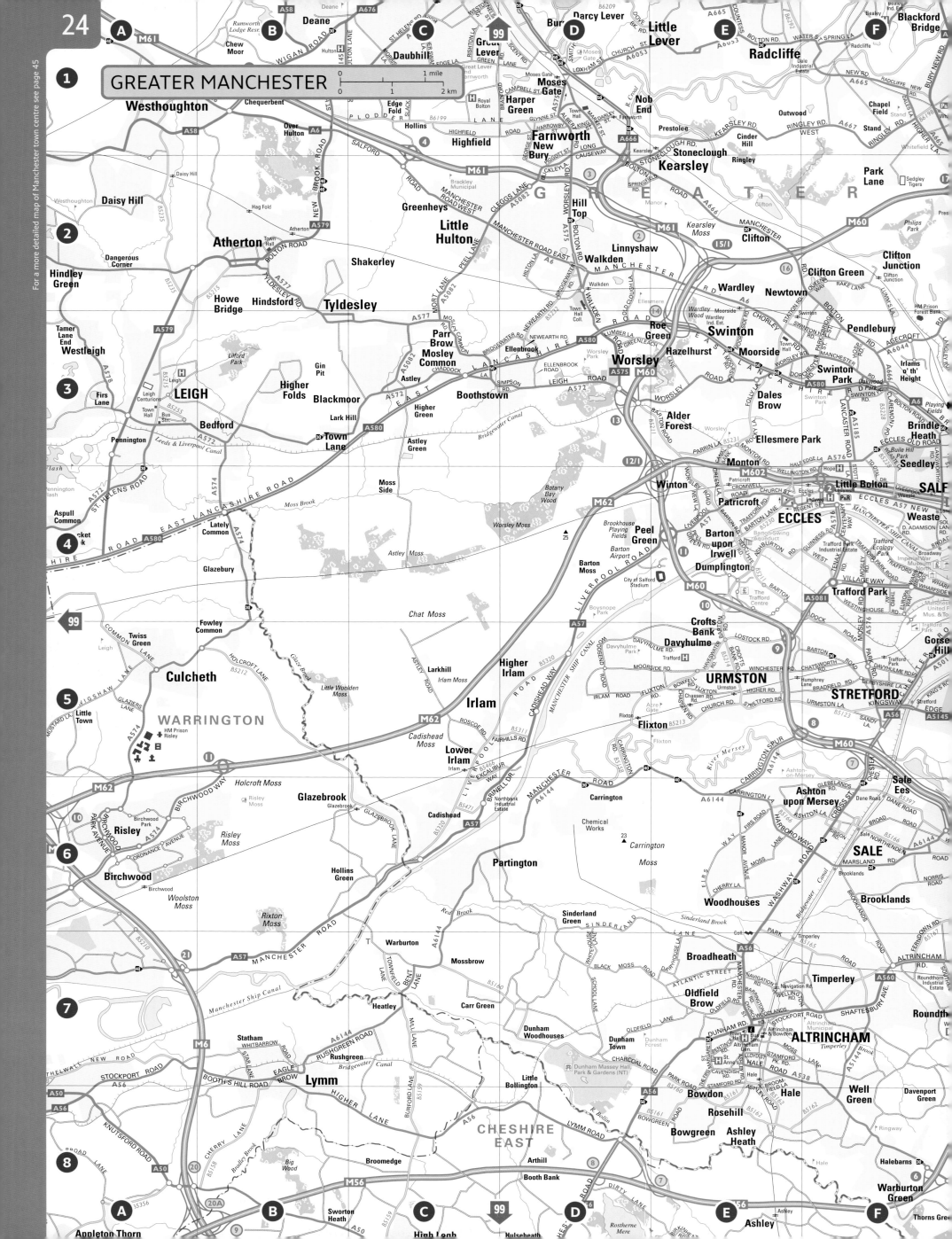

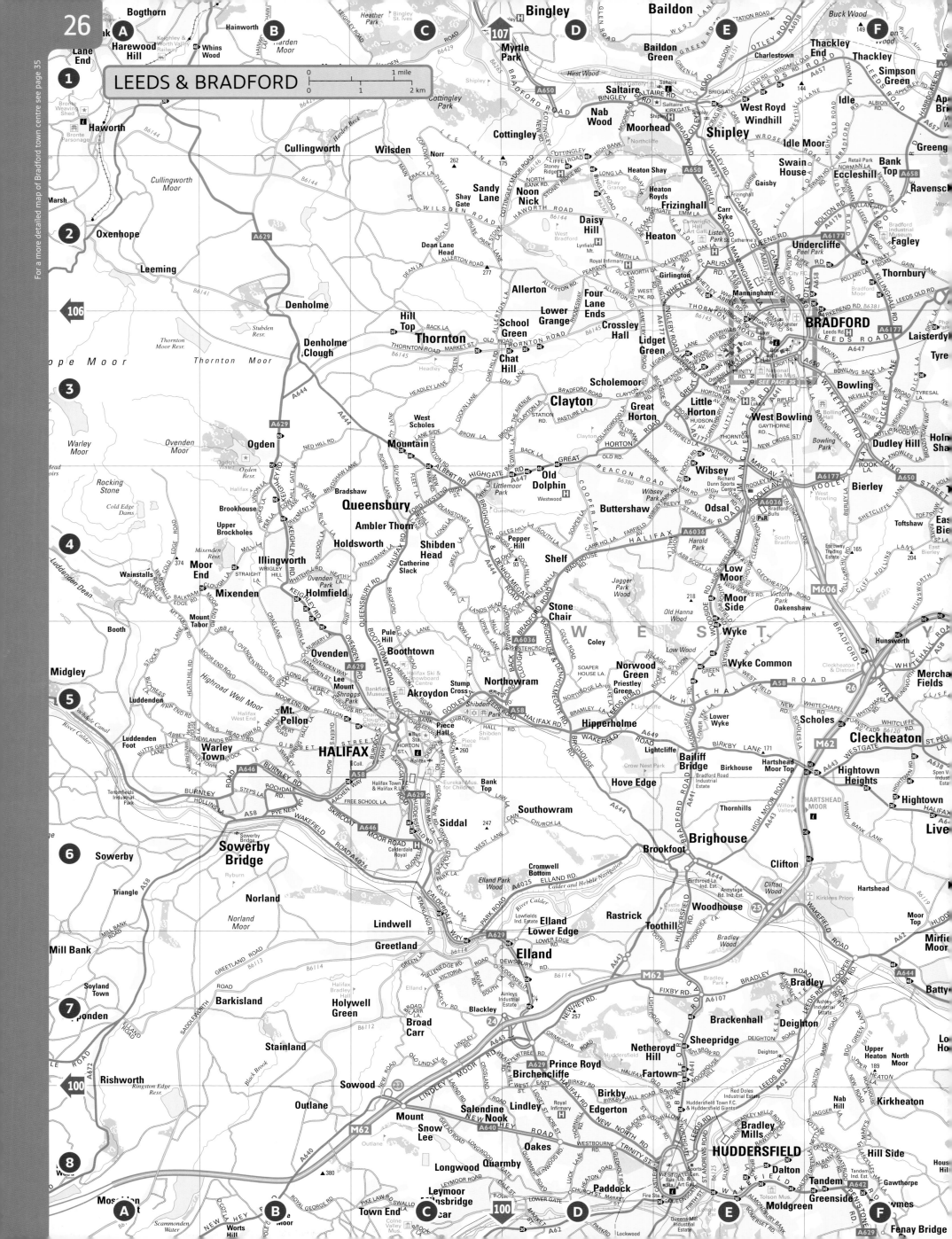

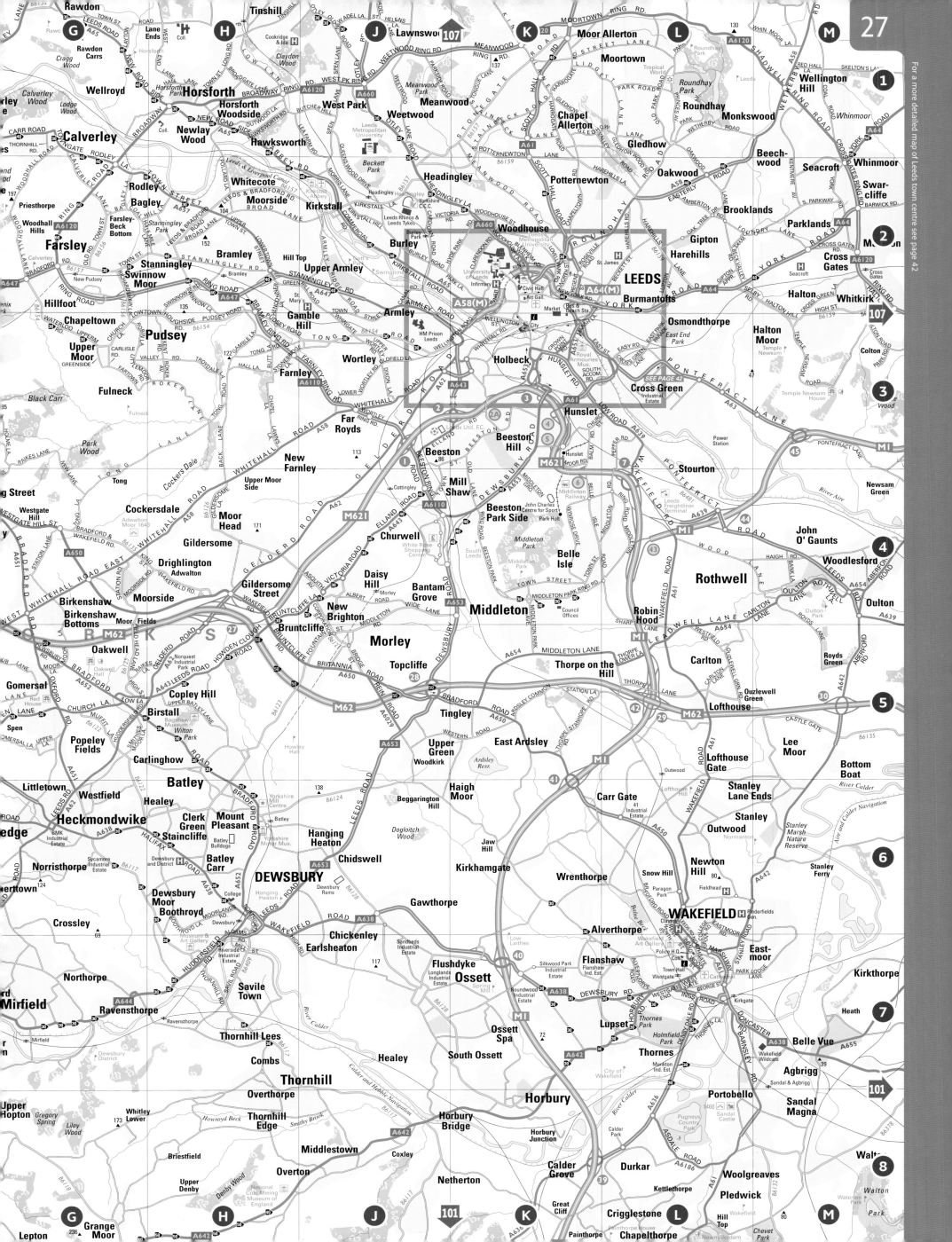

NEWCASTLE UPON TYNE & SUNDERLAND

For a more detailed map of Newcastle upon Tyne town centre see page 41 and of Sunderland town centre see page 48

MIDDLESBROUGH

0		1 mile
0	1	2 km

For a more detailed map of Middlesbrough town centre see page 41

Redcar
Marske-by-the-Sea
New Marske
Guisborough
Upleatham
Dunsdale
Wilton
Lazenby
Kirkleatham
Warrenby
Coatham
Dormanstown
Teesport
Seal Sands
Port Clarence
Haverton Hill
South Bank
Grangetown
Eston
Normanby
Ormesby
Nunthorpe
North Ormesby
Pallister
Berwick Hills
Park End
Coulby Newham
Marton
Tollesby
Acklam
Thornaby-on-Tees
Stockton-on-Tees
Norton
Roseworth
Billingham
Fairfield

REDCAR AND CLEVELAND

NORTH YORK MOORS NATIONAL PARK

New Silksworth
Ryhope
Tunstall
Grangetown
East Herrington
New Herrington
Newbottle
Penshaw
Shiney Row
Bournmoor
Washington
Biddick
Birtley
Chester-le-Street
Pelton
Ouston
Urpeth
Kibblesworth
Beamish
West Pelton
Newfield
Grange Villa
Stanley
Tanfield
Tantobie
Shield Row
Doxford Park
Thorney Close
Oxclose
Rickleton
Lambton

DURHAM
STOCKTON-ON-TEES

RIVER TEES

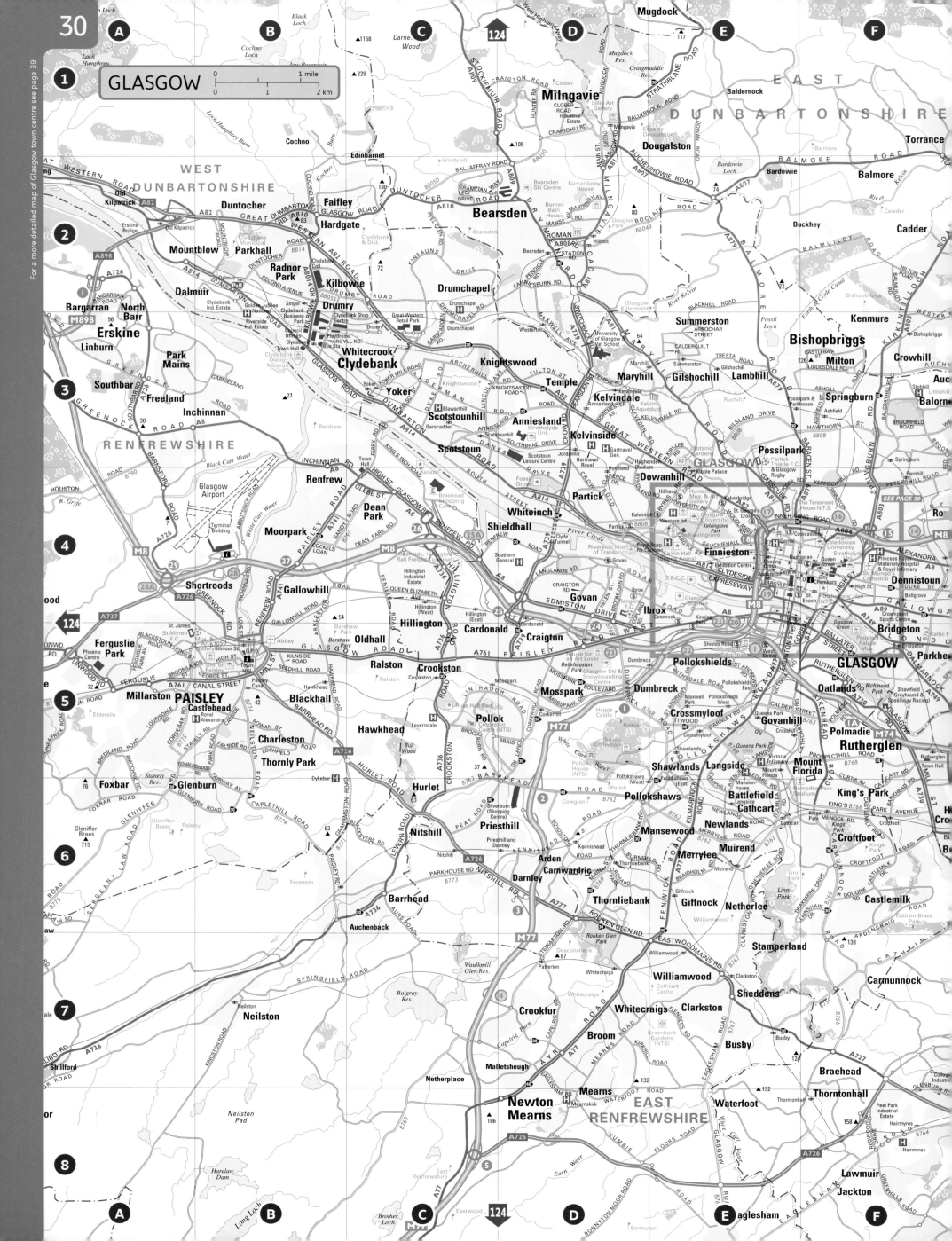

For a more detailed map of Edinburgh town centre see page 38

EDINBURGH

0   1 mile
0   1   2 km

FIRTH OF FORTH

EAST LOTHIAN

MIDLOTHIAN

PENTLAND HILLS REGIONAL PARK

Major places:
EDINBURGH, Leith, Musselburgh, Dalkeith, Bonnyrigg, Lasswade, Loanhead, Penicuik, Newtongrange, Eskbank, Newbattle, Easthouses, Gorebridge, Arniston, Milton Bridge, Auchendinny, Roslin, Bilston, Straiton, Gilmerton, Liberton, Gracemount, Fairmilehead, Colinton, Juniper Green, Currie, Balerno, Baberton, Wester Hailes, Sighthill, Stenhouse, Corstorphine, Clermiston, Barnton, Cramond, Davidson's Mains, Silverknowes, Muirhouse, Drylaw, West Pilton, Pilton, Granton, Newhaven, Trinity, Inverleith, Warriston, Comely Bank, Craigleith, Ravelston, Blackhall, Murrayfield, Dalry, Merchiston, Morningside, Craiglockhart, Oxgangs, Colinton Mains, Swanston, Torphin, Longstone, Saughton, North Gyle, South Gyle, Gogar, Turnhouse, Craigiehall, Cramond Bridge, Long Hermiston, Newington, Prestonfield, Duddingston, Bingham, Niddrie, Craigmillar, Moredun, Inch, Newcraighall, Monktonhall, Whitecraig, Inveresk, Newhailes, Joppa, Portobello, Restalring, Newton, Danderhall, Edmonstone, Millerhill, Whitehill, Dolphingstone, Cousland

Outlying villages: Dalmeny, Delteny, Crichton, Edgehead, Chesterhill, Dewartown, Mayfield, Easter Cowden, Southfi, Hunterfield, Newlandrig, Rosewell, Polton, Easter Bush, Boghall, Hillend, Dreghorn, Bonaly, Baberton, Middle Kinleith, Wester Kinleith, Easter Kinleith, Mansfield, Malleny Mills, Cockburnhill, East Rigg, Wester Bavelaw, Easter Bavelaw, Cockburnhill

Arthur's Seat 250
Scald Law 579
Middle Craig
Black Rocks
Eastern Craigs

Roads: A1, A7, A8, A68, A70, A71, A72, A90, A199, A701, A702, A703, A720, A768, A772, A899, A900, A901, A902, A903, A904, A6094, A6095, A6106, A6124, B701, B704, M8, M9

Street maps

Symbols used on the map

M8	Motorway
A4	Primary route dual / single carriageway / Junction
A40	'A' road dual / single carriageway
B507	'B' road dual / single carriageway
Toll	Other road dual / single carriageway / Toll
	One way street / Orbital route
	Access restriction
	Pedestrian street / Street market
	Minor road / Track
FB	Footpath / Footbridge
	Road under construction
	Extent of London congestion charging zone

	Main / other National Rail station
	London Underground / Overground station
	Light Rail / Station
	Bus / Coach station
P&R	Park and Ride site - rail operated (runs at least 5 days a week)
Dublin 8hrs	Vehicle / Pedestrian ferry
P	Car park
	Theatre
	Major hotel
	Public House
Pol	Police station
Lib	Library
PO	Post Office

	Visitor information centre (open all year / seasonally)
	Toilet
JAPAN	Embassy
	Cinema
	Cathedral / Church
Mormon	Mosque / Synagogue / Other place of worship
	Park / Garden / Sports ground
	Cemetery

	Leisure & tourism
	Shopping
	Administration & law
	Health & welfare
	Education
	Industry / Office
	Other notable building

Street maps

Locator map

ABERDEEN
Appears on main map page 135

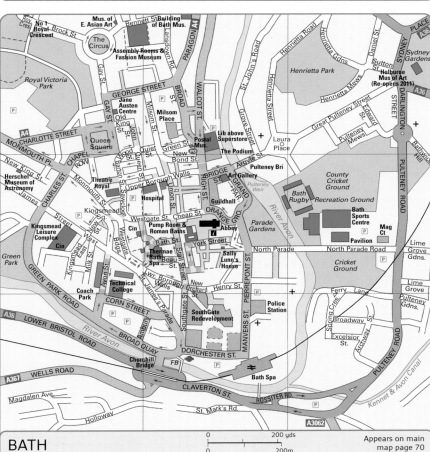

BATH
Appears on main map page 70

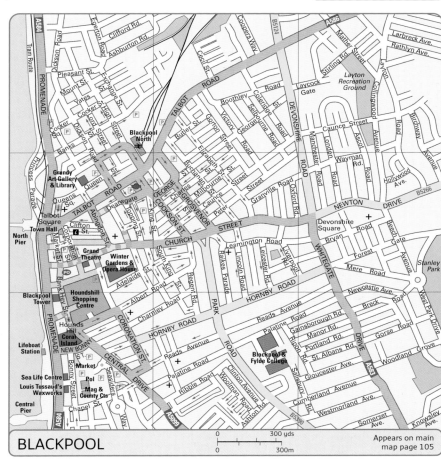

BLACKPOOL
Appears on main map page 105

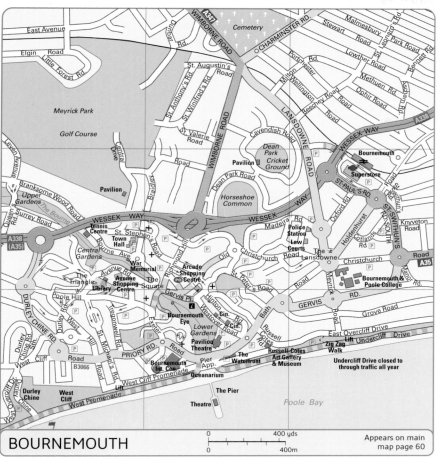

BOURNEMOUTH

| | 400 yds |
| | 400m |

Appears on main
map page 60

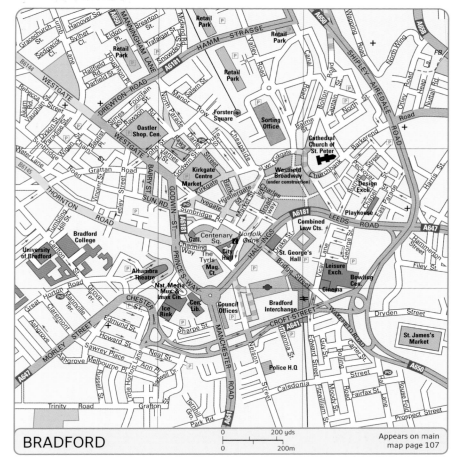

BRADFORD

| | 200 yds |
| | 200m |

Appears on main
map page 107

BRIGHTON

| | 200 yds |
| | 200m |

Appears on main
map page 63

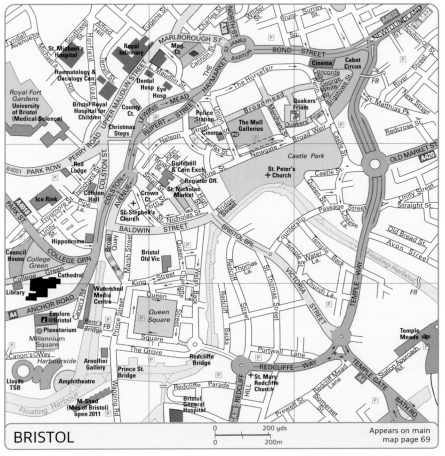

BRISTOL

| | 200 yds |
| | 200m |

Appears on main
map page 69

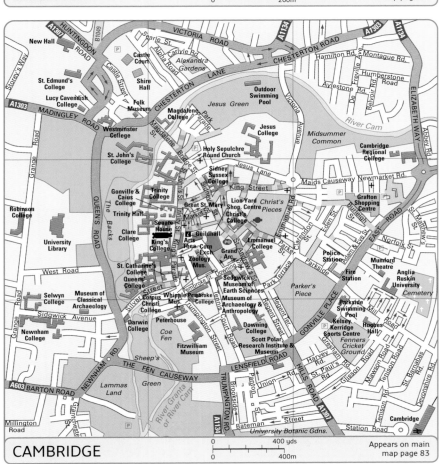

CAMBRIDGE

| | 400 yds |
| | 400m |

Appears on main
map page 83

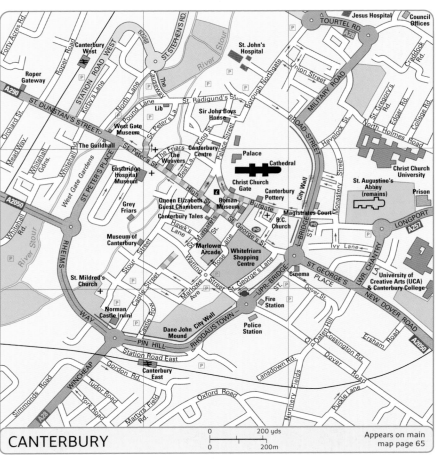

CANTERBURY

| | 200 yds |
| | 200m |

Appears on main
map page 65

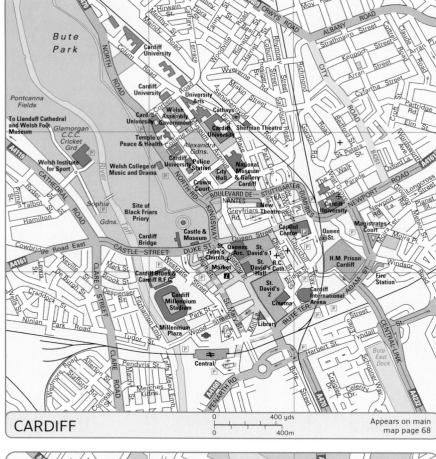

CARDIFF

0   400 yds
0   400m

Appears on main
map page 68

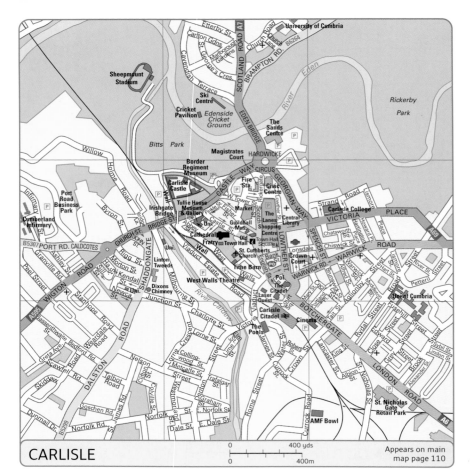

CARLISLE

0   400 yds
0   400m

Appears on main
map page 110

CHELTENHAM

0   300 yds
0   300m

Appears on main
map page 79

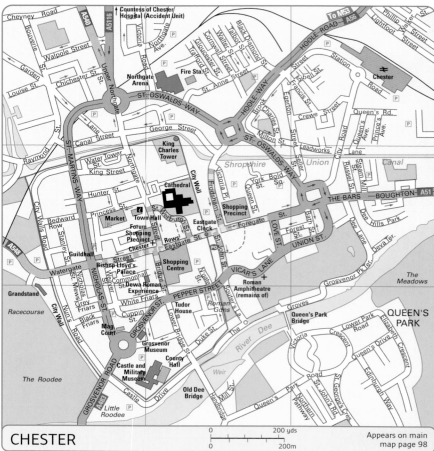

CHESTER

0   200 yds
0   200m

Appears on main
map page 98

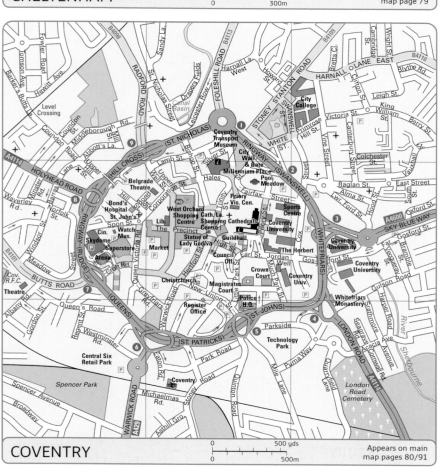

COVENTRY

0   500 yds
0   500m

Appears on main
map pages 80/91

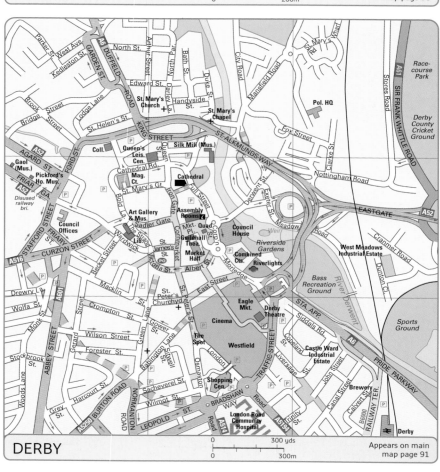

DERBY

0   300 yds
0   300m

Appears on main
map page 91

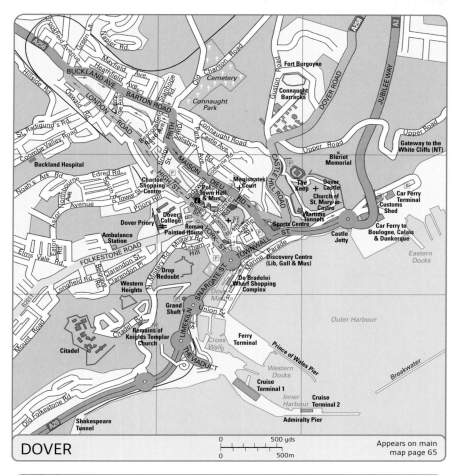

DOVER

Appears on main map page 65

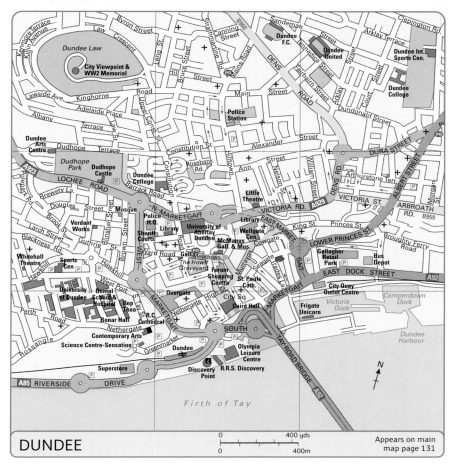

DUNDEE

Appears on main map page 131

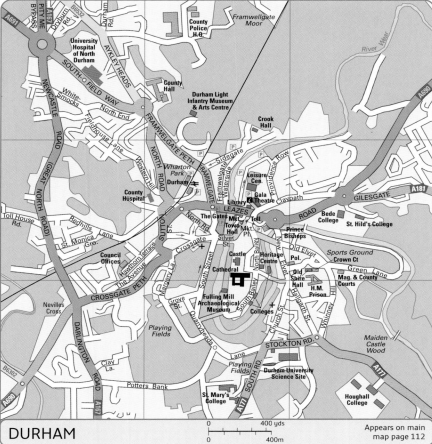

DURHAM

Appears on main map page 112

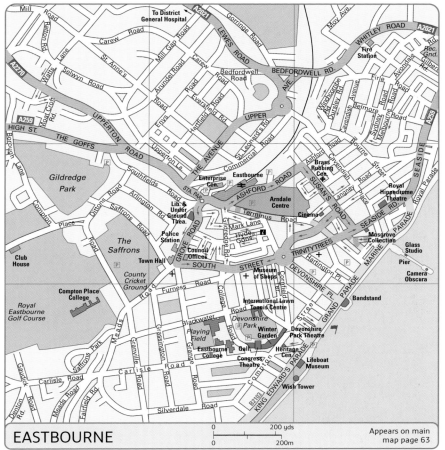

EASTBOURNE

Appears on main map page 63

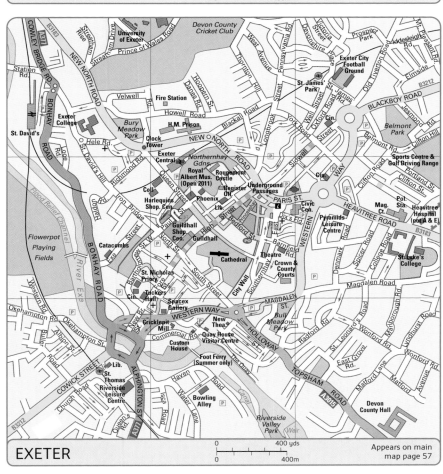

EXETER

Appears on main map page 57

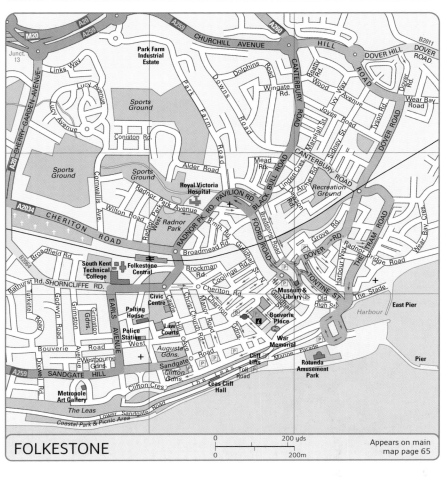

FOLKESTONE

Appears on main map page 65

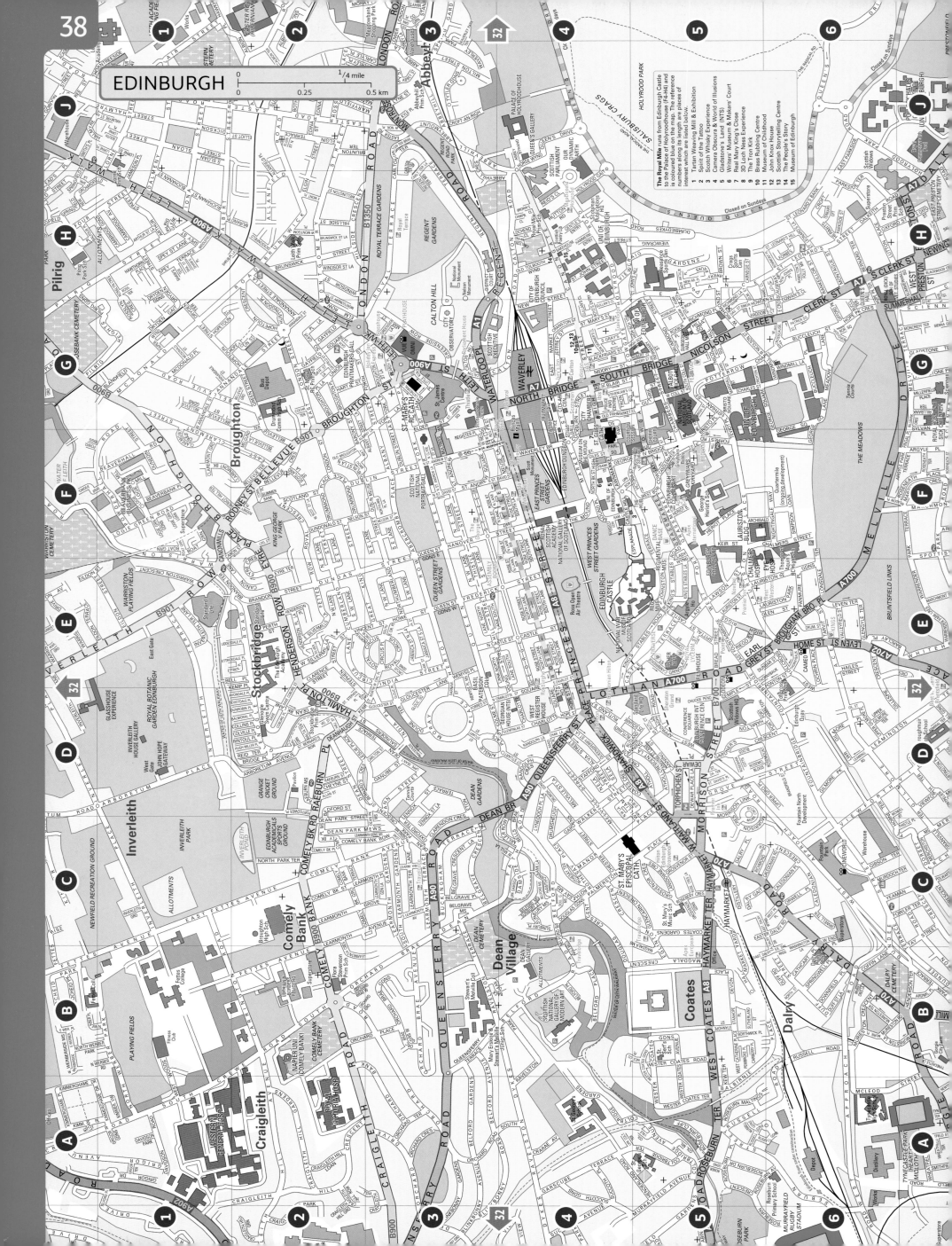

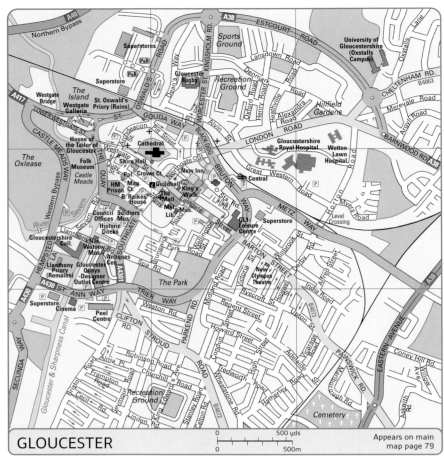

GLOUCESTER

0 — 500 yds
0 — 500m

Appears on main map page 79

GUILDFORD

0 — 200 yds
0 — 200m

Appears on main map page 72

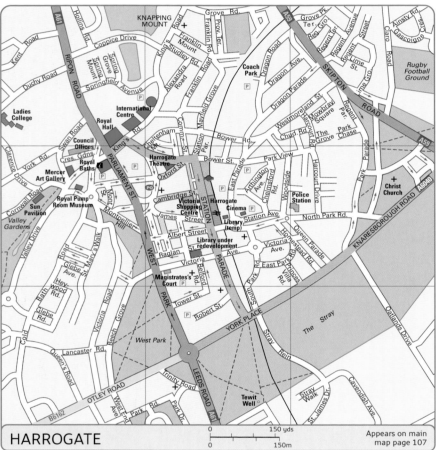

HARROGATE

0 — 150 yds
0 — 150m

Appears on main map page 107

HASTINGS

0 — 500 yds
0 — 500m

Appears on main map page 64

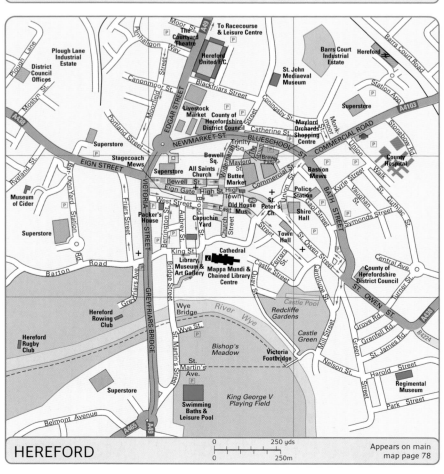

HEREFORD

0 — 250 yds
0 — 250m

Appears on main map page 78

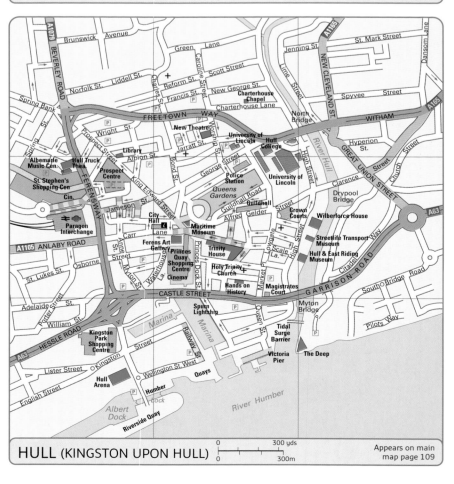

HULL (KINGSTON UPON HULL)

0 — 300 yds
0 — 300m

Appears on main map page 109

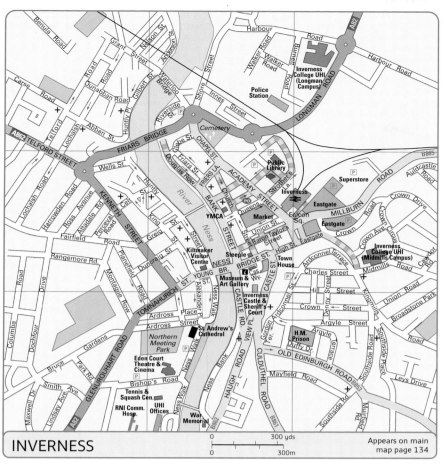

INVERNESS

0   300 yds
0   300m

Appears on main
map page 134

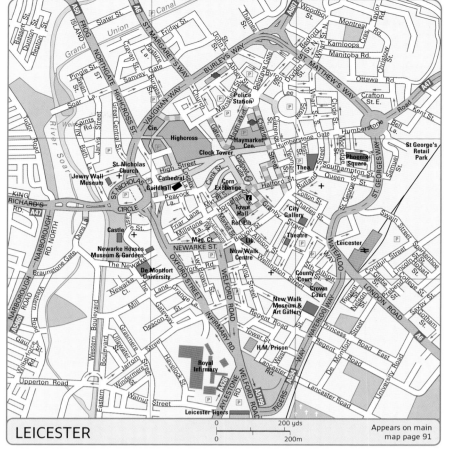

LEICESTER

0   200 yds
0   200m

Appears on main
map page 91

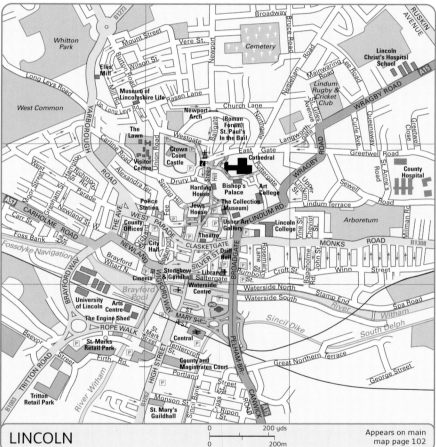

LINCOLN

0   200 yds
0   200m

Appears on main
map page 102

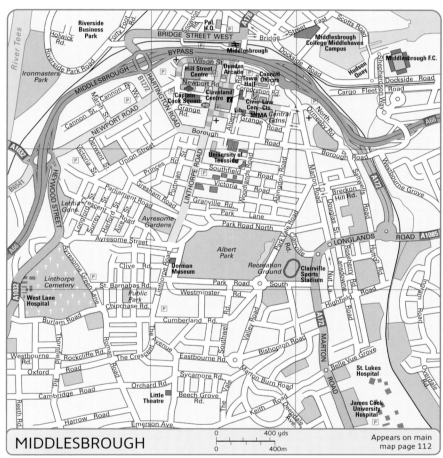

MIDDLESBROUGH

0   400 yds
0   400m

Appears on main
map page 112

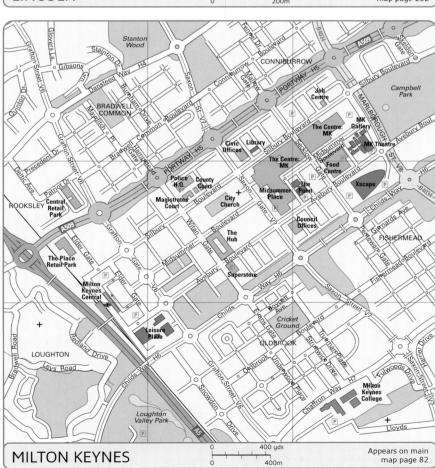

MILTON KEYNES

0   400 yds
0   400m

Appears on main
map page 82

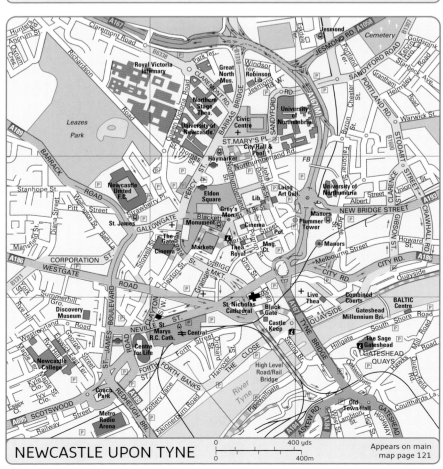

NEWCASTLE UPON TYNE

0   400 yds
0   400m

Appears on main
map page 121

MANCHESTER

1/4 mile

0   0.25   0.5 km

NORWICH

Appears on main map page 95

NOTTINGHAM

Appears on main map page 91

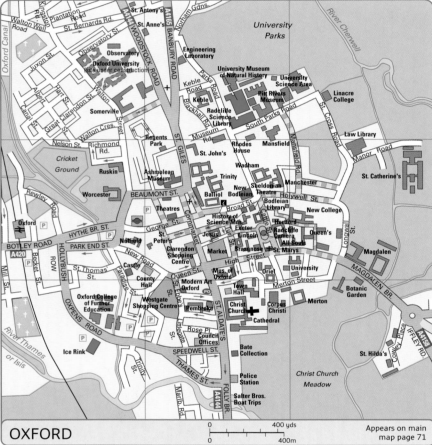

OXFORD

Appears on main map page 71

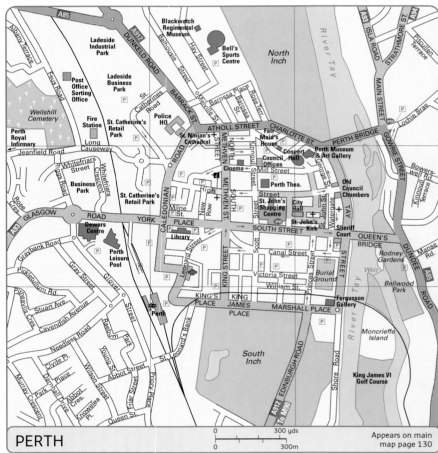

PERTH

Appears on main map page 130

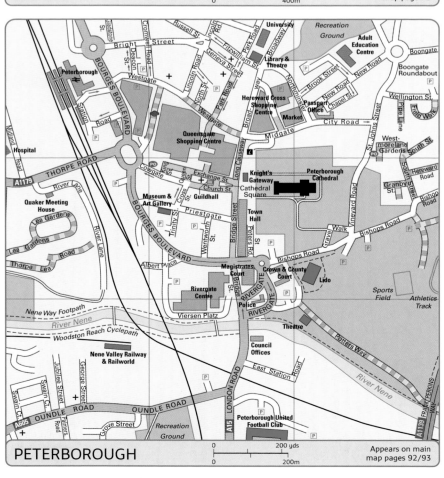

PETERBOROUGH

Appears on main map pages 92/93

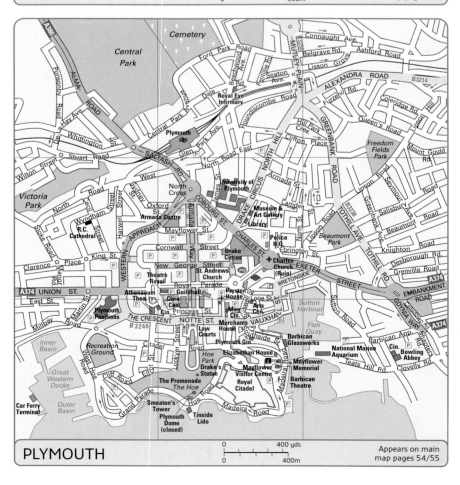

PLYMOUTH

Appears on main map pages 54/55

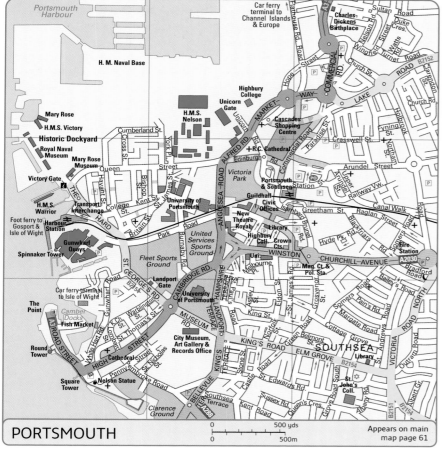

PORTSMOUTH

Appears on main
map page 61

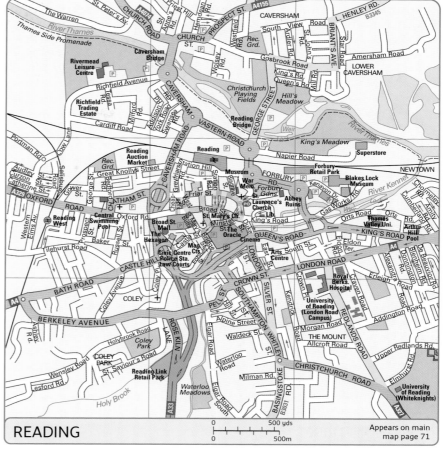

READING

Appears on main
map page 71

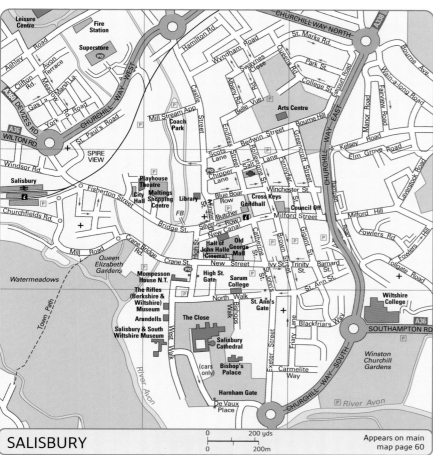

SALISBURY

Appears on main
map page 60

SCARBOROUGH

Appears on main
map page 109

SHEFFIELD

Appears on main
map page 101

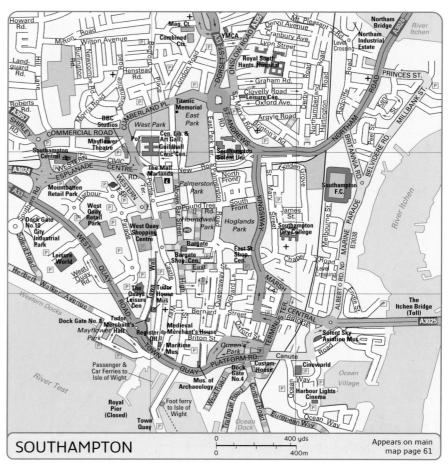

SOUTHAMPTON

Appears on main
map page 61

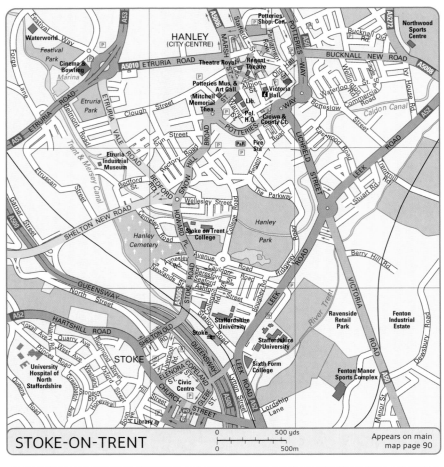

STOKE-ON-TRENT

0 — 500 yds
0 — 500m

Appears on main map page 90

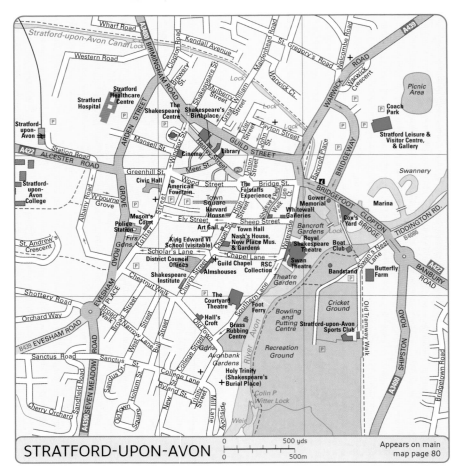

STRATFORD-UPON-AVON

0 — 500 yds
0 — 500m

Appears on main map page 80

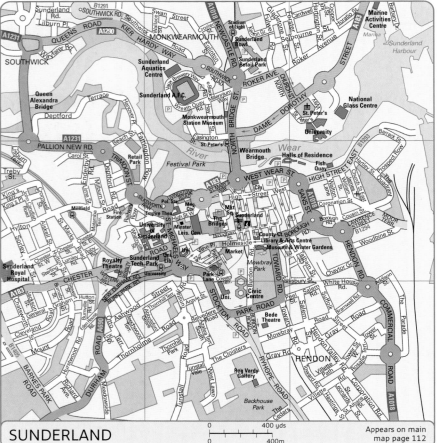

SUNDERLAND

0 — 400 yds
0 — 400m

Appears on main map page 112

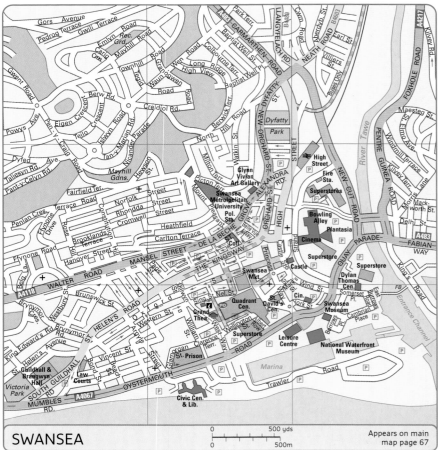

SWANSEA

0 — 500 yds
0 — 500m

Appears on main map page 67

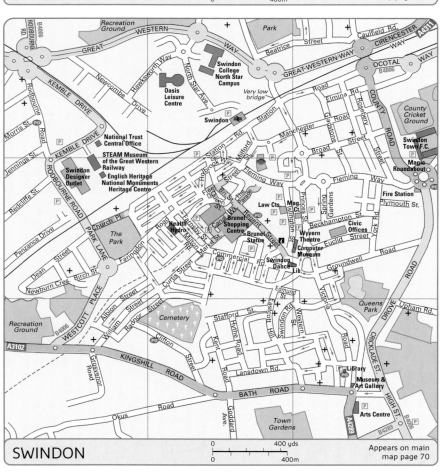

SWINDON

0 — 400 yds
0 — 400m

Appears on main map page 70

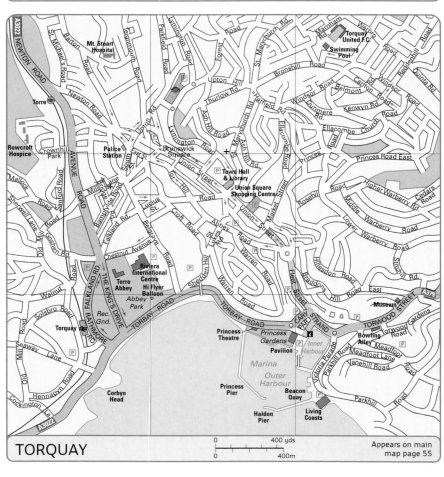

TORQUAY

0 — 400 yds
0 — 400m

Appears on main map page 55

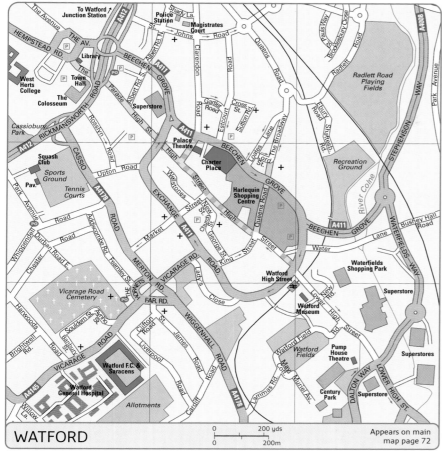

WATFORD

Appears on main map page 72

0 200 yds
0 200m

WESTON-SUPER-MARE

Appears on main map page 69

0 400 yds
0 400m

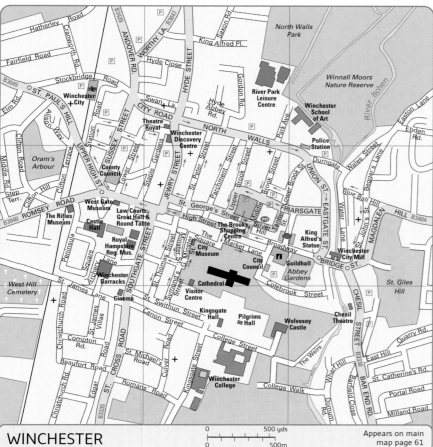

WINCHESTER

Appears on main map page 61

0 500 yds
0 500m

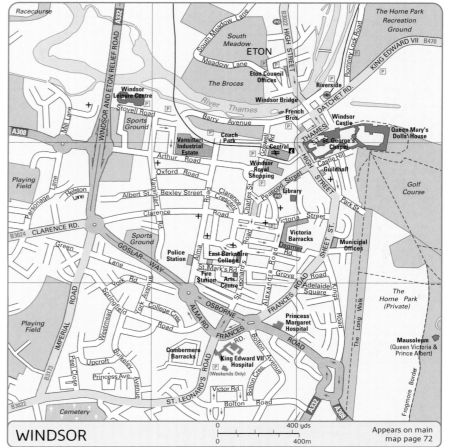

WINDSOR

Appears on main map page 72

0 400 yds
0 400m

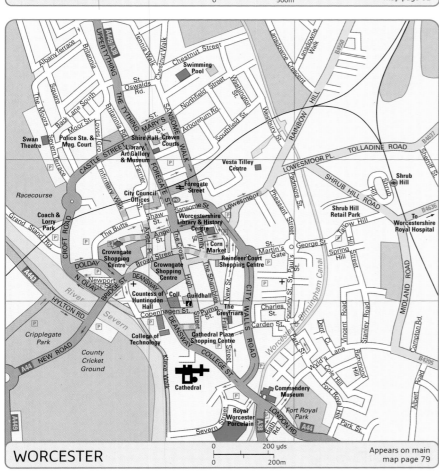

WORCESTER

Appears on main map page 79

0 200 yds
0 200m

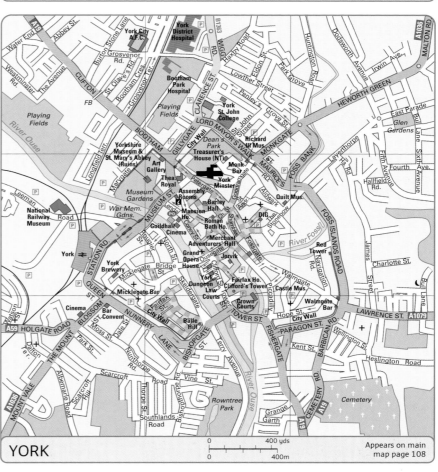

YORK

Appears on main map page 108

0 400 yds
0 400m

Key to map symbols 🅿 Short stay car park 🅿 Mid stay car park 🅿 Long stay car park 🅿 Other car park ▢ Airport terminal building

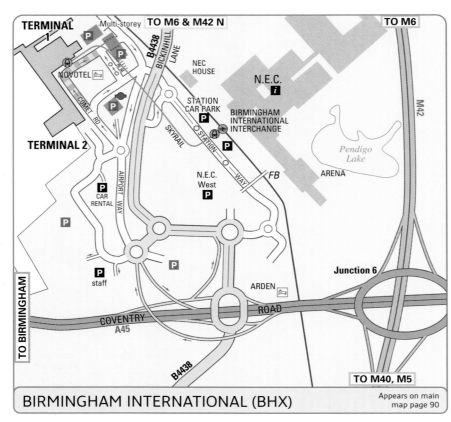

BIRMINGHAM INTERNATIONAL (BHX)

Appears on main map page 90

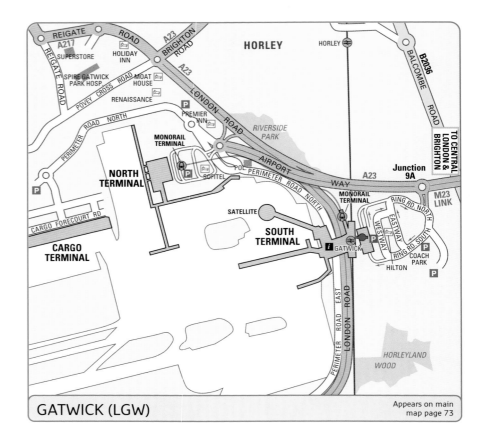

GATWICK (LGW)

Appears on main map page 73

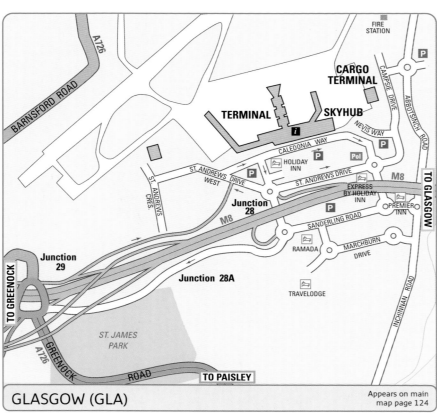

GLASGOW (GLA)

Appears on main map page 124

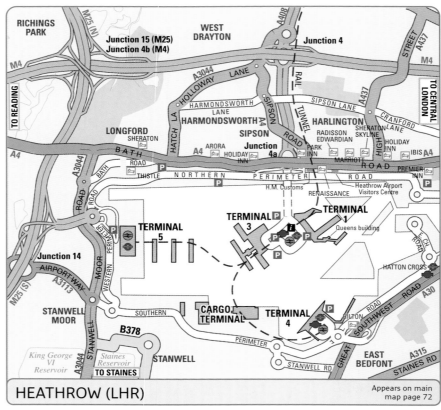

HEATHROW (LHR)

Appears on main map page 72

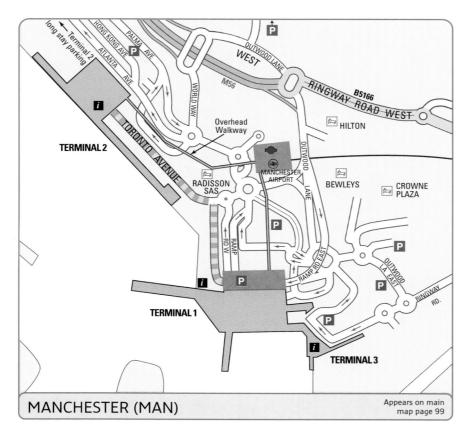

MANCHESTER (MAN)

Appears on main map page 99

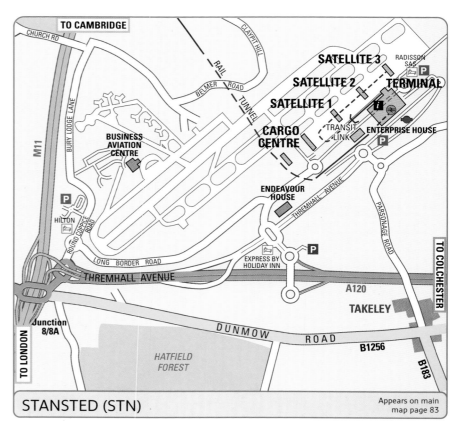

STANSTED (STN)

Appears on main map page 83

Map scale

A scale bar appears at the bottom of every page to help with measurements.

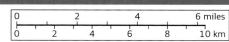

0		2		4		6 miles
0	2	4		6		10 km

England, Wales & Southern Scotland are at a scale of 1:200,000 or 3.2 miles to 1 inch
Northern Scotland is at a scale of 1:316,800 or 5 miles to 1 inch.
Orkney & Shetland are at a scale of 1:411,840 or 6.5 miles to 1 inch

Symbols used on the map

M5	Motorway
M6 Toll	Toll motorway
8 / 9	Motorway junction with full / limited access (in congested areas there is just a numbered symbol)
Maidstone Birch Sarn	Motorway service area with off road / full / limited access
A556	Primary route dual / single carriageway
	24 hour service area on primary route
Peterhead	Primary route destination Primary route destinations are places of major traffic importance linked by the primary route network. They are shown on a green background on direction signs.
A30	'A' road dual / single carriageway
B1403	'B' road dual / single carriageway
	Minor road
	Road with restricted access
	Roads with passing places
	Road proposed or under construction
33	Multi-level junction with full / limited access (with junction number)
	Roundabout
4	Road distance in miles between markers
	Road tunnel
	Steep hill (arrows point downhill)
Toll	Level crossing / Toll
St. Malo 8hrs	Car ferry route with journey times
	Railway line / station / tunnel
South Downs Way	National Trail / Long Distance Route

30 V	Fixed safety camera / fixed average-speed safety camera. Speed shown by number within camera, a V indicates a variable limit.
30 90	
✈ ✈	Airport with / without scheduled services
H	Heliport
P&R P&R	Park and Ride site operated by bus / rail (runs at least 5 days a week)
	Built up area
□ □ □	Town / Village / Other settlement
Hythe	Seaside destination
	National boundary
KENT	County / Unitary Authority boundary and name
	Heritage Coast
	National Park
	Regional / Forest Park boundary
	Woodland
Danger Zone	Military range
468 ▲ 941	Spot / Summit height (in metres)
	Lake / Dam / River / Waterfall
	Canal / Dry canal / Canal tunnel
	Lighthouse
	Beach
SEE PAGE 3	Area covered by urban area map
190	National Grid reference figures
SY	National Grid reference letters

Places of interest

A selection of tourist detail is shown on the mapping. It is advisable to check with the local tourist information centre regarding opening times and facilities available.

Any of the following symbols may appear on the map in maroon ★ which indicates that the site has World Heritage status.

i	Tourist information centre (open all year)
i	Tourist information centre (open seasonally)
m	Ancient monument
	Aquarium
	Aqueduct / Viaduct
	Arboretum
⚔ 1643	Battlefield
	Blue flag beach
▲	Camp site / Caravan site
	Castle
	Cave
	Country park
	County cricket ground
	Distillery
	Ecclesiastical feature
	Event venue
	Farm park
	Garden
	Golf course
	Historic house

	Historic ship
	Major football club
£	Major shopping centre / Outlet village
	Major sports venue
	Motor racing circuit
	Mountain bike trail
	Museum / Art gallery
	Nature reserve (NNR indicates a National Nature Reserve)
	Racecourse
	Rail Freight Terminal
	Ski slope (artificial / natural)
	Spotlight nature reserve (Best sites for access to nature)
	Steam railway centre / preserved railway
	Surfing beach
	Theme park
	University
	Vineyard
	Wildlife park / Zoo
★	Other interesting feature
(NT) (NTS)	National Trust / National Trust for Scotland property

Reading our maps

Multi-level junctions
Non-motorway junctions where slip roads are used to access the main roads

Distances
Blue numbers give distances in miles between junctions shown with a blue marker

Park & Ride
Sites are shown that operate at least 5 days a week. Bus operated sites have a yellow symbol and rail operated sites a pink symbol.

Motorway service area

World Heritage site
Places of interest defined by UNESCO as special on a world scale

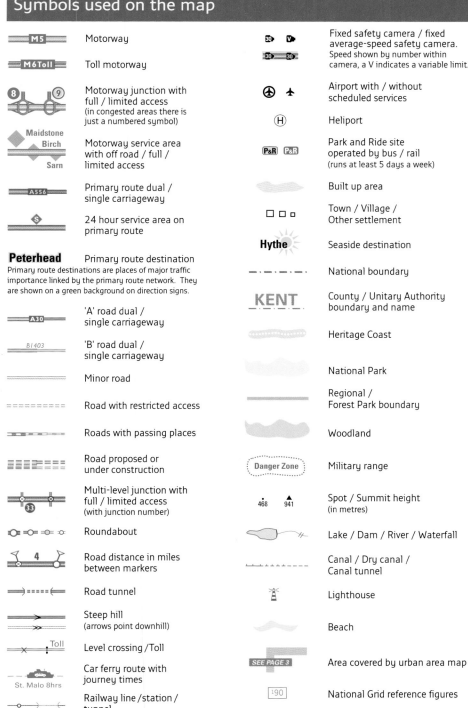

Places of interest
Blue symbols indicate places of interest. See the section at the bottom of the page for the different types of feature represented on the map.

Safety Camera
The number inside the camera shows the speed limit at the camera location.

More detailed maps
Green boxes indicate busy built-up areas. More detailed mapping is available.

Map pages

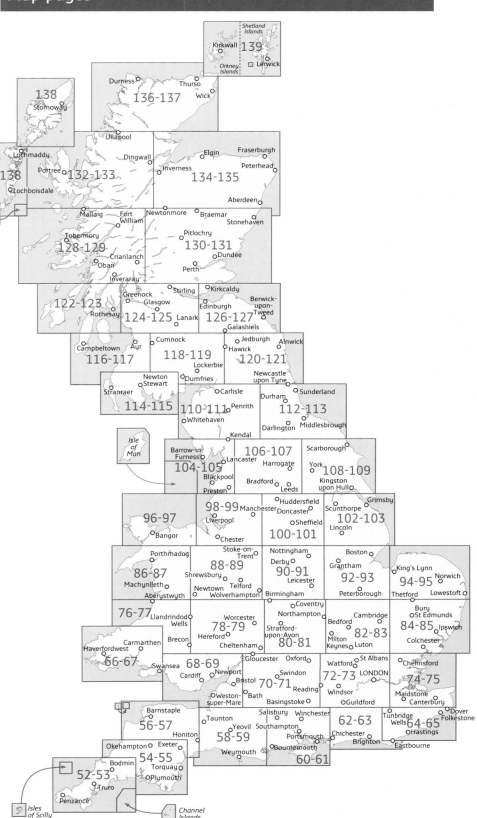

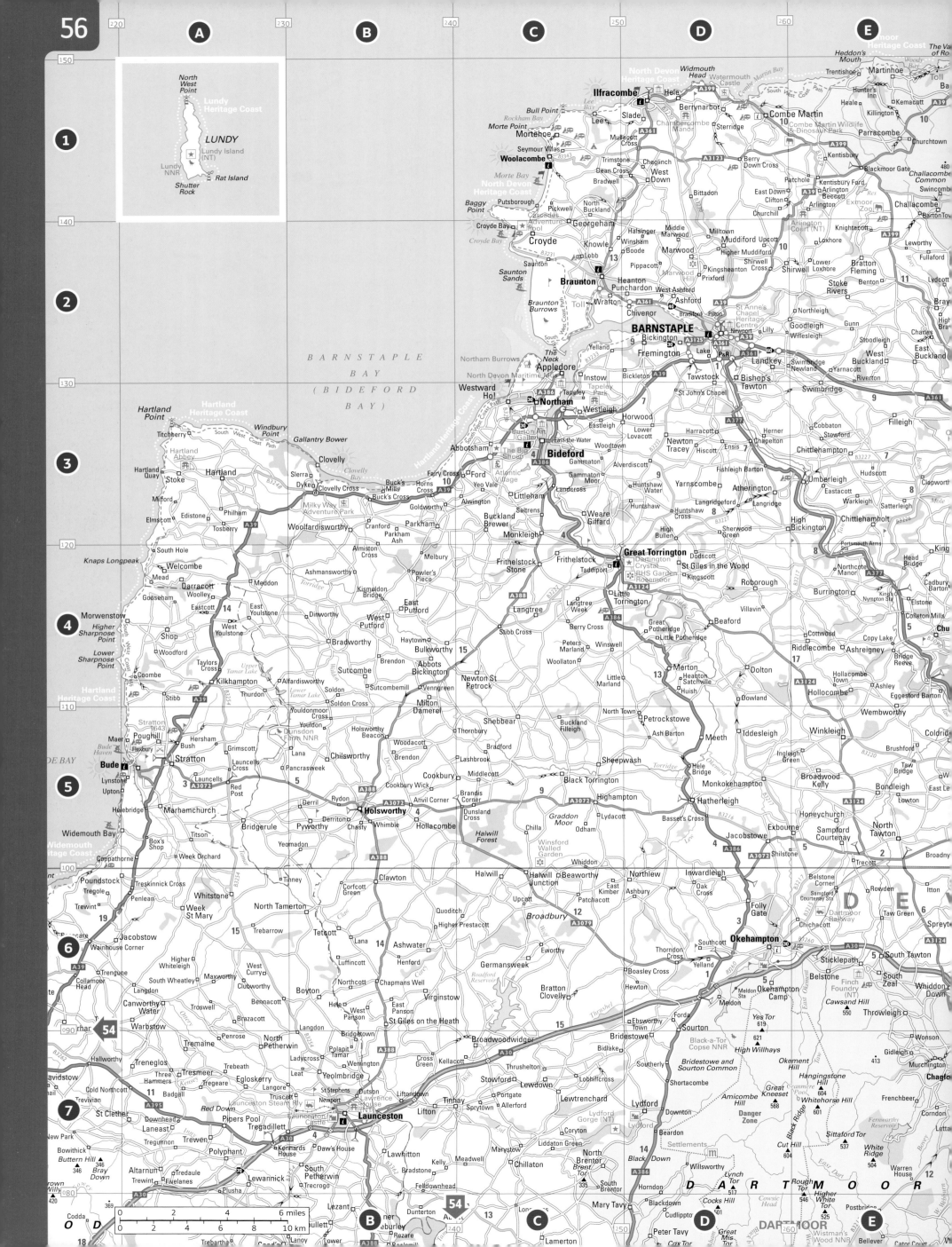

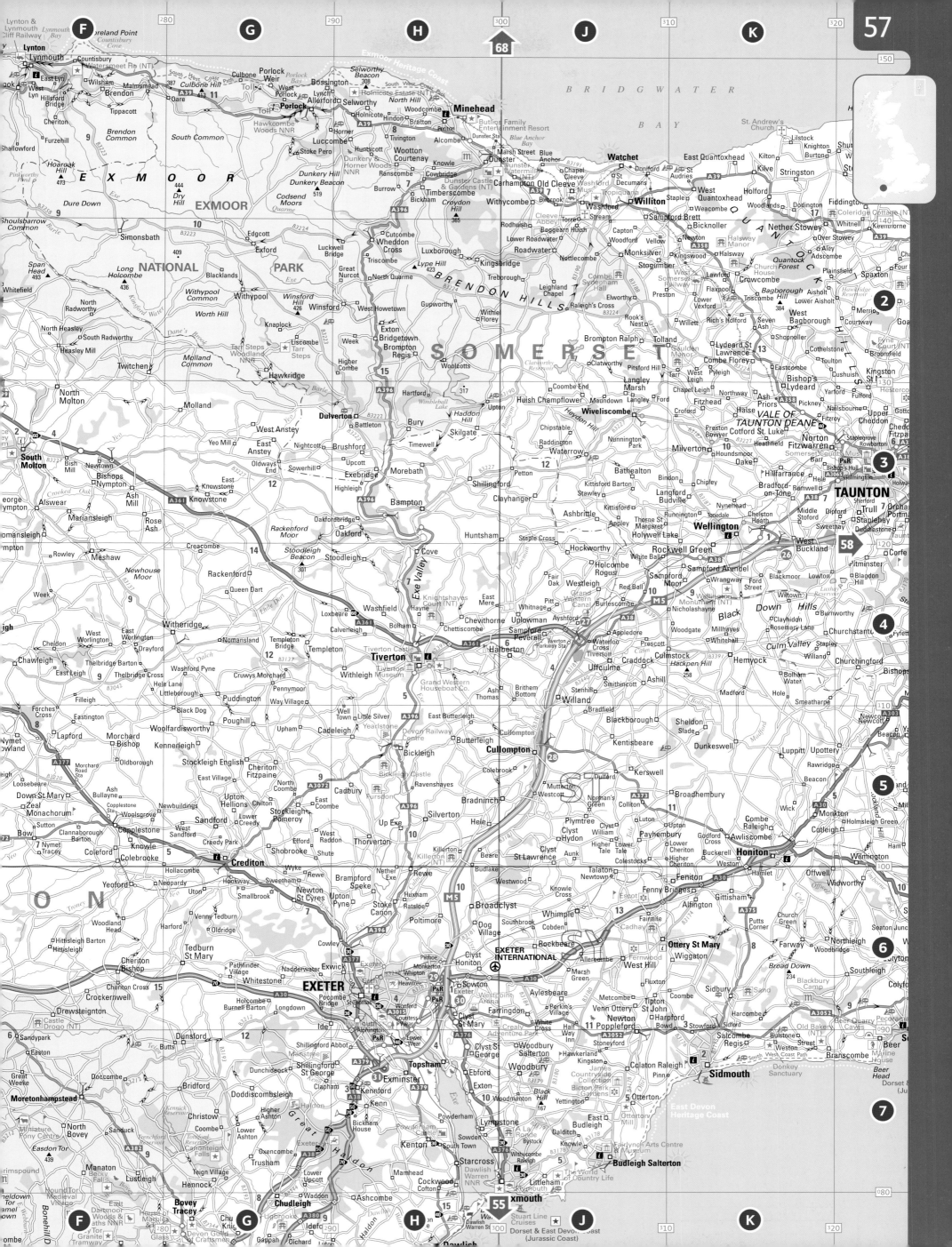

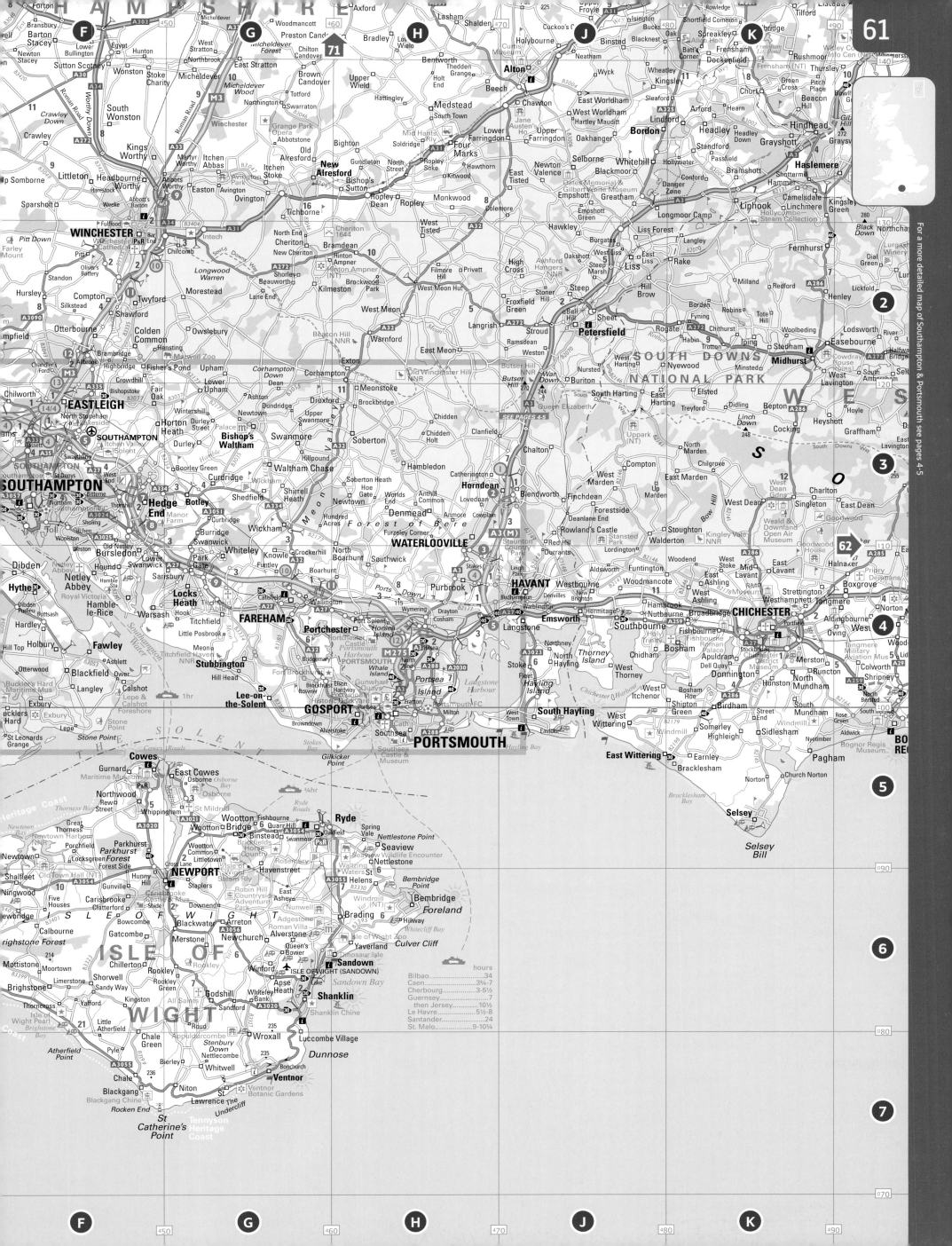

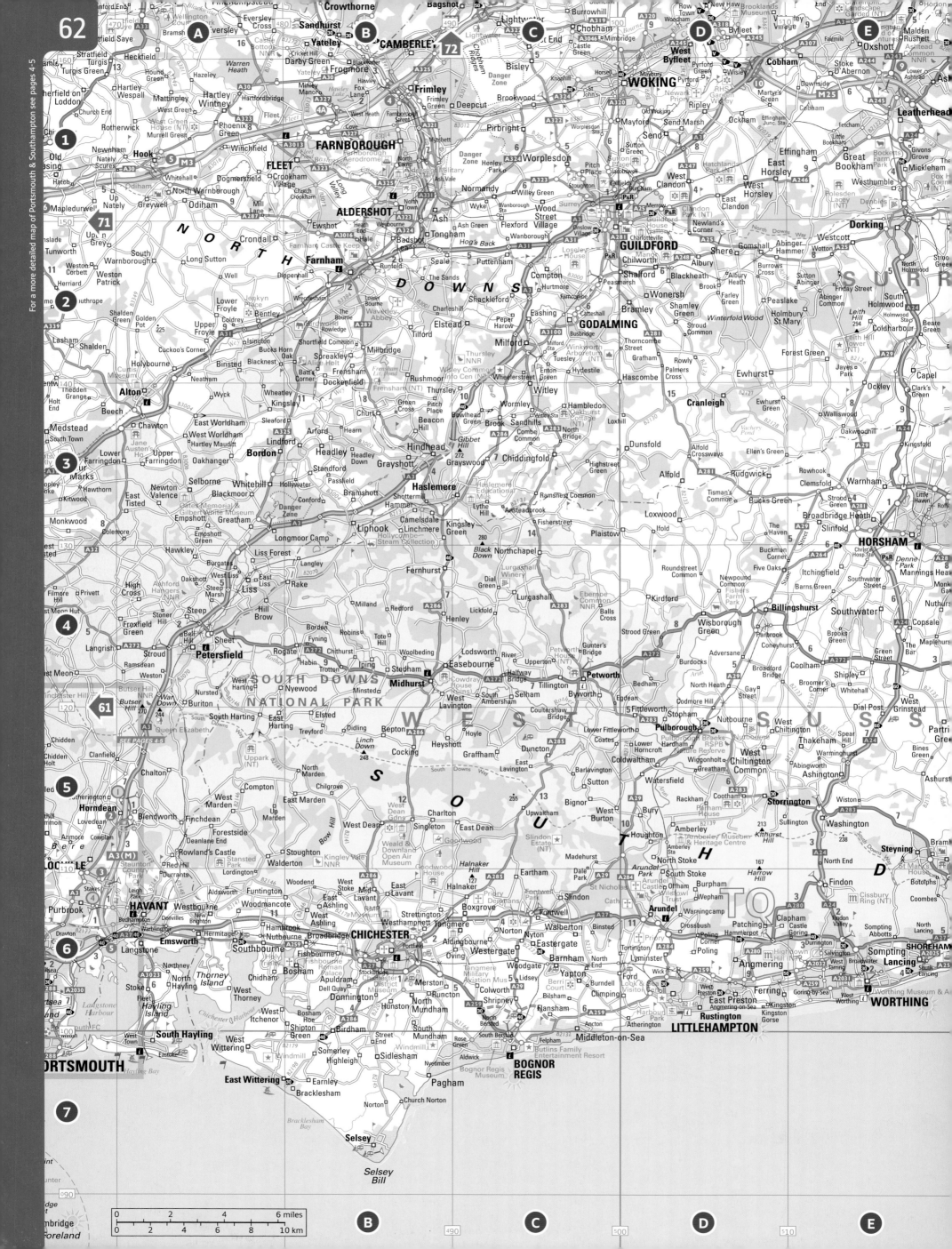

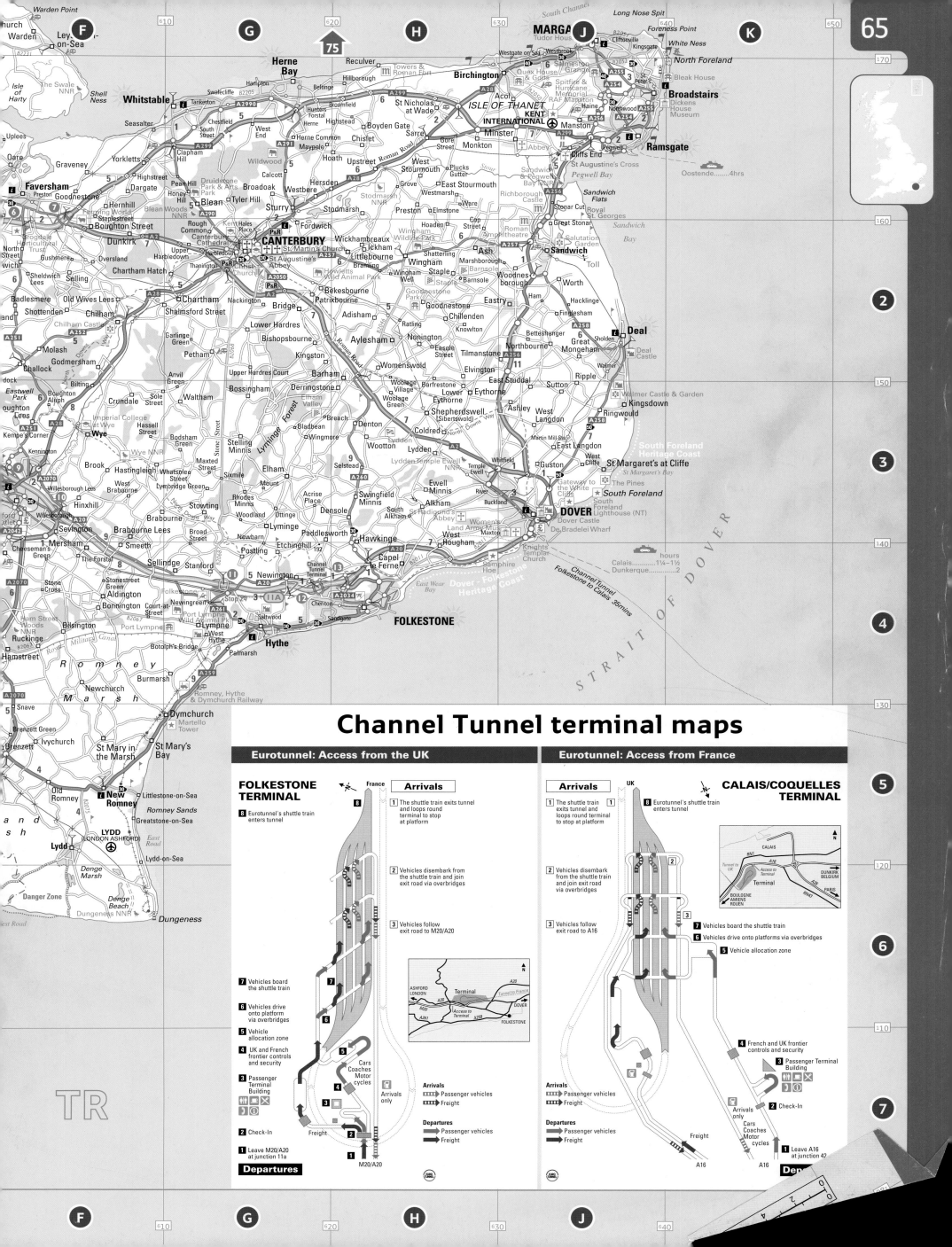

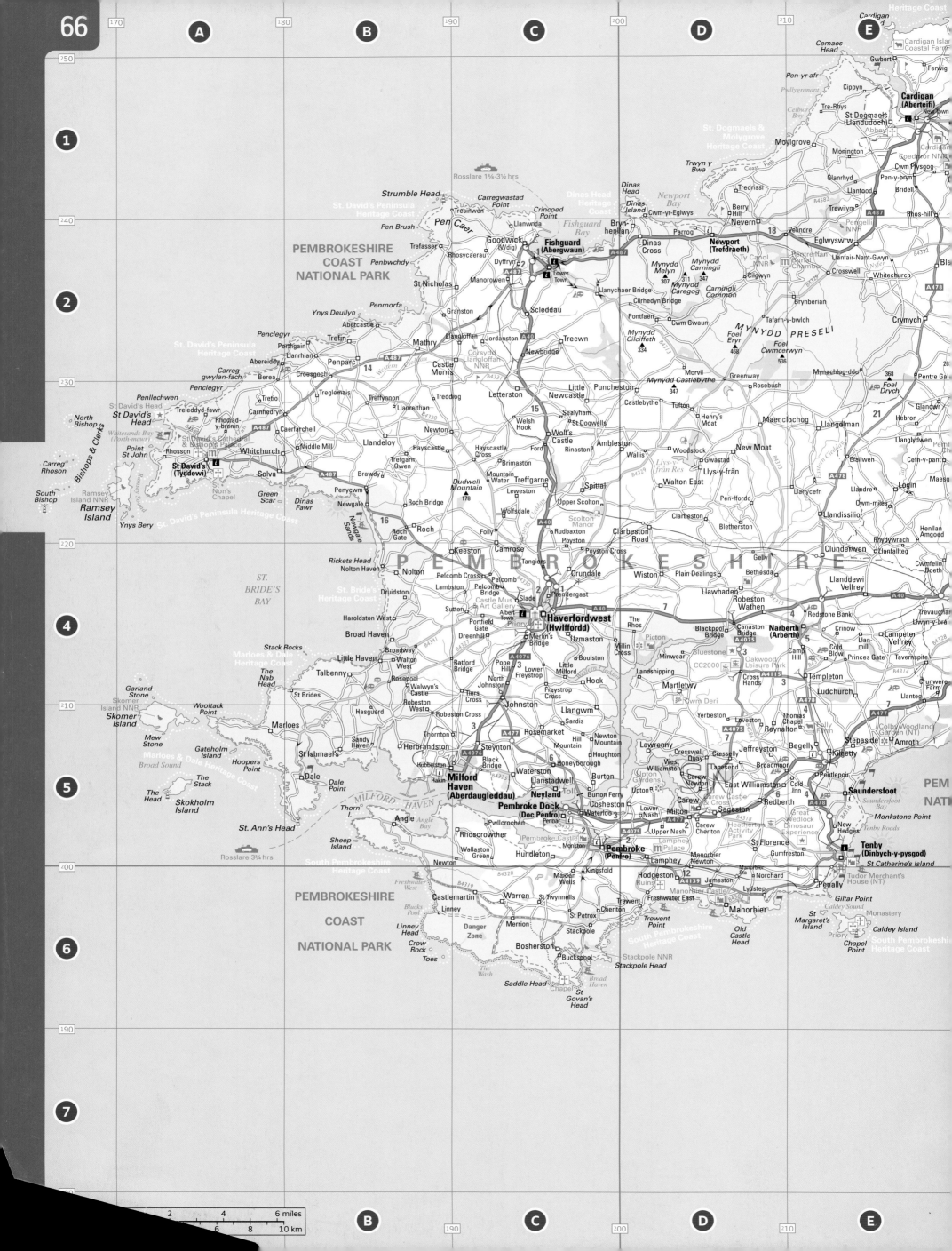

GLOUCESTERSHIRE

COTSWOLDS

SOUTH GLOUCESTERSHIRE

BATH & NORTH EAST SOMERSET

WILTSHIRE

SALISBURY PLAIN

VALE OF PEWSEY

SWINDON

STROUD

Cirencester

Swindon

Wootton Bassett

Malmesbury

Tetbury

Nailsworth

Dursley

Wotton-under-Edge

Chipping Sodbury

Yate

Chippenham

Calne

Marlborough

Avebury

Corsham

Bath

Melksham

Devizes

Bradford-on-Avon

Trowbridge

Westbury

Radstock

Frome

Warminster

Amesbury

Pewsey

For a more detailed map of Bristol see page 8

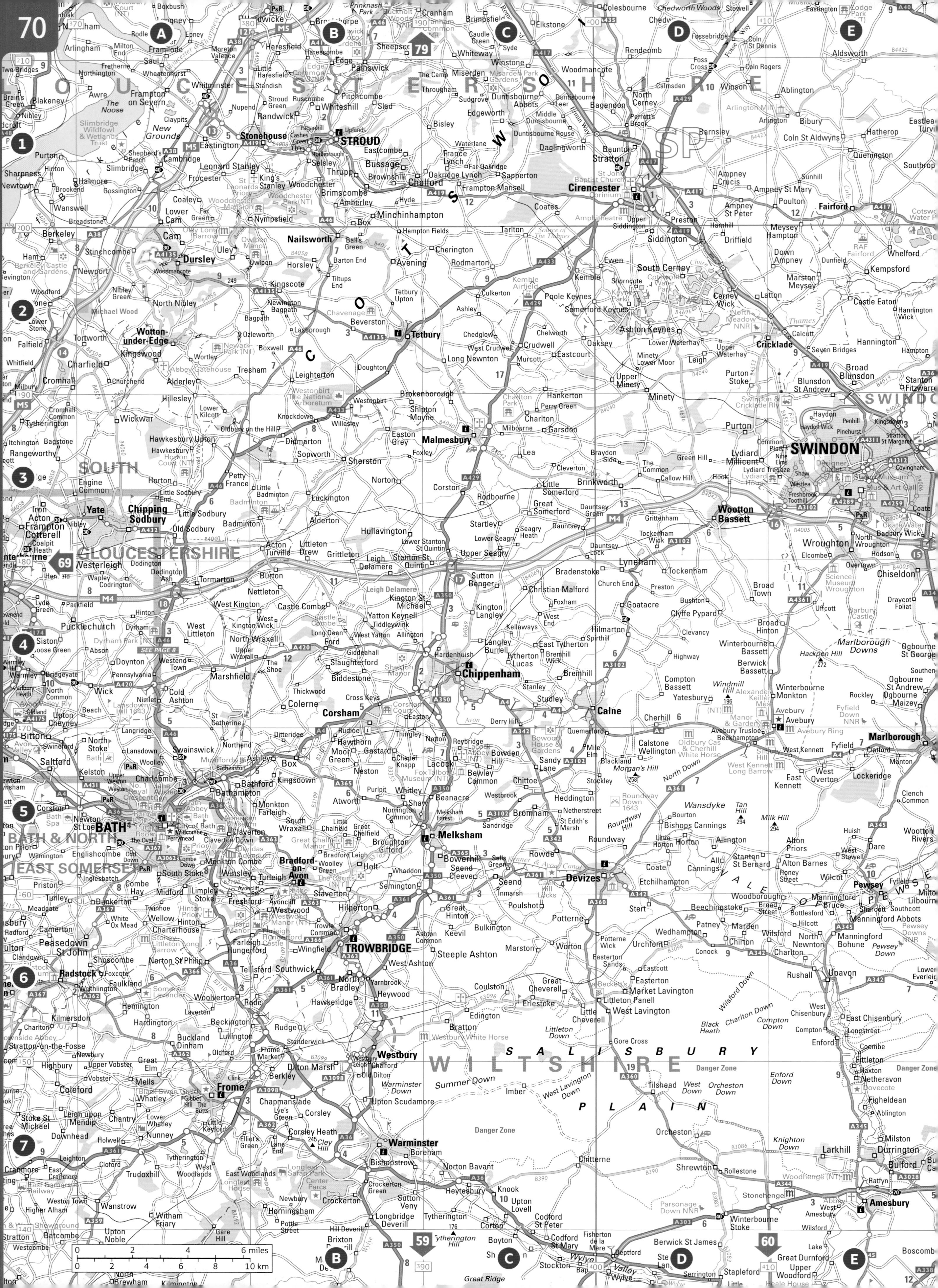

SEE PAGE 8

0 2 4 6 miles
0 2 4 6 8 10 km

For a more detailed map of West Midlands see pages 14-15 and of Coventry see page 16

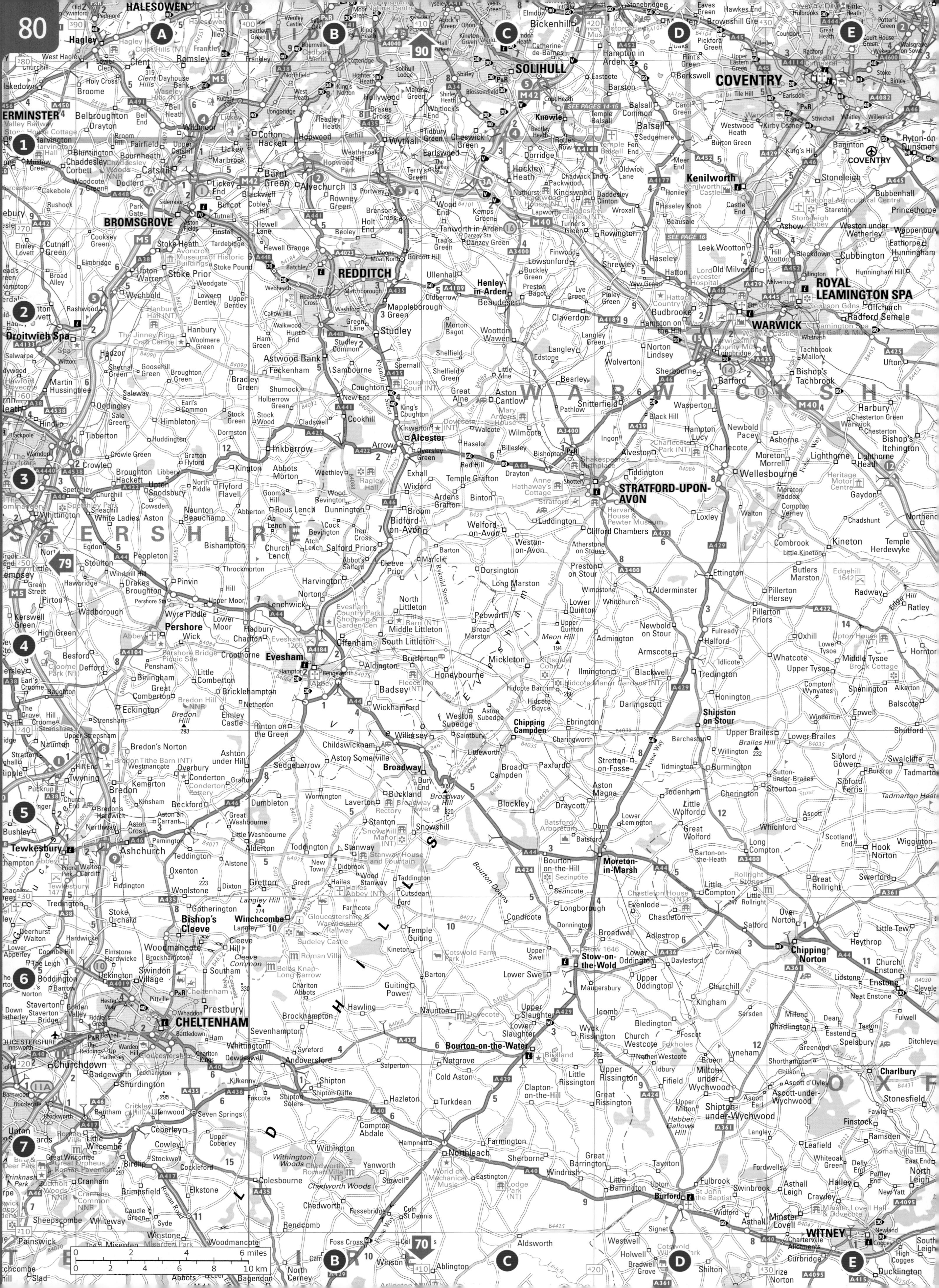

HALESOWEN

Hagley

KIDDERMINSTER

BROMSGROVE

Droitwich Spa

SOLIHULL

COVENTRY

Knowle

Kenilworth

ROYAL LEAMINGTON SPA

WARWICK

REDDITCH

Henley-in-Arden

Alcester

STRATFORD-UPON-AVON

Pershore

Evesham

Shipston on Stour

Tewkesbury

Broadway

Chipping Campden

Moreton-in-Marsh

Chipping Norton

Winchcombe

Bishop's Cleeve

Stow-on-the-Wold

Bourton-on-the-Water

CHELTENHAM

Northleach

Burford

WITNEY

WORCESTERSHIRE

WARWICKSHIRE

GLOUCESTERSHIRE

OXFORDSHIRE

M5 · M42 · M40 · M6

A46 · A44 · A429 · A422 · A435 · A40 · A361

0   2   4   6 miles
0 2 4 6 8 10 km

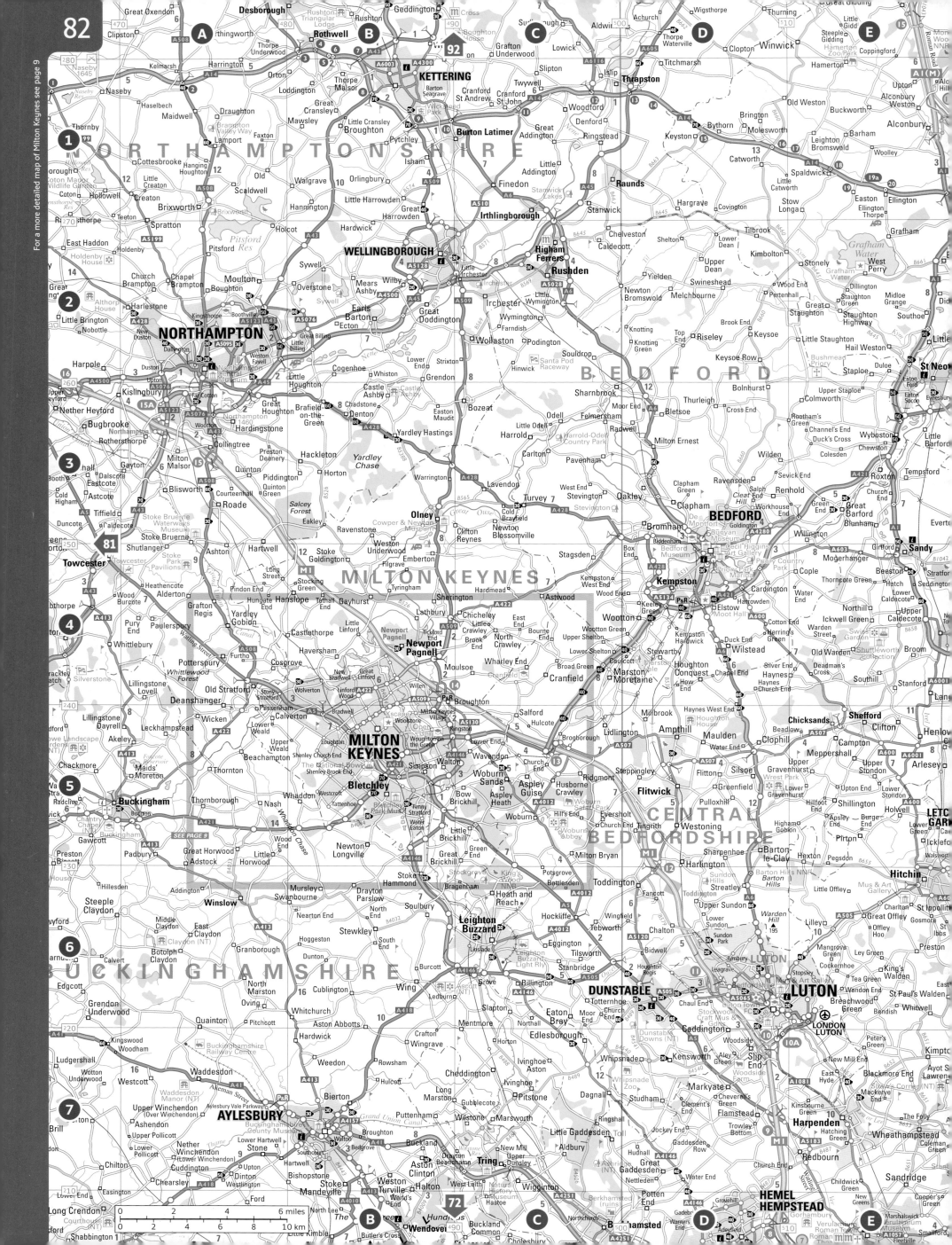

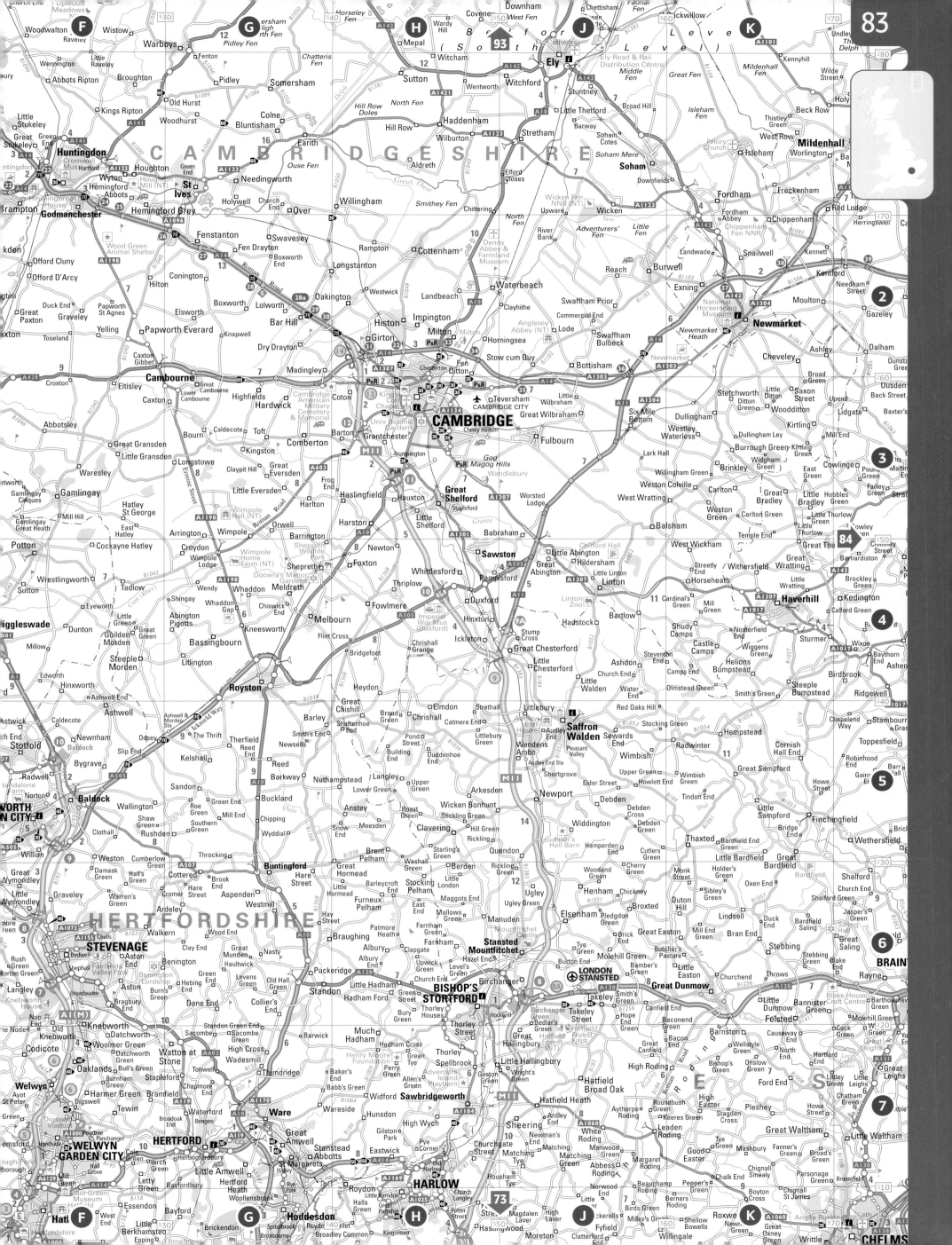

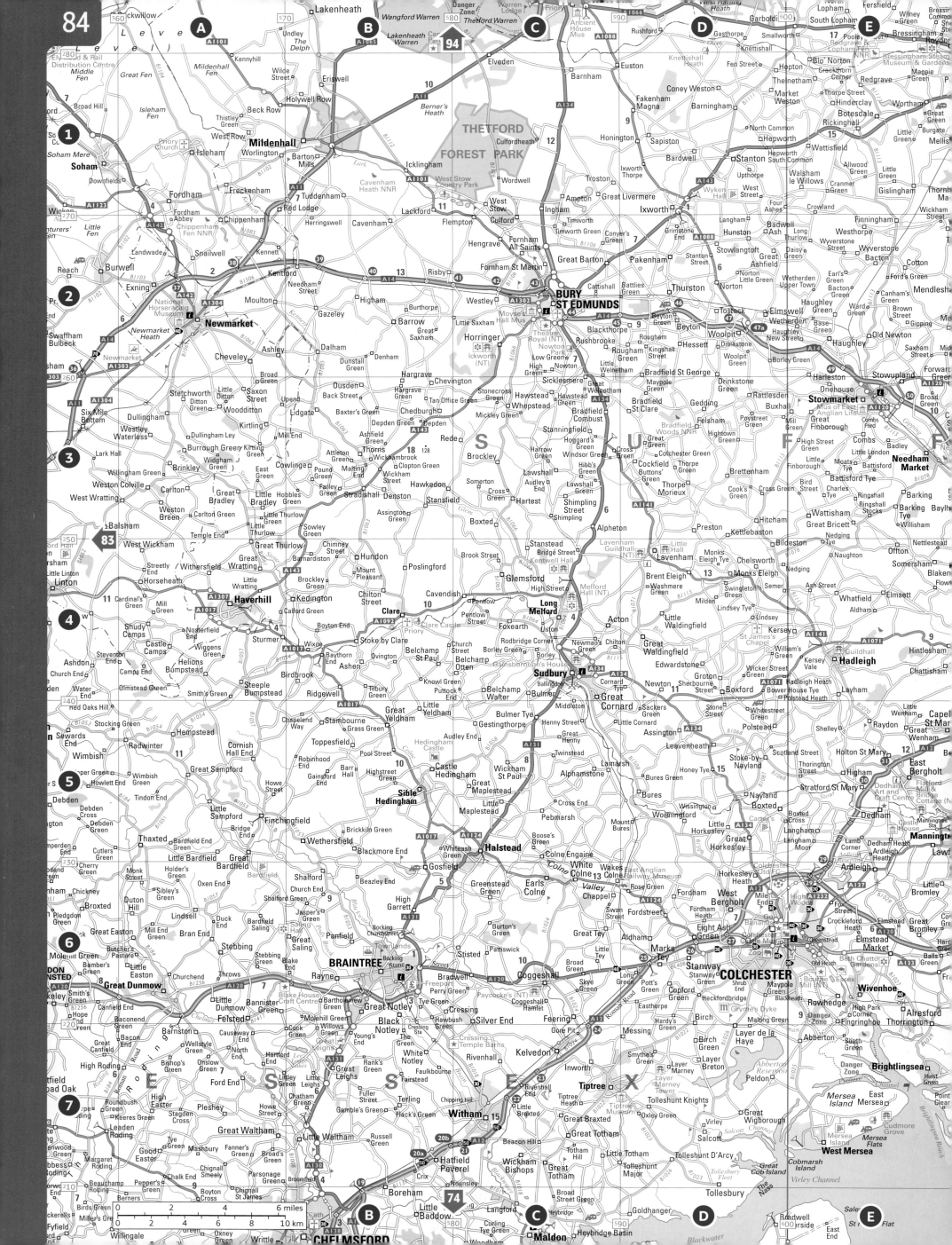

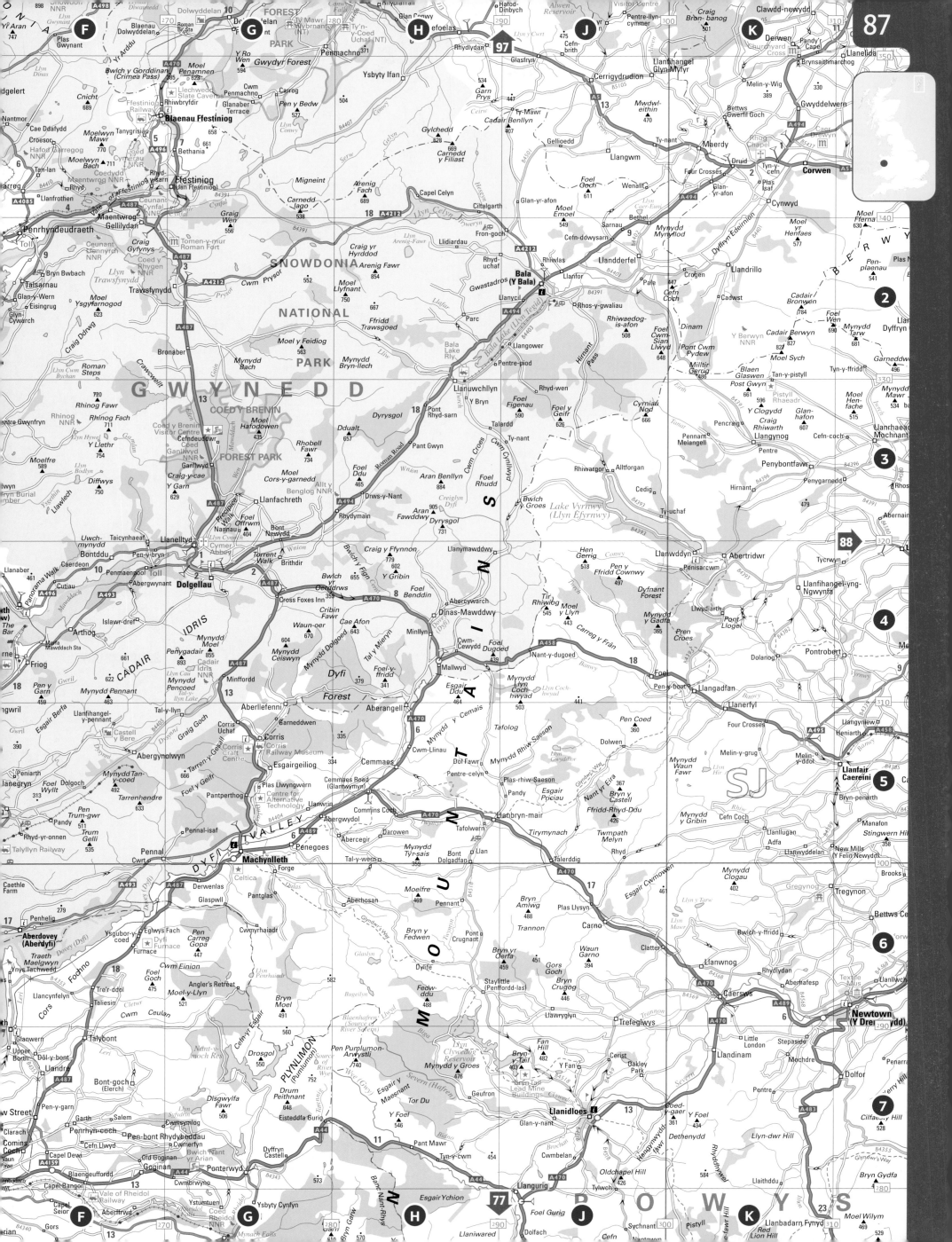

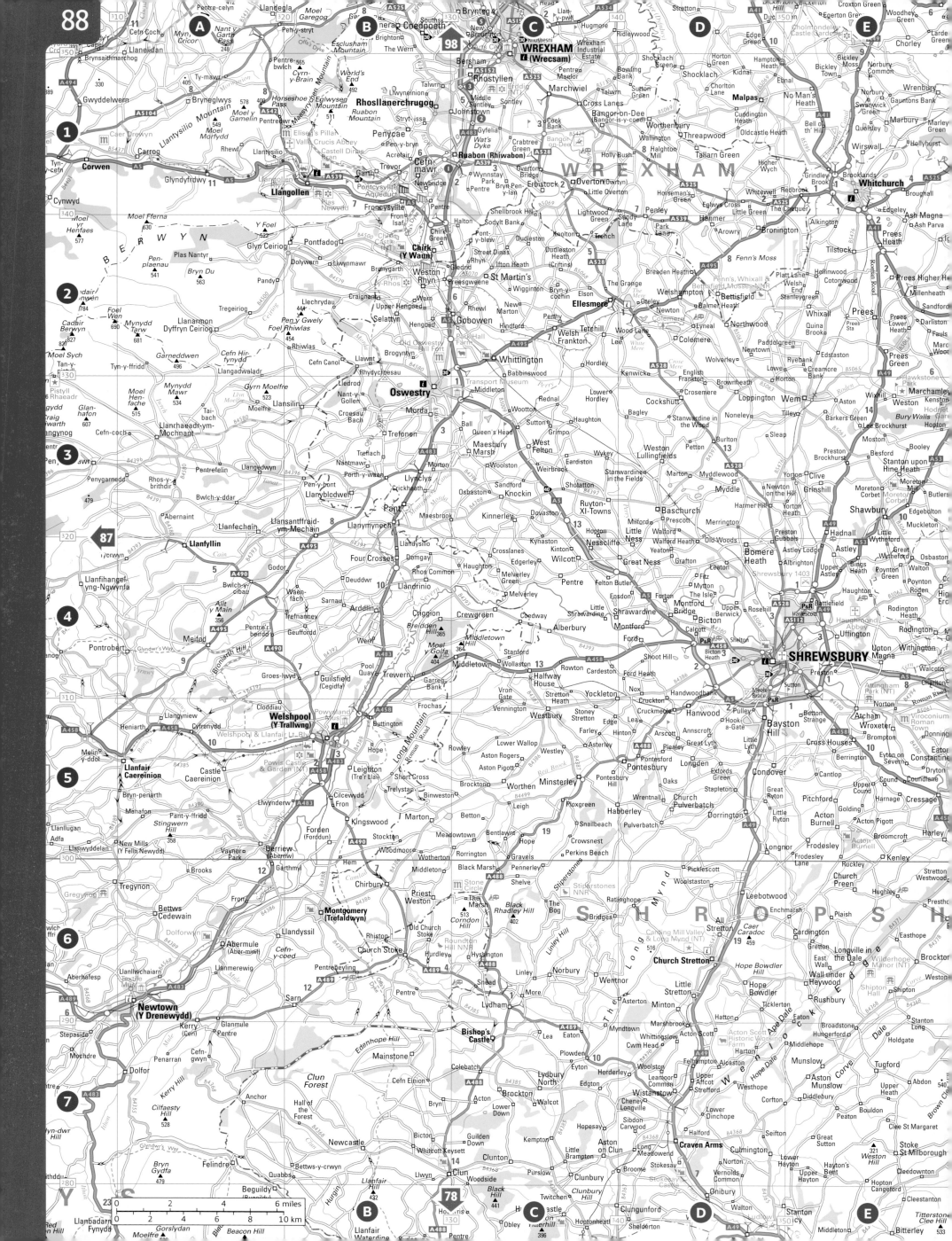

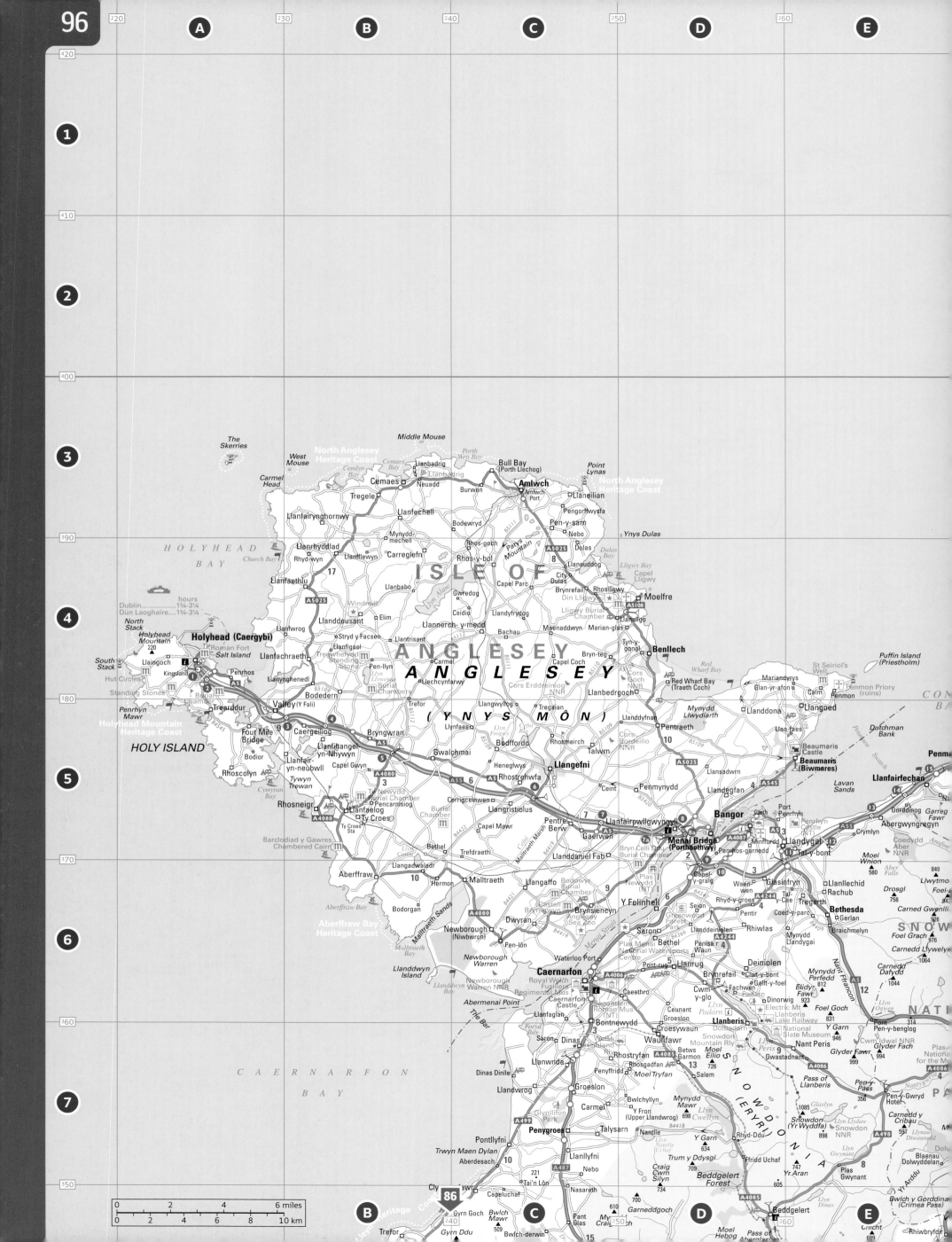

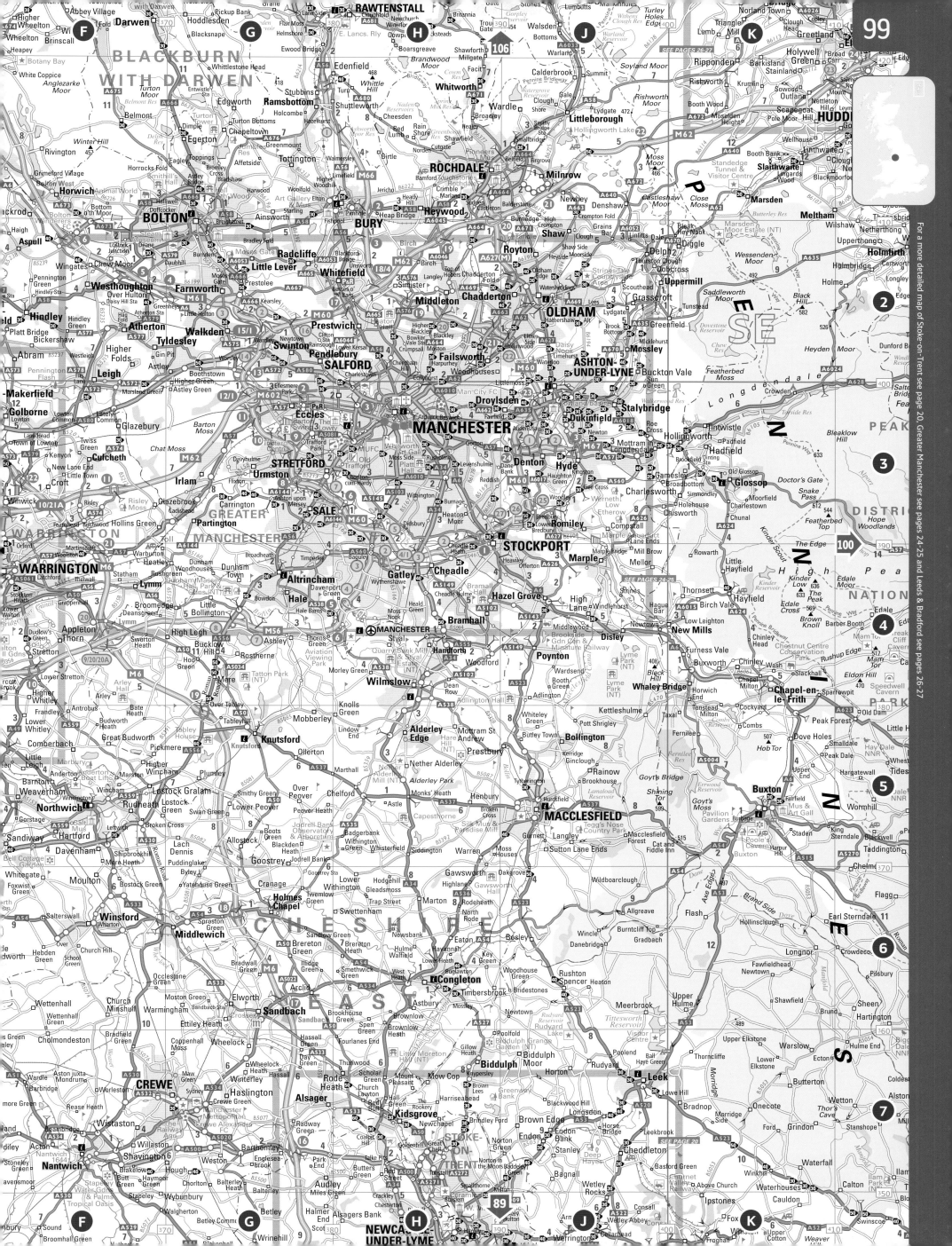

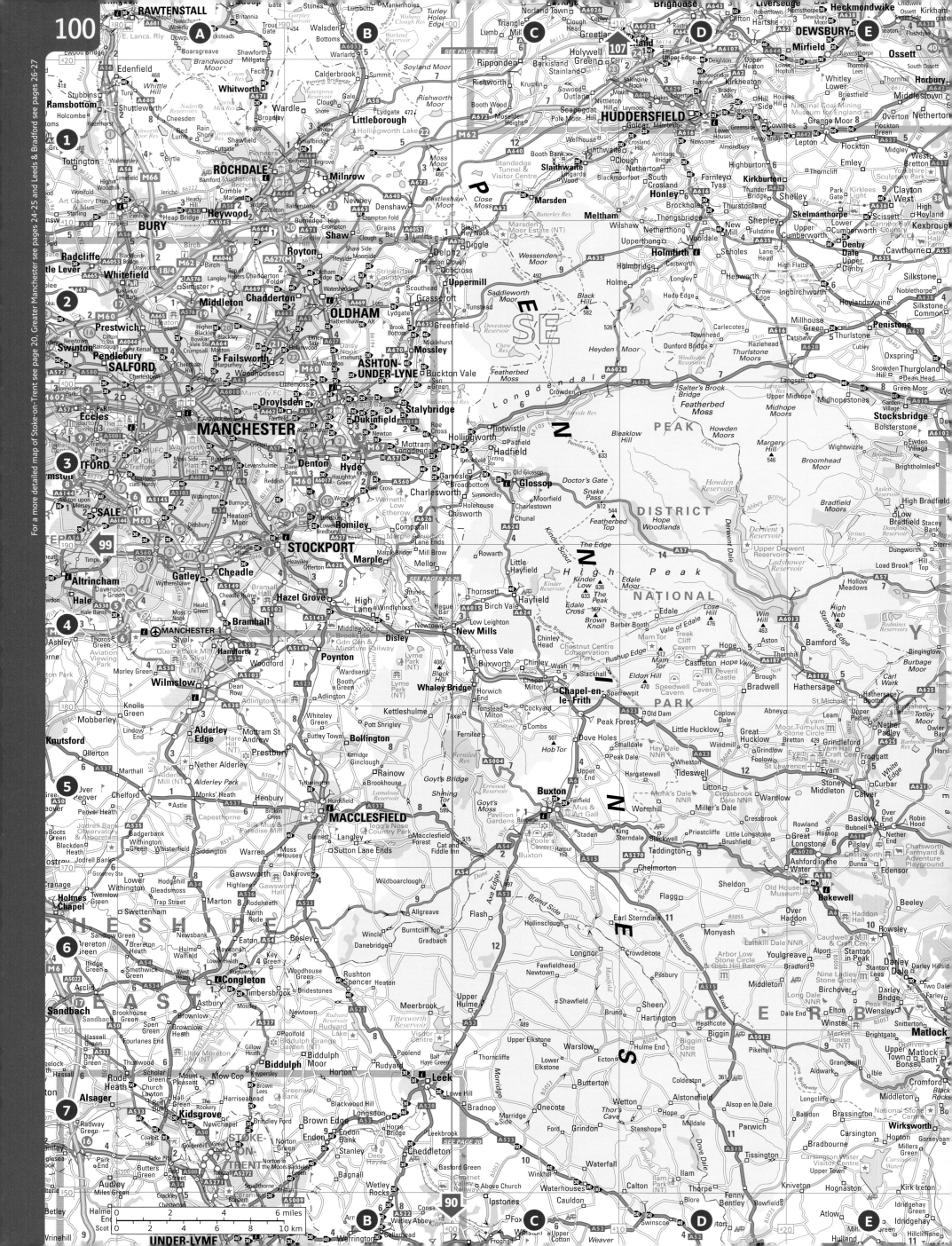

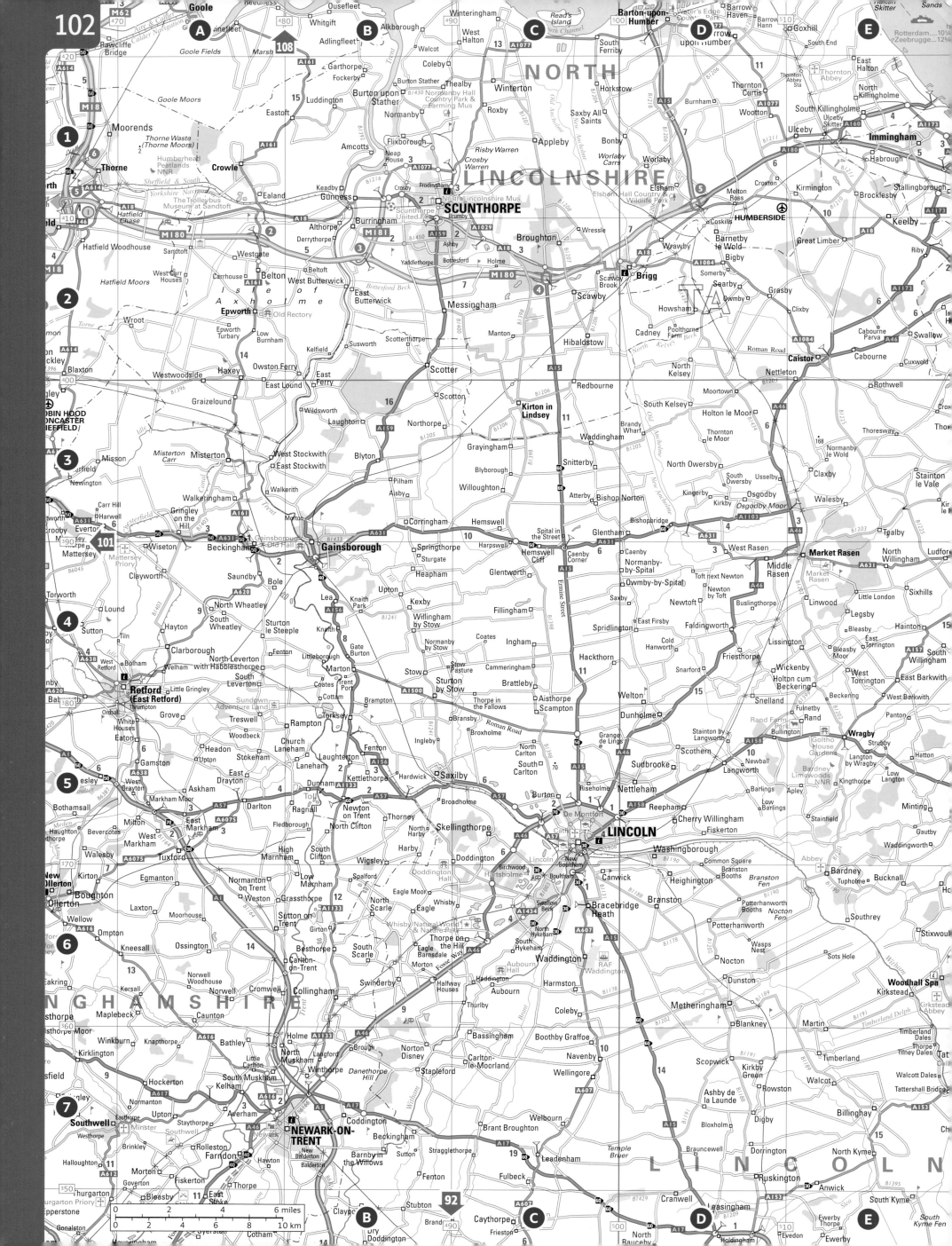

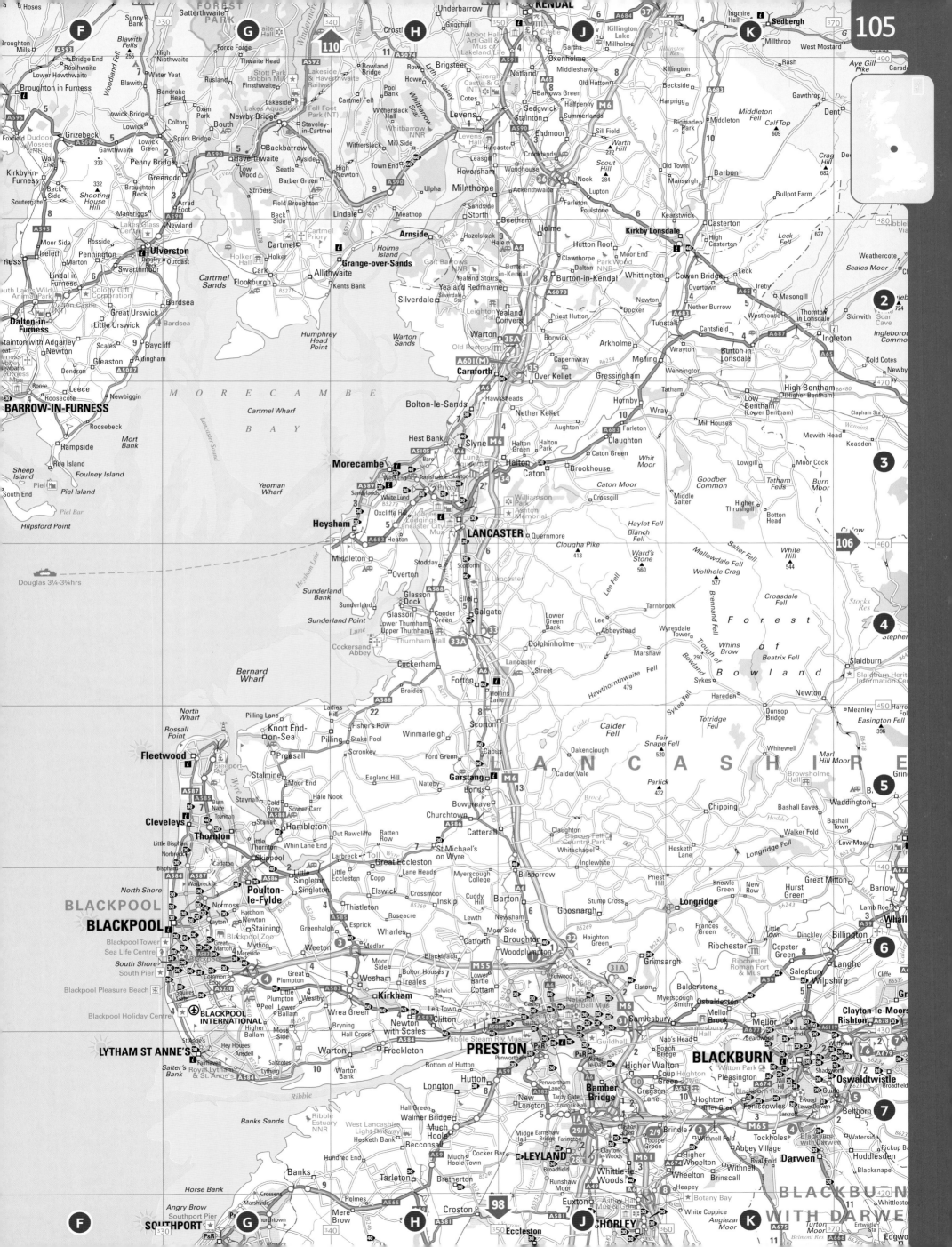

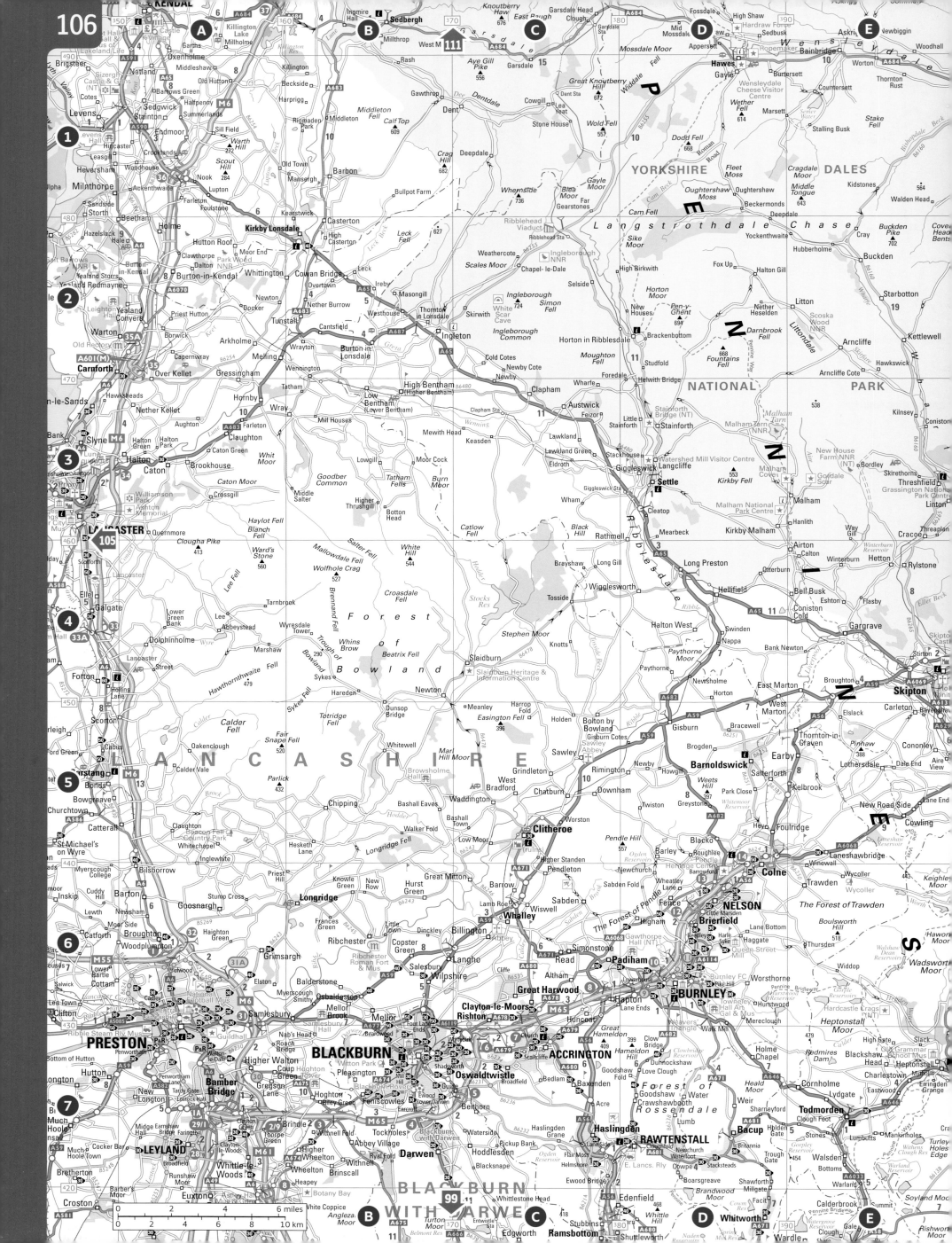

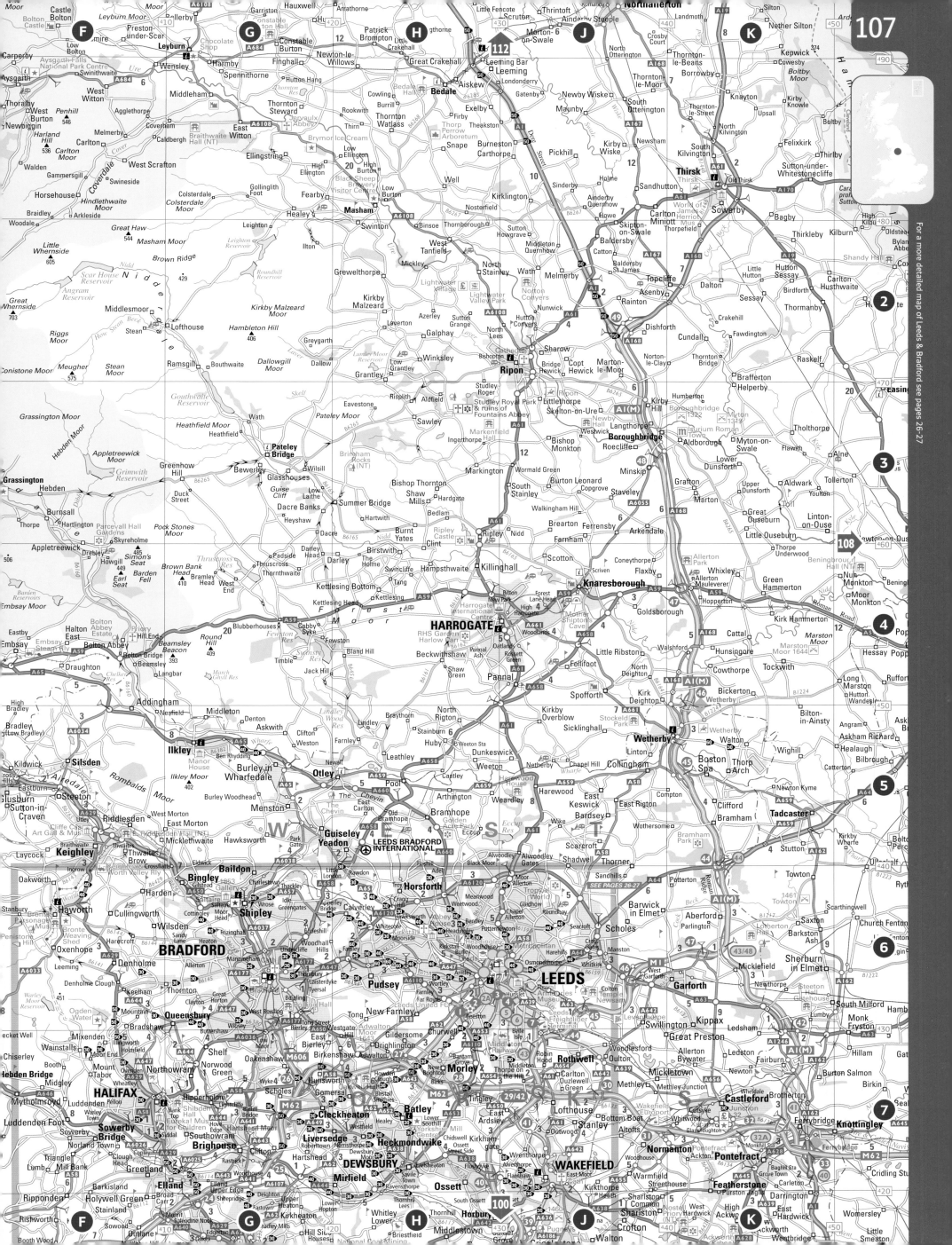

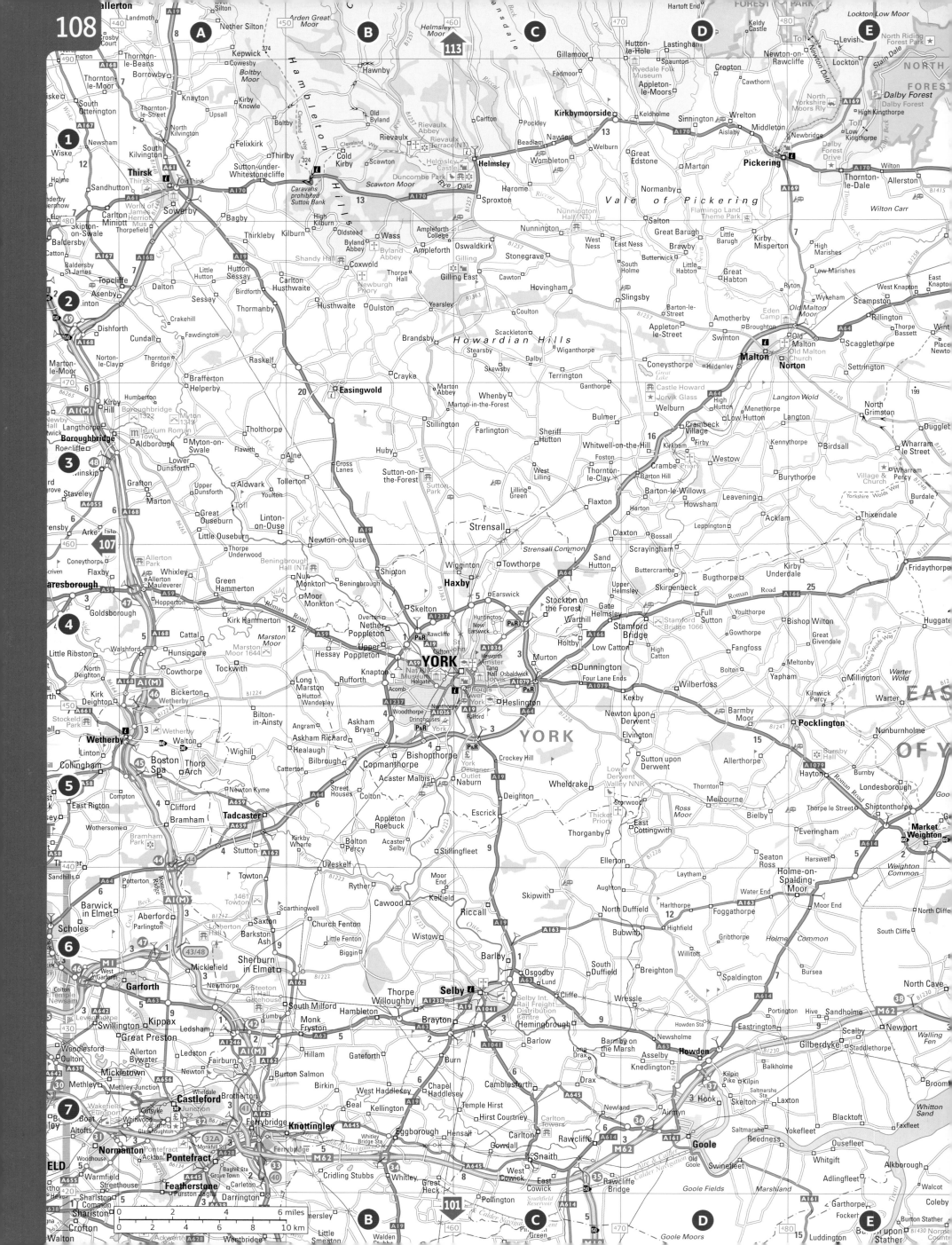

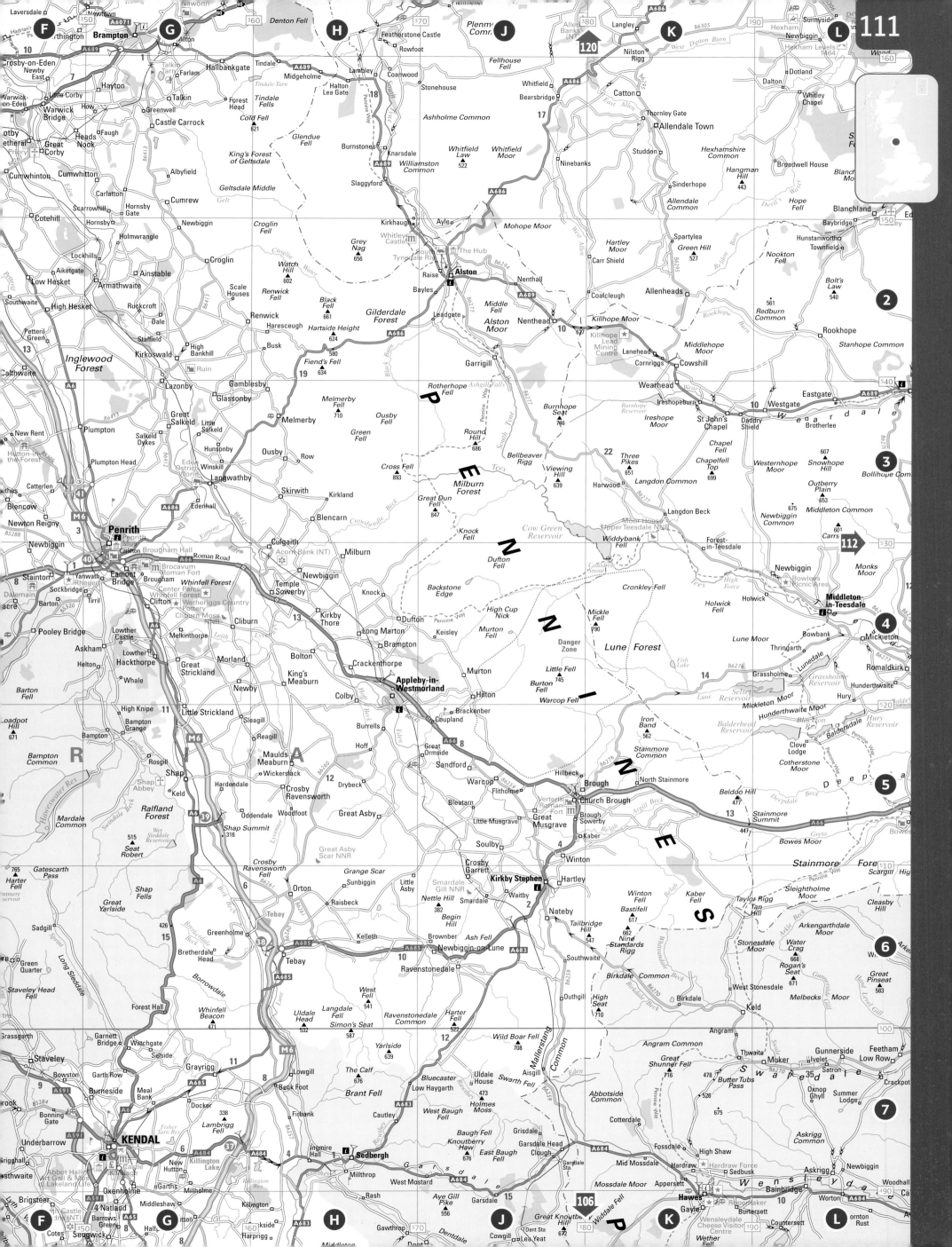

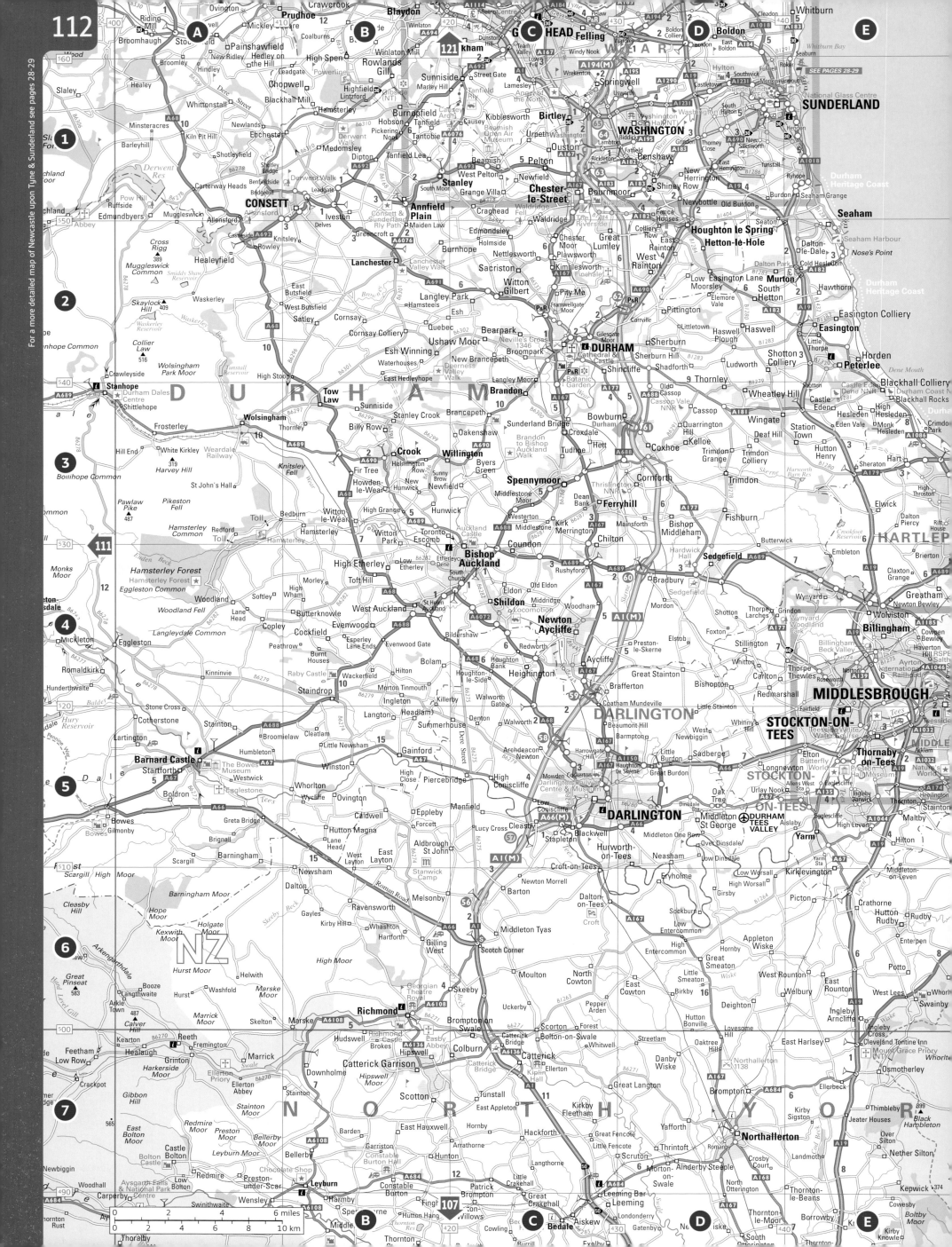

Ailsa Craig

SOUTH
AYRSHIRE

CARRICK

Girvan

Kennedy's Pass

Black Neuk

Pinminnoch

Grey Hill

Dowhill
Dipple
Low
Craighead
Old Dailly
Dailly
Penkill
Hadyard Hill
324
Garleffin Fell
429
Linfern
Loch
Craiglee
Loch
Doon
Waterhead
523
Shiel
Hill
508
Loch
Riecawr
Loch
Finlas

Houdston
Saugh Hill
296
Glendoune
Glendrissaig
Pemwhappie
Reservoir
Glengennet
Barr
North
Balloch
Changue
Forest
Nick of the
Balloch Pass
341
Shalloch
542
Polmaddie
Hill
Shalloch
on Minnoch
Carlin's
Cairn
Rhinns
Cors

12
Lendalfoot
Motte
Carleton
Fishery
Aldons
Daljarrock
Pinwherry
Pinmore
479
Kirrieroch
Hill
786
Merrick
843
Loch
Enoch

Bennane
Head
Colmonell
9
Dalreoch
Glenduisk
Black Clauchrie
Garwall
Hill
349
Palgowan
Craignaw
Silver
Flowe
NNR
Loch

Knockdolian
265
Craigneil
Balochmorrie
Buchan
Hill
493
Glen Trool Lodge
1307
557
Mulldonoch
Loch
Dee

Ballantrae
Mains of Tig
Balkissock
Shiel Hill
230
Barrhill
Eldrick
Corwar
House
22
Glentrool
Lamachan
Hill
716
Larg
Hill
675
Millfore
656
GALLOWAY FOR

Glenapp Castle
Downan
Point
Smyrton
Lochton
Bargrennan
Garlick
Hill
445
Wild
Goat
Park

Craigie
Fell
Beneraird
439
Chirmorrie
Drumlamford
House
Clachaneasy
Larg

Carlock
Hill
323
Milljoan
Hill
403
Altimeg
Hill
Markdhu
Standing
Stones
Polbae
Knockville
Cordorcan

Glen App
Finnarts
Point
Miltonise
Southern Upland Way
Knowe

Corsewall
Point
Dalnigap
Glenwhilly
Urrall
Fell
184
Penninghame
Barlies Castle
Dallash

Barnhills
North C
116
South
Cairn
Kirkcolm
Corsewall
Cairnryan
Cairn
Point
Braid
Fell
235
Artfield
Fell
Glenrazie
Boreland
Cumloden

Airies
Ervie
St Mary's
Croft
Soleburn
7
Innermessan
Carseriggan
Challoch
Newton
Stewart
Minnigaff
Creebridge

Knocknain
Leswalt
Lochinch Castle
Auchmantle
New
Luce
Culvennan
Fell
213
Shennanton
Nether
Barr

Lochnaw
Stranraer
Castle Kennedy
Galdenoch
Tarf Bridge
15
Benfield
Baltersan

Portslogan
Whiteleys
Lochans
Castle Kennedy
10
Dunragit
Moor
Glenluce
Abbey
Craiglaw
Kirkcowan
Barlae
Craighlaw
Barraer
Spittal

Black
Head
Cairn Pat
182
Kildrochet
House
Colfin
Genoch
Genoch Square
Dunragit
Whitecrook
Glenluce
Whitecairn
Carscreugh
Causeway End
Carsegowan
Barholm Mains
Creetown

Portpatrick
Dinvin
Awhirk
Stoneykirk
Sands of Luce
Milton
8
Knock Moss
175
Knock
Fell
Spittal
Culquhirk
Wigtown
Sands
Cassencar

Dunskey
Balgreggan
Sandhead
Crow's Nest
Auchenmalg
Barnbarroch
Culmalzie
11
Bladnoch
Wigtown
Baldoon
Sands
Carsluith

Money Head
Kirkmaiden
Stones
Alticry
Loch Head
Barrachan
Whauphill
Stewarton
12
Eggerness

Cairngarroch Bay
14
Ardwell
House
Ardwell
Chapel
Finian
Elrig
Mochrum
6
Motte of
Druchtag
Kirkland of
Longcastle
Airyhassen
Sorbie
Galliestoun

Clachanmore
Chapel Rossan
Balgowan
Barr Point
Barsalloch
Point
Monreith
Animal
World
Barwinnock
Castlewigg
Cults

Drumbreddan
Bay
Logan
House
Logan
Botanic
Gardens
New England Bay
Port
William
Monreith
Craigdhu
THE
MACHARS

Mull of Logan
Port Logan
Terally
Danger Zone
Barsalloch
Point
Monreith Bay
Rispain
Camp
Whithorn

LUCE BAY

Kilstay
Drummore
Cairndoon
Glasserton
10
Whithorn
Priory
Portyerrock

NX
Kirkmaiden
Damnaglaur
Maryport
St. Ninian's Cave
Fell of
Carleton
Kidsdale
Isle of Whithorn

Laggantalluch
Head
Dunman
160
Crammag Head
Nick of
Kindram
Cailiness Point
Burrow Head
Devil's
Bridge

East Tarbet
West Tarbet
Mull of Galloway

Cairnryan-Larne........ 1-1¼ hours
Stranraer-Belfast........ 2-3¼

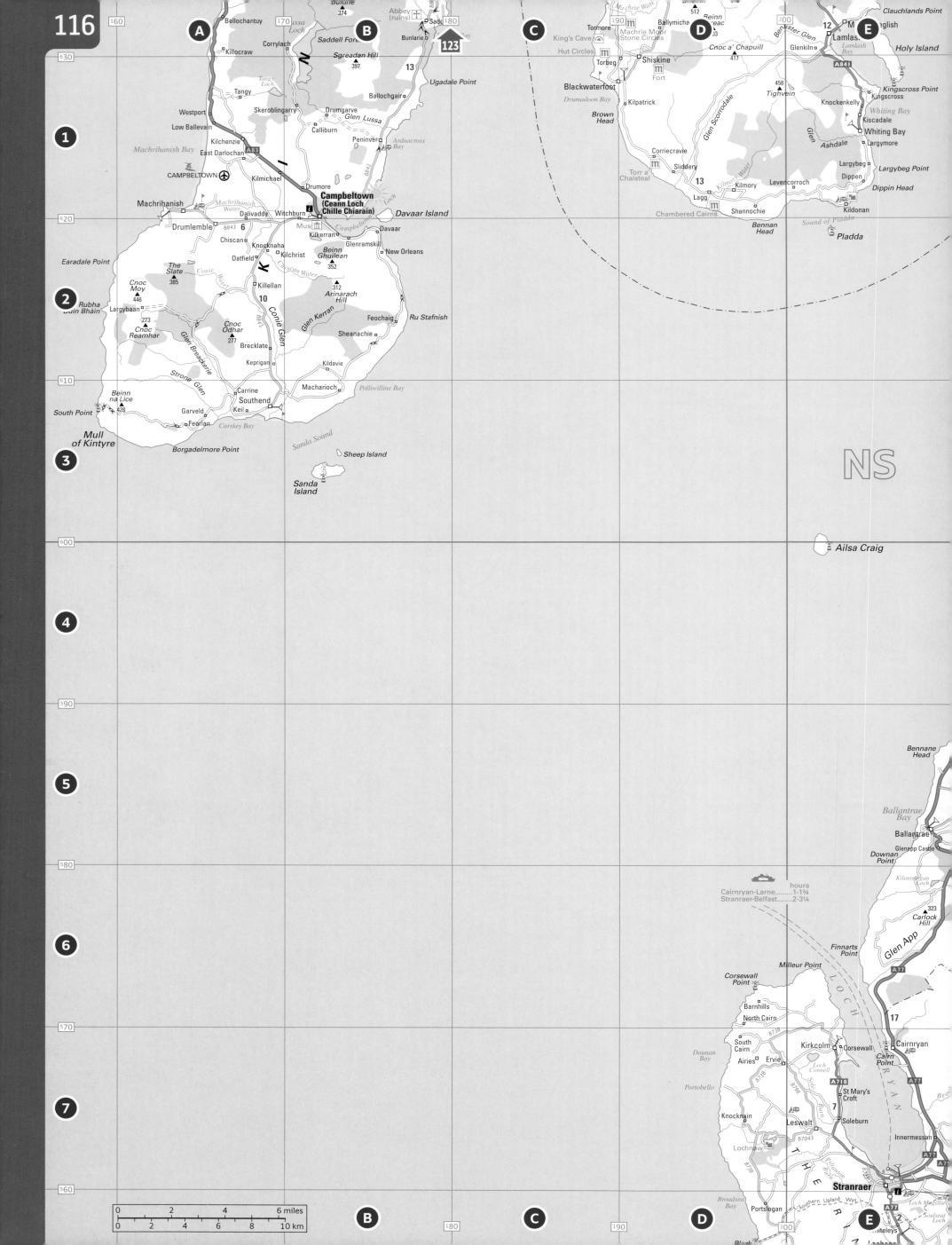

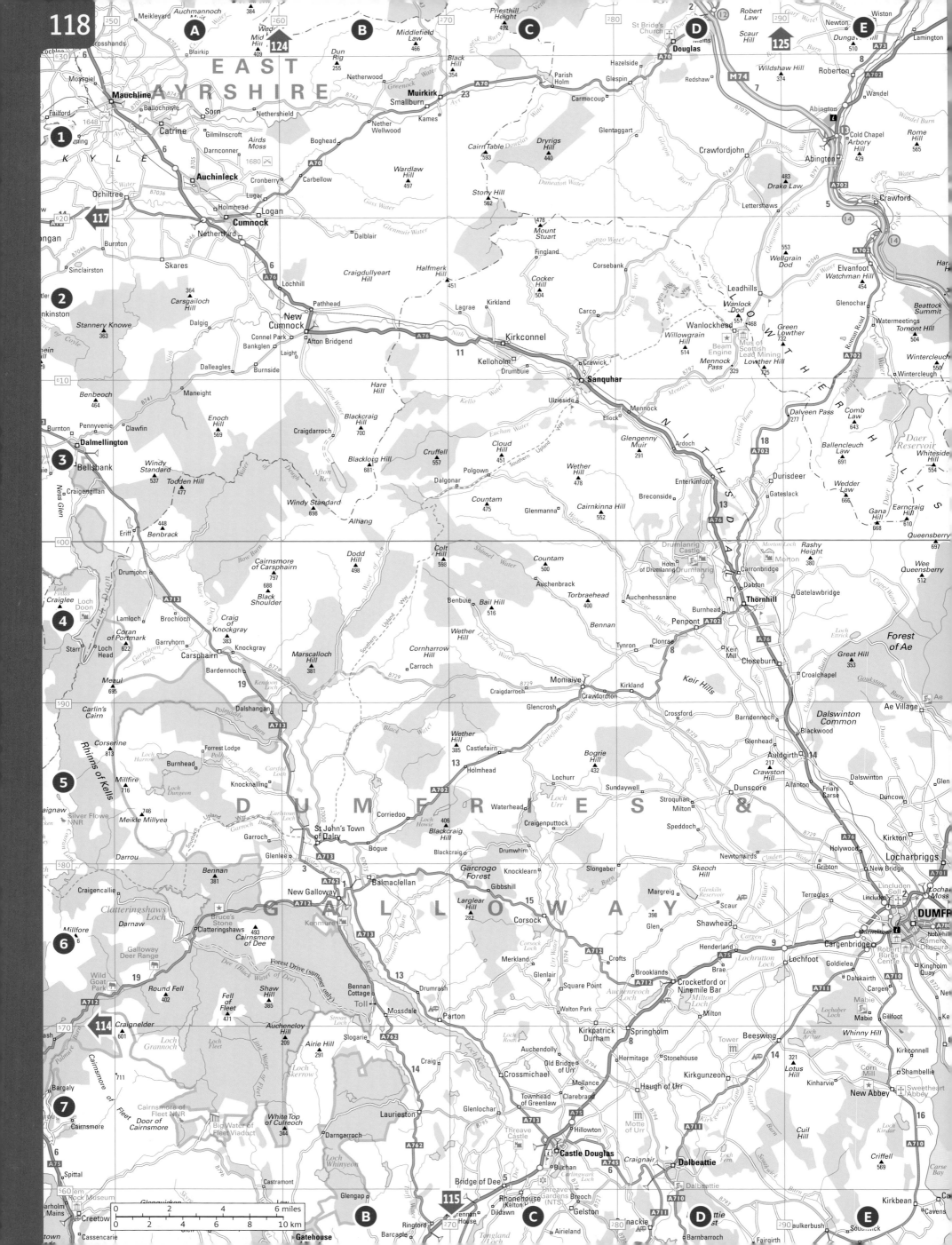

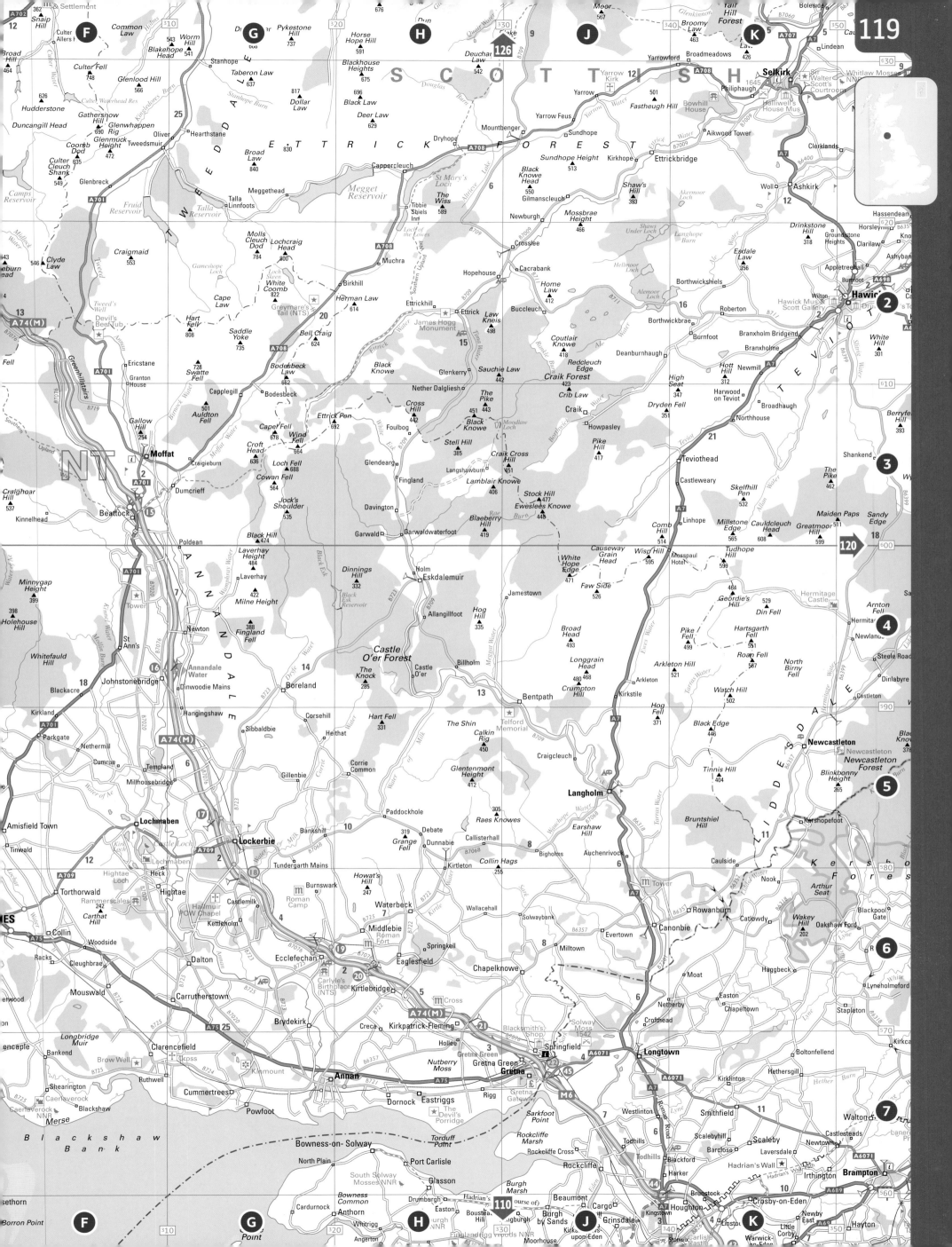

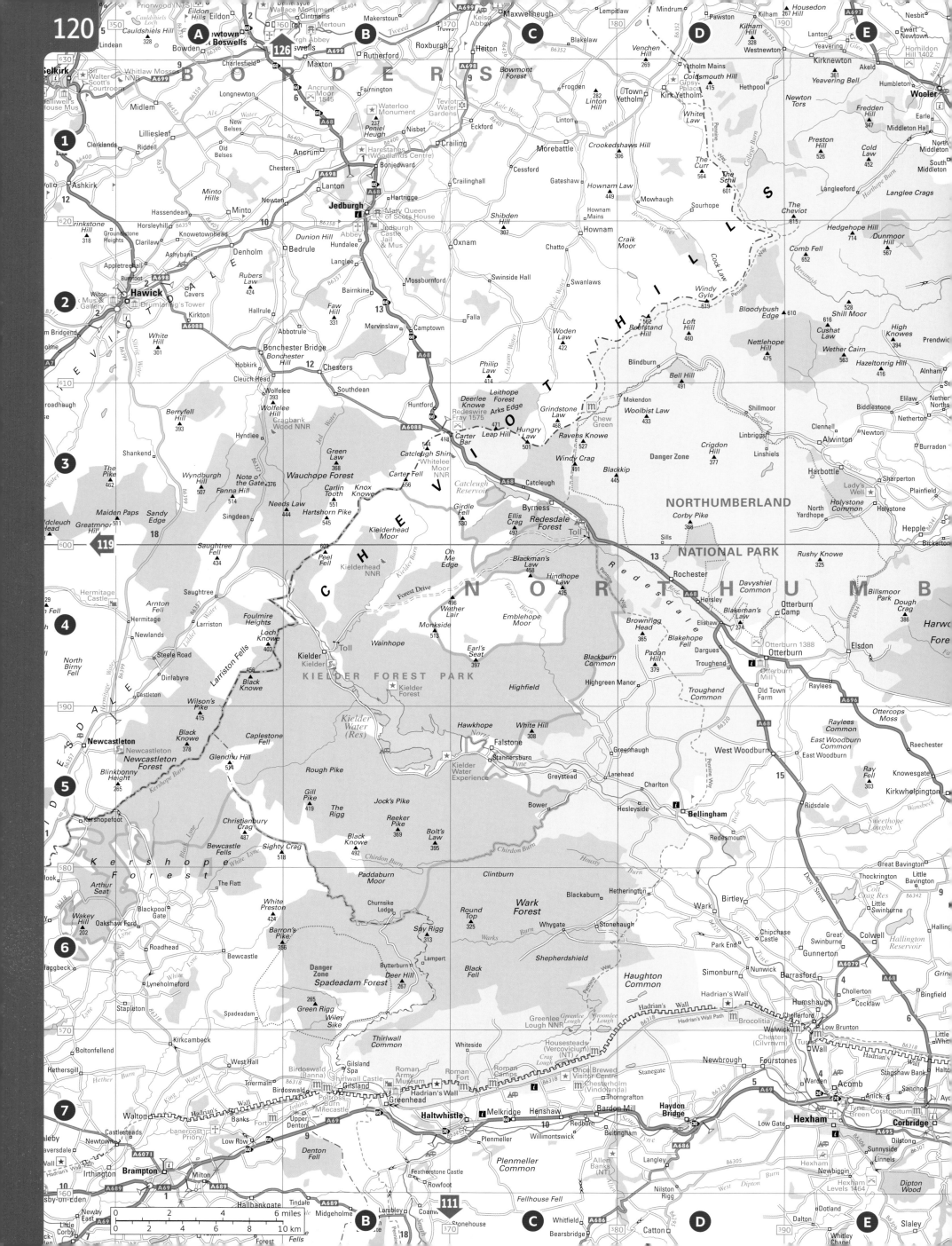

For a more detailed map of Newcastle upon Tyne & Sunderland see pages 28-29

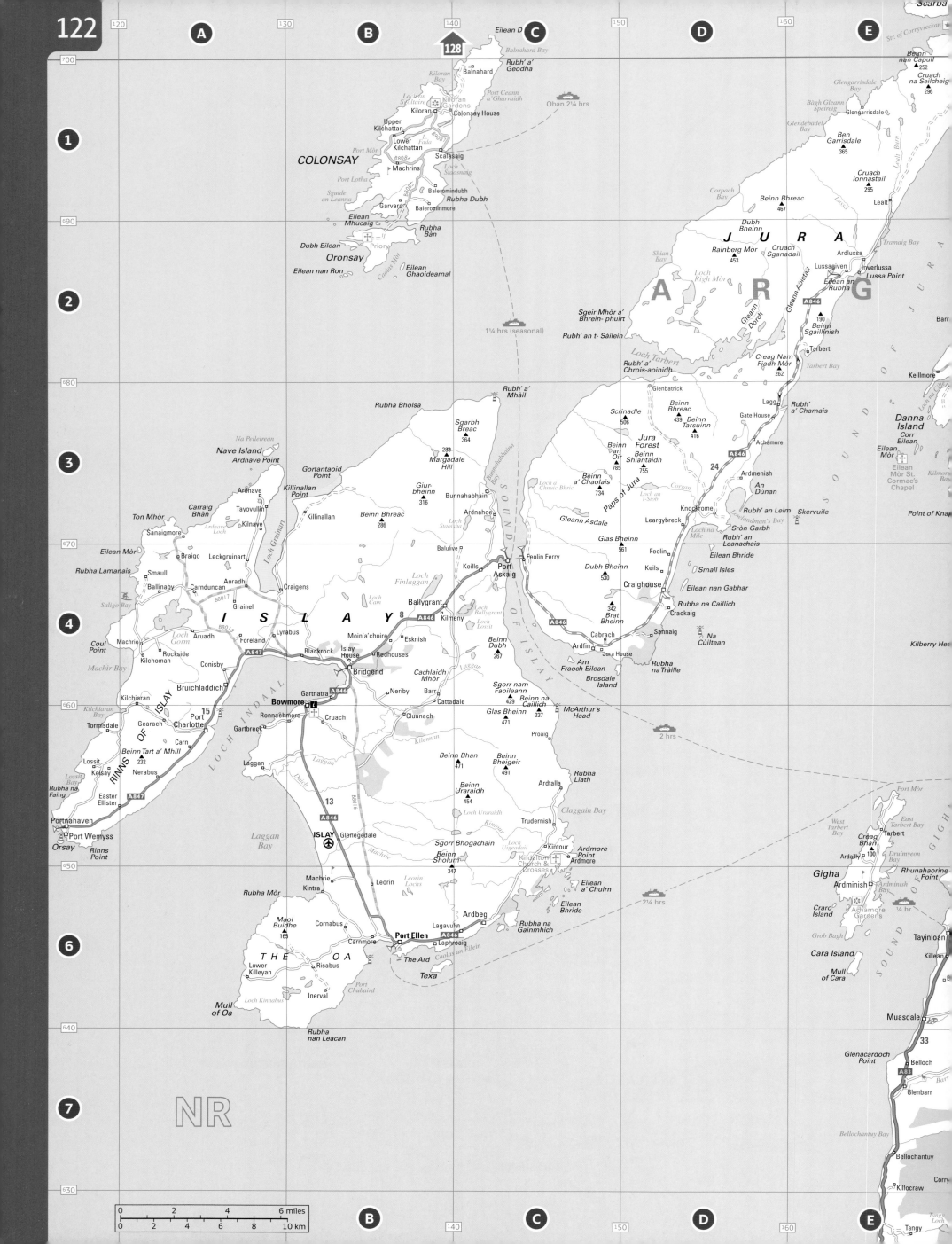

COLONSAY

Kiloran Bay
Balnahard
Eilean D
Balnahard Bay
Rubh' a' Geodha
Port Ceann a' Gharraidh
Oban 2¼ hrs
Loch an Sgoltaire
Kiloran Gardens
Kiloran
Colonsay House
Upper Kilchattan
Lower Kilchattan
Scalasaig
Loch Staosnaig
Port Mòr
Fada
Machrins
Balerominbubh
Garvard
Rubha Dubh
Balerominmore
Port Lotha
Sguide an Leanna
Eilean Mhucaig
Rubha Bàn
Dubh Eilean
Priory
Oronsay
Eilean nan Ron
Caolas Mòr
Eilean Ghaoideamal

JURA
ARG

Oban 2¼ hrs

1¼ hrs (seasonal)

Scarba
Str. of Corryvreckan
Beinn nan Capull
Cruach na Seilcheig 296
252
Glengarrisdale Bay
Bàgh Gleann Speireig
Glengarrisdale
Glendebadel Bay
Ben Garrisdale 365
Corpach Bay
Cruach Ionnastail 295
Beinn Bhreac 467
Dubh Bheinn
Rainberg Mòr 453
Cruach Sganadail
Lealt
Tramaig Bay
Ardlussa
Lussagiven
Inverlussa
Lussa Point
Eilean an Rubha
Shian Bay
Loch Righ Mòr
Gleann Aoistail
Barr
Beinn Sgaillinish 190
Tarbert
Keillmore
Danna Island
Corr Eilean
Eilean Mòr
Eilean Mòr St. Cormac's Chapel
Gleann Dorch
Loch Tarbert
Rubh' a' Chrois-aoinidh
Creag Nam Fiadh Mòr 262
Tarbert Bay
Glenbatrick
Scrinadle
Beinn Bhreac 439
Beinn Tarsuinn 416
Beinn an Oir 785
Beinn Shiantaidh 755
Jura Forest
24
Gate House
Lagg
Rubh' a' Chamais
Achamore
Ardmenish
An Dùnan
Rubh' an Leim
Skervuile
Point of Knap

Rubha Bholsa
Rubh' a' Mhàil
Sgarbh Breac 364
Sgorr nam 283
Margadale Hill
Na Peileirean
Nave Island
Ardnave Point
Gortantaoid Point
Giur-bheinn 316
Bunnahabhain
Loch a' Chnuic Bhric
Beinn a' Chaolais 734
Paps of Jura
Corran
Gleann Asdale
Leargybreck
Knockrome
Loch na Mile
An Dùnan
Ardnave
Killinallan Point
Killinallan
Ardnave Loch
Beinn Bhreac 286
Ardhoe
Glas Bheinn 561
Feolin
Eilean Bhride
Carraig Bhàn
Tayovullin
Kilnave
Braigo
Ballinaby
Eilean Mòr
Rubha Lamanais
Smaull
Leckgruinart
Aoradh
Craigens
Balulive
Keills
Loch Finlaggan
Loch Cam
Feolin Ferry
Port Askaig
Dubh Bheinn 530
Keils
Small Isles
ISLAY
Lyrabus
Grainel
Saligo Bay
Coul Point
Machrie
Aruadh
Foreland
Loch Gorm
B8018
Blackrock
Islay House
Redhouses
Esknish
Moin'a'choire
Loch Ballygrant
Loch Lossit
Beinn Dubh 267
Ardfin
Jura House
Crackaig
Cabrach
Sannaig
Na Cùiltean
Dubh Bheinn
Brat Bheinn 342
Kilchoman
Rockside
Conisby
Bruichladdich
Bridgend
Cachlaidh Mhòr
Barr
Cattadale
Sgorr nam Faoileann 429
Brosdale Island
Rubha na Tràille
Kilberry Head
Kilchiaran Bay
Kilchiaran
Gearach
Port Charlotte
Carn
Gartbreck
Ronnachmore
Cruach
Bowmore
Gartnatra
Neriby
Cluanach
Glas Bheinn 471
Beinn na Caillich 337
McArthur's Head
2 hrs
Tormisdale
Lossit
Kelsay
Nerabus
Easter Ellister
RINNS OF ISLAY
Beinn Tart a' Mhill 232
Laggan
13
Duich
Laggan
B8016
Kilennan
Beinn Bhan 471
Beinn Bheigeir 491
Beinn Uraraidh 454
Loch Uraraidh
Ardtalla
Rubha Liath
Claggain Bay
Portnahaven
Port Wemyss
Orsay
Rinns Point
Laggan Bay
ISLAY
Glenegedale
Machrie
Sgorr Bhogachain
Loch Uigeadail
Kintour
Kilnaughton Church & Crosses
Ardmore Point
Ardmore
West Tarbert Bay
Creag Bhàn 100
Druimyeon Bay
Tarbert
East Tarbert Bay
Ardaily
Gigha
Ardminish
Ardminish Bay
Port Mòr
Machrie
Kintra
Leorin
Leorin Lochs
Beinn Sholum 347
Eilean a' Chuirn
Rubha Mòr
Rubha na Gainmhich
Eilean Bhride
2¼ hrs
Ardbeg
Lagavulin
Laphroaig
Port Ellen
Craro Island
Achamore Gardens
¼ hr
Grob Bagh
Maol Buidhe 165
Cornabus
Carnmore
The Ard
Caolas an Eilein
Texa
Cara Island
Tayinloan
Killean
THE OA
Lower Killeyan
Risabus
Port Chubaird
Mull of Cara
Muasдale
Inerval
Loch Kinnabus
Mull of Oa
Rubha nan Leacan
Glenacardoch Point
Belloch
Glenbarr
33
Bellochantuy Bay
Bellochantuy
Corry
Killocraw

NR

For a more detailed map of Glasgow see pages 30-31

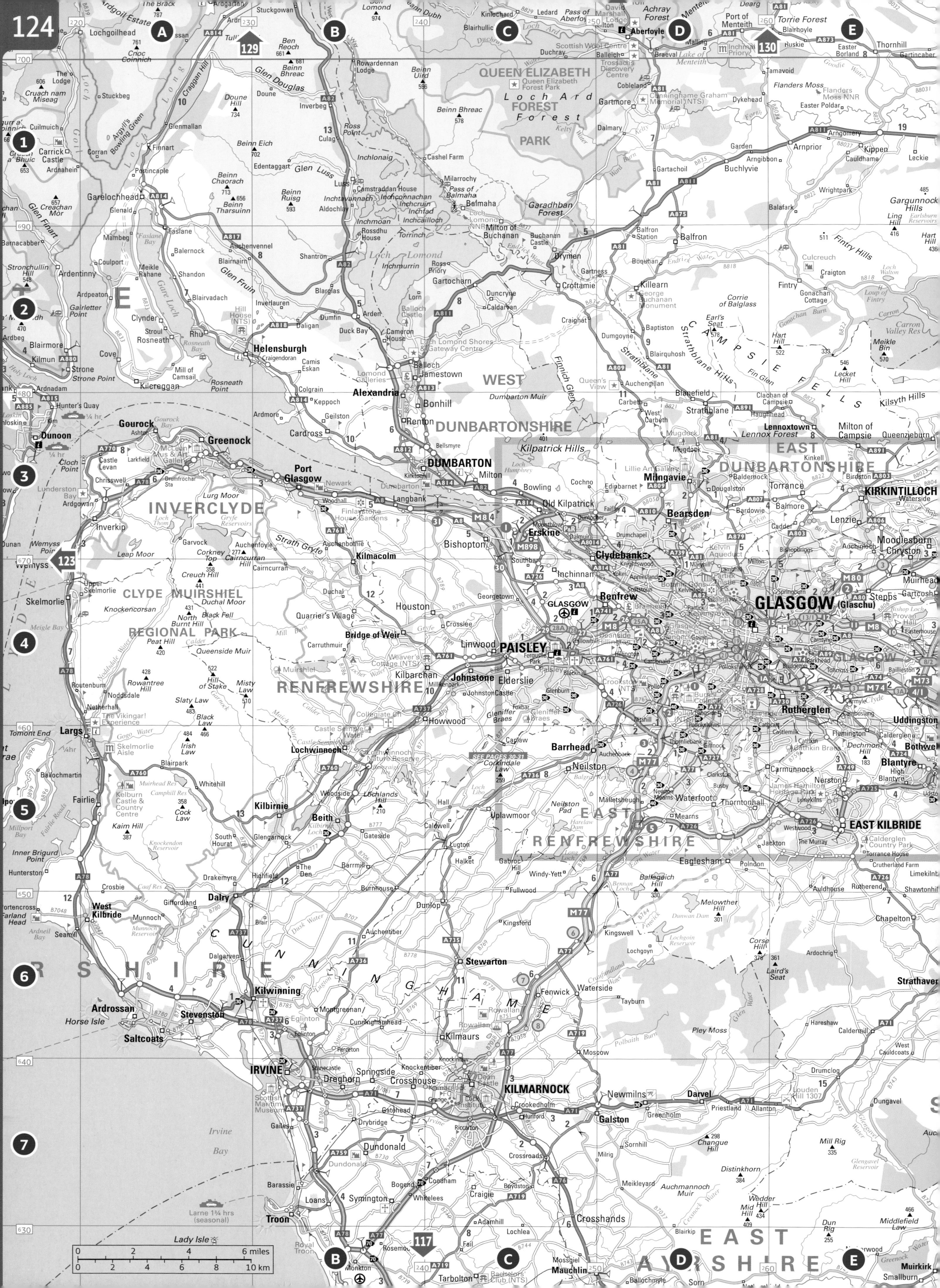

GLASGOW (Glaschu)

PAISLEY

DUMBARTON

Helensburgh

Greenock

Port Glasgow

Gourock

Dunoon

Largs

Irvine

KILMARNOCK

KIRKINTILLOCH

EAST KILBRIDE

Rutherglen

Barrhead

Johnstone

Bridge of Weir

Kilmacolm

Alexandria

Ardrossan

Saltcoats

Stevenston

Kilwinning

Troon

Dalry

Beith

Kilbirnie

West Kilbride

Fairlie

INVERCLYDE

WEST DUNBARTONSHIRE

EAST DUNBARTONSHIRE

RENFREWSHIRE

EAST RENFREWSHIRE

CLYDE MUIRSHIEL REGIONAL PARK

QUEEN ELIZABETH FOREST PARK

Loch Ard FOREST

Loch Lomond

CUNNINGHAME

NORTH AYRSHIRE

EAST AYRSHIRE

CAMPSIE FELLS

Aberfoyle

Bearsden

Milngavie

Clydebank

Renfrew

Erskine

Bishopton

Strathblane

Lennoxtown

Balloch

Drymen

Balfron

Kippen

Fintry

Gartmore

Stewarton

Fenwick

Galston

Newmilns

Darvel

Mauchlin

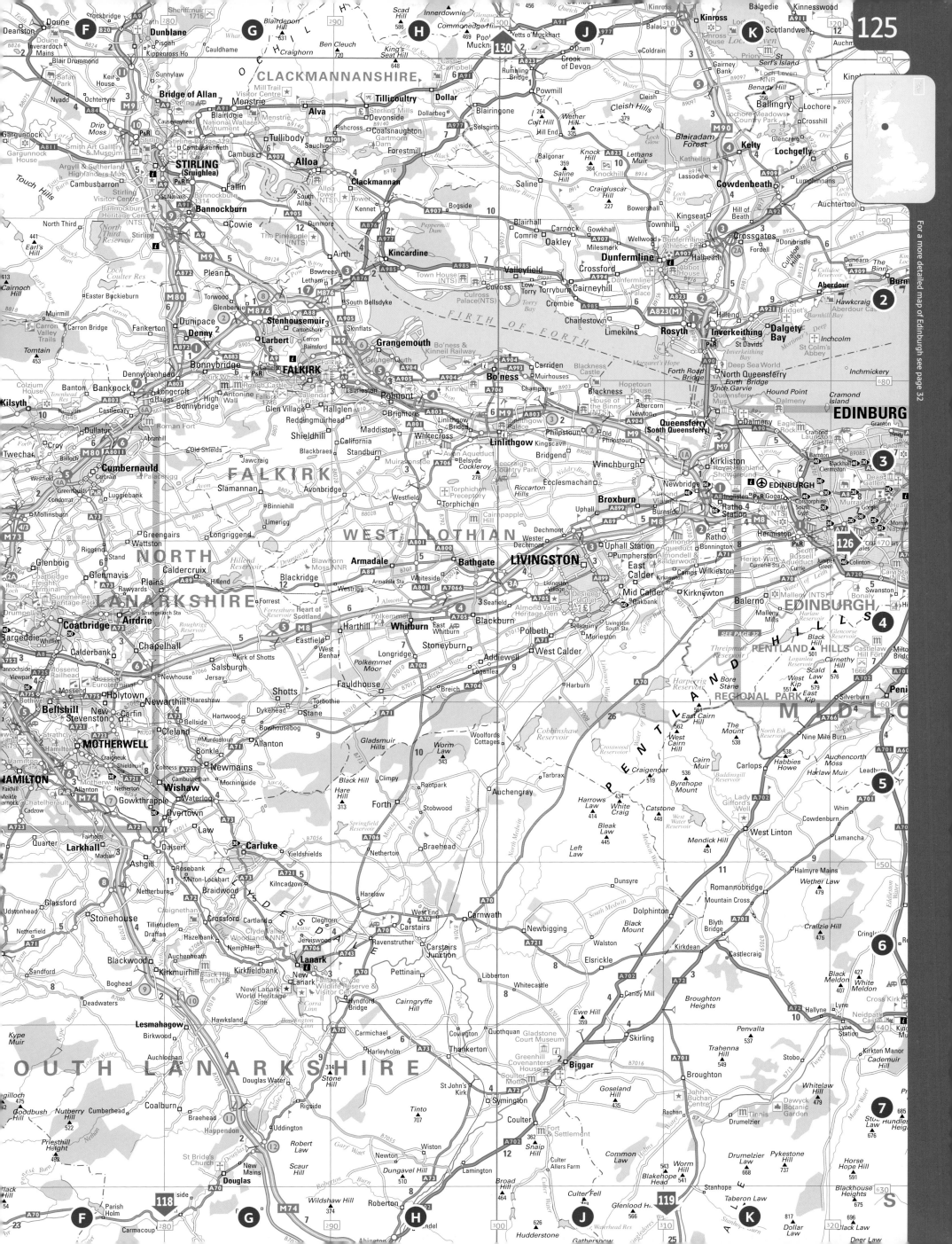

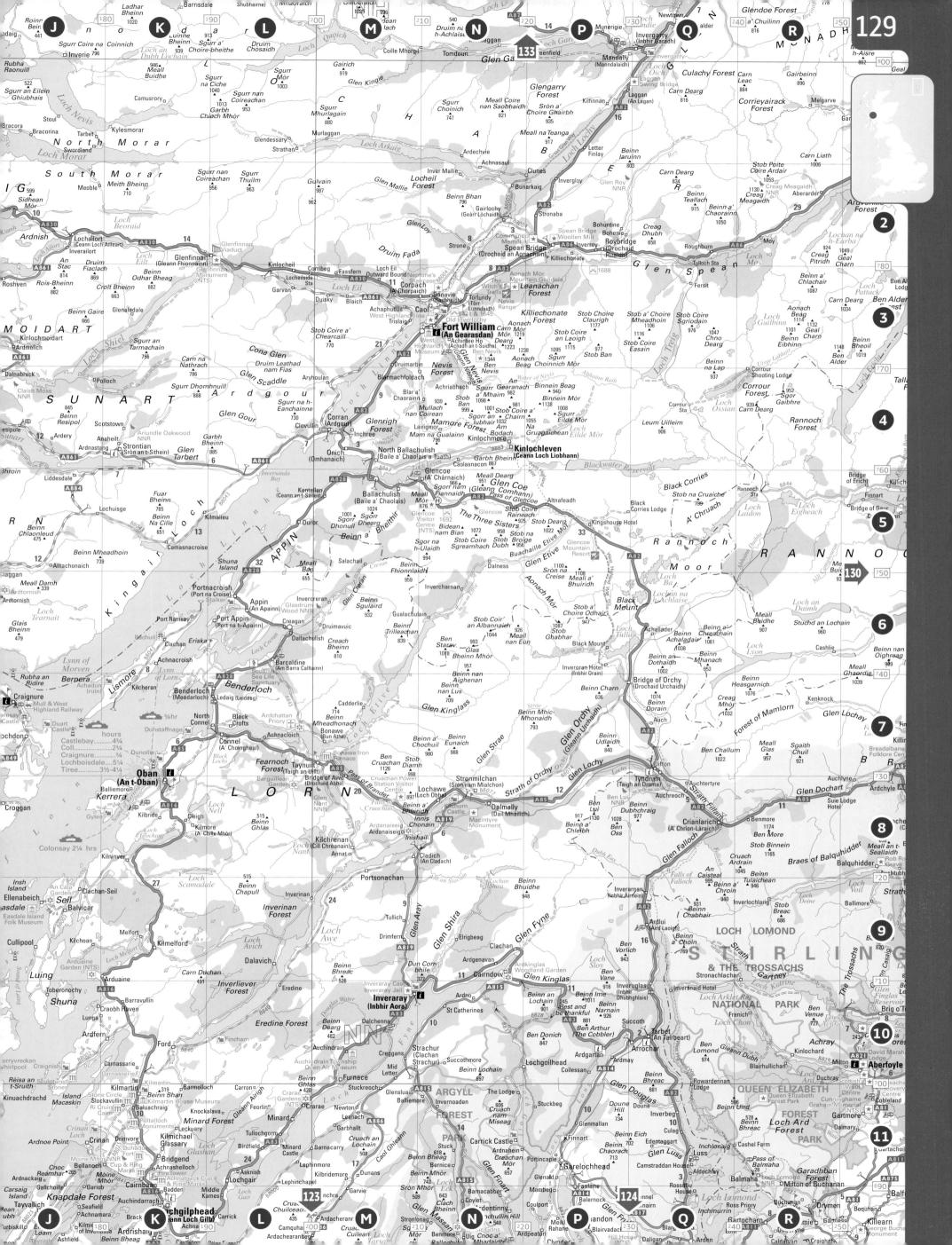

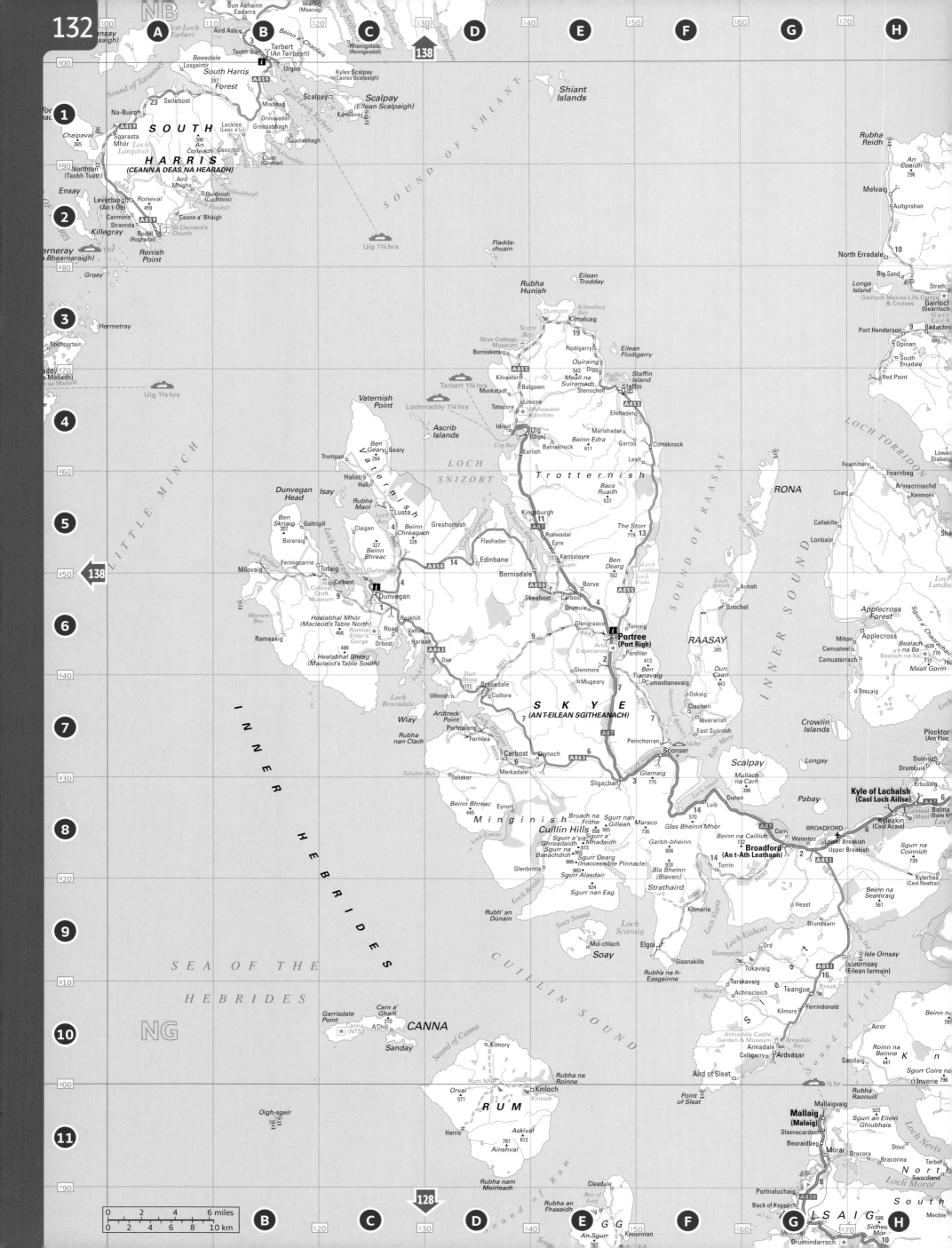

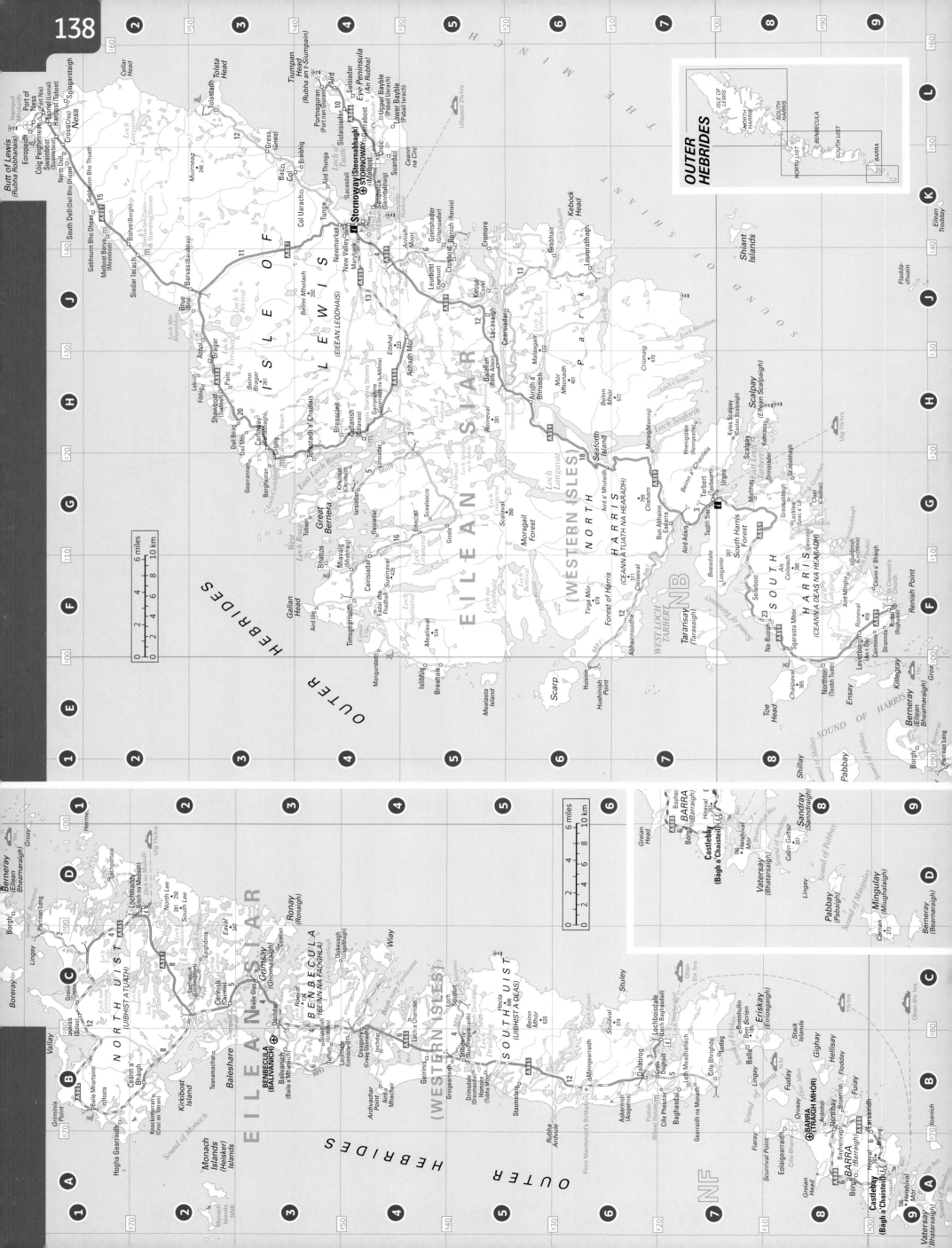

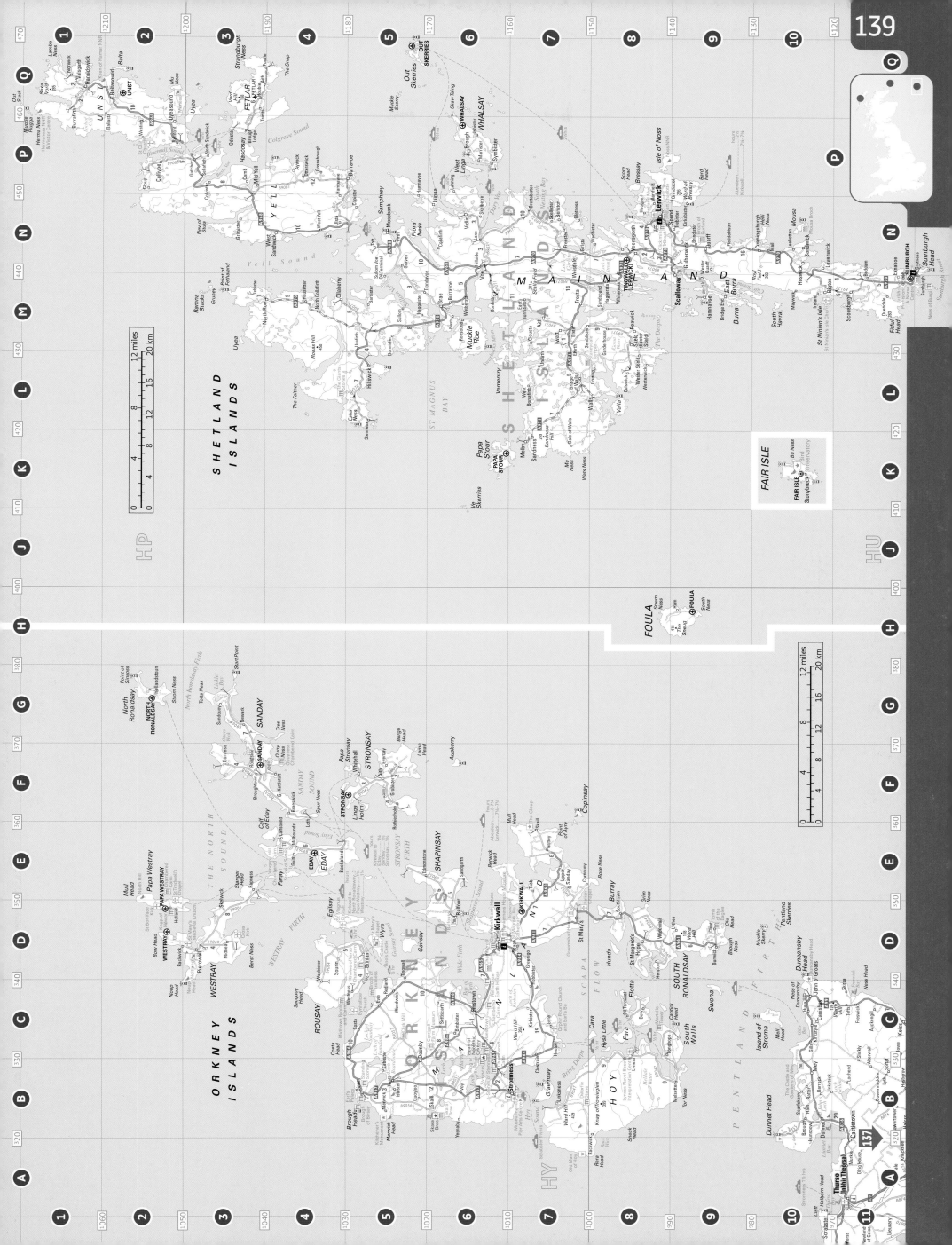

Using the index

Place and place of interest names are followed by a **page number** and a grid reference in black type. The feature can be found on the map somewhere within the grid square shown.

Where two or more places have the same name the abbreviated county or unitary authority names are shown to distinguish between them. A list of these abbreviated names appears below.

The top 1000 most visited places of interest are shown within the index in blue type. Their postcode information is supplied after the county names to aid integration with satnav systems.

A&B	Argyll & Bute	Midlo	Midlothian
Aber	Aberdeenshire	Mon	Monmouthshire
B&H	Brighton & Hove	N'hants	Northamptonshire
B&NESom	Bath & North East Somerset	N'umb	Northumberland
B'burn	Blackburn with Darwen	NAyr	North Ayrshire
B'pool	Blackpool	NELincs	North East Lincolnshire
BGwent	Blaenau Gwent	NLan	North Lanarkshire
Bed	Bedford	NLincs	North Lincolnshire
Bourne	Bournemouth	NPT	Neath Port Talbot
BrackF	Bracknell Forest	NSom	North Somerset
Bucks	Buckinghamshire	NYorks	North Yorkshire
Caerp	Caerphilly	Norf	Norfolk
Cambs	Cambridgeshire	Nott	Nottingham
Carmar	Carmarthenshire	Notts	Nottinghamshire
CenBeds	Central Bedfordshire	Ork	Orkney
Cere	Ceredigion	Oxon	Oxfordshire
Chanl	Channel Islands	P&K	Perth & Kinross
ChesE	Cheshire East	Pembs	Pembrokeshire
ChesW&C	Cheshire West & Chester	Peter	Peterborough
Corn	Cornwall	Plym	Plymouth
Cumb	Cumbria	Ports	Portsmouth
D&G	Dumfries & Galloway	R&C	Redcar & Cleveland
Darl	Darlington	RCT	Rhondda Cynon Taff
Denb	Denbighshire	Read	Reading
Derbys	Derbyshire	Renf	Renfrewshire
Dur	Durham	Rut	Rutland
EAyr	East Ayrshire	S'end	Southend-on-Sea
EDun	East Dunbartonshire	SAyr	South Ayrshire
ELoth	East Lothian	SGlos	South Gloucestershire
ERenf	East Renfrewshire	SLan	South Lanarkshire
ERid	East Riding of Yorkshire	SYorks	South Yorkshire
ESuss	East Sussex	ScBord	Scottish Borders
Edin	Edinburgh	Shet	Shetland
ESiar	Eilean Siar (Western Isles)	Shrop	Shropshire
		Slo	Slough
Falk	Falkirk	Som	Somerset
Flints	Flintshire	Soton	Southampton
Glas	Glasgow	Staffs	Staffordshire
Glos	Gloucestershire	Stir	Stirling
GtLon	Greater London	Stock	Stockton-on-Tees
GtMan	Greater Manchester	Stoke	Stoke-on-Trent
Gwyn	Gwynedd	Suff	Suffolk
Hants	Hampshire	Surr	Surrey
Hart	Hartlepool	Swan	Swansea
Here	Herefordshire	Swin	Swindon
Herts	Hertfordshire	T&W	Tyne & Wear
High	Highland	Tel&W	Telford & Wrekin
Hull	Kingston upon Hull	Thur	Thurrock
Invcly	Inverclyde	VGlam	Vale of Glamorgan
IoA	Isle of Anglesey	W&M	Windsor & Maidenhead
IoM	Isle of Man	W'ham	Wokingham
IoS	Isles of Scilly	WBerks	West Berkshire
IoW	Isle of Wight	WDun	West Dunbartonshire
Lancs	Lancashire	WLoth	West Lothian
Leic	Leicester	WMid	West Midlands
Leics	Leicestershire	WSuss	West Sussex
Lincs	Lincolnshire	WYorks	West Yorkshire
MK	Milton Keynes	Warks	Warwickshire
MTyd	Merthyr Tydfil	Warr	Warrington
Med	Medway	Wilts	Wiltshire
Mersey	Merseyside	Worcs	Worcestershire
Middl	Middlesbrough	Wrex	Wrexham

1	Bath & North East Somerset
2	Blaenau Gwent
3	Bournemouth
4	Bracknell Forest
5	Bridgend
6	Bristol
7	Caerphilly
8	Cardiff
9	Clackmannanshire
10	Darlington
11	Dundee
12	East Dunbartonshire
13	East Renfrewshire
14	Glasgow
15	Halton
16	Hartlepool
17	Inverclyde
18	Luton
19	Merthyr Tydfil
20	Middlesbrough
21	Monmouthshire
22	Neath Port Talbot
23	Newport
24	North Lanarkshire
25	Plymouth
26	Poole
27	Portsmouth
28	Reading
29	Redcar And Cleveland
30	Renfrewshire
31	Rhondda Cynon Taff
32	Slough
33	South Gloucestershire
34	Southampton
35	Stockton-on-Tees
36	Telford & Wrekin
37	Torfaen
38	Vale Of Glamorgan
39	Warrington
40	West Dunbartonshire
41	Windsor & Maidenhead
42	Wokingham

Bosworth Battlefield Country Park *Leics* CV13 0AD **91** G5
Botallack **52** A5
Botanic Garden *Oxon* OX1 4AZ **46** Oxford
Botany Bay **73** G2
Botany Bay *Lancs* PR6 9AF **98** E1
Botcheston **91** G5
Botesdale **84** E1
Bothal **121** H5
Bothamsall **101** J5
Bothel **110** C3
Bothenhampton **58** D5
Bothwell **125** F5
Botley *Bucks* **72** C1
Botley *Hants* **61** G3
Botley *Oxon* **71** H1
Botloe's Green **79** G6
Botolph Claydon **81** J6
Botolphs **62** E6
Botolph's Bridge **65** G4
Bottesford *Leics* **92** B2
Bottesford *NLincs* **102** B2
Bottisham **83** J2
Bottlesford **70** E6
Bottom Boat **107** J7
Bottom of Hutton **105** H7
Bottom o'th'Moor **99** F1
Bottoms **106** E7
Botton Head **106** B3
Botusfleming **54** E4
Botwnnog **86** B2
Bough Beech **73** H7
Boughrood **78** A5
Boughspring **69** J2
Boughton *N'hants* **81** J2
Boughton *Norf* **94** B5
Boughton *Notts* **101** J6
Boughton Aluph **65** G3
Boughton Lees **65** F3
Boughton Malherbe **64** D3
Boughton Monchelsea **64** C2
Boughton Street **65** F2
Boulby **113** H5
Bouldnor **60** E6
Bouldon **88** E7
Boulge **85** G3
Boulmer **121** H2
Boulston **66** C4
Boultenstone Hotel **135** J9
Boultham **102** C6
Boundary *Derbys* **91** F4
Boundary *Staffs* **90** B1
Bourn **83** G3
Bourne End *Bucks* **72** B3
Bourne End *CenBeds* **82** C4
Bourne End *Herts* **72** D1
Bournebridge **73** J2
Bournemouth **60** B5
Bournemouth Airport **60** C5
Bournemouth International Centre BH2 5BH **35** Bournemouth
Bournheath **79** J1
Bournmoor **112** D1
Bournville **90** C7
Bourton *Bucks* **81** J5
Bourton *Dorset* **59** G1
Bourton *NSom* **69** G5
Bourton *Oxon* **71** E3
Bourton *Shrop* **88** E6
Bourton *Wilts* **70** D5
Bourton on Dunsmore **81** F1
Bourton-on-the-Hill **80** C5
Bourton-on-the-Water **80** C6
Boustead Hill **110** D1
Bouth **105** G1
Bouthwaite **107** G2
Boveney **72** C4
Boveridge **60** B3
Boverton **68** C5
Bovey Tracey **55** J3
Bovingdon **72** D1
Bovinger **73** J1
Bovington Camp **59** H6
Bow *Cumb* **110** E1
Bow *Devon* **57** F5
Bow *Devon* **55** J5
Bow *Ork* **139** C8
Bow Brickhill **82** C5
Bow Street *Cere* **87** F7
Bow Street *Norf* **94** E6
Bowbank **111** L4
Bowburn **112** D3
Bowcombe **61** F6
Bowd **57** K6
Bowden *Devon* **55** J6
Bowden *ScBord* **126** D7
Bowden Hill **70** C5
Bowdon **99** G4
Bower **120** C5
Bower Hinton **58** D3
Bower House Tye **84** D4
Bowerchalke **60** B2
Bowerhill **70** C5
Bowermadden **137** Q3
Bowers **90** A2
Bowers Gifford **74** D3
Bowershall **125** J1
Bowertower **137** Q3
Bowes **111** L5
Bowgreave **105** H5
Bowhousebog **125** G5
Bowithick **54** B2
Bowker's Green **98** D2
Bowland Bridge **105** H1
Bowley **78** E3
Bowley Town **78** E3
Bowlhead Green **62** C3
Bowling *WDun* **124** C3
Bowling *WYorks* **107** G6
Bowling Bank **88** C1
Bowlish **69** K7
Bowmanstead **110** E7
Bowmore **122** B4
Bowness-on-Solway **119** H7
Bowness-on-Windermere **110** F7
Bowood House & Gardens *Wilts* SN11 0LZ **70** C5
Bowscale **110** E3
Bowsden **127** H6
Bowside Lodge **137** L3
Bowston **111** F7
Bowthorpe **95** F5
Bowtrees **125** H2
Box *Glos* **70** B1
Box *Wilts* **70** B5
Box End **82** D4
Boxbush *Glos* **79** G7
Boxbush *Glos* **79** F6
Boxford *Suff* **84** D4
Boxford *WBerks* **71** H4
Boxgrove **62** C6
Boxley **64** C2
Boxmoor **72** D1
Box's Shop **56** A5
Boxted *Essex* **84** D5
Boxted *Suff* **84** C3
Boxted Cross **84** D5
Boxwell **70** B2
Boxworth **83** G2
Boxworth End **83** G2
Boyden Gate **75** J5
Boydston **124** C7
Boylestone **90** D2
Boyndie **135** L4
Boynton **109** H3
Boys Hill **59** F4
Boyton *Corn* **56** B6
Boyton *Suff* **85** H4
Boyton *Wilts* **59** J1
Boyton Cross **74** C1
Boyton End **84** B4
Bozeat **82** C3
Braaid **104** C6
Braal Castle **137** P3
Brabling Green **85** G2
Brabourne **65** F3
Brabourne Lees **65** F3
Bracadale **132** D7
Braceborough **92** D4
Bracebridge Heath **102** C6
Braceby **92** D2
Bracewell **106** D5
Brachla **133** R7
Brackenber **111** J5
Brackenbottom **106** D2
Brackenfield **101** F7
Bracklesham **62** B7
Brackley *A&B* **123** G2
Brackley *N'hants* **81** G5
Brackley Gate **91** F1
Brackley Hatch **81** H4
Bracknell **72** B5
Braco **130** D10
Bracon Ash **95** F6
Bracora **132** H11
Bracorina **132** H11
Bradbourne **100** E7
Bradbury **112** D4
Bradda **104** A6
Bradden **81** H4
Braddock **54** B4
Bradenham *Bucks* **72** B2
Bradenham *Norf* **94** D5
Bradenstoke **70** D4
Bradfield *Devon* **57** J5
Bradfield *Essex* **85** F5
Bradfield *Norf* **95** G2
Bradfield *WBerks* **71** K4
Bradfield Combust **84** C3
Bradfield Green **99** F7
Bradfield Heath **85** F6
Bradfield St. Clare **84** D3
Bradfield St. George **84** D2
Bradfield Southend (Southend) **71** J4
Bradford *Corn* **54** B3
Bradford *Derbys* **100** E6
Bradford *Devon* **56** C5
Bradford *N'umb* **127** K7
Bradford *N'umb* **121** F6
Bradford *WYorks* **107** G6
Bradford Abbas **58** E3
Bradford Cathedral Church of St. Peter *WYorks* BD1 4EH **35** Bradford
Bradford Leigh **70** B5
Bradford Peverell **59** F5
Bradford-on-Avon **70** B5
Bradford-on-Tone **57** K3
Bradgate Park *Leics* LE6 0HE **17** C4
Bradiford **56** D2
Brading **61** H6
Bradley *ChesW&C* **98** E5
Bradley *Derbys* **90** E1
Bradley *Hants* **71** K7
Bradley *NELincs* **103** F2
Bradley (Low Bradley) *NYorks* **107** F5
Bradley *Staffs* **90** A4
Bradley *WMid* **90** B6
Bradley Fold **99** G2
Bradley Green *Warks* **90** E5
Bradley Green *Worcs* **79** J2
Bradley in the Moors **90** C1
Bradley Mills **100** D1
Bradley Stoke **69** K3
Bradlingill **110** C4
Bradmore *Notts* **91** H2
Bradmore *WMid* **90** A6
Bradney **58** C1
Bradninch **57** J5
Bradnop **100** C7
Bradnor Green **78** B3
Bradpole **58** D5
Bradshaw *GtMan* **99** G1
Bradshaw *WYorks* **107** F6
Bradstone **56** B7
Bradwall Green **99** G6
Bradwell *Derbys* **100** D4
Bradwell *Devon* **56** C1
Bradwell *Essex* **84** C6
Bradwell *MK* **82** B5
Bradwell *Norf* **95** K5
Bradwell Grove **71** F1
Bradwell Waterside **75** F1
Bradwell-on-Sea **75** G1
Bradworthy **56** B4
Brae *D&G* **115** J3
Brae *High* **136** G9
Brae *Shet* **139** M6
Brae of Achnahaird **136** C8
Braeantra **133** R3
Braedownie **130** H3
Braegrum **130** F8
Braehead *D&G* **114** E5
Braehead *Glas* **124** D4
Braehead *SLan* **125** G7
Braehead *SLan* **125** H5
Braehead of Lunan **131** M5
Braeleny **130** B9
Braemar **134** F11
Braemore *High* **137** N6
Braemore *High* **133** M3
Braeswick **139** F4
Brafferton *Darl* **112** C4
Brafferton *NYorks* **107** K2
Brafield-on-the-Green **82** B3
Bragar **138** H3
Bragbury End **83** F6
Bragenham **82** C6
Braichmelyn **96** E6
Braides **105** H4
Braidley **107** F1
Braidwood **125** G6
Braigo **122** A4
Brailsford **90** E1
Brain's Green **69** K1
Braintree **84** B6
Braiseworth **85** F1
Braishfield **60** E2
Braithwaite *Cumb* **110** D4
Braithwaite *SYorks* **101** J1
Braithwaite *WYorks* **107** F5
Braithwell **101** H3
Bramber **62** E5
Brambletye **63** H3
Brambridge **61** F2
Bramcote *Notts* **91** H2
Bramcote *Warks* **91** G7
Bramdean **61** H2
Bramerton **95** G5
Bramfield *Herts* **83** F7
Bramfield *Suff* **85** H1
Bramford **85** F4
Bramhall **99** H4
Bramham **107** K5
Bramhope **107** H5
Bramley *Hants* **71** K6
Bramley *Surr* **72** D7
Bramley *SYorks* **101** G3
Bramley Corner **71** K6
Bramley Head **107** G4
Bramley Vale **101** G6
Bramling **65** H2
Brampford Speke **57** H6
Brampton *Cambs* **83** F1
Brampton *Cumb* **120** A7
Brampton *Cumb* **111** H4
Brampton *Derbys* **101** F5
Brampton *Lincs* **102** B5
Brampton *Norf* **95** G3
Brampton *Suff* **95** J7
Brampton *SYorks* **101** G2
Brampton Abbotts **79** F6
Brampton Ash **92** A7
Brampton Bryan **78** C1
Brampton en le Morthen **101** G4
Brampton Street **95** J7
Brampton Valley Way Country Park *N'hants* NN6 9DG **81** J1
Bramshall **90** C2
Bramshaw **60** D3
Bramshill **72** A5
Bramshott **62** B3
Bramwell **58** D2
Bran End **83** K6
Brancaster **94** B1
Brancaster Staithe **94** B1
Brancepeth **112** C3
Branchill **134** E5
Brand Green **79** G6
Brandelhow **110** D4
Branderburgh **134** G3
Brandesburton **109** H5
Brandeston **85** G2
Brandis Corner **56** C5
Brandiston **95** F3
Brandlingill **110** C4
Brandon *Dur* **112** C3
Brandon *Lincs* **92** C1
Brandon *N'umb* **121** F2
Brandon *Suff* **94** B7
Brandon *Warks* **81** F1
Brandon Bank **94** A7
Brandon Creek **94** A6
Brandon Park *Suff* IP27 0SU **94** B7
Brandon Parva **94** E5
Brandon to Bishop Auckland Walk *Dur* DH7 7RJ **112** C3
Brandsby **108** B2
Brandy Wharf **102** D3
Brane **52** B6
Branksome **60** B5
Branksome Park **60** B5
Bransbury **71** H7
Bransby **102** B5
Branscombe **57** K7
Bransford **79** G3
Bransford Bridge **79** H3
Bransgore **60** C5
Bransholme **109** H6
Branson's Cross **80** B1
Branston *Leics* **92** B3
Branston *Lincs* **102** D6
Branston *Staffs* **90** E3
Branston Booths **102** D6
Branston Water Park *Staffs* DE14 3EZ **90** E3
Brant Broughton **102** C7
Brantham **85** F5
Branthwaite *Cumb* **110** D3
Branthwaite *Cumb* **110** B4
Brantingham **109** F7
Branton *N'umb* **121** F2
Branton *SYorks* **101** J2
Brantwood **110** E7
Branxholm Bridgend **119** K2
Branxholme **119** K2
Branxton **127** G7
Brassey Green **98** E6
Brassington **100** E7
Brasted **73** H6
Brasted Chart **73** H6
Bratoft **103** H6
Brattleby **102** C4
Bratton *Som* **57** H1
Bratton *Tel&W* **89** F4
Bratton *Wilts* **70** C6
Bratton Clovelly **56** C6
Bratton Fleming **56** E2
Bratton Seymour **59** F2
Braughing **83** G6
Brauncewell **102** D7
Braunston *N'hants* **81** G2
Braunston *Rut* **92** B5
Braunstone **91** H5
Braunton **56** C2
Brawby **108** D2
Brawdy **66** B3
Brawith **113** F6
Brawl **137** L3
Brawlbin **137** N4
Bray **72** C4
Bray Shop **54** D3
Bray Wick **72** B4
Braybrooke **92** A7
Braydon Side **70** D3
Brayford **56** E2
Brayshaw **106** C4
Braythorn **107** H5
Brayton **108** C6
Braywoodside **72** B4
Brazacott **54** C1
Brea **52** D4
Breach *Kent* **74** E5
Breach *Kent* **65** G3
Breachwood Green **82** E6
Breaden Heath **88** D2
Breadsall **91** F2
Breadstone **70** A1
Breage **52** D6
Bream **69** K1
Breamore **60** C3
Brean **69** F6
Breanais **138** E5
Brearton **107** J3
Breascleit **138** H4
Breaston **91** G2
Brechfa **67** J2
Brechin **131** M4
Brecklate **116** A2
Breckles **94** D6
Brecon (Aberhonddu) **77** K6
Brecon Beacons Visitor Centre *Powys* LD3 8ER **77** J6
Breconside **118** D3
Bredbury **99** J3
Brede **64** D6
Bredenbury **79** F3
Bredfield **85** G3
Bredgar **74** E5
Bredhurst **74** D5
Bredon **79** J5
Bredon's Hardwick **79** J5
Bredon's Norton **79** J5
Bredwardine **78** C4
Breedon on the Hill **91** G3
Breibhig **138** K4
Breich **125** H4
Breightmet **99** G2
Breighton **108** D6
Breinton **78** D5
Breinton Common **78** D5
Bremhill **70** C4
Bremhill Wick **70** C4
Brenchley **73** K7
Brendon *Devon* **57** F1
Brendon *Devon* **56** B4
Brendon *Devon* **56** B5
Brenkley **121** H6
Brent Eleigh **84** D4
Brent Knoll **69** G6
Brent Pelham **83** H5
Brentford **72** E4
Brentingby **92** A4
Brentwood **73** J2
Brenzett **65** F5
Brenzett Green **65** F5
Breoch **115** H5
Brereton **90** C4
Brereton Green **99** G6
Brereton Heath **99** H6
Breretonhill **90** C4
Bressay **139** P8
Bressingham **94** E7
Bressingham Common **94** E7
Bressingham Steam Museum & Gardens *Norf* IP22 2AA **94** E7
Bretby **90** E3
Bretford **81** F1
Bretforton **80** B4
Bretherdale Head **111** G6
Bretherton **105** H7
Brettabister **139** N7
Brettenham *Norf* **94** D7
Brettenham *Suff* **84** D3
Bretton *Derbys* **100** D5
Bretton *Flints* **98** C6
Bretton *Peter* **92** E5
Brevig **138** A9
Brewood **90** A5
Briantspuddle **59** H5
Brick End **83** J6
Brickendon **73** G1
Bricket Wood **72** E1
Brickfields Horse Country *IoW* PO33 3TH **61** G5
Brickkiln Green **84** B5
Bricklehampton **79** J4
Bride **104** D3
Bridekirk **110** C3
Bridell **66** E1
Bridestones **99** J6
Bridestowe **56** D7
Brideswell **135** K7
Bridford **57** G7
Bridge *Corn* **52** D4
Bridge *Kent* **65** G2
Bridge End *Cumb* **105** F1
Bridge End *Devon* **55** G6
Bridge End *Essex* **83** K5
Bridge End *Lincs* **92** E2
Bridge End *Shet* **139** M9
Bridge Hewick **107** J2
Bridge of Alford **135** K9
Bridge of Allan **125** F1
Bridge of Avon **134** F7
Bridge of Awe (Drochaid Abha) **129** M7
Bridge of Balgie **130** A6
Bridge of Brewlands **130** G4
Bridge of Brown **134** F8
Bridge of Cally **130** G5
Bridge of Canny **135** L11
Bridge of Craigisla **130** H5
Bridge of Dee **115** H4
Bridge of Don **135** P10
Bridge of Dun **131** M5
Bridge of Dye **131** M2
Bridge of Earn **130** G9
Bridge of Ericht **130** A5
Bridge of Forss **137** N3
Bridge of Gaur **130** A5
Bridge of Orchy (Drochaid Urchaidh) **129** P7
Bridge of Tynet **134** H4
Bridge of Walls **139** L7
Bridge of Weir **124** B4
Bridge Reeve **56** E4
Bridge Sollers **78** D4
Bridge Street **84** C4
Bridge Trafford **98** D5
Bridgefoot *Angus* **131** J7
Bridgefoot *Cambs* **83** H4
Bridgefoot *Cumb* **110** B4
Bridgehampton **58** E2
Bridgehill **112** A1
Bridgemary **61** G4
Bridgemere **89** G1
Bridgend *A&B* **122** B4
Bridgend *A&B* **123** G1
Bridgend *Aber* **135** M6
Bridgend *Angus* **131** L4
Bridgend (Pen-y-bont ar Ogwr) *Bridgend* **68** C4
Bridgend *Corn* **54** B5
Bridgend *Cumb* **110** F5
Bridgend *Moray* **134** H7
Bridgend *WLoth* **125** J3
Bridgend of Lintrathen **130** H5
Bridgerule **56** A5
Bridges **88** C6
Bridgeton **124** E4
Bridgetown *Corn* **56** B7
Bridgetown *Som* **57** H2
Bridgewater Hall, Manchester *GtMan* M2 3WS **45** E5
Bridgeyate **69** K4
Bridgham **94** D7
Bridgnorth **89** G6
Bridgnorth Cliff Railway *Shrop* WV16 4AH **89** G6
Bridgtown **90** B5
Bridgwater **58** B1
Bridlington **109** H3
Bridport **58** D5
Bridstow **78** E6
Brierfield **106** D6
Brierley *Glos* **79** F7
Brierley *Here* **78** D3
Brierley *SYorks* **101** G1
Brierley Hill **90** B7
Brierton **112** E4
Briestfield **100** E1
Brig o'Turk **130** A10
Brigg **102** D2
Briggate **95** H3
Briggswath **113** J6
Brigham *Cumb* **110** B3
Brigham *ERid* **109** G4
Brighouse **107** G7
Brighstone **61** F6
Brightgate **100** E7
Brighthampton **71** G1
Brightholmlee **100** E3
Brightling **63** K4
Brightlingsea **84** E7
Brighton *B&H* **63** G6
Brighton *Corn* **53** G3
Brighton Centre, The *B&H* BN1 2GR **35** Brighton
Brighton Museum & Art Gallery *B&H* BN1 1EE **35** Brighton
Brighton Pier *B&H* BN2 1TW **35** Brighton
Brightons **125** H3
Brightwalton **71** H4
Brightwalton Green **71** H4
Brightwell **85** G4
Brightwell Baldwin **71** K2
Brightwell Upperton **71** K2
Brightwell-cum-Sotwell **71** J2
Brignall **112** A5
Brigsley **103** F2
Brigsteer **105** H1
Brigstock **92** C7
Brill *Bucks* **81** H7
Brill *Corn* **52** E6
Brilley **78** B4
Brilley Mountain **78** B3
Brimaston **66** C3
Brimfield **78** E2
Brimington **101** G5
Brimington Common **101** G5
Brimley **55** J3
Brimpsfield **79** J7
Brimpton **71** J5
Brimscombe **70** B1
Brimstage **98** C4
Brindham **69** J7
Brindister **139** N9
Brindle **105** J7
Brindley Ford **99** H7
Brineton **90** A4
Bringhurst **92** B6
Brington **82** D1
Brinian **139** D5
Briningham **94** E2
Brinkhill **103** G5
Brinkley *Cambs* **83** K3
Brinkley *Notts* **101** K7
Brinklow **81** F1
Brinkworth **70** D3
Brinscall **106** B7
Brinsea **69** H5
Brinsley **91** G1
Brinsop **78** D4
Brinsworth **101** G3
Brinton **94** E2
Brisco **110** F1
Brisley **94** D3
Brislington **69** K4
Brissenden Green **64** E4
Bristol **69** J4
Bristol Cathedral BS1 5TJ **35** Bristol
Bristol City Museum & Art Gallery *Bristol* BS8 1RL **8** C4
Bristol Filton Airport **69** J3
Bristol International Airport **69** J5
Bristol Zoo *Bristol* BS8 3HA **8** C4
Briston **94** E2
Britain At War Experience *GtLon* SE1 2TF **13** B7
Britannia **106** D7
Britford **60** C2
Brithdir *Caerp* **68** E1
Brithdir *Gwyn* **87** G4
Brithem Bottom **57** J4
British Empire & Commonwealth Museum BS1 6QH **35** Bristol
British Library (St. Pancras) *GtLon* NW1 2DB **12** A6
British Museum *GtLon* WC1B 3DG **44** E1
Briton Ferry (Llansawel) **68** A2
Britwell **72** C3
Britwell Salome **71** K2
Brixham **55** K5
Brixton *Devon* **55** F5
Brixton *GtLon* **73** G4
Brixton Deverill **59** H1
Brixworth **81** J1
Brixworth Country Park *N'hants* NN6 9DG **81** J1
Brize Norton **71** F1
Broad Alley **79** H2
Broad Blunsdon **70** E2
Broad Campden **80** C5
Broad Carr **100** C1
Broad Chalke **60** B2
Broad Ford **64** C4
Broad Green *Cambs* **83** K3
Broad Green *CenBeds* **82** C4
Broad Green *Essex* **84** C6
Broad Green *Essex* **83** H5
Broad Green *Mersey* **98** D3
Broad Green *Suff* **84** E3
Broad Green *Worcs* **79** G3
Broad Haven **66** B4
Broad Hill **83** J1
Broad Hinton **70** E4
Broad Laying **71** H5
Broad Marston **80** C4
Broad Oak *Carmar* **67** J3
Broad Oak *Cumb* **110** C7
Broad Oak *ESuss* **64** D6
Broad Oak *ESuss* **63** K4
Broad Oak *Here* **78** D6
Broad Road **85** G1
Broad Street *ESuss* **64** D6
Broad Street *Kent* **64** D2
Broad Street *Kent* **65** G4
Broad Street *Wilts* **70** E6
Broad Street Green **74** E1
Broad Town **70** D4
Broadbottom **99** J3
Broadbridge **62** B6
Broadbridge Heath **62** E3
Broadclyst **57** H6
Broadfield *Lancs* **106** C7
Broadfield *Lancs* **105** J7
Broadford (An t-Ath Leathann) **132** G8
Broadford Airport **132** G8
Broadford Bridge **62** D4
Broadgate **104** E1
Broadhaugh **119** K3
Broadheath *GtMan* **99** G4
Broadheath *Worcs* **79** F2
Broadhembury **57** K5
Broadhempston **55** J4
Broadholme **102** B5
Broadland Row **64** D6
Broadlay **67** G5
Broadley *Lancs* **99** H1
Broadley *Moray* **134** H4
Broadley Common **73** H1
Broadmayne **59** G6
Broadmeadows **126** C7
Broadmere **71** K7
Broadmoor **66** D5
Broadnymett **57** F5
Broadoak *Dorset* **58** D5
Broadoak *Glos* **79** F7
Broadoak *Kent* **75** H5
Broadoak End **83** G7
Broad's Green **83** K7
Broadstairs **75** K5
Broadstone *Poole* **60** B5
Broadstone *Shrop* **88** E7
Broadstreet Common **69** G3
Broadwas **79** G3
Broadwater *Herts* **83** F6
Broadwater *WSuss* **62** E6
Broadwater Down **63** J3
Broadwaters **79** H1
Broadway *Carmar* **67** G5
Broadway *Carmar* **67** F4
Broadway *Pembs* **66** B4
Broadway *Som* **58** C3
Broadway *Suff* **85** H1
Broadway *Worcs* **80** C5
Broadwell *Glos* **80** D6
Broadwell *Oxon* **71** F1
Broadwell *Warks* **81** F2
Broadwell House **111** L1
Broadwey **59** F6
Broadwindsor **58** D4
Broadwood Kelly **56** E5
Broadwoodwidger **56** C7
Brobury **78** C4
Brocastle **68** C4
Brochel **132** F6
Brochloch **117** K4
Brockamin **79** G3
Brockbridge **61** H3
Brockdish **85** G1
Brockenhurst **60** D4
Brockford Green **85** F2
Brockford Street **85** F2
Brockhall **81** H2
Brockham **72** E7
Brockhampton *Glos* **80** B6
Brockhampton *Glos* **79** J6
Brockhampton *Here* **78** E5
Brockhampton *Here* **79** F3
Brockhampton Green **59** G4
Brockholes **100** D1
Brockhurst *Hants* **61** G4
Brockhurst *WSuss* **63** H3
Brocklebank **110** E2
Brocklesby **102** E1
Brockley *NSom* **69** H5
Brockley *Suff* **84** C3
Brockley Green **84** B4
Brock's Green **71** J5
Brockton *Shrop* **88** E6
Brockton *Shrop* **89** G5
Brockton *Shrop* **88** C5
Brockton *Shrop* **88** C7
Brockton *Tel&W* **89** G4
Brockweir **69** J1
Brockwood Park **61** H2
Brockworth **79** H7
Brocton **90** B4
Brodick **123** J7
Brodsworth **101** H2
Brogborough **82** C5
Brogden **106** D5
Brogyntyn **88** B2
Broken Cross *ChesE* **99** H5
Broken Cross *ChesW&C* **99** F5
Brokenborough **70** C3
Brokes **112** B7
Bromborough **98** C4
Brome **85** F1
Brome Street **85** F1
Bromeswell **85** H3
Bromfield *Cumb* **110** C2
Bromfield *Shrop* **78** D1
Bromham *Bed* **82** D3
Bromham *Wilts* **70** C5
Bromley *GtLon* **73** H5
Bromley *SYorks* **101** F3
Bromley Cross **99** G1
Bromley Green **64** E4
Brompton *Med* **74** D5
Brompton *NYorks* **112** D7
Brompton *NYorks* **109** F1
Brompton *Shrop* **88** E5
Brompton on Swale **112** C7
Brompton Ralph **57** J2
Brompton Regis **57** H2
Bromsash **79** F6
Bromsberrow **79** G5
Bromsberrow Heath **79** G5
Bromsgrove **79** J1
Bromstead Heath **90** A4
Bromyard **79** F3
Bromyard Downs **79** F3
Bronaber **87** G2
Brondesbury **73** F3
Brongest **67** G1
Bronington **88** D2
Bronllys **78** A5
Bronnant **77** F2
Brontë Weaving Shed *WYorks* BD22 8EP **26** A1
Bronwydd Arms **67** H3
Bronydd **78** B4
Bron-y-gaer **67** G4
Bronygarth **88** B2
Brook *Carmar* **67** F5
Brook *Hants* **60** E2
Brook *Hants* **60** D3
Brook *IoW* **60** E6
Brook *Kent* **65** F3
Brook *Surr* **62** C3
Brook *Surr* **72** D7
Brook Bottom **99** J2
Brook End *Bed* **82** D2
Brook End *Herts* **83** G6
Brook End *MK* **82** C4
Brook End *Worcs* **79** H4
Brook Hill **60** D3
Brook Street *Essex* **73** J2
Brook Street *Kent* **64** E4
Brook Street *Suff* **84** C4
Brook Street *WSuss* **63** G4
Brooke *Norf* **95** G6
Brooke *Rut* **92** B5
Brookend *Glos* **69** J2
Brookend *Glos* **69** K1
Brookfield **100** C3
Brookhampton **71** K2
Brookhouse *ChesE* **99** J5
Brookhouse *Denb* **97** J6
Brookhouse *Lancs* **105** J3
Brookhouse *SYorks* **101** H4
Brookhouse Green **99** H6
Brookhouses **90** B1
Brookland **64** E5
Brooklands *D&G* **115** J3
Brooklands *Shrop* **88** E1
Brooklands Museum *Surr* KT13 0QN **72** D5
Brookmans Park **73** F1
Brooks **88** A6
Brooks Green **62** E4
Brooksby **91** J4
Brookside Miniature Railway *ChesE* SK12 1BZ **25** L8
Brookthorpe **79** H7
Brookwood **72** C6
Broom *CenBeds* **82** E4
Broom *Fife* **131** J10
Broom *Warks* **80** B3
Broom Green **94** D3
Broom Hill *Dorset* **60** B4
Broom Hill *Worcs* **79** J1
Broomcroft **88** E5
Broome *Norf* **95** H6
Broome *Shrop* **88** D7
Broome *Worcs* **79** J1
Broome Wood **121** G2
Broomedge **99** G4
Broomer's Corner **62** E4
Broomfield *Essex* **84** B7
Broomfield *Kent* **75** H5
Broomfield *Kent* **64** D2
Broomfield *Som* **58** B1
Broomfleet **108** E7
Broomhall Green **89** F1
Broomhaugh **121** F7
Broomhill *Bristol* **69** K4
Broomhill *N'umb* **121** H3
Broomielaw **112** A5
Broomley **121** F7
Broompark **112** C2
Broom's Green **79** G5
Brora **137** M9
Broseley **89** F5
Brotherlee **111** L3
Brothertoft **93** F1
Brotherton **107** K7
Brotton **113** G5
Broubster **137** N3
Brough *Cumb* **111** J5
Brough *Derbys* **100** D4
Brough *ERid* **109** F7
Brough *High* **137** Q2
Brough *Notts* **102** B7
Brough *Shet* **139** P6
Brough Lodge **139** P3
Brough Sowerby **111** J5
Broughall **88** E1
Brougham **111** G4
Brougham Hall *Cumb* CA10 2DE **111** G4
Broughton *Bucks* **82** B7
Broughton *Cambs* **83** F1
Broughton *Flints* **98** C6
Broughton *Hants* **60** E1
Broughton *Lancs* **105** J6
Broughton *MK* **82** B4
Broughton *N'hants* **82** B1
Broughton *NLincs* **102** C2
Broughton *NYorks* **108** D2
Broughton *NYorks* **106** E4
Broughton *Oxon* **81** F5
Broughton *ScBord* **125** K7
Broughton *VGlam* **68** C4
Broughton Astley **91** H6
Broughton Beck **105** F1
Broughton Gifford **70** B5
Broughton Green **79** J2
Broughton Hackett **79** J3
Broughton in Furness **105** F1
Broughton Mills **110** D7
Broughton Moor **110** B3
Broughton Poggs **71** F1
Broughtown **139** F3
Broughty Ferry **131** K7
Brown Candover **61** G1
Brown Edge *Lancs* **98** C1
Brown Edge *Staffs* **99** J7
Brown Heath **98** D6
Brown Lees **99** H7
Brown Street **84** E2
Brownber **111** J6
Browndown **61** G5
Brownheath **88** D3
Brownhills **90** C5
Brownieside **121** G1
Brownlow **99** H6
Brownlow Heath **99** H6
Brown's Bank **89** F1
Brownsea Island *Dorset* BH13 7EE **60** B6
Brownshill **70** B1
Brownshill Green **91** F7
Brownsover **81** G1
Brownston **55** G5
Browston Green **95** J5
Broxa **113** K7
Broxbourne **73** G1
Broxburn *ELoth* **126** E3
Broxburn *WLoth* **125** J3
Broxholme **102** C5
Broxted **83** J6
Broxton **98** D7
Broxwood **78** C3
Broyle Side **63** H5
Brue (Brù) **138** J3
Bruera **98** D6
Bruern **80** D6
Bruernish **138** B8
Bruichladdich **122** A4
Bruisyard **85** H2
Bruisyard Street **85** H2
Brumby **102** C1
Brund **100** D6
Brundall **95** H5
Brundish *Norf* **95** H6
Brundish *Suff* **85** G2
Brundish Street **85** G1
Brunstock **110** F1
Brunswick Village **121** H6
Bruntingthorpe **91** J6
Brunton *Fife* **131** J8
Brunton *N'umb* **121** H1
Brunton *Wilts* **71** F6
Brushford *Devon* **56** E5
Brushford *Som* **57** H3
Bruton **59** F1
Bryanston **59** H4
Bryant's Bottom **72** B2
Brydekirk **119** G6
Brymbo **98** B7
Brymor Ice Cream *NYorks* HG4 4PG **107** G1
Brympton **58** E3
Bryn *Caerp* **68** E2
Bryn *Carmar* **67** J5
Bryn *ChesW&C* **99** F5
Bryn *GtMan* **98** E2
Bryn *NPT* **68** B2
Bryn *Shrop* **88** B7
Bryn Bach Country Park *BGwent* NP22 3AY **68** E1
Bryn Bwbach **87** F2
Bryn Gates **98** E2
Bryn Pen-y-lan **88** C1
Brynamman **77** G7
Brynberian **66** E2
Bryncae **68** C3
Bryncethin **68** C3
Bryncir **86** D1
Bryncoch *Bridgend* **68** C3
Bryn-côch *NPT* **68** A2
Bryncroes **86** B2
Bryncrug **87** F5
Bryneglwys **88** A1
Brynford **97** K5
Bryngwran **96** B5
Bryngwyn *Mon* **69** G1
Bryngwyn *Powys* **78** A4
Bryn-henllan **66** D2
Brynhoffnant **76** C3
Bryning **105** H6
Brynithel **69** F1
Brynmawr *BGwent* **78** A7
Bryn-mawr *Gwyn* **86** B2
Brynmelyn **78** A1
Brynmenyn **68** C3
Brynna **68** C3
Brynnau Gwynion **68** C3
Brynog **76** E3
Bryn-penarth **88** A5
Brynrefail *Gwyn* **96** D6
Brynrefail *IoA* **96** C4
Brynsadler **68** D3
Brynsaithmarchog **97** J7
Brynsiencyn **96** C6
Bryn-teg *IoA* **96** C4
Brynteg *Wrex* **98** C7
Bryn-y-cochin **88** C2
Brynygwenin **78** C7
Bryn-y-maen **97** G5
Bubbenhall **80** E1
Bubnell **100** E5
Bubwith **108** D6
Buccleuch **119** J2
Buchan **115** H4
Buchanan Castle **124** C2
Buchanty **130** E8
Buchlyvie **124** D1
Buckabank **110** E2
Buckby Wharf **81** H2
Buckden *Cambs* **82** E2
Buckden *NYorks* **106** E2
Buckenham **95** H5
Buckerell **57** K5
Buckfast **55** H4
Buckfast Abbey *Devon* TQ11 0EE **55** H4
Buckfastleigh **55** H4
Buckhaven **126** B1
Buckholm **126** C7
Buckholt **78** E7
Buckhorn Weston **59** G2
Buckhurst Hill **73** H2
Buckie **135** J4
Buckingham **81** H5
Buckingham Palace *GtLon* SW1A 1AA **44** B5
Buckland *Bucks* **82** B7
Buckland *Devon* **55** G6
Buckland *Glos* **80** B5
Buckland *Hants* **60** E5
Buckland *Here* **78** E3
Buckland *Herts* **83** G5
Buckland *Kent* **65** J3
Buckland *Oxon* **71** G2
Buckland *Surr* **73** F6
Buckland Brewer **56** C3
Buckland Common **72** C1
Buckland Dinham **70** A6
Buckland Filleigh **56** C5
Buckland in the Moor **55** H3
Buckland Monachorum **54** E4
Buckland Newton **59** F4
Buckland Ripers **59** F6
Buckland St. Mary **58** B3
Buckland-tout-Saints **55** H6
Bucklebury **71** J4
Bucklers Hard **61** F5
Bucklesham **85** G4
Buckley (Bwcle) **98** B6
Buckley Green **80** C2
Bucklow Hill **99** G4
Buckman Corner **62** E4
Buckminster **92** B3
Bucknall **102** E6
Bucknell *Oxon* **81** G6
Bucknell *Shrop* **78** C1
Buckridge **79** G1
Buck's Cross **56** B3
Bucks Green **62** D3
Bucks Hill **72** D1
Bucks Horn Oak **72** B7
Buck's Mills **56** B3
Bucksburn **135** N10
Buckspool **66** C6
Buckton *ERid* **109** H2
Buckton *Here* **78** C1
Buckton *N'umb* **127** J7
Buckton Vale **99** J2
Buckworth **82** E1
Budbrooke **80** D2
Budby **101** J5
Bude **56** A5
Budge's Shop **54** D5
Budlake **57** H5
Budle **127** K7
Budleigh Salterton **57** J7
Budock Water **52** E5
Budworth Heath **99** F5
Buerton **89** F1
Bugbrooke **81** H3
Buglawton **99** H6
Bugle **54** A5
Bugthorpe **108** D4
Building End **83** H5
Buildwas **89** F5
Builth Road **77** K3
Builth Wells (Llanfair-ym-Muallt) **77** K3
Bulby **92** D3
Bulcote **91** J1
Buldoo **137** M3
Bulford **70** E7
Bulford Camp **70** E7
Bulkeley **98** E7
Bulkington *Warks* **91** F7
Bulkington *Wilts* **70** C6
Bulkworthy **56** B4
Bull Bay (Porth Llechog) **96** C3
Bull Green **64** E4
Bullbridge **101** F7
Bullbrook **72** B5
Bullen's Green **73** F1
Bulley **79** G7
Bullington **102** D5
Bullpot Farm **106** B1
Bulls Cross **73** G2
Bull's Green *Herts* **83** F7
Bull's Green *Norf* **95** J6
Bullwood **123** K3
Bulmer *Essex* **84** C4
Bulmer *NYorks* **108** C3
Bulmer Tye **84** C5
Bulphan **74** C3
Bulstone **57** K7
Bulverhythe **64** C7
Bulwell **91** H1
Bulwick **92** C6
Bumble's Green **73** H1
Bun Abhainn Eadarra **138** G7
Bunarkaig **129** N2
Bunbury **98** E7
Bunbury Heath **98** E7
Bunchrew **134** A6
Bundalloch **133** J8
Bunessan **128** E8
Bungay **95** H7
Bunker's Hill **103** F7
Bunlarie **123** F7
Bunmhullin **138** B7
Bunnahabhain **122** C3
Bunny **91** H3
Buntait **133** P7
Buntingford **83** G6
Bunwell **95** F6
Bunwell Street **95** F6
Burbage *Derbys* **100** C5
Burbage *Leics* **91** G6
Burbage *Wilts* **71** F5
Burbage Common *Leics* LE10 3DD **91** G6
Burchett's Green **72** B3
Burcombe **60** B1
Burcot *Oxon* **71** J2
Burcot *Worcs* **79** J1
Burcott **82** B6
Burdale **108** E3
Burdocks **62** D4
Burdon **112** D1
Burdrop **80** E5
Bure Valley Railway *Norf* NR11 6BW **95** G3
Bures **84** D5
Bures Green **84** D5
Burfa **78** B2
Burford *Oxon* **80** D7
Burford *Shrop* **78** E2
Burg **128** E6
Burgate **84** E1
Burgess Hill **63** G5
Burgh **85** G3
Burgh by Sands **110** E1
Burgh Castle **95** J5
Burgh Heath **73** F6
Burgh le Marsh **103** H6
Burgh next Aylsham **95** G3
Burgh on Bain **103** F4
Burgh St. Margaret (Fleggburgh) **95** J4
Burgh St. Peter **95** J6
Burghclere **71** H5
Burghead **134** F4
Burghfield **71** K5
Burghfield Common **71** K5
Burghfield Hill **71** K5
Burghill **78** D4
Burghwallis **101** H1
Burham **74** D5
Buriton **61** J2
Burland **99** F7
Burlawn **53** G2
Burleigh **72** C5
Burlescombe **57** J4
Burleston **59** G5
Burley *Hants* **60** D4
Burley *Rut* **92** B4
Burley *WYorks* **107** H6
Burley Gate **78** E4
Burley in Wharfedale **107** G5
Burley Street **60** D4
Burley Woodhead **107** G5
Burleydam **89** F1
Burlingjobb **78** B3
Burlow **63** J5
Burlton **88** D3
Burmarsh **65** G4
Burmington **80** D5
Burn **108** B7
Burn Naze **105** G5
Burnage **99** H3
Burnaston **90** E2
Burnby **108** E5
Burncross **101** F3
Burndell **62** C6
Burnden **99** G2
Burnedge **99** J1
Burneside **111** G7
Burness **139** F3
Burneston **107** J1
Burnett **69** K5
Burnfoot *ScBord* **120** A2
Burnfoot *ScBord* **119** K2
Burnham *Bucks* **72** C3
Burnham *NLincs* **102** D1
Burnham Deepdale **94** C1
Burnham Green **83** F7
Burnham Market **94** C1
Burnham Norton **94** C1
Burnham Overy Staithe **94** C1
Burnham Overy Town **94** C1
Burnham Thorpe **94** C1
Burnham-on-Crouch **75** F2
Burnham-on-Sea **69** G7
Burnhaven **135** R6
Burnhead *D&G* **117** K5
Burnhead *D&G* **118** D4
Burnhervie **135** M9
Burnhill Green **89** G5
Burnhope **112** B2
Burnhouse **124** C5
Burniston **113** K7
Burnley **106** D6
Burnmouth **127** H4
Burnopfield **112** B1
Burn's Green **83** G6
Burns National Heritage Park *SAyr* KA7 4PQ **117** H2
Burnsall **107** F3
Burnside *EAyr* **117** K2
Burnside *WLoth* **125** J3
Burnstones **111** H1
Burnswark **119** G6
Burnt Hill **71** J4
Burnt Houses **112** B4
Burnt Oak **73** F2
Burnt Yates **107** H3
Burntcliff Top **99** J6
Burntisland **126** A2
Burnton *EAyr* **117** J2
Burnton *EAyr* **117** J3
Burntwood **90** C5
Burntwood Green **90** C5
Burnworthy **57** K4
Burpham *Surr* **72** D6
Burpham *WSuss* **62** D6
Burra **139** M9
Burradon *N'umb* **120** E3
Burradon *T&W* **121** H6
Burrafirth **139** Q1
Burras **52** D5
Burraton *Corn* **54** E4
Burraton *Corn* **54** E5
Burravoe *Shet* **139** P5
Burravoe *Shet* **139** M6
Burrell Collection *Glas* G43 1AT **30** D5
Burrells **111** H5
Burrelton **130** H7
Burridge *Devon* **58** C4
Burridge *Hants* **61** G3
Burrill **107** H1
Burringham **102** B2
Burrington *Devon* **56** E4
Burrington *Here* **78** D1
Burrington *NSom* **69** H6
Burrough Green **83** K3
Burrough on the Hill **92** A4
Burrow *Som* **57** H1
Burrow *Som* **58** D3
Burrow Bridge **58** C1
Burrowhill **72** C5
Burrows Cross **72** D7
Burry **67** H6
Burry Green **67** H6
Burry Port **67** H5
Burscough **98** D1
Burscough Bridge **98** D1
Bursea **108** E6
Burshill **109** G5
Bursledon **61** F4
Burslem **90** A1
Burstall **85** F4
Burstock **58** D4
Burston *Norf* **95** F7
Burston *Staffs* **90** B2
Burstow **73** G7
Burstwick **109** J7
Burtersett **106** D1
Burthorpe **84** B2
Burthwaite **110** F2
Burtle **69** H7
Burtle Hill **69** G7
Burton *ChesW&C* **98** C5
Burton *ChesW&C* **98** E6
Burton *Dorset* **60** C5
Burton *Lincs* **102** C5
Burton *N'umb* **127** K7
Burton *Pembs* **66** C5
Burton *Som* **57** K1
Burton *Wilts* **70** B4
Burton *Wilts* **59** H1
Burton Agnes **109** H3
Burton Bradstock **58** D6
Burton Coggles **92** C3
Burton End **83** J6
Burton Ferry **66** C5
Burton Fleming **109** G2
Burton Green *Warks* **80** D1
Burton Green *Wrex* **98** C7
Burton Hastings **91** G7
Burton in Lonsdale **106** B2
Burton Joyce **91** J1
Burton Latimer **82** C1
Burton Lazars **92** A4
Burton Leonard **107** J3
Burton on the Wolds **91** H3
Burton Overy **91** J6
Burton Pedwardine **92** E1
Burton Pidsea **109** J6
Burton Salmon **107** K7
Burton Stather **102** B1
Burton upon Stather **102** B1
Burton upon Trent **90** E3
Burton-in-Kendal **105** J2
Burton's Green **84** C6
Burtonwood **98** E3
Burwardsley **98** E7
Burwarton **89** F7
Burwash **63** K4
Burwash Common **63** K4
Burwash Weald **63** K4
Burwell *Cambs* **83** J2
Burwell *Lincs* **103** G5
Burwen **96** C3
Burwick **139** D9
Bury *Cambs* **93** F7
Bury *GtMan* **99** H1
Bury *Som* **57** H3
Bury *WSuss* **62** D5
Bury End **80** B5
Bury Green **83** H6
Bury St. Edmunds **84** C2
Buryas Bridge **52** B6
Burythorpe **108** D3
Busbridge **72** C7
Busby **124** D5
Buscot **71** F2
Bush **56** A5
Bush Bank **78** D3
Bush Crathie **134** G11
Bush Green **95** G7
Bushbury **90** B5
Bushby **91** J5
Bushey **72** E2
Bushey Heath **72** E2
Bushley **79** H5
Bushley Green **79** H5
Bushton **70** D4
Bushy Common **94** D4
Business Design Centre, Islington *GtLon* N1 0QH **12** B6
Busk **111** H2
Buslingthorpe **102** D4
Bussage **70** B1

Busta 139 M6
Butcher's Common 95 H3
Butcher's Cross 63 J4
Butcher's Pasture 83 K6
Butcombe 69 J5
Bute 123 J4
Bute Town 68 E1
Butleigh 58 E1
Butleigh Wootton 58 E1
Butler's Cross 72 B1
Butler's Hill 91 H1
Butlers Marston 80 E4
Butlersbank 88 E3
Butley 85 H3
Butley Abbey 85 H4
Butley Low Corner 85 H4
Butley Mills 85 H3
Butley Town 99 J5
Butt Green 99 F7
Butt Lane 99 H7
Butterburn 120 B6
Buttercrambe 108 D4
Butterknowle 112 B4
Butterleigh 57 H5
Butterley 101 G7
Buttermere Cumb 110 C5
Buttermere Wilts 71 G5
Butters Green 99 H7
Buttershaw 107 G6
Butterstone 130 F6
Butterton Staffs 100 C7
Butterton Staffs 90 A1
Butterwick Dur 112 D4
Butterwick Lincs 93 G1
Butterwick NYorks 109 F2
Butterwick NYorks 108 D2
Buttington 88 B5
Buttonbridge 79 G1
Buttonoak 79 G1
Buttons' Green 84 D3
Butts 57 G7
Butt's Green Essex 74 D1
Butt's Green Hants 60 D2
Buttsash 61 F4
Buxhall 84 E3
Buxted 63 H4
Buxton Derbys 100 C5
Buxton Norf 95 G3
Buxton Heath 95 F3
Buxworth 100 C4
Bwlch 78 A6
Bwlch-clawdd 67 G2
Bwlch-derwin 86 D1
Bwlchgwyn 98 B7
Bwlch-llan 76 E3
Bwlchnewydd 67 G3
Bwlchtocyn 86 C3
Bwlch-y-cibau 88 A4
Bwlch-y-ddar 88 A3
Bwlchyfadfa 67 H1
Bwlch-y-ffridd 87 K6
Bwlch-y-groes 67 F2
Bwlchyllyn 96 D7
Bwlchymynydd 67 J6
Bwlch-y-sarnau 77 K1
Byers Green 112 C3
Byfield 81 G3
Byfleet 72 D5
Byford 78 C4
Bygrave 83 F5
Byker 121 H7
Byland Abbey 108 B2
Bylane End 54 C5
Bylchau 97 H6
Byley 99 G6
Bynea 67 J6
Byrness 120 C3
Bystock 57 J7
Bythorn 82 D1
Byton 78 C2
Bywell 121 F7
Byworth 62 C4

C

Cabourne 102 E2
Cabourne Parva 102 E2
Cabrach A&B 122 C4
Cabrach Moray 134 H8
Cabus 105 H5
Cackle Street ESuss 64 D6
Cackle Street ESuss 63 H4
Cacrabank 119 J2
Cadbury 57 H5
Cadbury Barton 56 E4
Cadbury Heath 69 K4
Cadbury World WMid B30 1JR 15 G7
Cadder 124 E3
Cadderlie 129 M7
Caddington 82 D7
Caddonfoot 126 C7
Cade Street 63 K4
Cadeby Leics 91 G5
Cadeby SYorks 101 H2
Cadeleigh 57 H5
Cader 97 J6
Cadgwith 52 E7
Cadishead 99 G3
Cadle 67 K6
Cadley Lancs 105 J6
Cadley Wilts 71 F5
Cadmore End 72 A2
Cadnam 60 D3
Cadney 102 D2
Cadole 98 B6
Cadover Bridge 55 F4
Cadoxton 68 E5
Cadoxton-Juxta-Neath 68 A2
Cadwell 82 E5
Cadwst 87 K2
Cadzow 125 F5
Cae Ddafydd 87 F1
Caeathro 96 D6
Caehopkin 77 H7
Caenby 102 D4
Caenby Corner 102 C4
Caer Llan 69 H1
Caerau Bridgend 68 B2
Caerau Cardiff 68 E4
Caerdeon 87 F4
Caerfarchell 66 A3
Caergeiliog 96 B5
Caergwrle 98 C7
Caer-Lan 77 H7
Caerleon 69 G2
Caernarfon 96 C6
Caernarfon Castle Gwyn LL55 2AY 96 C6
Caerphilly 68 E3
Caersws 87 K6
Caerwedros 76 C3
Caerwent 69 H2
Caerwys 97 K5
Caethle Farm 87 F6
Caggan 134 C9
Caggle Street 78 C7
Caim 96 E4
Caio 67 K2
Cairisiadar 138 F4
Cairminis 138 F9
Cairnbaan 123 G1
Cairnbulg 135 Q4
Cairncross Angus 131 L3
Cairncross ScBord 127 G4
Cairncurran 124 B4
Cairndoon 114 D7
Cairndow 129 N9
Cairness 135 Q4
Cairneyhill 125 J2
Cairngorm Mountain High PH22 1RB 134 D10
Cairnie 135 J6
Cairnorrie 135 N6
Cairnryan 114 A4
Cairnsmore 114 E4
Caister-on-Sea 95 K4
Caistor 102 E2
Caistor St. Edmund 95 G5
Caistron 120 E3
Caithness Crystal Visitor Centre Norf PE30 4NE 94 A4
Cake Street 94 E6
Cakebole 79 H1
Calbourne 61 F6
Calceby 103 G5
Calcoed 97 K5
Calcot 71 K4
Calcot Kent 75 H5
Calcott Shrop 88 D4
Calcotts Green 79 G7
Calcutt 70 E2
Caldarvan 124 C2
Caldbeck 110 E3
Caldbergh 107 F1
Caldecote Cambs 83 G3
Caldecote Cambs 82 E1
Caldecote Herts 83 F5
Caldecote N'hants 81 H3
Caldecote Warks 91 F6
Caldecott N'hants 82 C2
Caldecott Oxon 71 H2
Caldecott Rut 92 B6
Calder Bridge 110 B6
Calder Grove 101 F1
Calder Vale 105 J5
Calderbank 125 F4
Calderbrook 99 J1
Caldercruix 125 G4
Calderglen 124 E5
Calderglen Country Park SLan G75 0QZ 31 H8
Caldermill 124 E6
Caldey Island 66 E6
Caldicot 69 H3
Caldwell Derbys 90 E4
Caldwell ERenf 124 C5
Caldwell NYorks 112 B5
Caldy 98 B4
Calebreck 110 E3
Caledrhydiau 76 D3
Calford Green 83 K4
Calfsound 139 E4
Calgary 128 E5
Califer 134 E5
California Falk 125 H3
California Norf 95 K4
California Suff 85 G4
California Country Park W'ham RG40 4HT 72 A5
Calke 91 F3
Calke Abbey Derbys DE73 7LE 91 F3
Callakille 132 G5
Callaly 121 F3
Callander 130 B10
Callanish (Calanais) 138 H4
Callaughton 89 F6
Callerton Lane End 121 G7
Calliburn 116 B1
Calligarry 132 G10
Callington 54 D4
Callingwood 90 D3
Callisterhall 119 H5
Callow 78 D5
Callow End 79 H4
Callow Hill Wilts 70 D3
Callow Hill Worcs 79 G1
Callow Hill Worcs 80 B2
Callows Grave 78 E2
Calmore 60 E3
Calmsden 70 D1
Calne 70 C4
Calow 101 G5
Calshot 61 F4
Calstock 54 E4
Calstone Wellington 70 D5
Calthorpe 95 F2
Calthwaite 111 F2
Calton NYorks 106 E4
Calton Staffs 100 D7
Calveley 98 E7
Calver 100 E5
Calver Hill 78 C4
Calverhall 89 F2
Calverleigh 57 H4
Calverley 107 H6
Calvert 81 H6
Calverton MK 81 J5
Calverton Notts 91 J1
Calvine 130 C4
Calvo 110 C1
Cam 70 A2
Camasnacroise 129 K5
Camastianavaig 132 F7
Camault Muir 133 R6
Camb 139 P3
Camber 64 E6
Camberley 72 B5
Camberwell 73 G4
Camblesforth 108 C7
Cambo 121 F5
Cambois 121 J5
Camborne 52 D5
Cambourne 83 G3
Cambridge Cambs 83 H3
Cambridge Glos 70 A1
Cambridge American Military Cemetery & Memorial Cambs CB23 7PH 83 G3
Cambridge City Airport 83 H3
Cambridge University Botanic Garden Cambs CB2 1JF 83 H3
Cambus 125 G1
Cambusbarron 125 F1
Cambuskenneth 125 G1
Cambuslang 124 E4
Cambusnethan 125 G5
Camden Town 73 F3
Camel Hill 58 E2
Camel Trail Corn PL27 7AL 53 G1
Camelford 54 B2
Camelon 125 G2
Camelot Theme Park Lancs PR7 5LP 98 E1
Camelsdale 62 B3
Camer 74 C5
Cameron House 124 B2
Camer's Green 79 G5
Camerton B&NESom 69 K6
Camerton Cumb 110 B3
Camerton ERid 109 J7
Camghouran 130 A5
Camis Eskan 124 B2
Cammachmore 135 P11
Cammeringham 102 C4
Camp Hill Pembs 66 E4
Camp Hill Warks 91 F6
Campbeltown (Ceann Loch Chille Chiarain) 116 B1
Campbeltown Airport 116 A1
Camperdown 121 H6
Camperdown Country Park Dundee DD2 4TF 131 J7
Camps 125 K4
Camps End 83 K4
Camps Heath 95 K6
Campsall 101 H1
Campsea Ashe 85 H3
Campton 82 E5
Camptown 120 B2
Camquhart 123 H2
Camrose 66 C3
Camserney 130 D6
Camstraddan House 124 B1
Camus-luinie 133 K8
Camusnoroy 133 J11
Camusteel 132 H6
Camusterrach 132 H6
Camusvrachan 130 B6
Canada 60 D3
Canaston Bridge 66 D4
Candlesby 103 H6
Candy Mill 125 J6
Cane End 71 K4
Canewdon 74 E2
Canfield End 83 J6
Canford Bottom 60 B4
Canford Cliffs 60 B6
Canford Heath 60 B5
Canford Magna 60 B5
Canham's Green 84 E2
Canisbay 137 R2
Canley 80 E1
Cann 59 H2
Cann Common 59 H2
Canna 132 C10
Cannard's Grave 69 K7
Cannich (Canaich) 133 P7
Canning Town 73 H3
Cannington 58 B1
Cannock 90 B5
Cannock Wood 90 C4
Cannon Hall Country Park SYorks S75 4AT 100 E2
Cannon Hall Farm SYorks S75 4AT 100 E2
Cannon Hill Park WMid B13 8RD 15 H6
Cannop 79 F7
Canon Bridge 78 D4
Canon Frome 79 F4
Canon Pyon 78 D4
Canonbie 119 J6
Canons Ashby 81 G3
Canon's Town 52 C5
Canterbury 65 G2
Canterbury Cathedral Kent CT1 2EH 35 Canterbury
Canterbury Tales, The Kent CT1 2TG 35 Canterbury
Cantley Norf 95 H5
Cantley SYorks 101 J2
Cantlop 88 E5
Canton 68 E4
Cantraydoune 134 B6
Cantsfield 106 B2
Canvey Island 74 D3
Canwell Hall 90 D5
Canwick 102 C6
Canworthy Water 54 C1
Caol 129 N3
Caolas 128 B6
Caolasnacon 129 N4
Capel Kent 73 K7
Capel Surr 72 E7
Capel Bangor 87 F7
Capel Betws Lleucu 77 F3
Capel Carmel 86 A3
Capel Celyn 87 H1
Capel Coch 96 C4
Capel Curig 97 F7
Capel Cynon 67 G1
Capel Dewi Carmar 67 H3
Capel Dewi Cere 87 F7
Capel Dewi Cere 67 H1
Capel Garmon 97 G7
Capel Gwyn Carmar 67 H3
Capel Gwyn IoA 96 B5
Capel Gwynfe 77 G6
Capel Hendre 67 J4
Capel Isaac 67 J3
Capel Iwan 67 F2
Capel le Ferne 65 H4
Capel Llanilltern 68 D3
Capel Mawr 96 C5
Capel Parc 96 C4
Capel St. Andrew 85 H4
Capel St. Mary 84 E5
Capel St. Silin 76 E3
Capel Seion 77 F1
Capel Tygwydd 67 F1
Capeluchaf 86 D1
Capelulo 97 F5
Capel-y-ffin 78 B5
Capel-y-graig 96 D6
Capenhurst 98 C5
Capernwray 105 J2
Capheaton 121 F5
Caplaw 124 C5
Capon's Green 85 G2
Cappercleuch 119 H1
Capplegill 119 G3
Capstone 74 D5
Capton Devon 55 J5
Capton Som 57 J2
Caputh 130 F6
Car Colston 92 A1
Caradon Town 54 C3
Carbellow 118 B1
Carbeth 124 D3
Carbis Bay 52 C5
Carbost High 132 E6
Carbost High 132 D7
Carbrain 125 F3
Carbrooke 94 D5
Carburton 101 J5
Carco 118 C2
Carcroft 101 H1
Cardenden 126 A1
Cardeston 88 C4
Cardew 110 E2
Cardiff (Caerdydd) 68 E4
Cardiff Bay Visitor Centre Cardiff CF10 4PA 7 C6
Cardiff Castle & Museum CF10 3RB 36 Cardiff
Cardiff International Airport 68 D5
Cardiff Millennium Stadium CF10 1GE 36 Cardiff
Cardigan (Aberteifi) 66 E1
Cardinal's Green 83 K4
Cardington Bed 82 D4
Cardington Shrop 88 E6
Cardinham 54 B4
Cardonald 124 D4
Cardoness 115 F5
Cardow 134 F6
Cardrona 126 A7
Cardross 124 B3
Cardurnock 110 C1
Careby 92 D4
Careston 131 L5
Carew 66 D5
Carew Cheriton 66 D5
Carew Newton 66 D5
Carey 78 E5
Carfin 125 F5
Carfrae 126 D4
Carfraemill 126 D5
Cargate Green 95 H4
Cargen 115 K3
Cargenbridge 115 K3
Cargill 130 G7
Cargo 110 E1
Cargreen 54 E4
Carham 127 F7
Carhampton 57 J1
Carharrack 52 E4
Carie P&K 130 B5
Carie P&K 130 B7
Carines 52 E3
Carinish (Cairinis) 138 C2
Carisbrooke 61 F6
Carisbrooke Castle & Museum IoW PO30 1XY 61 F6
Cark 105 G2
Carkeel 54 E4
Carland Cross 53 F3
Carlatton 111 G1
Carlby 92 D4
Carlecotes 100 D2
Carleen 52 D6
Carleton Cumb 110 F1
Carleton Cumb 111 G4
Carleton Lancs 105 G5
Carleton NYorks 106 E5
Carleton WYorks 107 K7
Carleton Fishery 117 F5
Carleton Forehoe 94 E5
Carleton Rode 95 F6
Carleton St. Peter 95 H5
Carlin How 113 H5
Carlisle 110 F1
Carlisle Cathedral Cumb CA3 8TZ 36 Carlisle
Carlisle Park, Morpeth N'umb NE61 1YD 121 G5
Carloggas 53 F2
Carlops 125 K5
Carloway (Càrlabhagh) 138 H3
Carlton Bed 82 C3
Carlton Cambs 83 K3
Carlton Leics 91 F5
Carlton Notts 91 J1
Carlton NYorks 108 C7
Carlton NYorks 107 F1
Carlton NYorks 108 C1
Carlton Stock 112 D4
Carlton Suff 85 H2
Carlton SYorks 101 F1
Carlton WYorks 107 J7
Carlton Colville 95 K6
Carlton Curlieu 91 J6
Carlton Green 83 K3
Carlton Husthwaite 107 K2
Carlton in Lindrick 101 H4
Carlton Miniott 107 J1
Carlton Scroop 92 C1
Carlton-in-Cleveland 113 F6
Carlton-le-Moorland 102 C7
Carlton-on-Trent 102 B6
Carluke 125 G5
Carlyon Bay 54 A5
Carmacoup 118 C1
Carmarthen (Caerfyrddin) 67 H3
Carmel Carmar 67 J4
Carmel Flints 97 K5
Carmel Gwyn 96 C7
Carmel IoA 96 B4
Carmichael 125 H7
Carmunnock 124 D5
Carmyle 124 E4
Carmyllie 131 L6
Carn 122 A5
Carn Brea Village 52 D4
Carnaby 109 H3
Carnach 133 L8
Carnassarie 129 K10
Carnbee 131 L10
Carnbo 130 F10
Carnduncan 122 A4
Carne 53 G5
Carnforth 105 H2
Carnhedryn 66 B3
Carnhell Green 52 D5
Carnkie Corn 52 D5
Carnkie Corn 52 E5
Carnmore 122 B6
Carno 87 J6
Carnoch High 133 P7
Carnoch High 133 N5
Carnoch High 134 C6
Carnock 125 J2
Carnon Downs 53 F4
Carnoustie 131 L7
Carntyne 124 E4
Carnwath 125 H6
Carnyorth 52 A5
Carol Green 80 D1
Carperby 107 F1
Carr 101 H3
Carr Hill 101 J3
Carr Houses 98 C2
Carr Shield 111 K2
Carr Vale 101 G5
Carradale 123 G7
Carrbridge 134 D8
Carrefour Selous 53 J7
Carreglefn 96 B4
Carreg-wen 67 F1
Carrhouse 101 K2
Carrick 123 H2
Carrick Castle 123 K1
Carriden 125 J2
Carrine 116 A3
Carrington GtMan 99 G3
Carrington Lincs 103 G7
Carrington Midlo 126 B4
Carroch 118 B4
Carrog Conwy 97 G7
Carrog Denb 88 A1
Carron Falk 125 G2
Carron Moray 134 G6
Carron Bridge 125 F2
Carronbridge 118 D4
Carronshore 125 G2
Carrow Hill 69 H2
Carrutherstown 119 G6
Carruthmuir 124 B4
Carrville 112 D2
Carry 123 H4
Carsaig 128 G8
Carscreugh 114 C4
Carse 123 F4
Carsegowan 114 E5
Carseriggan 114 D4
Carsethorn 115 K5
Carshalton 73 F5
Carshalton Beeches 73 F5
Carsie 130 G6
Carsington 100 E7
Carsington Water Derbys DE6 1ST 100 E7
Carsluith 114 E5
Carsphairn 117 K4
Carstairs 125 H6
Carstairs Junction 125 H6
Carswell Marsh 71 G2
Carter's Clay 60 E2
Carterton 71 F1
Carterway Heads 112 A1
Carthew 54 A5
Carthorpe 107 J1
Cartington 121 F3
Cartland 125 G6
Cartmel 105 G2
Cartmel Fell 105 H1
Cartworth 100 D2
Carway 67 H5
Cascades Adventure Pool Devon EX33 1NZ 56 C2
Cascob 78 B2
Cashel Farm 124 C1
Cashes Green 70 B1
Cashlie 129 R6
Cashmoor 59 J3
Cassencarie 114 E5
Cassington 81 F7
Cassop 112 D3
Castell 97 F6
Castell Gorfod 67 F3
Castell Howell 67 H1
Castellau 68 D3
Castell-y-bwch 69 F2
Casterton 106 B2
Castle Acre 94 C4
Castle Ashby 82 B3
Castle Bolton 112 A7
Castle Bromwich 90 D7
Castle Bytham 92 C4
Castle Caereinion 88 A5
Castle Camps 83 K4
Castle Carrock 111 G1
Castle Cary 59 F1
Castle Combe 70 B4
Castle Donington 91 G3
Castle Douglas 115 H4
Castle Drogo Devon EX6 6PB 57 F6
Castle Eaton 70 E2
Castle Eden 112 E3
Castle Eden Dene National Nature Reserve Dur SR8 1NJ 112 E3
Castle End 80 D1
Castle Frome 79 F4
Castle Gate 52 B5
Castle Goring 62 E6
Castle Green 72 C5
Castle Gresley 90 E4
Castle Heaton 127 H6
Castle Hedingham 84 B5
Castle Hill Kent 73 K7
Castle Hill Suff 85 F4
Castle Howard NYorks YO60 7DA 108 D3
Castle Kennedy 114 B5
Castle Levan 124 A3
Castle Madoc 77 K5
Castle Morris 66 C2
Castle O'er 119 H4
Castle Rising 94 A3
Castle Semple Water Country Park Renf PA12 4HJ 124 B5
Castlebay (Bàgh a'Chaisteil) 138 A9
Castlebythe 66 D3
Castlecary 125 F3
Castlecraig High 134 C4
Castlecraig ScBord 125 K6
Castlefairn 118 C5
Castleford 107 K7
Castlemartin 66 C6
Castlemilk D&G 119 G6
Castlemilk Glas 124 E5
Castlemorton 79 G5
Castlerigg 110 D4
Castleside 112 A2
Castlesteads 120 A7
Castlethorpe 81 J4
Castleton A&B 123 G2
Castleton Derbys 100 D4
Castleton GtMan 99 H1
Castleton Newport 69 F3
Castleton NYorks 113 G6
Castleton ScBord 120 A4
Castletown Dorset 59 F7
Castletown High 137 P3
Castletown IoM 104 B7
Castletown T&W 112 D1
Castleweary 119 K3
Castlewigg 114 E6
Castley 107 H5
Caston 94 D6
Castor 92 E6
Castramont 115 F4
Caswell 67 J7
Cat & Fiddle Inn 100 C5
Catacol 123 H6
Catbrain 69 J3
Catbrook 69 J1
Catchall 52 B6
Catcleugh 120 C3
Catcliffe 101 G4
Catcott 58 C1
Caterham 73 G6
Catfield 95 H3
Catford 73 G4
Catforth 105 H6
Cathays 68 E4
Cathcart 124 D4
Cathedine 78 A6
Catherine-de-Barnes 90 D7
Catherington 61 H3
Catherston Leweston 58 C5
Catherton 79 F1
Cathkin 124 E5
Catisfield 61 G4
Catlodge 134 A11
Catlowdy 119 K6
Catmere End 83 H5
Catmore 71 H3
Caton Devon 55 H3
Caton Lancs 105 J3
Caton Green 105 J3
Cator Court 55 G3
Catrine 117 K1
Cat's Ash 69 G2
Catsfield 64 C6
Catsfield Stream 64 C6
Catshaw 100 E2
Catshill 79 J1
Cattadale 122 B4
Cattal 107 K4
Cattawade 84 E5
Catterall 105 J5
Catterick 112 C7
Catterick Bridge 112 C7
Catterick Garrison 112 B7
Catterlen 111 F3
Catterline 131 P3
Catterton 108 B5
Catteshall 72 C7
Catthorpe 81 G1
Cattishall 84 C2
Cattistock 58 E4
Catton N'umb 111 K1
Catton Norf 95 G4
Catton NYorks 107 J2
Catton Hall 90 E4
Catwick 109 H5
Catworth 82 D1
Caudle Green 79 J7
Caudwell's Mill & Craft Centre Derbys DE4 2EB 100 E6
Caulcott CenBeds 82 D4
Caulcott Oxon 81 G6
Cauldhame Stir 124 E1
Cauldhame Stir 130 D10
Cauldon 90 C1
Caulkerbush 115 K5
Caulside 119 K5
Caundle Marsh 59 F3
Caunsall 90 A7
Caunton 101 K6
Causeway End D&G 114 E4
Causeway End Essex 83 K7
Causeway End Lancs 98 D1
Causewayhead Cumb 110 C1
Causewayhead Stir 125 G1
Causey 112 C1
Causey Arch Picnic Area Dur NE16 5EG 29 A7
Causey Park 121 G4
Cautley 111 H7
Cavendish 84 C4
Cavendish Bridge 91 G3
Cavenham 84 B2
Cavens 115 K5
Cavers 120 A2
Caversfield 81 G6
Caversham 72 A4
Caverswall 90 B1
Cawdor 134 C5
Cawkeld 109 F4
Cawkwell 103 F4
Cawood 108 B6
Cawsand 54 E6
Cawston Norf 95 F3
Cawston Warks 81 F1
Cawthorn 108 D1
Cawthorne 100 E2
Cawthorpe 92 D3
Cawton 108 C2
Caxton 83 G3
Caxton Gibbet 83 F2
Caynham 78 E1
Caythorpe Lincs 92 C1
Caythorpe Notts 91 J1
Cayton 109 G1
CC2000 Pembs SA67 8DD 66 D4
Ceallan 138 C3
Ceann a' Bhàigh ESiar 138 B2
Ceann a' Bhàigh ESiar 138 F9
Cearsiadar 138 J6
Cedig 87 J3
Cefn Berain 97 H6
Cefn Canol 88 B2
Cefn Cantref 77 K6
Cefn Coch Denb 97 K7
Cefn Coch Powys 87 K5
Cefn Cribwr 68 B3
Cefn Cross 68 B3
Cefn Einion 88 B7
Cefn Hengoed 68 E2
Cefn Llwyd 87 F7
Cefn Rhigos 68 C1
Cefn-brith 97 H7
Cefn-caer-Ferch 86 D1
Cefn-coch 88 A3
Cefn-coed-y-cymmer 68 D1
Cefn-ddwysarn 87 J2
Cefndeuddwr 87 G3
Cefneithin 67 J4
Cefn-gorwydd 77 J4
Cefn-gwyn 88 A7
Cefn-mawr 88 B1
Cefnpennar 68 D1
Cefn-y-bedd 98 C7
Cefn-y-pant 66 E3
Ceidio 96 C4
Ceidio Fawr 86 B2
Ceint 96 C5
Cellan 67 K1
Cellarhead 90 B1
Cemaes 96 B3
Cemmaes 87 H5
Cemmaes Road (Glantwymyn) 87 H5
Cenarth 67 F1
Cennin 86 D1
Centre for Life T&W NE1 4EP 41 Newcastle upon Tyne
Ceramica Stoke ST6 3DS 20 D3
Ceres 131 K9
Cerist 87 J7
Cerne Abbas 59 F4
Cerney Wick 70 D2
Cerrigceinwen 96 C5
Cerrigydrudion 87 J1
Cessford 120 C1
Ceunant 96 D6
Chaceley 79 H5
Chacewater 52 E4
Chackmore 81 H5
Chacombe 81 F4
Chad Valley 90 C7
Chadderton 99 J2
Chadderton Fold 99 H2
Chaddesden 91 F2
Chaddesley Corbett 79 H1
Chaddleworth 71 H4
Chadlington 80 E6
Chadshunt 80 E3
Chadstone 82 B3
Chadwell Leics 92 A3
Chadwell Shrop 89 G4
Chadwell St. Mary 74 C4
Chadwick End 80 D1
Chaffcombe 58 C3
Chafford Hundred 74 C4
Chagford 57 F7
Chailey 63 G5
Chainhurst 64 C3
Chalbury 60 B4
Chalbury Common 60 B4
Chaldon 73 G6
Chaldon Herring (East Chaldon) 59 G6
Chale 61 F7
Chale Green 61 F6
Chalfont Common 72 D2
Chalfont St. Giles 72 C2
Chalfont St. Peter 72 D2
Chalford Glos 70 B1
Chalford Wilts 70 B7
Chalgrove 71 K2
Chalk 74 C4
Chalk End 83 K7
Challaborough 55 G6
Challacombe 56 E1
Challoch 114 D4
Challock 65 F2
Chalmington 58 E4
Chalton CenBeds 82 D6
Chalton Hants 61 J3
Chalvey 72 C4
Chalvington 63 J6
Champany 125 J3
Chancery 76 E1
Chandler's Cross 72 D2
Chandler's Ford 61 F2
Channel Islands 53 G7
Channel's End 82 E3
Chantry Som 70 A7
Chantry Suff 85 F4
Chapel 126 A1
Chapel Allerton Som 69 H6
Chapel Allerton WYorks 107 J6
Chapel Amble 53 G1
Chapel Brampton 81 J2
Chapel Chorlton 90 A2
Chapel Cleeve 57 J1
Chapel Cross 63 K4
Chapel End 82 D4
Chapel Green Warks 90 E7
Chapel Green Warks 81 F2
Chapel Haddlesey 108 B7
Chapel Hill Aber 135 Q7
Chapel Hill Lincs 103 F7
Chapel Hill Mon 69 J1
Chapel Hill NYorks 107 J5
Chapel Knapp 70 B5
Chapel Lawn 78 C1
Chapel Leigh 57 K3
Chapel Milton 100 C4
Chapel of Garioch 135 M8
Chapel Rossan 114 B6
Chapel Row Essex 74 D1
Chapel Row WBerks 71 J5
Chapel St. Leonards 103 J5
Chapel Stile 110 E6
Chapel Town 53 F3
Chapeldonan 117 F3
Chapelend Way 84 B5
Chapel-en-le-Frith 100 C4
Chapelgate 93 H3
Chapelhall 125 F4
Chapelhill P&K 130 H8
Chapelhill P&K 130 F7
Chapelknowe 119 J6
Chapel-le-Dale 106 C2
Chapelthorpe 101 F1
Chapelton Angus 131 M6
Chapelton Devon 56 E3
Chapelton SLan 124 E6
Chapeltown B'burn 99 G1
Chapeltown Cumb 119 K6
Chapeltown Moray 134 G8
Chapeltown SYorks 101 F3
Chapmans Well 56 B6
Chapmanslade 70 B7
Chapmore End 83 G7
Chappel 84 C6
Charaton 54 D4
Chard 58 C4
Chard Junction 58 C4
Chardleigh Green 58 C3
Chardstock 58 C4
Charfield 70 A2
Charing 64 E3
Charing Cross 60 C3
Charing Heath 64 E3
Charingworth 80 C5
Charlbury 80 E7
Charlcombe 70 A5
Charlecote 80 D3
Charles 56 E2
Charles Tye 84 E3
Charlesfield 120 A1
Charleshill 72 B7
Charleston 131 J6
Charlestown Aberdeen 135 P10
Charlestown Corn 54 A5
Charlestown Derbys 100 C3
Charlestown Dorset 59 F7
Charlestown Fife 125 J2
Charlestown GtMan 99 H2
Charlestown High 133 J3
Charlestown High 134 A6
Charlestown WYorks 107 G6
Charlestown WYorks 106 E7
Charlestown of Aberlour (Aberlour) 134 G6
Charlesworth 100 C3
Charlinch 58 B1
Charlotteville 72 D7
Charlton GtLon 73 H4
Charlton Hants 71 G7
Charlton Herts 82 E6
Charlton N'hants 81 G5
Charlton N'umb 120 D5
Charlton Oxon 71 H3
Charlton Som 69 K6
Charlton Som 69 K7
Charlton Som 58 B2
Charlton Tel&W 88 E4
Charlton Wilts 59 J2
Charlton Wilts 70 C3
Charlton Wilts 70 E6
Charlton Worcs 80 B4
Charlton WSuss 62 B5
Charlton Abbots 80 B6
Charlton Adam 58 E2
Charlton Down 59 F5
Charlton Horethorne 59 F2
Charlton Kings 79 J6
Charlton Mackrell 58 E2
Charlton Marshall 59 H4
Charlton Musgrove 59 G2
Charlton on the Hill 59 H4
Charlton-All-Saints 60 C2
Charlton-on-Otmoor 81 G7
Charltons 113 G5
Charlwood 73 F7
Charminster 59 F5
Charmouth 58 C5
Charndon 81 H6
Charney Bassett 71 G2
Charnock Richard 98 E1
Charsfield 85 G3
Chart Corner 64 C3
Chart Sutton 64 D3
Charter Alley 71 J6
Charterhouse 69 H6
Charterville Allotments 71 G1
Chartham 65 G2
Chartham Hatch 65 G2
Chartridge 72 C1
Chartwell Kent TN16 1PS 73 H6
Charvil 72 A4
Charwelton 81 G3
Chase End Street 79 G5
Chase Terrace 90 C5
Chasetown 90 C5
Chastleton 80 D6
Chasty 56 B5
Chatburn 106 C5
Chatcull 89 G2
Chatelherault Country Park SLan ML3 7UE 31 K8
Chatham 74 D5
Chatham Green 84 B7
Chatham Historic Dockyard Med ME4 4TZ 74 D5
Chathill 121 G1
Chatsworth Farmyard & Adventure Playground Derbys DE45 1PP 100 E5
Chatsworth House Derbys DE45 1PP 100 E5
Chattenden 74 D4
Chatteris 93 G7
Chattisham 84 E4
Chatto 120 C2
Chatton 121 F1
Chaul End 82 D6
Chavey Down 72 B5
Chawleigh 57 F4
Chawley 71 H1
Chawston 82 E3
Chawton 61 J1
Chazey Heath 71 K4
Cheadle GtMan 99 H4
Cheadle Staffs 90 C1
Cheadle Heath 99 H4
Cheadle Hulme 99 H4
Cheam 73 F5
Cheapside 72 C5
Chearsley 81 J7
Chebsey 90 A3
Checkendon 71 K3
Checkley ChesE 89 G1
Checkley Here 78 E5
Checkley Staffs 90 C2
Checkley Green 89 G1
Chedburgh 84 B3
Cheddar 69 H6
Cheddar Caves & Gorge Som BS27 3QF 69 H6
Cheddington 82 C7
Cheddleton 99 J7
Cheddon Fitzpaine 58 B2
Chedglow 70 C2
Chedgrave 95 H6
Chedington 58 D4
Chediston 85 H1
Chediston Green 85 H1
Chedworth 80 B7
Chedzoy 58 C1
Cheesden 99 H1
Cheeseman's Green 65 F4
Cheetham Hill 99 H2
Cheglinch 56 D1
Cheldon 57 F4
Chelford 99 H5
Chellaston 91 F2
Chells 83 F6
Chelmarsh 89 G7
Chelmondiston 85 G5
Chelmorton 100 D6
Chelmsford 74 D1
Chelmsford Cathedral Essex CM1 1TY 74 D1
Chelmsley Wood 90 D7
Chelsea 73 F4
Chelsfield 73 H5
Chelsham 73 G6
Chelsworth 84 D4
Cheltenham 79 J6
Chelveston 82 C2
Chelvey 69 H5
Chelwood 69 K5
Chelwood Common 63 H4
Chelwood Gate 63 H4
Chelworth 70 C2
Cheney Longville 88 D7
Chenies 72 D2
Chepstow (Cas-gwent) 69 J2
Cherhill 70 D4
Cherington Glos 70 C2
Cherington Warks 80 D5
Cheriton Devon 57 F1
Cheriton Hants 61 G2
Cheriton Kent 65 G4
Cheriton Pembs 66 C6
Cheriton Swan 67 H6
Cheriton Bishop 57 F6
Cheriton Cross 57 F6
Cheriton Fitzpaine 57 G5
Cherrington 89 F3
Cherry Burton 109 F5
Cherry Green 83 J6
Cherry Hinton 83 H3
Cherry Willingham 102 D5
Chertsey 72 D5
Cheselbourne 59 G5
Chesham 72 C1
Chesham Bois 72 C1
Cheshire Farm Ice Cream, Tattenhall ChesW&C CH3 9NE 98 D7
Cheshunt 73 G1
Cheslyn Hay 90 B5
Chessington 72 E5
Chessington World of Adventures GtLon KT9 2NE 72 E5
Chestall 90 C4
Chester 98 D6
Chester Cathedral ChesW&C CH1 2HU 36 Chester
Chester Moor 112 C2
Chester Zoo ChesW&C CH2 1LH 98 D5
Chesterblade 69 K7
Chesterfield Derbys 101 F5
Chesterfield Staffs 90 D5
Chester-le-Street 112 C1
Chesters ScBord 120 B2
Chesters ScBord 120 B1
Chesterton Cambs 83 H2
Chesterton Cambs 92 E6
Chesterton Oxon 81 G6
Chesterton Shrop 89 G6
Chesterton Staffs 90 A1
Chesterton Warks 80 E3
Chesterton Green 80 E3
Chestfield 75 H5
Cheston 55 G5
Cheswardine 89 G3
Cheswick 127 J6
Cheswick Buildings 127 J6
Cheswick Green 80 C1
Chetnole 59 F4
Chettiscombe 57 H4
Chettisham 93 J7
Chettle 59 J3
Chetton 89 F6
Chetwode 81 H6
Chetwynd Aston 89 G4
Chetwynd Park 89 G3
Cheveley 83 K2
Chevening 73 H6
Cheverell's Green 82 D7
Chevin Forest Park WYorks LS21 3JL 107 H5
Chevington 84 B3
Chevithorne 57 H4
Chew Magna 69 J5
Chew Moor 99 F2
Chew Stoke 69 J5
Chewton Keynsham 69 K5
Chewton Mendip 69 J6
Chichacott 56 E6
Chicheley 82 C4
Chichester 62 B6
Chichester Cathedral WSuss PO19 1PX 62 B6
Chickerell 59 F6
Chickering 85 G1
Chicklade 59 J1
Chickney 83 J6
Chicksands 82 E5
Chidden 61 H3
Chidden Holt 61 H3
Chiddingfold 62 C3
Chiddingly 63 J5
Chiddingstone 73 H7
Chiddingstone Causeway 73 J7
Chiddingstone Hoath 73 H7
Chideock 58 D5
Chidham 62 A6
Chidswell 107 H7
Chieveley 71 H4
Chignall St. James 74 C1
Chignall Smealy 83 K7
Chigwell 73 H2
Chigwell Row 73 H2
Chilbolton 71 G7
Chilcomb 61 G2
Chilcombe 58 E5
Chilcompton 69 K6
Chilcote 90 E4
Child Okeford 59 H3
Childer Thornton 98 C5
Childerditch 74 C3
Childrey 71 G3
Child's Ercall 89 F3
Childs Hill 73 F3
Childswickham 80 B5
Childwall 98 D4
Childwick Green 82 E7
Chilfrome 58 E5
Chilgrove 62 B5
Chilham 65 F2
Chilhampton 60 B1
Chilla 56 C5
Chillaton 56 C7
Chillenden 65 H2
Chillerton 61 F6
Chillesford 85 H3
Chilley 55 H5
Chillingham 121 F1
Chillington Devon 55 H6
Chillington Som 58 C3
Chilmark 59 J1
Chilson Oxon 80 E7
Chilson Som 58 C4
Chilsworthy Corn 54 E3
Chilsworthy Devon 56 B5
Chilthorne Domer 58 E3
Chilton Bucks 81 H7
Chilton Devon 57 G5
Chilton Dur 112 C4
Chilton Oxon 71 H3
Chilton Suff 84 C4
Chilton Candover 61 G1
Chilton Cantelo 58 E2
Chilton Foliat 71 G4
Chilton Polden 58 C1
Chilton Street 84 B4
Chilton Trinity 58 B1
Chilvers Coton 91 F6
Chilwell 91 H2
Chilworth Hants 61 F3
Chilworth Surr 72 D7
Chimney 71 G1
Chimney Street 84 B4
Chineham 71 K6
Chingford 73 G2
Chinley 100 C4
Chinley Head 100 C4
Chinnor 72 A1
Chipchase Castle 120 D6
Chipley 57 K3
Chipnall 89 G2
Chippenham Cambs 83 K2
Chippenham Wilts 70 C4
Chipperfield 72 D1
Chipping Herts 83 G5
Chipping Lancs 106 B5
Chipping Campden 80 C5
Chipping Hill 84 C7
Chipping Norton 80 E6
Chipping Ongar 73 J1
Chipping Sodbury 70 A3
Chipping Warden 81 F4
Chipstable 57 J3
Chipstead Kent 73 J6
Chipstead Surr 73 F6
Chirbury 88 B6
Chirk (Y Waun) 88 B2
Chirk Green 88 B2
Chirmorrie 114 C3
Chirnside 127 G5
Chirnsidebridge 127 G5
Chirton T&W 121 J7
Chirton Wilts 70 D6
Chisbury 71 F5
Chiscan 116 A2
Chiselborough 58 D3
Chiseldon 70 E4
Chiserley 107 F7
Chislehampton 71 J2
Chislehurst 73 H4
Chislet 75 J5
Chiswell Green 72 E1
Chiswick 73 F4
Chiswick End 83 G4
Chisworth 99 J3
Chithurst 62 B4
Chittering 83 H1
Chitterne 70 C7
Chittlehamholt 56 E3
Chittlehampton 56 E3
Chittoe 70 C5
Chivelstone 55 H7
Chivenor 56 D2
Chobham 72 C5
Choicelee 127 F5
Cholderton 71 F7
Cholesbury 72 C1
Chollerford 120 E6
Chollerton 120 E6
Cholmondeston 99 F7
Cholsey 71 J3
Cholstrey 78 D3
Cholwell B&NESom 69 K6
Cholwell Devon 54 E3
Chop Gate 113 F7
Choppington 121 H5
Chopwell 112 B1
Chorley ChesE 98 E7
Chorley Lancs 98 E1
Chorley Shrop 89 F7
Chorley Staffs 90 C4
Chorleywood 72 D2
Chorlton 99 G7
Chorlton Lane 88 D1
Chorlton-cum-Hardy 99 H3
Chowley 98 D7
Chrishall 83 H5
Chrishall Grange 83 H4
Chrisswell 124 A3
Christ Church Oxon OX1 1DP 46 Oxford
Christchurch Cambs 93 H6
Christchurch Dorset 60 C5
Christchurch Glos 78 E7
Christchurch Newport 69 G3
Christian Malford 70 C4
Christleton 98 D6
Christmas Common 72 A2
Christon 69 G6
Christon Bank 121 H1
Christow 57 G7
Chryston 124 E3
Chudleigh 55 J3
Chudleigh Knighton 55 J3
Chulmleigh 56 E4
Chunal 100 C3
Church 106 C7
Church Aston 89 G4
Church Brampton 81 J2
Church Brough 111 J5
Church Broughton 90 E2
Church Charwelton 81 G3
Church Common 85 H3
Church Crookham 72 B6
Church Eaton 90 A4
Church End Cambs 93 G5
Church End Cambs 83 G1
Church End Cambs 93 F7
Church End CenBeds 82 E5
Church End CenBeds 82 C6
Church End CenBeds 82 E3
Church End CenBeds 82 C5
Church End ERid 109 G4
Church End Essex 83 J4
Church End Essex 84 B6
Church End Glos 79 H5
Church End Hants 71 K6
Church End Herts 82 E7
Church End Herts 83 H6
Church End Lincs 93 F2
Church End Lincs 103 H3
Church End Warks 90 E6
Church End Wilts 70 D4
Church Enstone 80 E6
Church Fenton 108 B6
Church Green 57 K6
Church Gresley 90 E4
Church Hanborough 81 F7
Church Hill ChesW&C 99 F6
Church Hill Derbys 101 G6
Church Houses 113 G7
Church Knowle 59 J6
Church Laneham 102 B5
Church Langley 73 H1
Church Langton 92 A6
Church Lawford 81 F1
Church Lawton 99 H7
Church Leigh 90 C2
Church Lench 80 B3
Church Mayfield 90 D1
Church Minshull 99 F6
Church Norton 62 B7
Church of St. Mary-in-Castro Kent CT16 1HU 37 Dover
Church Preen 88 E6
Church Pulverbatch 88 D5
Church Stoke 88 B6
Church Stowe 81 H3
Church Street Essex 84 B4
Church Street Kent 74 D4
Church Stretton 88 D6
Church Town Leics 91 F4
Church Town Surr 73 G6
Church Village 68 D3
Church Warsop 101 H6
Church Westcote 80 D6
Church Wilne 91 G2
Churcham 79 G7
Churchdown 79 H7
Churchend Essex 83 K6
Churchend Essex 75 G2
Churchend SGlos 70 A2
Churchfield 90 C6
Churchgate 73 G1
Churchgate Street 83 H7
Churchill Devon 56 D1
Churchill Devon 58 B4
Churchill NSom 69 H6
Churchill Oxon 80 D6
Churchill Worcs 79 J3
Churchill Worcs 79 H1
Churchill Museum & Cabinet War Rooms GtLon SW1A 2AQ 44 D5
Churchingford 58 B3
Churchover 91 H7
Churchstanton 57 K4
Churchstow 55 H6
Churchtown Devon 56 E1
Churchtown IoM 104 D4
Churchtown Lancs 105 H5
Churchtown Mersey 98 C1
Churnsike Lodge 120 B6
Churston Ferrers 55 K5
Churt 62 B3
Churton 98 D7
Churwell 107 H7
Chute Cadley 71 G6
Chute Standen 71 G6
Chwilog 86 D2
Chyandour 52 B5
Chysauster 52 B5
Cilan Uchaf 86 B3
Cilcain 97 K6
Cilcennin 76 E2
Cilcewydd 88 B5
Cilfrew 68 A1

Crossway Green
Mon 69 J2
Crossway Green
Worcs 79 H2
Crossways *Dorset* 59 G6
Crosswell *Glos* 78 E3
Crosswell 66 E2
Crosthwaite 110 F7
Croston 98 E6
Crostwick 95 H6
Crostwight 95 H3
Crothair 138 F4
Crouch 73 K6
Crouch End 73 F3
Crouch Hill 59 G3
Croucheston 60 B2
Croughton 81 G5
Crovie 135 N4
Crow 60 C4
Crow Edge 100 D2
Crow Green 73 J2
Crow Hill 79 F6
Crowan 52 G3
Crowborough 63 J3
Crowborough
Warren 63 J3
Crowcombe 57 K2
Crowdecote 100 D6
Crowden 100 C3
Crowdhill 61 F2
Crowell 72 A2
Crowfield *N'hants* 81 H4
Crowfield *Suff* 85 F3
Crowhurst *Surr* 73 G2
Crowhurst *Surr* 73 G2
Crowhurst Lane
End 73 G2
Crowland *Lincs* 93 F4
Crowland *Suff* 84 E1
Crowlas 52 F3
Crowle *NLincs* 101 K1
Crowle *Worcs* 79 J3
Crowle Green 79 J3
Crowmarsh Gifford 71 K3
Crown Corner 85 H2
Crownhill 54 E5
Crownthorpe 94 E5
Crowntown 52 D3
Crow's Nest 54 C4
Crows-an-wra 52 A6
Crowsnest 88 C5
Crowthorne 72 B5
Crowton 98 E5
Croxall 90 E4
Croxby 102 E3
Croxdale 112 C3
Croxden 90 C2
Croxley Green 72 D2
Croxteth Country
Park
Mersey L12 0BH 22 E2
Croxteth Hall *Mersey*
L12 0DH 22 E2
Croxton *Cambs* 83 F3
Croxton *NLincs* 102 D1
Croxton *Norf* 94 C7
Croxton *Staffs* 89 G2
Croxton Kerrial 92 B3
Croxton Green 98 E7
Croxtonbank 89 G2
Croy *High* 134 B6
Croy *NLan* 125 F3
Croyde 56 C2
Croyde Bay 56 C2
Croydon *GtLon* 73 G5
Cruach 122 B5
Cruckmeole 88 D5
Cruckton 88 D4
Cruden Bay 135 Q7
Crudgington 89 F4
Crudwell 70 C2
Crug 78 A1
Crugmeer 53 G1
Crugybar 67 K2
Crumlin 69 H2
Crumpsall 99 H2
Crumpsbrook 79 F1
Crundale *Kent* 65 F3
Crundale *Pembs* 66 C4
Crunwere Farm 66 C4
Crutherland
Farm 124 E5
Cruwys Morchard 57 G4
Crux Easton 71 H6
Crwbin 67 H4
Cryers Hill 72 B2
Crymlyn 96 C5
Crymych 66 E2
Crynant 68 A1
Crystal Palace 73 G4
Crystal Palace Park *GtLon*
SE20 8DT 13 B10
Cuaig 132 H5
Cubbington 80 E2
Cubert 52 E3
Cubley 100 E2
Cublington
Bucks 82 B6
Cublington *Here* 78 D5
Cuckfield 63 G4
Cucklington 59 G2
Cuckney 101 H5
Cuckold's Green 95 J7
Cuckoo Bridge 93 F3
Cuckoo's Corner 72 A7
Cuckoo's Nest 98 C6
Cuddesdon 71 J1
Cuddington
Bucks 81 J7
Cuddington
ChesW&C 98 E5
Cuddington Heath 88 D1
Cuddy Hill 105 H6
Cudham 73 H5
Cudlipptown 55 H7
Cudmore Grove Country
Park *Essex*
CO5 8UE 84 E7
Cudworth *Som* 58 C3
Cudworth *SYorks* 101 F2
Cuerdley Cross 98 E4
Cuffley 73 G1
Cuilmuich 123 K1
Culbo 134 A4
Culbokie
(Cùil Bhàicidh) 134 A5
Culbone 57 G1
Culburnie 133 Q6
Culcabock 134 A6
Culcheth 99 F3
Culdrain 135 K7
Culford 84 C2
Culfordheath 84 C1
Culgaith 111 H4
Culham 71 J2
Culindrach 123 H5
Culkein 136 C6
Culkerton 70 C2
Cullen 135 K4
Cullercoats 121 J6
Culliculden 134 A4
Culligran 133 P6
Cullingworth 107 F6
Cullipool 129 J9
Cullivoe 139 P2
Culloch 130 C2
Culloden 134 B6
Cullompton 57 J4

Culmstock 57 K4
Culnacraig 136 C9
Culnaknock 132 F4
Dagdale 90 C2
Daggons 60 C2
Dagenham 73 H3
Daglingworth 70 C1
Dagnall 82 C7
Dail Beag 138 H3
Dail Bho Dheas 138 L1
Dail Mór 138 H3
Dailly 117 G3
Dainton 55 J4
Dairsie
(Osnaburgh) 131 K9
Dairy House 109 J7
Daisy Bank 90 C7
Daisy Green 84 E2
Dalabrog 138 B7
Dalavich 129 L9
Dalballoch 134 C10
Dalblair 118 B2
Dalbreck 137 K8
Dalbury 90 E2
Dalby *IoM* 104 B6
Dalby *Lincs* 103 H6
Dalby *NYorks* 108 C2
Dalby Forest Drive *NYorks*
YO18 7LT 108 E1
Dalcairnie 117 J3
Dalchalm 137 L7
Dalchenna 129 M10
Dalchork 136 H8
Dalchreichart 133 N9
Dalchruin 130 C9
Dalderby 103 F6
Dalditch 57 J7
Daldowie 134 G10
Dale *Cumb* 111 F1
Dale *GtMan* 99 J2
Dale *Pembs* 66 B5
Dale Abbey 91 G2
Dale End *Derbys* 100 E6
Dale End *NYorks* 106 E5
Dale Head 110 F5
Dale of Walls 139 K7
Dale Park 62 C5
Dalehouse 113 H5
Daless 134 C7
Dalganachan 137 N5
Dalgarven 124 A6
Dalgety Bay 125 K2
Dalgig 117 K2
Dalginross 130 C8
Dalgonar 118 C3
Dalguise 130 E6
Dalhalvaig 137 L4
Dalham 84 B2
Daligan 124 B2
Dalinlongart 123 K2
Dalivaddy 116 H4
Daljarrock 117 F5
Dalkeith 126 B4
Dallachulish 129 L6
Dallas 134 F5
Dallash 134 C1
Dalleagles 117 K2
Dallinghoo 85 G3
Dallington *ESuss* 63 K5
Dallington *N'hants* 81 J2
Dallow 107 G2
Dalmadilly 135 M9
Dalmally
(Dail Mhàilidh) 129 N8
Dalmary 124 D1
Dalmellington 117 J3
Dalmeny 125 K3
Dalmichy 136 H8
Dalmigavie 134 B8
Dalmore 136 H8
Dalmuir 124 C3
Dalmunzie House
Hotel 130 E3
Dalnabreck 129 J4
Dalnahaitnach 134 C9
Dalnavert 134 C10
Dalnavie 134 A3
Dalness 129 N5
Dalnessie 137 J8
Dalnigap 114 B3
Dalqueich 130 F10
Dalreoch 117 F5
Dalroy 134 A6
Dalrulzian 130 F5
Dalry 124 A6
Dalrymple 117 H2
Dalscote 81 H3
Dalserf 125 F5
Dalshangan 117 K3
Dalskairth 115 K3
Dalston 110 E1
Dalswinton 118 E5
Daltomach 134 B8
Dalton *Cumb* 105 J2
Dalton *Lancs* 98 D2
Dalton *D&G* 119 G6
Dalton *N'umb* 121 G6
Dalton *N'umb* 111 L1
Dalton *NYorks* 107 K1
Dalton *NYorks* 112 B2
Dalton *SYorks* 101 G3
Dalton Magna 101 G3
Dalton Piercy 112 E3
Dalton-in-
Furness 105 J2
Dalton-le-Dale 112 E2
Dalton-on-Tees 112 C6
Daltote 123 F1
Daltra 134 D6
Dalveich 130 B7
Dalvennan 117 H2
Dalwhinnie 130 B3
Dalwood 58 B4
Dam Green 94 E7
Damask Green 83 F6
Damerham 60 C3
Damgate 95 J5
Damnaglaur 114 B7
Danaway 74 D1
Danbury 74 D1
Danby 113 H6
Danby Wiske 112 D7
Dancers Hill 73 F2
Dandaleith 134 G6
Danderhall 126 B4
Dane Bank 99 J3
Dane End 83 G6
Dane Hills 91 H5
Danebridge 99 J6
Danehill 63 H4
Danesmoor 101 G6
Daniel's Water 64 E3
Danskine 126 D4
Danthorpe 109 J6
Danzey Green 80 C2
Darby End 90 B7
Darby Green 72 B5
Darenth 73 J4
Daresbury 98 E4
Darfield 101 G2
Dargate 75 G5
Dargues 120 D3
Darite 54 C4
Darland 74 D5
Darlaston 90 B6
Darley 107 H4
Darley Bridge 100 E6
Darley Dale 100 E6
Darley Head 107 G4
Darley Hillside 100 E6
Darlingscott 80 D4
Darlington 112 C5
Darliston 88 E2
Darlton 101 K5
Darnall 101 F4
Darnconner 117 K2
Darngarroch 115 G4

Eachwick 121 G6
Eadar dha
Fhadhail 138 F4
Eagland Hill 105 H5
Eagle 102 B6
Eagle Barnsdale 102 B6
Eagle Moor 102 B6
Eaglescliffe 112 E5
Eaglesfield
Cumb 110 B4
Eaglesfield *D&G* 119 H6
Eaglesham 124 D5
Eaglethorpe 92 D6
Eairy 104 B6
Eakley 82 B3
Eakring 101 J6
Ealand 101 K1
Ealing 72 E3
Eals 111 L1
Eamont Bridge 111 G4
Earby 106 E5
Earcroft 106 C7
Eardington 89 G6
Eardisland 78 D3
Eardisley 78 C4
Eardiston *Shrop* 88 C3
Eardiston *Worcs* 79 F2
Earith 83 G1
Earl Shilton 91 G6
Earl Soham 85 G2
Earl Sterndale 100 C6
Earl Stonham 85 F3
Earle 120 E1
Earlestown 98 E3
Earley 72 A4
Earlham 95 F5
Earlish 132 D4
Earls Barton 82 B2
Earls Colne 84 C6
Earl's Common 79 J3
Earl's Court 73 F4
Earls Court Exhibition
Centre *GtLon*
SW5 9TA 11 G8
Earl's Croome 79 H4
Earls Green 84 E2
Earlsdon 80 E1
Earlsferry 131 K10
Earlsford 135 N7
Earlsheaton 107 H7
Earlston 126 D7
Earlswood *Mon* 69 H2
Earlswood *Surr* 73 F2
Earlswood *Warks* 80 C1
Earnley 62 B7
Earnshaw Bridge 105 J7
Earsdon 121 J6
Earsdon Moor 121 G4
Earsham 95 H7
Earswick 108 C4
Eartham 62 C6
Earthcott Green 69 K3
Easby 113 F6
Easdale 129 J9
Easebourne 62 B4
Easenhall 81 F1
Eashing 72 C7
Easington *Bucks* 81 H7
Easington *Dur* 112 E2
Easington *ERid* 103 G1
Easington
N'umb 127 K7
Easington *Oxon* 71 K2
Easington *Oxon* 81 F5
Easington *R&C* 113 H5
Easington
Colliery 112 E2
Easington Lane 112 D2
Easingwold 108 B3
Easole Street 65 H2
Eassie 131 J6
East Aberthaw 68 D5
East Acton 73 F3
East Allington 55 H6
East Anstey 57 G3
East Anton 71 G7
East Appleton 112 C7
East Ardsley 107 H7
East Ashey 61 G6
East Ashling 62 B6
East Ayton 109 F1
East Barkwith 102 E4
East Barming 64 C2
East Barnby 113 J5
East Barnet 73 F2
East Barsham 94 D2
East Beckham 95 F2
East Bedfont 72 D4
East Bergholt 84 E5
East Bierley 107 G6
East Bilney 94 D4
East Blatchington 63 H7
East Boldon 121 J7
East Boldre 60 E4
East Bower 58 C1
East Brent 69 G6
East Bridge 85 J2
East Bridgford 91 J1
East Buckland 56 E2
East Budleigh 57 J7
East Burnham 72 C3
East Burra 139 M9
East Burrafirth 139 M7
East Burton 59 H6
East Butsfield 112 B2
East Butterleigh 57 H5
East Butterwick 102 B2
East Calder 125 J4
East Carleton 95 F5
East Carlton
N'hants 92 B7
East Carlton
WYorks 107 H5
East Carlton Countryside
Park *N'hants*
LE16 8YF 92 B7
East Chaldon (Chaldon
Herring) 59 G6
East Challow 71 G3
East Charleton 55 H6
East Chelborough 58 E4
East Chiltington 63 G5
East Chinnock 58 D3
East Chisenbury 70 E6
East Clandon 72 D6

East Claydon 81 J6
East Coker 58 E3
East Compton Dorset 59 H3
East Compton Som 69 K7
East Coombe 57 G5
East Cornworthy 55 J5
East Cottingwith 108 D5
East Cowes 61 G5
East Cowick 108 C7
East Cowton 112 D6
East Cramlington 121 H6
East Cranmore 69 K7
East Creech 59 J6
East Darlochan 116 A1
East Dean ESuss 63 J7
East Dean Hants 60 D2
East Dean WSuss 62 C5
East Dereham (Dereham) 94 D4
East Down 56 D1
East Drayton 101 K5
East Dundry 69 J5
East Ella 109 G7
East End ERid 109 H6
East End ERid 109 J7
East End Essex 75 G1
East End Hants 71 H5
East End Hants 60 E5
East End Herts 83 H6
East End Kent 64 D4
East End Kent 75 F4
East End MK 82 C4
East End NSom 69 H4
East End Oxon 80 E7
East End Poole 59 J5
East End Som 69 K6
East End Suff 85 F5
East End Suff 85 F3
East Farleigh 64 C2
East Farndon 92 A7
East Ferry 102 B3
East Firsby 102 D4
East Fleetham 121 H1
East Fortune 126 D3
East Garston 71 G4
East Ginge 71 H3
East Goscote 91 J4
East Grafton 71 F5
East Green Suff 85 J2
East Green Suff 83 K3
East Grimstead 60 D2
East Grinstead 63 G3
East Guldeford 64 E5
East Haddon 81 H2
East Hagbourne 71 J3
East Halton 102 E1
East Ham 73 H3
East Hanney 71 H2
East Hanningfield 74 D1
East Hardwick 101 G1
East Harling 94 D7
East Harlsey 112 E7
East Harnham 60 C2
East Harptree 69 J6
East Hartford 121 H6
East Harting 61 J3
East Hatch 59 J2
East Hatley 83 F3
East Hauxwell 112 B7
East Haven 131 L7
East Heckington 92 E1
East Hedleyhope 112 B2
East Hendred 71 H3
East Herrington 112 D1
East Heslerton 109 F2
East Hewish 69 H5
East Hoathly 63 J5
East Holme 59 H6
East Horndon 74 C3
East Horrington 69 J7
East Horsley 72 D6
East Horton 127 J7
East Howe 60 B5
East Huntspill 69 G7
East Hyde 82 E7
East Ilsley 71 H3
East Keal 103 G6
East Kennett 70 E5
East Keswick 107 J5
East Kilbride 124 E5
East Kimber 56 C6
East Kirkby 103 G6
East Knapton 108 E2
East Knighton 59 H6
East Knowstone 57 G3
East Knoyle 59 H1
East Kyloe 127 J7
East Lambrook 58 D3
East Lancashire Railway Lancs BL9 0EY 106 D7
East Langdon 65 J3
East Langton 92 A6
East Langwell 137 K9
East Lavant 62 B6
East Lavington 62 C5
East Layton 112 B5
East Leake 91 H3
East Learmouth 127 G7
East Leigh Devon 57 F5
East Leigh Devon 57 F4
East Leigh Devon 55 H5
East Leigh Devon 55 G5
East Lexham 94 C4
East Lilburn 121 F1
East Linton 126 D3
East Liss 61 J2
East Lockinge 71 H3
East Looe 54 C5
East Lound 101 K2
East Lulworth 59 H6
East Lutton 109 F3
East Lydford 58 E1
East Lyn 57 F1
East Lyng 58 C2
East Malling 64 C2
East Malling Heath 73 K6
East Marden 62 B5
East Markham 101 K5
East Martin 60 B3
East Marton 106 E4
East Meon 61 H2
East Mere 57 H4
East Mersea 84 E7
East Midlands Airport 91 G3
East Molesey 72 E5
East Moor 107 J7
East Morden 59 J5
East Morriston 126 E6
East Morton 107 G5
East Ness 108 C2
East Newton 109 J6
East Norton 92 A5
East Oakley 71 J6
East Ogwell 55 J3
East Orchard 59 H3
East Ord 127 H5
East Panson 56 B6
East Parley 60 C5
East Peckham 73 K7
East Pennard 58 E1
East Point Pavilion, Lowestoft Suff NR33 0AP 95 K6
East Portlemouth 55 H7
East Prawle 55 H7
East Preston 62 D6
East Pulham 59 G4
East Putford 56 B4
East Quantoxhead 57 K1
East Rainton 112 D2
East Ravendale 103 F3
East Raynham 94 C3
East Retford (Retford) 101 K4
East Rigton 107 J5
East Rolstone 69 G5
East Rounton 112 E6
East Row 113 J5
East Rudham 94 C3
East Runton 95 G1
East Ruston 95 H3
East Saltoun 126 C4
East Shefford 71 G4
East Sleekburn 121 H5
East Somerton 95 J4
East Stockwith 101 K3
East Stoke Dorset 59 H6
East Stoke Notts 92 A1
East Stour 59 H2
East Stourmouth 75 J5
East Stratton 71 J7
East Street 58 E1
East Studdal 65 J3
East Suisnish 132 F7
East Taphouse 54 B4
East Thirston 121 G4
East Tilbury 74 C4
East Tisted 61 J1
East Torrington 102 E4
East Town 69 K7
East Tuddenham 94 E4
East Tytherley 60 E2
East Tytherton 70 C4
East Village 57 G5
East Wall 88 E6
East Walton 94 B4
East Wellow 60 E2
East Wemyss 126 B1
East Whitburn 125 H4
East Wickham 73 H4
East Williamston 66 D5
East Winch 94 A4
East Winterslow 60 D1
East Wittering 61 J5
East Witton 107 G1
East Woodburn 120 E5
East Woodhay 71 H5
East Woodlands 70 A7
East Worldham 61 J1
East Worlington 57 F4
East Youlstone 56 A4
Eastacott 56 E3
Eastbourne 63 K7
Eastbourne Pier ESuss BN21 3EL 37 Eastbourne
Eastbrook 68 E4
Eastburn ERid 109 F4
Eastburn WYorks 107 F5
Eastbury Herts 72 E2
Eastbury WBerks 71 G4
Eastby 107 F4
Eastchurch 75 F4
Eastcombe Glos 70 B1
Eastcombe Som 57 K2
Eastcote GtLon 72 E3
Eastcote N'hants 81 H3
Eastcote WMid 80 C1
Eastcott Corn 56 A4
Eastcott Wilts 70 D6
Eastcourt 70 C2
Eastdown 55 J6
Eastend 80 E6
Easter Ardross 134 A3
Easter Balmoral 134 G11
Easter Buckieburn 125 F2
Easter Compton 69 J3
Easter Drummond 133 Q9
Easter Ellister 122 A5
Easter Fearn 134 A2
Easter Howlaws 127 F6
Easter Kinkell 133 R5
Easter Lednathie 131 J4
Easter Poldar 124 E1
Easter Skeld (Skeld) 139 M8
Easter Suddie 134 A5
Eastergate 62 C6
Easterhouse 124 E4
Easterton 70 D6
Easterton Sands 70 D6
Eastertown 69 G6
Eastfield Bristol 69 J4
Eastfield NLan 125 G4
Eastfield NYorks 109 G1
Eastfield Hall 121 H3
Eastgate Dur 111 L3
Eastgate Lincs 92 E4
Eastgate Norf 95 F3
Easthall 83 F6
Eastham Mersey 98 C4
Eastham Worcs 79 F2
Easthampstead 72 B5
Easthampton 78 D2
Easthaugh 94 E4
Eastheath 72 B5
Easthope 88 E6
Easthorpe Essex 84 D6
Easthorpe Leics 92 B2
Easthorpe Notts 101 K7
Easthouses 126 B4
Eastington Devon 57 F5
Eastington Glos 80 C7
Eastington Glos 70 A1
Eastleach Martin 71 F1
Eastleach Turville 71 F1
Eastleigh Devon 56 C3
Eastleigh Hants 61 F3
Eastling 64 E2
Eastmoor Derbys 101 F5
Eastmoor Norf 94 B5
Eastnor 79 G5
Eastoft 102 B1
Eastoke 61 J5
Easton Cambs 82 E1
Easton Cumb 119 G6
Easton Cumb 110 D1
Easton Devon 57 F7
Easton Dorset 59 F7
Easton Hants 61 G1
Easton IoW 60 E6
Easton Lincs 92 C3
Easton Norf 95 F4
Easton Som 69 J7
Easton Suff 85 G3
Easton Wilts 70 B4
Easton Grey 70 B3
Easton Maudit 82 B3
Easton on the Hill 92 D5
Easton Royal 71 F5
Easton-in-Gordano 69 J4
Eastrea 93 F6
Eastriggs 119 H7
Eastrington 108 D6
Eastry 65 J2
East-the-Water 56 C3
Eastville 69 K4
Eastwell 92 A3
Eastwick 83 H7
Eastwood Notts 91 G1
Eastwood S'end 74 E3
Eastwood SYorks 101 G3
Eastwood WYorks 106 E7
Eastwood End 93 H6
Eathorpe 80 E2
Eaton ChesE 99 H6
Eaton ChesW&C 98 E6
Eaton Leics 92 A3
Eaton Norf 95 G5
Eaton Norf 94 A2
Eaton Notts 101 K5
Eaton Oxon 71 H1
Eaton Shrop 88 E6
Eaton Shrop 88 C7
Eaton Bishop 78 D5
Eaton Bray 82 C6
Eaton Constantine 89 F5
Eaton Ford 82 E3
Eaton Hall 98 D6
Eaton Hastings 71 F2
Eaton Socon 82 E3
Eaton upon Tern 89 F3
Eaves Green 90 D7
Eavestone 107 H3
Ebberston 108 E1
Ebbesborne Wake 59 J2
Ebbw Vale (Glynebwy) 68 E1
Ebchester 112 B1
Ebdon 69 G5
Ebford 57 H7
Ebley 70 B1
Ebnal 88 D1
Ebrington 80 C4
Ebsworthy Town 56 D6
Ecchinswell 71 H6
Ecclaw 127 F4
Ecclefechan 119 G6
Eccles GtMan 99 G3
Eccles Kent 74 D5
Eccles ScBord 127 F6
Eccles Green 78 C4
Eccles Road 94 E6
Ecclesfield 101 F3
Ecclesgreig 131 N4
Eccleshall 90 A3
Eccleshill 107 G6
Ecclesmachan 125 J3
Eccles-on-Sea 95 J3
Eccleston ChesW&C 98 D6
Eccleston Lancs 98 E1
Eccleston Mersey 98 D3
Eccup 107 H5
Echt 135 M10
Eckford 120 C1
Eckington Derbys 101 G5
Eckington Worcs 79 J4
Ecton N'hants 82 B2
Ecton Staffs 100 C7
Edale 100 D4
Eday 139 E4
Eday Airfield 139 E4
Edburton 63 F5
Edderside 110 C2
Edderton 134 B2
Eddington 71 G5
Eddleston 126 A6
Eden Camp NYorks YO17 6RT 108 E2
Eden Park 73 G5
Eden Project Corn PL24 2SG 54 A5
Eden Vale 112 E3
Edenbridge 73 H7
Edenfield 99 G1
Edenhall 111 G3
Edenham 92 D3
Edensor 100 E5
Edentaggart 124 B1
Edenthorpe 101 J2
Edern 86 B2
Edgarley 58 E1
Edgbaston 90 C7
Edgcote 81 G4
Edgcott Bucks 81 H6
Edgcott Som 57 G2
Edgcumbe 52 E5
Edge Glos 70 B1
Edge Shrop 88 C5
Edge End 78 E7
Edge Green ChesW&C 98 D7
Edge Green GtMan 98 E3
Edge Green Norf 94 E7
Edgebolton 88 E3
Edgefield 94 E2
Edgehead 126 B4
Edgeley 88 E1
Edgerley 88 C4
Edgerton 100 D1
Edgeworth 70 C1
Edginswell 55 J4
Edgmond 89 G4
Edgmond Marsh 89 G3
Edgton 88 C7
Edgware 73 F2
Edgworth 99 G1
Edinample 130 B8
Edinbane 132 D5
Edinbarnet 124 D3
Edinburgh 126 A3
Edinburgh Airport 125 K3
Edinburgh Castle Edin EH1 2NG 38 E4
Edinburgh Zoo Edin EH12 6TS 32 C2
Edinchip 130 A8
Edingale 90 E4
Edingley 101 J7
Edingthorpe 95 H2
Edingthorpe Green 95 H2
Edington Som 58 C1
Edington Wilts 70 C6
Edistone 56 A3
Edith Weston 92 C5
Edithmead 69 G7
Edlaston 90 D1
Edlesborough 82 C7
Edlingham 121 G3
Edlington 103 F5
Edmondsham 60 B3
Edmondsley 112 C2
Edmondstown 68 D2
Edmondthorpe 92 B4
Edmonstone 139 E5
Edmonton Corn 53 G1
Edmonton GtLon 73 G2
Edmundbyers 112 A1
Ednam 127 F7
Ednaston 90 E1
Edney Common 74 C1
Edrom 127 G5
Edstaston 88 E2
Edstone 80 C2
Edvin Loach 79 F3
Edwalton 91 H2
Edwardstone 84 D4
Edwardsville 68 D2
Edwinsford 67 K2
Edwinstowe 101 J6
Edworth 83 F4
Edwyn Ralph 79 F3
Edzell 131 M4
Efail Isaf 68 D3
Efail-fâch 68 A2
Efailnewydd 86 C2
Efailwen 66 E3
Efenechtyd 97 K7
Effingham 72 E6
Effirth 139 M7
Efflinch 90 D4
Efford 57 G5
Egbury 71 H6
Egdean 62 C4
Egdon 79 J3
Egerton GtMan 99 G1
Egerton Kent 64 E3
Egerton Forstal 64 D3
Egerton Green 98 E7
Egg Buckland 54 E5
Eggborough 108 B7
Eggerness 114 E6
Eggesford Barton 56 E4
Eggington 82 C6
Egginton 90 E3
Egglescliffe 112 E5
Eggleston 111 L4
Egham 72 D4
Egham Wick 72 C4
Egilsay 139 D5
Egleton 92 B5
Eglingham 121 G2
Eglinton 124 B6
Egloshayle 54 A3
Egloskerry 54 C2
Eglwys Cross 88 D1
Eglwys Fach 87 F6
Eglwys Nunydd 68 B3
Eglwysbach 97 G5
Eglwys-Brewis 68 D5
Eglwyswrw 66 E2
Egmanton 101 K6
Egmere 94 D2
Egremont 110 B5
Egton 113 J6
Egton Bridge 113 J6
Egypt 71 H7
Eigg 128 F2
Eight Ash Green 84 D6
Eilanreach 133 J9
Eildon 126 D7
Eilean Donan Castle High IV40 8DX 133 J8
Eilean Shona 128 H3
Einacleit 138 G5
Eisingrug 87 F2
Eisteddfa Gurig 87 G7
Elan Valley Visitor Centre Powys LD6 5HP 77 J2
Elan Village 77 J2
Elberton 69 K3
Elborough 69 G6
Elburton 55 F5
Elcombe 70 E3
Elder Street 83 J5
Eldernell 93 G6
Eldersfield 79 G5
Elderslie 124 C4
Eldon 112 C4
Eldrick 117 G5
Eldroth 106 C3
Eldwick 107 G5
Elemore Vale 112 D2
Elford N'umb 127 K7
Elford Staffs 90 D4
Elford Closes 83 J1
Elgin 134 G4
Elgol 132 F9
Elham 65 G3
Elie 131 K10
Elilaw 120 E3
Elim 96 B4
Eling Hants 60 E3
Eling WBerks 71 J4
Eling Tide Mill Hants SO40 9HF 4 A3
Eliock 118 D3
Elishader 132 E4
Elishaw 120 D4
Elkesley 101 J5
Elkington 81 H1
Elkstone 79 J7
Elland 107 G7
Elland Upper Edge 107 G7
Ellary 123 F3
Ellastone 90 D1
Ellbridge 54 E4
Ellel 105 H4
Ellemford 127 F4
Ellenabeich 129 J9
Ellenborough 110 B3
Ellenhall 90 A3
Ellen's Green 62 D3
Ellerbeck 112 E7
Ellerby 113 H5
Ellerdine 89 F3
Ellerdine Heath 89 F3
Ellerker 109 F7
Ellerton ERid 108 D5
Ellerton NYorks 112 C7
Ellerton Shrop 89 G3
Ellerton Abbey 112 A7
Ellesborough 72 B1
Ellesmere 88 C2
Ellesmere Park 99 G3
Ellesmere Port 98 D5
Ellingham Hants 60 C4
Ellingham N'umb 121 G1
Ellingham Norf 95 H6
Ellingstring 107 G1
Ellington Cambs 82 E1
Ellington N'umb 121 H4
Ellington Thorpe 82 E1
Elliot 131 M7
Elliot's Green 70 A7
Ellisfield 71 K7
Ellistown 91 G4
Ellon 135 P7
Ellonby 110 F3
Ellough 95 J7
Ellough Moor 95 J7
Elloughton 109 F7
Ellwood 69 J1
Elm 93 H5
Elm Park 73 J3
Elmbridge 79 J2
Elmdon Essex 83 H5
Elmdon WMid 90 D7
Elmdon Heath 90 D7
Elmers End 73 G5
Elmer's Green 98 D2
Elmesthorpe 91 G6
Elmhurst 90 D4
Elmley Castle 79 J4
Elmley Lovett 79 H2
Elmore 79 G7
Elmore Back 79 G7
Elmscott 56 A3
Elmsett 84 E4
Elmstead Essex 84 E6
Elmstead GtLon 73 H4
Elmstead Market 84 E6
Elmstone 75 J5
Elmstone Hardwicke 79 J6
Elmswell ERid 109 F4
Elmswell Suff 84 D2
Elmton 101 H5
Elphin 136 E8
Elphinstone 126 B3
Elrick 135 N10
Elrig 114 D6
Elrigbeag 129 N9
Elsdon 120 E4
Elsecar 101 F2
Elsecar Heritage Centre SYorks S74 8HJ 101 F3
Elsenham 83 J6
Elsfield 81 G7
Elsham 102 D1
Elsing 94 E4
Elslack 106 E5
Elson Hants 61 H4
Elson Shrop 88 C2
Elsrickle 125 J6
Elstead 72 C7
Elsted 62 B5
Elsthorpe 92 D3
Elstob 112 D4
Elston Lancs 105 J6
Elston Notts 92 A1
Elstone 56 E4
Elstow 82 D4
Elstree 72 E2
Elstronwick 109 J6
Elswick 105 H6
Elsworth 83 G2
Elterwater 110 E6
Eltham 73 H4
Eltisley 83 F3
Elton Cambs 92 D6
Elton ChesW&C 98 D5
Elton Derbys 100 E6
Elton Glos 79 G7
Elton GtMan 99 G1
Elton Here 78 D1
Elton Notts 92 A2
Elton Stock 112 E5
Elton Green 98 D5
Elvanfoot 118 E2
Elvaston 91 G2
Elvaston Castle Country Park Derbys DE72 3EP 18 D6
Elveden 84 C1
Elvingston 126 C3
Elvington Kent 65 H2
Elvington York 108 D5
Elwick Hart 112 E3
Elwick N'umb 127 K7
Elworth 99 G6
Elworthy 57 J2
Ely Cambs 83 J1
Ely Cardiff 68 E4
Emberton 82 B4
Emberton Country Park MK MK46 5FJ 82 B3
Embleton Cumb 110 C3
Embleton Hart 112 E4
Embleton N'umb 121 H1
Embo 134 C1
Embo Street 134 C1
Emborough 69 K6
Embsay 107 F4
Embsay Steam Railway NYorks BD23 6AF 107 F4
Emerson Park 73 J3
Emery Down 60 D4
Emley 100 E1
Emmington 72 A1
Emneth 93 H5
Emneth Hungate 93 J5
Empingham 92 C5
Empshott 61 J1
Empshott Green 61 J1
Emsworth 61 J4
Enborne 71 H5
Enborne Row 71 H5
Enchmarsh 88 E6
Enderby 91 H6
Endmoor 105 J1
Endon 99 J7
Endon Bank 99 J7
Enfield 73 G2
Enfield Wash 73 G2
Enford 70 E6
Engine Common 69 K3
Englefield 71 K4
Englefield Green 72 C4
Englesea-brook 99 G7
English Bicknor 78 E7
English Frankton 88 D3
Englishcombe 70 A5
Enham Alamein 71 G7
Enmore 58 B1
Ennerdale Bridge 110 B5
Enniscaven 53 G3
Ennochdhu 130 F4
Ensdon 88 D4
Ensis 56 D3
Enson 90 B3
Enstone 80 E6
Enterkinfoot 118 D3
Enterpen 112 E6
Enton Green 72 C7
Enville 90 A7
Eolaigearraidh 138 B8
Eoropaidh 138 L1
Epney 79 G7
Epperstone 91 J1
Epping 73 H1
Epping Green Essex 73 H1
Epping Green Herts 73 F1
Epping Upland 73 H1
Eppleby 112 B5
Eppleworth 109 G6
Epsom 73 F5
Epwell 80 E4
Epworth 101 K2
Epworth Turbary 101 K2
Erbistock 88 C1
Erbusaig 132 H8
Erchless Castle 133 Q6
Erdington 90 D6
Eredine 129 L10
Eriboll 136 G4
Ericstane 119 F2
Eridge Green 63 J3
Eriff 117 K3
Erines 123 G3
Erisey Barton 52 E7
Eriskay (Eiriosgaigh) 138 B7
Eriswell 84 B1
Erith 73 J4
Erlestoke 70 C6
Ermington 55 G5
Ernesettle 54 E4
Erpingham 95 F2
Erringden Grange 106 E7
Errogie (Earagaidh) 133 R8
Errol 130 H8
Erskine 124 C3
Ervie 116 D7
Erwarton 85 G5
Erwood 77 K4
Eryholme 112 D6
Eryrys 98 B7
Escart 123 G4
Escart Farm 123 G5
Escomb 112 B4
Escrick 108 C5
Esgair 67 G3
Esgairgeiliog 87 G5
Esgyryn 97 G5
Esh 112 B2
Esh Winning 112 B2
Esher 72 E5
Eshott 121 H4
Eshton 106 E4
Eskadale 133 Q7
Eskbank 126 B4
Eskdale Green 110 C6
Eskdalemuir 119 H4
Eskham 103 G3
Esknish 122 B4
Esperley Lane Ends 112 B4
Espley Hall 121 G4
Esprick 105 H6
Essendine 92 D4
Essendon 73 F1
Essich 134 A7
Essington 90 B5
Eston 113 F5
Etal 127 H7
Etchilhampton 70 D5
Etchingham 64 C5
Etchinghill Kent 65 G4
Etchinghill Staffs 90 C4
Etherdwick Grange 109 J6
Etherley Dene 112 B4
Etherow Country Park GtMan SK6 5JQ 25 M6
Ethie Mains 131 M6
Eton 72 C4
Eton Wick 72 C4
Etteridge 134 A11
Ettiley Heath 99 G6
Ettington 80 D4
Etton ERid 109 F5
Etton Peter 92 E5
Ettrick 119 H2
Ettrickbridge 119 J1
Ettrickhill 119 H2
Etwall 90 E2
Eudon George 89 F7
Eureka! Museum for Children WYorks HX1 2NE 26 C5
Euston 84 C1
Euxton 98 E1
Evanstown 68 C3
Evanton 134 A4
Evedon 92 D1
Evelix 134 B1
Evenjobb 78 B2
Evenley 81 G5
Evenlode 80 D6
Evenwood 112 B4
Evenwood Gate 112 B4
Everbay 139 F5
Evercreech 59 F1
Everdon 81 G3
Everingham 108 E5
Everleigh 71 F6
Everley 109 F1
Eversholt 82 C5
Evershot 58 E4
Eversley 72 A5
Eversley Cross 72 A5
Everthorpe 109 F6
Everton CenBeds 83 F3
Everton Hants 60 D5
Everton Mersey 98 C3
Everton Notts 101 J3
Evertown 119 J6
Eves Corner 75 F2
Evesbatch 79 F4
Evesham 80 B4
Evesham Country Park Shopping & Garden Centre Worcs WR11 4TP 80 B4
Evie 139 C5
Evington 91 J5
Ewart Newtown 127 H7
Ewden Village 100 E3
Ewell 73 F5
Ewell Minnis 65 H3
Ewelme 71 K2
Ewen 70 D2
Ewenny 68 C4
Ewerby 92 E1
Ewerby Thorpe 92 E1
Ewhurst 72 D7
Ewhurst Green ESuss 64 C5
Ewhurst Green Surr 62 D3
Ewloe 98 C6
Ewloe Green 98 B6
Ewood 106 B7
Ewood Bridge 106 C7
Eworthy 56 C6
Ewshot 72 B7
Ewyas Harold 78 C6
Exbourne 56 E5
Exbury 61 F4
Exbury Gardens Hants SO45 1AZ 4 C8
Exceat 63 J7
Exebridge 57 H3
Exelby 107 H1
Exeter 57 H6
Exeter Cathedral Devon EX1 1HS 37 Exeter
Exeter International Airport 57 H6
Exford 57 G2
Exfords Green 88 D5
Exhall Warks 80 C3
Exhall Warks 91 F7
Exlade Street 71 K3
Exminster 57 H7
Exmouth 57 J7
Exnaboe 139 M11
Exning 83 K2
Explore-At-Bristol BS1 5DB 35 Bristol
Exton Devon 57 H7
Exton Hants 61 H2
Exton Rut 92 C4
Exton Som 57 H2
Exwick 57 H6
Eyam 100 E5
Eydon 81 G4
Eye Here 78 D2
Eye Peter 93 F5
Eye Suff 85 F1
Eye Green 93 F5
Eyemouth 127 H4
Eyeworth 83 F4
Eyhorne Street 64 D2
Eyke 85 H3
Eynesbury 82 E3
Eynort 132 D8
Eynsford 73 J5
Eynsham 71 H1
Eype 58 D5
Eyre 132 E5
Eythorne 65 H3
Eyton Here 78 D2
Eyton Shrop 88 C7
Eyton on Severn 88 E5
Eyton upon the Weald Moors 89 F4
Eywood 78 C3

F

Faccombe 71 G6
Faceby 112 E6
Fachwen 96 D6
Facit 99 H1
Faddiley 98 E7
Fadmoor 108 C1
Faebait 133 Q5
Faifley 124 D3
Fail 117 J1
Failand 69 J4
Failford 117 J1
Failsworth 99 H2
Fair Isle 139 K10
Fair Isle Airstrip 139 K10
Fair Oak Devon 57 J4
Fair Oak Hants 61 F3
Fair Oak Hants 71 J5
Fair Oak Green 71 K5
Fairbourne 87 F4
Fairburn 107 K7
Fairfield Derbys 100 C5
Fairfield GtMan 99 J3
Fairfield Kent 64 E5
Fairfield Mersey 98 B4
Fairfield Stock 112 E5
Fairfield Worcs 79 J1
Fairfield Halls, Croydon GtLon CR9 1DG 13 B12
Fairford 70 E1
Fairgirth 115 J5
Fairhaven 105 G7
Fairhill 125 F5
Fairholm 125 F5
Fairlands Valley Park Herts SG2 0BL 83 F6
Fairley 135 N10
Fairlie 124 A5
Fairlight 64 D6
Fairlight Cove 64 D6
Fairmile Devon 57 J6
Fairmile Surr 72 E5
Fairmilehead 126 A4
Fairnington 120 B1
Fairoak 89 G2
Fairseat 74 C5
Fairstead 84 B7
Fairwarp 63 H4
Fairwater 68 E4
Fairy Cross 56 C3
Fairyhill 67 H6
Fakenham 94 D3
Fakenham Magna 84 D1
Fala 126 C4
Fala Dam 126 C4
Falahill 126 B5
Faldingworth 102 D4
Falfield 69 K2
Falin-Wnda 67 G1
Falkenham 85 G5
Falkirk 125 G3
Falkirk Wheel Falk FK1 4RS 125 G2
Falkland 130 H10
Falla 120 C2
Fallgate 101 F6
Fallin 125 G1
Falmer 63 G6
Falmouth 53 F5
Falsgrave 109 G1
Falstone 120 C5
Famous Grouse Experience, Glenturret Distillery P&K PH7 4HA 130 D8
Fanagmore 136 D5
Fancott 82 D6
Fangdale Beck 113 F7
Fangfoss 108 D4
Fankerton 125 F2
Fanmore 128 F6
Fanner's Green 83 K7
Fans 126 E6
Fantasy Island Lincs PE25 1RH 103 J6
Far Cotton 81 J3
Far Forest 79 G1
Far Gearstones 106 C1
Far Green 70 A1
Far Moor 98 E2
Far Oakridge 70 C1
Far Royds 107 H6
Far Sawrey 110 E7
Farcet 93 F6
Farden 78 E1
Fareham 61 G4
Farewell 90 C4
Farforth 103 G5
Faringdon 71 F2
Farington 105 J7
Farlam 111 G1
Farlary 137 K9
Farleigh NSom 69 J5
Farleigh Surr 73 G5
Farleigh Hungerford 70 B6
Farleigh Wallop 71 K7
Farlesthorpe 103 H5
Farleton Cumb 105 J1
Farleton Lancs 105 J3
Farley Derbys 100 E6
Farley Shrop 88 C5
Farley Staffs 90 C1
Farley Wilts 60 D2
Farley Green Suff 84 B3
Farley Green Surr 72 D7
Farley Hill 72 A5
Farleys End 79 G7
Farlington 108 C3
Farlow 89 F7
Farm Town 91 F4
Farmborough 69 K5
Farmcote 80 B6
Farmington 80 C7
Farmoor 71 H1
Farmtown 135 K5
Farnborough GtLon 73 H5
Farnborough Hants 72 B6
Farnborough Warks 81 F4
Farnborough WBerks 71 H3
Farnborough Street 72 B6
Farncombe 72 C7
Farndish 82 C2
Farndon ChesW&C 98 D7
Farndon Notts 101 K7
Farne Islands 127 K7
Farnell 131 M5
Farnham Dorset 59 J3
Farnham Essex 83 H6
Farnham NYorks 107 J3
Farnham Suff 85 H2
Farnham Surr 72 B7
Farnham Common 72 C3
Farnham Green 83 H6
Farnham Royal 72 C3
Farningham 73 J5
Farnley NYorks 107 H5
Farnley WYorks 107 H6
Farnley Tyas 100 D1
Farnsfield 101 J7
Farnworth GtMan 99 G2
Farnworth Halton 98 E4
Farr High 137 K3
Farr High 134 A7
Farr High 134 C10
Farraline 133 R8
Farringdon 57 J6
Farrington Gurney 69 K6
Farsley 107 H6
Farthing Corner 74 E5
Farthing Green 64 D3
Farthinghoe 81 G5
Farthingstone 81 H3
Farthorpe 103 F5
Fartown 100 D1
Farway 57 K6
Fascadale 128 G3
Fashion Museum B&NESom BA1 2QH 33 Bath
Faslane 124 A2
Fasnakyle 133 P8
Fassfern 129 M3
Fatfield 112 D1
Faugh 111 G1
Fauldhouse 125 H4
Faulkbourne 84 B7
Faulkland 70 A6
Fauls 88 E2
Faulston 60 B2
Faversham 75 G5
Fawdington 107 K2
Fawdon 121 H7
Fawfieldhead 100 C6
Fawkham Green 73 J5
Fawler 80 E7
Fawley Bucks 72 A3
Fawley Hants 61 F4
Fawley WBerks 71 G3
Fawley Chapel 78 E6
Faxfleet 108 E7
Faxton 81 J1
Faygate 63 F3
Fazakerley 98 C3
Fazeley 90 E5
Fearby 107 G1
Fearnan 130 C6
Fearnbeg 132 H5
Fearnhead 99 F3
Fearnmore 132 H4
Fearnoch A&B 123 J3
Fearnoch A&B 123 H2
Featherstone Staffs 90 B5
Featherstone WYorks 107 K7
Featherstone Castle 120 B7
Feckenham 80 B2
Feering 84 C6
Feetham 111 L7
Feizor 106 C3
Felbridge 63 G3
Felbrigg 95 G2
Felcourt 73 G7
Felden 72 D1
Felhampton 88 D7
Felindre Carmar 77 G6
Felindre Carmar 67 J3
Felindre Carmar 67 G2
Felindre Carmar 67 K2
Felindre Cere 76 E3
Felindre Powys 88 A7
Felindre Powys 78 A6
Felindre Swan 67 K5
Felinfach Cere 76 E3
Felinfach Powys 77 K5
Felinfoel 67 J5
Felingwmisaf 67 J3
Felingwmuchaf 67 J3
Felixkirk 107 K1
Felixstowe 85 H5
Felixstowe Ferry 85 H5
Felkington 127 H6
Felldownhead 56 B7
Felling 121 H7
Felmersham 82 C3
Felmingham 95 G3
Felpham 62 C7
Felsham 84 D3
Felsted 83 K6
Feltham 72 E4
Felthamhill 72 E4
Felthorpe 95 F4
Felton Here 78 E4
Felton N'umb 121 G3
Felton NSom 69 J5
Felton Butler 88 C4
Feltwell 94 B6
Fen Ditton 83 H2
Fen Drayton 83 G2
Fen End 80 D1
Fen Street Norf 94 D6
Fen Street Norf 84 E1
Fen Street Suff 84 D1
Fen Street Suff 85 F2
Fenay Bridge 100 D1
Fence 106 D6
Fence Houses 112 D1
Fencott 81 G7
Fendike Corner 103 H6
Fenham 127 J6
Fenhouses 93 F1
Feniscowles 106 B7
Feniton 57 K6
Fenn Street 74 D4
Fenni-fach 77 K6
Fenny Bentley 100 D7
Fenny Bridges 57 K6
Fenny Compton 81 F3
Fenny Drayton 91 F6
Fenny Stratford 82 B5
Fenrother 121 G4
Fenstanton 83 G2
Fenton Cambs 83 G1
Fenton Lincs 102 B5
Fenton Lincs 102 B7
Fenton N'umb 127 H7
Fenton Notts 101 K4
Fenton Stoke 90 A1
Fenton Barns 126 D2
Fenwick EAyr 124 C6
Fenwick N'umb 121 F6
Fenwick N'umb 127 J6
Fenwick SYorks 101 H1
Feochaig 116 B2
Feock 53 F5
Feolin 122 D4
Feolin Ferry 122 C4
Feorlan 116 A3
Feorlin 123 H1
Ferens Art Gallery HU1 3RA 40 Kingston upon Hull
Ferguslie Park 124 C4
Feriniquarrie 132 B5
Fern 131 K4
Ferndale 68 C2
Ferndown 60 B4
Ferness 134 D6
Fernham 71 F2
Fernhill Heath 79 H3
Fernhurst 62 B4
Fernilea 132 D7
Fernilee 100 C5
Fernybank 131 L3
Ferrensby 107 J3
Ferrers Centre for Arts & Crafts Leics LE65 1RU 91 F3
Ferrindonald 132 G10
Ferring 62 D6
Ferry Hill 93 G7
Ferrybridge 107 K7
Ferryden 131 N5
Ferryhill 112 C3
Ferryside (Glanyferi) 67 G4
Fersfield 94 E7
Fersit 129 Q3
Ferwig 66 E1
Feshiebridge 133 C10
Festival Park BGwent NP23 8FP 68 E1
Fetcham 72 E6
Fetlar 139 Q3
Fetlar Airport 139 Q3
Fetterangus 135 P5
Fettercairn 131 M3
Feus of Caldhame 131 M4
Fewcott 81 G6
Fewston 107 G4
Ffairfach 67 K3
Ffair-Rhos 77 G2
Ffaldybrenin 67 K1
Ffarmers 67 K1
Ffawyddog 78 B7
Ffestiniog (Llan Ffestiniog) 87 G1
Ffestiniog Railway Gwyn LL49 9NF 87 F1
Ffordd-las Denb 97 K6
Fforddlas Powys 78 B5
Fforest 67 J5
Fforest-fach 67 K6
Ffostrasol 67 G1
Ffos-y-ffin 76 D2
Ffridd Uchaf 96 D7
Ffrith Denb 97 J4
Ffrith Flints 98 B7
Ffrwdgrech 77 K6
Ffynnon 67 G4
Ffynnongroyw 97 K4
Fibhig 138 H3
Fiddington Glos 79 J5
Fiddington Som 69 F7
Fiddleford 59 H3
Fiddler's Green Glos 79 J6
Fiddler's Green Here 78 E5
Fiddler's Green Norf 94 C4
Fiddler's Green Norf 94 E6
Fiddlers Hamlet 73 H1
Field 90 C2
Field Broughton 105 G1
Field Dalling 94 E2
Field Head 91 G5
Fife Keith 135 J5
Fifehead Magdalen 59 G2
Fifehead Neville 59 G3
Fifehead St. Quintin 59 G3
Fifield Oxon 80 D7
Fifield W&M 72 C4
Fifield Bavant 60 B2
Figheldean 70 E7
Filby 95 J4
Filey 109 H1
Filgrave 82 B4
Filham 55 G5
Filkins 71 F1
Filleigh Devon 56 E3
Filleigh Devon 57 F4
Fillingham 102 C4
Fillongley 90 E7
Filmore Hill 61 H2
Filton 69 K4
Fimber 108 E3
Finavon 131 K5
Fincham 94 A5
Finchampstead 72 A5
Finchdean 61 J3
Finchingfield 83 K5
Finchley 73 F2
Findern 91 F2
Findhorn 134 E4
Findochty 135 J4
Findon Aber 135 P11
Findon WSuss 62 E6
Findon Mains 134 A4
Findon Valley 62 E6
Finedon 82 C1
Finegand 130 G4
Fingal Street 85 G1
Fingerpost 79 G1
Fingest 72 A2
Finghall 107 G1
Fingland Cumb 110 D1
Fingland D&G 119 H3
Fingland D&G 118 C2
Finglesham 65 J2
Fingringhoe 84 E6
Finkle Street 101 F3
Finlarig 130 A7
Finmere 81 H5
Finnart A&B 124 A1
Finnart P&K 130 A5
Finney Hill 91 G4
Finningham 84 E2
Finningley 101 J3
Finnygaud 135 L5
Finsbury 73 G3
Finstall 79 J1
Finsthwaite 105 G1
Finstock 80 E7
Finstown 139 C6
Fintry Aber 135 M5
Fintry Stir 124 E2
Finwood 80 C2
Fionnphort 128 D8
Fir Tree 112 B3
Firbank 111 H7
Firbeck 101 H4
Firby NYorks 107 H1
Firby NYorks 108 D3
Firgrove 99 J1
Firs Lane 99 F2
Firsby 103 H6
Firsdown 60 D1
Firth 139 N5
Fishbourne IoW 61 G5
Fishbourne WSuss 62 B6
Fishburn 112 D3
Fishcross 125 H1
Fisherford 135 L7
Fishers Farm Park WSuss RH14 0EG 62 D4
Fisher's Pond 61 F2
Fisher's Row 105 H5
Fishersgate 63 F6
Fisherstreet 62 C3
Fisherton High 134 B5
Fisherton SAyr 117 G2
Fisherton de la Mere 59 J1
Fishguard (Abergwaun) 66 C2
Fishlake 101 J1
Fishleigh Barton 56 D3
Fishley 95 J4
Fishnish 128 H6
Fishpond Bottom 58 C5
Fishponds 69 K4
Fishpool 99 H2
Fishtoft 93 G1
Fishtoft Drove 93 G1
Fishtown of Usan 131 N5
Fishwick 127 H5
Fiskerton Lincs 102 D5
Fiskerton Notts 101 K7
Fitling 109 J6
Fittleton 70 E7
Fittleworth 62 D5
Fitton End 93 H4
Fitz 88 D4
Fitzhead 57 K3
Fitzroy 57 K3
Fitzwilliam 101 G1
Fitzwilliam Museum Cambs CB2 1RB 35 Cambridge
Fiunary 128 H6
Five Acres 78 E7
Five Ash Down 63 H4
Five Ashes 63 J4
Five Bridges 79 F4
Five Houses 61 F6
Five Lanes 69 H2
Five Oak Green 73 K7
Five Oaks Chanl 53 K7
Five Oaks WSuss 62 D4
Five Roads 67 H5
Five Turnings 78 B1
Five Wents 64 D2
Fivehead 58 C2
Fivelanes 54 C2
Flack's Green 84 B7
Flackwell Heath 72 B3
Fladbury 79 J4
Fladdabister 139 N9
Flagg 100 D6
Flambards Experience, The Corn TR13 0QA 52 D6
Flamborough 109 J2
Flamingo Land Theme Park NYorks YO17 6UX 108 D1
Flamingo Park, Hastings ESuss TN34 3AR 64 D7
Flamstead 82 D7
Flamstead End 73 G1
Flansham 62 C6
Flanshaw 107 J7
Flasby 106 E4
Flash 100 C6
Flashader 132 D5
Flask Inn 113 K6
Flatts Lane Woodland Country Park R&C TS6 0NN 29 E4
Flaunden 72 D1
Flawborough 92 A1
Flawith 107 K3
Flax Bourton 69 J5
Flax Moss 106 C7
Flaxby 107 J4
Flaxholme 91 F1
Flaxlands 95 F6
Flaxley 79 F7
Flaxpool 57 K2
Flaxton 108 C3
Fleckney 91 J6
Flecknoe 81 G2
Fledborough 102 B5
Fleet Hants 72 B6
Fleet Hants 61 J4
Fleet Lincs 93 G3
Fleet Air Arm Museum Som BA22 8HT 58 E2
Fleet Hargate 93 G3
Fleetville 72 E1
Fleetwood 105 G5
Fleggburgh (Burgh St. Margaret) 95 J4
Flemingston 68 D4
Flemington 124 E5
Flempton 84 C2
Fletchersbridge 54 B4
Fletchertown 110 D2
Fletching 63 H4
Fleur-de-lis 68 E2
Flexbury 56 A5
Flexford 72 C6
Flimby 110 B3
Flimwell 64 C4
Flint (Y Fflint) 98 B5
Flint Cross 83 H4
Flint Mountain 98 B5
Flintham 92 A1
Flinton 109 J6
Flint's Green 90 E7
Flishinghurst 64 C4
Flitcham 94 B3
Flitholme 111 J5
Flitton 82 D5
Flitwick 82 D5
Flixborough 102 B1
Flixton GtMan 99 G3
Flixton NYorks 109 G2
Flixton Suff 95 H7
Flockton 100 E1
Flockton Green 100 E1
Flodden 127 H7
Flodigarry 132 E3
Flood's Ferry 93 G6
Flookburgh 105 G2
Flordon 95 F6
Flore 81 H2
Flotta 139 C8
Flotterton 121 F3
Flowton 84 E4
Flushdyke 107 H7
Flushing Corn 53 F5
Flushing Corn 52 E6
Fluxton 57 J6
Flyford Flavell 79 J3
Foals Green 85 G1
Fobbing 74 D3
Fochabers 134 H5
Fochriw 68 E1
Fockerby 102 B1
Fodderletter 134 F8
Fodderty 133 R5
Foddington 58 E2
Foel 87 J4
Foelgastell 67 J4
Foggathorpe 108 D6
Fogo 127 F6
Fogorig 127 F6
Fogwatt 134 G5
Foindle 136 D5
Folda 130 G4
Fole 90 C2
Foleshill 91 F7
Folke 59 F3
Folkestone 65 H4
Folkingham 92 D2
Folkington 63 J6
Folksworth 92 E7
Folkton 109 G2
Folla Rule 135 M7
Follifoot 107 J4
Folly Dorset 59 G4
Folly Pembs 66 C3
Folly Farm, Begelly Pembs SA68 0XA 66 E5
Folly Gate 56 D6
Fonmon 68 D5
Fonthill Bishop 59 J1
Fonthill Gifford 59 J1
Fontmell Magna 59 H3
Fontmell Parva 59 H3
Fontwell 62 C6
Font-y-gary 68 D5
Foolow 100 D5
Footherley 90 D5
Foots Cray 73 H4

Force Forge 110 E7
Force Green 73 H6
Forcett 112 B5
Forches Cross 57 F5
Ford A&B 129 K10
Ford Bucks 72 A1
Ford Devon 55 G5
Ford Devon 56 C3
Ford Devon 55 H6
Ford Glos 80 B6
Ford Mersey 98 C3
Ford Midlo 126 B4
Ford N'umb 127 H7
Ford Pembs 66 C3
Ford Plym 54 E5
Ford Shrop 88 D4
Ford Som 57 J3
Ford Staffs 100 C7
Ford Wilts 70 B4
Ford WSuss 62 C6
Ford End 83 K7
Ford Green 105 H5
Ford Heath 88 D4
Ford Street 57 K4
Forda 56 D6
Fordbridge 90 D7
Fordcombe 73 J7
Fordell 125 K2
Forden (Forddun) 88 B5
Forder Green 55 H4
Fordgate 58 C1
Fordham Cambs 83 K1
Fordham Essex 84 D6
Fordham Norf 94 A6
Fordham Abbey 83 K2
Fordham Heath 84 D6
Fordhouses 90 B5
Fordingbridge 60 C3
Fordon 109 G2
Fordoun 131 N3
Ford's Green 84 E2
Fordstreet 84 D6
Fordwells 80 E7
Fordwich 65 G2
Fordyce 135 K4
Forebridge 90 B3
Foredale 106 D3
Foreland 122 A4
Foremark 91 F3
Foremark Reservoir Derbys DE65 6EG 91 F3
Forest 112 C6
Forest Coal Pit 78 B6
Forest Gate 73 H3
Forest Green 72 E7
Forest Hall Cumb 111 G6
Forest Hall T&W 121 H7
Forest Head 111 G1
Forest Hill GtLon 73 G4
Forest Hill Oxon 71 J1
Forest Lane Head 107 J4
Forest Lodge 130 E3
Forest Row 63 H3
Forest Side 61 F6
Forest Town 101 H6
Forestburn Gate 121 F4
Forest-in-Teesdale 111 K4
Forestmill 125 H1
Forestside 61 J3
Forfar 131 K5
Forfar Loch Country Park Angus DD8 1BT 131 K5
Forgandenny 130 F9
Forge 87 G6
Forgie 134 H5
Forhill 80 B1
Formby 98 B2
Forncett End 95 F6
Forncett St. Mary 95 F6
Forncett St. Peter 95 F6
Fornham All Saints 84 C2
Fornham St. Martin 84 C2
Forres 134 E5
Forrest 125 G4
Forrest Lodge 117 K5
Forsbrook 90 B1
Forsinain 137 M5
Forsinard 137 L5
Forston 59 F5
Fort Augustus (Cille Chuimein) 133 P10
Fort Fun, Eastbourne ESuss BN22 7LQ 63 K6
Fort George 134 B5
Fort William (An Gearasdan) 129 N3
Forter 130 G4
Forteviot 130 F9
Forth 125 H5
Forthampton 79 H5
Fortingall 130 C6
Fortis Green 73 F3
Forton Hants 71 H7
Forton Lancs 105 H4
Forton Shrop 88 D4
Forton Som 58 C4
Forton Staffs 89 G3
Fortrie 135 L6
Fortrose (A'Chananaich) 134 B5
Fortuneswell 59 F7
Forty Green 72 C2
Forty Hill 73 G2
Forward Green 84 E3
Fosbury 71 G6
Foscot 80 D6
Fosdyke 93 G2
Foss 130 C5
Foss Cross 70 D1
Fossdale 111 K7
Fossebridge 80 B7
Foster Street 73 H1
Fosterhouses 101 J1
Foster's Booth 81 H3
Foston Derbys 90 D2
Foston Leics 91 J6
Foston Lincs 92 B1
Foston NYorks 108 C3
Foston on the Wolds 109 H4
Fotherby 103 G3
Fotheringhay 92 D6
Foul Mile 63 K5
Foula 139 H9
Foula Airstrip 139 H9
Foulbog 119 H3
Foulden Norf 94 B6
Foulden ScBord 127 H5
Foulness Island 75 G2
Foulridge 106 D5
Foulsham 94 E3
Foulstone 105 J1
Fountainhall 126 C6
Four Ashes Staffs 90 B5
Four Ashes Staffs 90 A7
Four Ashes Suff 84 D1
Four Crosses Denb 87 K1
Four Crosses Powys 88 B4
Four Crosses Powys 87 K5
Four Crosses Staffs 90 B5
Four Elms 73 H7
Four Forks 58 B1
Four Gotes 93 H4
Four Lane Ends B'burn 106 B7
Four Lane Ends ChesW&C 98 E6
Four Lane Ends York 108 C4
Four Lanes 52 D5
Four Marks 61 H1
Four Mile Bridge 96 A5
Four Oaks ESuss 64 D5
Four Oaks Glos 79 F6
Four Oaks WMid 90 E7
Four Oaks WMid 90 D6
Four Oaks Park 90 D6
Four Roads 67 H5
Four Throws 64 C5
Fourlane Ends 101 F7
Fourlanes End 99 H7
Fourstones 120 D7
Fovant 60 B2
Foveran House 135 P8
Fowey 54 B5
Fowlis 131 J7
Fowlis Wester 130 E8
Fowlmere 83 H4
Fownhope 78 E5
Fox Hatch 73 J2
Fox Lane 72 B6
Fox Street 84 E6
Fox Up 106 D2
Foxbar 124 C4
Foxcombe Hill 71 H1
Foxcote Glos 80 B7
Foxcote Som 70 A6
Foxdale 104 B6
Foxearth 84 C4
Foxfield 105 F1
Foxham 70 C4
Foxhole 53 G3
Foxholes 109 G2
Foxhunt Green 63 J5
Foxley Here 78 D4
Foxley N'hants 81 H3
Foxley Norf 94 E3
Foxley Wilts 70 B3
Foxt 90 C1
Foxton Cambs 83 H4
Foxton Dur 112 D4
Foxton Leics 91 J6
Foxton Locks Leics LE16 7RA 91 J7
Foxwist Green 99 F6
Foy 78 E6
Foyers (Foithir) 133 Q8
Fraddam 52 C5
Fraddon 53 G3
Fradley 90 D4
Fradswell 90 B2
Fraisthorpe 109 H3
Framfield 63 H4
Framingham Earl 95 G5
Framingham Pigot 95 G5
Framlingham 85 G2
Frampton Dorset 59 F5
Frampton Lincs 93 G2
Frampton Cotterell 69 K3
Frampton Mansell 70 C1
Frampton on Severn 70 A1
Frampton West End 93 F1
Framsden 85 G3
Framwellgate Moor 112 C2
France Lynch 70 C1
Frances Green 106 B6
Franche 79 H1
Frandley 99 F5
Frankby 98 B4
Frankfort 95 H3
Frankley 90 B7
Franksbridge 78 A3
Frankton 81 F1
Frant 63 J3
Fraserburgh 135 P4
Frating 84 E6
Fratton 61 H4
Freasley 90 E6
Freathy 54 D5
Freckenham 83 K1
Freckleton 105 H7
Freeby 92 B3
Freefolk 71 H7
Freehay 90 C1
Freeland 81 F7
Freester 139 N7
Freethorpe 95 J5
Freethorpe Common 95 J5
Freiston 93 G1
Freiston Shore 93 G1
Fremington Devon 56 D2
Fremington NYorks 112 A7
French Brothers Cruises W&M SL4 5JH 72 C4
Frenchay 69 K4
Frenchbeer 56 E7
Frenich 129 R10
Frensham 72 B7
Fresgoe 137 M3
Freshbrook 70 E3
Freshfield 98 B2
Freshford 70 A6
Freshwater 60 E6
Freshwater Bay 60 E6
Freshwater East 66 D6
Fressingfield 85 G1
Freston 85 F5
Freswick 137 R3
Fretherne 70 A1
Frettenham 95 G4
Freuchie 130 H10
Freystrop Cross 66 C4
Friars Carse 118 E5
Friar's Gate 63 H3
Friars, The, Aylesford Kent ME20 7BX 64 C2
Friday Bridge 93 H5
Friday Street ESuss 63 K6
Friday Street Suff 85 G3
Friday Street Suff 85 H3
Friday Street Surr 72 E7
Fridaythorpe 108 E4
Friern Barnet 73 F2
Friesthorpe 102 D4
Frieston 92 C1
Frieth 72 A2
Frilford 71 H2
Frilsham 71 J4
Frimley 72 B6
Frimley Green 72 B6
Frindsbury 74 D5
Fring 94 B2
Fringford 81 H6
Friningham 64 D2
Frinsted 64 D2
Frinton-on-Sea 85 G7
Friockheim 131 L6
Friog 87 F4
Frisby on the Wreake 91 J4
Friskney 103 H7
Friskney Eaudyke 103 H7
Friston ESuss 63 J7
Friston Suff 85 J2
Fritchley 101 F7
Frith 64 E2
Frith Bank 93 G1
Frith Common 79 F2
Fritham 60 D3
Frithelstock 56 C4
Frithelstock Stone 56 C4
Frithville 103 G7
Frittenden 64 D3
Frittiscombe 55 J6
Fritton Norf 95 G6
Fritton Norf 95 J5
Fritwell 81 G6
Frizinghall 107 G6
Frizington 110 B5
Frocester 70 A1
Frochas 88 B5
Frodesley 88 E5
Frodesley Lane 88 E5
Frodingham 102 B1
Frodsham 98 E5
Frog End 83 H3
Frog Pool 79 G2
Frogden 120 C1
Froggatt 100 E5
Froghall 90 C1
Frogham 60 C3
Frogland Cross 69 K3
Frogmore Devon 55 H6
Frogmore Hants 72 B6
Frogmore Herts 72 E1
Frogwell 54 D4
Frolesworth 91 H6
Frome 70 A7
Frome Market 70 B6
Frome St. Quintin 58 E4
Frome Whitfield 59 F5
Fromes Hill 79 F4
Fron Gwyn 86 C2
Fron Powys 88 B5
Fron Powys 77 K2
Fron Powys 88 A6
Fron Isaf 88 B2
Froncysyllte 88 B1
Fron-goch 87 J2
Frostenden 95 J7
Frosterley 112 A3
Froxfield 71 G5
Froxfield Green 61 J2
Fruitmarket Gallery Edin EH1 1DF 38 G4
Fryerning 74 C1
Fugglestone St. Peter 60 C1
Fulbeck 102 C7
Fulbourn 83 J3
Fulbrook 80 D7
Fulflood 61 F2
Fulford Som 58 B2
Fulford Staffs 90 B2
Fulford York 108 C5
Fulham 73 F4
Fulking 63 F5
Full Sutton 108 D4
Fullaford 56 E2
Fuller Street 84 B7
Fuller's Moor 98 D7
Fullerton 60 E1
Fulletby 103 F5
Fullwood 124 C5
Fulmer 72 D3
Fulmodeston 94 D2
Fulnetby 102 E5
Fulready 80 D4
Fulstone 100 D2
Fulstow 103 G3
Fulwell Oxon 80 E6
Fulwell T&W 112 D1
Fulwood Lancs 105 J6
Fulwood SYorks 101 F4
Fun Farm, Spalding Lincs PE12 6JU 93 F3
Fundenhall 95 F6
Fundenhall Street 95 F6
Funtington 62 B6
Funtley 61 G4
Funzie 139 Q3
Furley 58 B4
Furnace A&B 129 M10
Furnace Carmar 67 J5
Furnace Cere 87 F6
Furnace End 90 E6
Furner's Green 63 H4
Furness Vale 100 C4
Furneux Pelham 83 H6
Furnham 58 C4
Further Quarter 64 D4
Furtho 81 J4
Furze Green 95 G7
Furze Platt 72 B3
Furzehill Devon 57 F1
Furzehill Dorset 60 B4
Furzeley Corner 61 H3
Furzey Lodge 60 E4
Furzley 60 D3
Fyfett 58 B3
Fyfield Essex 73 J1
Fyfield Glos 71 F1
Fyfield Hants 71 F7
Fyfield Oxon 71 H2
Fyfield Wilts 70 E5
Fyfield Wilts 70 E5
Fylingthorpe 113 K6
Fyning 62 B4
Fyvie 135 M7

G

Gabalfa 68 E4
Gabhsunn Bho Dheas 138 K2
Gabhsunn Bho Thuath 138 K2
Gabroc Hill 124 C5
Gaddesby 91 J4
Gaddesden Row 82 D7
Gadebridge 72 D1
Gadshill 74 D4
Gaer Newport 69 F3
Gaer Powys 78 A6
Gaer-fawr 69 H2
Gaerllwyd 69 H2
Gaerwen 96 C5
Gagingwell 81 F6
Gaick Lodge 130 C2
Gailes 124 B7
Gailey 90 B4
Gainford 112 B5
Gainsborough 102 B3
Gainsford End 84 B5
Gairloch (Geàrrloch) 132 H3
Gairlochy (Geàrr Lòchaidh) 129 N2
Gairney Bank 125 K1
Gaitsgill 110 E2
Galabank 126 C6
Galashiels 126 C7
Galdenoch 114 B4
Gale 99 J1
Galgate 105 H4
Galhampton 59 F2
Gallantry Bank 98 E7
Gallatown 126 A1
Gallchoille 123 F1
Gallery of Modern Art Glas G1 3AH 39 F4
Galley Common 91 F6
Galleyend 74 D1
Galleywood 74 D1
Gallowfauld 131 K6
Gallowhill 124 C4
Gallows Green 90 C1
Gallowstree Common 71 K3
Gallowstree Elm 90 A7
Galltair 133 J8
Gallt-y-foel 96 D6
Gallypot Street 63 H3
Galmington 58 B2
Galmisdale 128 F2
Galmpton Devon 55 G6
Galmpton Torbay 55 J5
Galmpton Warborough 55 J5
Galphay 107 H2
Galston 124 C7
Galtrigill 132 B5
Gamble's Green 84 B7
Gamblesby 111 H3
Gamelsby 110 D1
Gamesley 100 C3
Gamlingay 83 F3
Gamlingay Cinques 83 F3
Gamlingay Great Heath 83 F3
Gammaton 56 C3
Gammaton Moor 56 C3
Gammersgill 107 F1
Gamston Notts 101 K5
Gamston Notts 91 J2
Ganarew 78 E7
Gang 54 D4
Ganllwyd 87 G3
Gannochy 131 M3
Ganstead 109 H6
Ganthorpe 108 C2
Ganton 109 F2
Ganwick Corner 73 F2
Gaodhail 128 H7
Gappah 55 J3
Gara Bridge 55 H5
Garbat 133 Q4
Garbhallt 123 J1
Garboldisham 94 E7
Garden 124 D1
Garden City 98 C6
Garden Village 100 E3
Gardeners Green 72 B5
Gardenstown 135 M4
Garderhouse 139 M8
Gardham 109 F5
Gare Hill 70 A7
Garelochhead 124 A1
Garford 71 H2
Garforth 107 K6
Gargrave 106 E4
Gargunnock 125 F1
Gariob 123 F2
Garlic Street 95 G7
Garlies Castle 114 E4
Garlieston 114 E6
Garlinge Green 65 G2
Garlogie 135 M10
Garmelow 90 A3
Garmond 135 N5
Garmony 128 H6
Garmouth 134 H4
Garmston 89 F5
Garnant 67 K4
Garndolbenmaen 86 D1
Garneddwen 87 G5
Garnett Bridge 111 G7
Garnfadryn 86 B2
Garnswllt 67 K5
Garrabost 138 L4
Garrachra 123 J2
Garras 52 E6
Garreg 87 F1
Garreg Bank 88 B4
Garrett's Green 90 D7
Garrick 130 D9
Garrigill 111 J2
Garriston 112 B7
Garroch 117 K5
Garrochty 123 J5
Garros 132 E4
Garrow 130 D7
Garryhorn 117 K4
Garrynahine (Gearraidh na h-Aibhne) 138 H4
Garsdale 106 C1
Garsdale Head 111 J7
Garsdon 70 C3
Garshall Green 90 B2
Garsington 71 J1
Garstang 105 H5
Garston 98 D4
Garswood 98 E3
Gartachoil 124 D1
Gartavaich 123 G5
Gartbreck 122 A5
Gartcosh 124 E4
Garth Bridgend 68 B2
Garth Cere 87 F7
Garth Gwyn 96 D5
Garth IoM 104 C6
Garth Powys 77 J4
Garth Wrex 88 B1
Garth Row 111 G7
Garthbrengy 77 K5
Gartheli 76 E3
Garthmyl 88 A6
Garthorpe Leics 92 B3
Garthorpe NLincs 102 B1
Garths 111 G7
Garthynty 77 G4
Gartly 135 K7
Gartmore 124 D1
Gartnagrenach 123 F5
Gartnatra 122 B4
Gartness 124 D2
Gartocharn 124 C2
Garton 109 J6
Garton-on-the-Wolds 109 F3
Gartymore 137 N8
Garvald 126 D3
Garvamore 133 R11
Garvan 129 L3
Garvard 122 B1
Garve (Clachan Ghairbh) 133 P4
Garveld 116 A3
Garvestone 94 E5
Garvie 123 J2
Garvock 124 A3
Garwald 119 H3
Garwaldwaterfoot 119 H3
Garway 78 D6
Garway Hill 78 D6
Gass 117 J3
Gastard 70 B5
Gasthorpe 94 D7
Gaston Green 83 J7
Gatcombe 61 F6
Gate Burton 102 B4
Gate Helmsley 108 C4
Gate House 122 D3
Gateacre 98 D4
Gateford 101 H4
Gateforth 108 B7
Gatehead 124 B7
Gatehouse of Fleet 115 G5
Gatelawbridge 118 E4
Gateley 94 D3
Gatenby 107 J1
Gatesgarth 110 C5
Gateshaw 120 C1
Gateshead 121 H7
Gatesheath 98 D6
Gateside Angus 131 K6
Gateside Fife 130 G10
Gateside NAyr 124 B5
Gateslack 118 D3
Gathurst 98 E2
Gatley 99 H4
Gattonside 126 D7
Gatwick Airport 73 F7
Gaufron 77 J2
Gaulby 91 J5
Gauldry 131 J8
Gauntons Bank 88 E1
Gaunt's Common 60 B4
Gaunt's Earthcott 69 K3
Gautby 102 E5
Gavinton 127 F5
Gawber 101 F2
Gawcott 81 H5
Gawsworth 99 H5
Gawthrop 106 B1
Gawthwaite 105 F1
Gay Bowers 74 D1
Gay Street 62 D4
Gaydon 80 E3
Gayhurst 82 B4
Gayle 106 D1
Gayles 112 B6
Gayton Mersey 98 B4
Gayton N'hants 81 J3
Gayton Norf 94 B4
Gayton Staffs 90 B3
Gayton le Marsh 103 H4
Gayton le Wold 103 F4
Gayton Thorpe 94 B4
Gaywood 94 A3
Gazeley 84 B2
Gearach 122 A5
Gearnsary 137 K6
Gearraidh na Monadh 138 B7
Gearrannan 138 G3
Geary 132 C4
Gedding 84 D3
Geddington 92 B7
Gedgrave Hall 85 J4
Gedling 91 J1
Gedney 93 H3
Gedney Broadgate 93 H3
Gedney Drove End 93 H3
Gedney Dyke 93 H3
Gedney Hill 93 G4
Gee Cross 99 J3
Geilston 124 B3
Geirinis 138 B4
Geisiadar 138 G4
Geldeston 95 H6
Gell Conwy 97 G6
Gell Gwyn 86 D2
Gelli 68 C2
Gelli Aur Country Park Carmar SA32 8LR 67 K3
Gelli Gynan 97 K7
Gellideg 68 D1
Gellifor 97 K6
Gelligaer 68 E2
Gellilydan 87 F2
Gellioedd 87 J1
Gelly 66 D4
Gellyburn 130 F7
Gellywen 67 F3
Gelston D&G 115 H5
Gelston Lincs 92 C1
Gembling 109 H4
Genoch 114 B5
Genoch Square 114 B5
Gentleshaw 90 C4
Geocrab 138 G8
George Green 72 D3
George Nympton 57 F3
Georgeham 56 C2
Georgetown 124 C4
Gerlan 96 E6
Germansweek 56 C6
Germoe 52 C6
Gerrans 53 F5
Gerrards Cross 72 D3
Gestingthorpe 84 C5
Geuffordd 88 B4
Geufron 87 H7
Gibbet Hill 70 A7
Gibbshill 115 H3
Gibraltar Lincs 103 J7
Gibraltar Suff 85 F3
Gibraltar Point National Nature Reserve Lincs PE24 4SU 103 J7
Gibside T&W NE16 6BG 28 A6
Giddeahall 70 B4
Giddy Green 59 H6
Gidea Park 73 J3
Gidleigh 56 E7
Giffnock 124 D5
Gifford 126 D4
Giffordland 124 A6
Giffordtown 130 H9
Giggleswick 106 D3
Gigha 122 E6
Gilberdyke 108 E7
Gilbert's End 79 H4
Gilchriston 126 C4
Gilcrux 110 C3
Gildersome 107 H7
Gildingwells 101 H4
Gilesgate Moor 112 C2
Gileston 68 D5
Gilfach 68 E2
Gilfach Goch 68 C3
Gilfachrheda 76 D3
Gilgarran 110 B4
Gill 110 F4
Gillamoor 108 C1
Gillenbie 119 G5
Gillfoot 115 K3
Gilling East 108 C2
Gilling West 112 B6
Gillingham Dorset 59 H2
Gillingham Med 74 D5
Gillingham Norf 95 J6
Gillock 137 Q4
Gillow Heath 99 H7
Gills 137 R2
Gill's Green 64 C4
Gilmanscleuch 119 J1
Gilmerton Edin 126 A4
Gilmerton P&K 130 D8
Gilmilnscroft 117 K1
Gilmonby 111 L5
Gilmorton 91 H7
Gilsland 120 B7
Gilsland Spa 120 B7
Gilson 90 D6
Gilstead 107 G6
Gilston 126 C5
Gilston Park 83 H7
Giltbrook 91 G1
Gilwern 78 B7
Gimingham 95 G2
Gin Pit 99 F2
Ginclough 99 J5
Ginger's Green 63 K5
Giosla 138 G5
Gipping 84 E2
Gipsey Bridge 93 F1
Girlsta 139 N7
Girsby 112 D6
Girtford 82 E4
Girthon 115 G5
Girton Cambs 83 H2
Girton Notts 102 B6
Girvan 117 F4
Gisburn 106 D5
Gisburn Cotes 106 D5
Gisleham 95 K7
Gislingham 84 E1
Gissing 95 F7
Gittisham 57 K6
Givons Grove 72 E6
Gladestry 78 B3
Gladsmuir 126 C3
Glaic 123 J3
Glais 68 A1
Glaisdale 113 H6
Glaister 123 H7
Glamis 131 J6
Glamis Castle Angus DD8 1QJ 131 J6
Glan Conwy 97 G7
Glanaber Terrace 87 G1
Glanaman 67 K4
Glanbran 77 H5
Glan-Denys 76 E3
Glandford 94 E1
Glan-Duar 67 J1
Glandwr 66 E3
Glan-Dwyfach 86 D1
Glangrwyney 78 B7
Glanllynfi 68 B2
Glanmule 88 A6
Glan-rhyd NPT 68 A1
Glanrhyd Pembs 66 E1
Glanton 121 F2
Glanton Pyke 121 F2
Glanvilles Wootton 59 F4
Glanwern 87 F7
Glanwydden 97 G4
Glan-y-don 97 K5
Glan-y-llyn 68 E3
Glan-y-nant 87 J7
Glan-yr-afon Gwyn 87 J1
Glan-yr-afon Gwyn 87 K1
Glan-yr-afon IoA 96 E4
Glan-y-Wern 87 F2
Glapthorn 92 D6
Glapwell 101 G6
Glasbury 78 A5
Glascoed Mon 69 G1
Glascoed Wrex 98 B7
Glascote 90 E5
Glascwm 78 A3
Glasfryn 97 H7
Glasgow (Glaschu) 124 D4
Glasgow Airport 124 C4
Glasgow Botanic Garden Glas G12 0UE 30 E3
Glasgow Prestwick Airport 117 H1
Glasgow Royal Concert Hall Glas G2 3NY 39 F3
Glasgow Science Centre Glas G51 1EA 39 A4
Glasinfryn 96 D6
Glasnacardoch 132 G11
Glasnakille 132 F9
Glaspant 67 F2
Glaspwll 87 G6
Glass Studio, Eastbourne Pier ESuss BN21 3EL 37 Eastbourne
Glassel 135 L11
Glassenbury 64 C4
Glasserton 114 E7
Glassford 125 F6
Glasshouse 79 G6
Glasshouses 107 G3
Glasson Cumb 119 H7
Glasson Lancs 105 H4
Glasson Dock 105 H4
Glassonby 111 G3
Glaston 92 B5
Glastonbury 58 D1
Glastonbury Abbey Som BA6 9EL 58 E1
Glatton 92 E7
Glazebrook 99 F3
Glazebury 99 F3
Glazeley 89 G7
Gleadless 101 F4
Gleadsmoss 99 H6
Gleaston 105 F2
Glecknabae 123 J4
Gledhow 107 J6
Gledrid 88 B2
Glemsford 84 C4
Glen D&G 115 J3
Glen D&G 115 F5
Glen Auldyn 104 D4
Glen Mona 104 D5
Glen Parva 91 H6
Glen Trool Lodge 117 J5
Glen Village 125 G3
Glen Vine 104 C6
Glenae 118 E5
Glenaladale 129 K3
Glenald 124 A1
Glenapp Castle 116 E5
Glenarm 131 J4
Glenbarr 122 E7
Glenbatrick 122 D3
Glenbeg 128 G4
Glenbervie Aber 131 N2
Glenbervie Falk 125 G2
Glenboig 125 F4
Glenborrodale 128 H4
Glenbranter 123 K1
Glenbreck 119 F1
Glenbrittle 132 E8
Glenburn 124 C4
Glencaple 115 K4
Glencarse 130 G8
Glencloy 123 J7
Glencoe (A' Chàrnaich) 129 N5
Glencoe Visitor Centre High PH49 4LA 129 N5
Glencraig 125 K1
Glencrosh 118 C5
Glendearg D&G 119 H3
Glendearg ScBord 126 D7
Glendessary 133 K11
Glendevon 130 E10
Glendoebeg 133 Q10
Glendoick 130 H8
Glendoll Lodge 130 H3
Glendoune 117 F4
Glendrissaig 117 F4
Glenduisk 117 G5
Glendye Lodge 131 M2
Gleneagles Hotel 130 E9
Gleneagles House 130 E10
Glenegedale 122 B5
Glenelg (Gleann Eilg) 133 J9
Glenfarg 130 G9
Glenfield 91 H5
Glenfinnan (Gleann Fhionnainn) 129 L2
Glengap 115 G5
Glengarnock 124 B5
Glengarrisdale 122 E1
Glengennet 117 G4
Glengrasco 132 E6
Glenhead 118 D5
Gleniffer Braes Country Park Renf PA2 8TE 30 A6
Glenkerry 119 H2
Glenkiln 123 J7
Glenkin 123 K2
Glenkindie 135 J9
Glenlair 115 H3
Glenlean 123 J2
Glenlee Angus 131 K3
Glenlee D&G 118 B5
Glenlochar 115 H4
Glenluce 114 B5
Glenmallan 124 A1
Glenmanna 118 C3
Glenmavis 125 F4
Glenmaye 104 B6
Glenmeanie 133 N5
Glenmore A&B 123 J4
Glenmore High 132 E6
Glenmore Forest Park Visitor Centre High PH22 1QY 134 D9
Glenmore Lodge 134 D10
Glenmoy 131 K4
Glenochar 118 E2
Glenprosen Village 131 J4
Glenramskill 116 B2
Glenrazie 114 D4
Glenridding 110 E5
Glenrisdell 123 G5
Glenrothes 130 H10
Glenshellish 123 K1
Glensluain 123 J1
Glentaggart 118 D1
Glentham 102 D3
Glenton 135 L8
Glentress 126 A7
Glentress Forest ScBord EH45 8NB 126 A6
Glentrool 114 D3
Glentruan 104 D3
Glentworth 102 C4
Glenuig 128 H3
Glenurquhart 134 B4
Glenwhilly 114 B3
Glespin 118 D1
Gletness 139 N7
Glewstone 78 E6
Glinton 92 E5
Glogue 67 F2
Glooston 92 A6
Glororum 127 K7
Glossop 100 C3
Gloster Hill 121 H3
Gloucester 79 H7
Gloucester Cathedral Glos GL1 2LR 40 Gloucester
Gloucester Historic Docks Glos GL1 2ER 40 Gloucester
Gloucestershire Airport 79 H6
Gloucestershire & Warwickshire Railway Glos GL54 5DT 80 B6
Gloup 139 P2
Gloweth 52 E4
Glusburn 107 F5
Glympton 81 F6
Glyn 97 F7
Glyn Ceiriog 88 B2
Glynarthen 67 G1
Glyncoch 68 D2
Glyncorrwg 68 B2
Glyn-Cywarch 87 F2
Glynde 63 H6
Glyndebourne 63 H5
Glyndyfrdwy 88 A1
Glynneath (Glyn-Nedd) 68 B1
Glynogwr 68 C3
Glyntaff 68 D3
Gnosall 90 A3
Gnosall Heath 90 A3
Go Bananas, Colchester Essex CO1 1BX 84 D6
Goadby 92 A6
Goadby Marwood 92 A3
Goatacre 70 D4
Goathill 59 F3
Goathland 113 J6
Goathurst 58 B1
Gobernuisgeach 137 M6
Gobowen 88 C2
Godalming 72 C7
Goddard's Corner 85 G2
Goddards Green 63 F4
Godden Green 73 J6
Goddington 73 H5
Godford Cross 57 K5
Godington 81 H6
Godleybrook 90 B1
Godmanchester 83 F1
Godmanstone 59 F5
Godmersham 65 F2
Godney 69 H7
Godolphin Cross 52 D5
Godor 88 B4
Godre'r-graig 68 A1
Godshill Hants 60 C3
Godshill IoW 61 G6
Godstone 73 G6
Godstone Farm Surr RH9 8LX 73 G6
Godwick 94 D3
Goetre 69 G1
Goff's Oak 73 G1
Gogar 125 K3
Gogarth 97 F4
Goginan 87 F7
Goirtein 123 H2
Golan 86 E1
Golant 54 B5
Golberdon 54 D3
Golborne 99 F3
Golcar 100 D1
Gold Hill Cambs 93 J6
Gold Hill Dorset 59 H3
Goldcliff 69 G3
Golden Acre Park WYorks LS16 8BQ 107 H5
Golden Cross 63 J5
Golden Green 73 K7
Golden Grove 67 J4
Golden Pot 72 A7
Golden Valley Derbys 101 G7
Golden Valley Glos 79 J6
Goldenhill 99 H7
Golders Green 73 F3
Goldhanger 75 F1
Goldielea 115 K3
Golding 88 E5
Goldington 82 D3
Goldsborough NYorks 113 J5
Goldsborough NYorks 107 J4
Goldsithney 52 C5
Goldstone 89 G3
Goldthorn Park 90 B6
Goldthorpe 101 G2
Goldworthy 56 B3
Goleulong 2000 Lightship Cardiff CF10 4PA 7 C6
Golford 64 C4
Gollinglith Foot 107 G1
Golspie 134 C1
Golval 137 L3
Gomeldon 60 C1
Gomersal 107 H7
Gometra 128 E6
Gomshall 72 D7
Gonachan Cottage 124 E2
Gonalston 91 J1
Gonerby Hill Foot 92 C2
Gonfirth 139 M6
Good Easter 83 K7
Gooderstone 94 B5
Goodleigh 56 E2
Goodmanham 108 E5
Goodmayes 73 H3
Goodnestone Kent 65 H2
Goodnestone Kent 75 G5
Goodrich 78 E7
Goodrington 55 J5
Goodshaw 106 D7
Goodshaw Fold 106 D7
Goodwick (Wdig) 66 C2
Goodworth Clatford 71 G7
Goodyers End 91 F7
Goole 108 D7
Goom's Hill 80 B3
Goonbell 52 E4
Goonhavern 52 E3
Goonvrea 52 E4
Goose Green Essex 85 F6
Goose Green Essex 85 F6
Goose Green GtMan 98 E2
Goose Green Kent 73 K6
Goose Green SGlos 69 K4
Goose Pool 78 D5
Gooseham 56 A4
Goosehill Green 79 J2
Goosewell 55 F5
Goosey 71 G2
Goosnargh 105 J6
Goostrey 99 G5
Gorcott Hill 80 B2
Gorddinog 96 E5
Gordon 126 E6
Gordonbush 137 L9
Gordonstown Aber 135 K5
Gordonstown Aber 135 M7
Gore Cross 70 D6
Gore End 71 H5
Gore Pit 84 C7
Gore Street 75 J5
Gorebridge 126 B4
Gorefield 93 H4
Gorey 53 K7
Gorgie 126 A3
Gorgie City Farm Edin EH11 2LA 32 C2
Goring 71 K3
Goring Heath 71 K4
Goring-by-Sea 62 E6
Gorleston-on-Sea 95 K5
Gorllwyn 67 G2
Gornalwood 90 B6
Gorran Churchtown 53 G4
Gorran Haven 54 A6
Gors 77 F1
Gorsedd 97 K5
Gorseinon 67 J6
Gorseybank 100 E7
Gorsgoch 76 D3
Gorslas 67 J4
Gorsley 79 F6
Gorsley Common 79 F6
Gorstage 99 F5
Gorstan 133 P4
Gorsty Hill 90 D3
Gorteneorn 128 H4
Gorton 99 H3
Gosbeck 85 F3
Gosberton 93 F2
Gosberton Clough 92 E3
Goseley Dale 91 F3
Gosfield 84 B6
Gosford Here 78 E2
Gosford Oxon 81 G7
Gosforth Cumb 110 B6
Gosforth T&W 121 H7
Gosland Green 98 E7
Gosmore 82 E6
Gospel End 90 A6
Gosport 61 H5
Gossabrough 139 P4
Gossington 70 A1
Gossops Green 63 F3
Goswick 127 J6
Gotham 91 H2
Gotherington 79 J6
Gothers 53 G3
Gott 139 N8
Gotton 58 B2
Goudhurst 64 C4
Goulceby 103 F5
Gourdon 131 P3
Gourock 124 A3
Govan 124 D4
Goverton 101 K7
Goveton 55 H6
Govilon 78 B7
Gowdall 108 C7
Gowerton 67 J6
Gowkhall 125 J2
Gowkthrapple 125 F5
Gowthorpe 108 D4
Goxhill ERid 109 H5
Goxhill NLincs 109 H7
Goytre 68 A3
Gozzard's Ford 71 H2
Grabhair 138 J6
Graby 92 D3
Gradbach 99 J6
Grade 52 E7
Gradeley Green 98 E7
Graffham 62 C5
Grafham Cambs 82 E2
Grafham Surr 72 D7
Grafham Water Cambs PE28 0BH 82 E2
Grafton Here 78 D5
Grafton NYorks 107 K3
Grafton Oxon 71 F1
Grafton Shrop 88 D4
Grafton Worcs 78 E2
Grafton Worcs 79 J5
Grafton Flyford 79 J3
Grafton Regis 81 J4
Grafton Underwood 92 C7
Grafty Green 64 D3
Graianrhyd 98 B7
Graig Carmar 67 H5
Graig Conwy 97 G5
Graig Denb 97 J5
Graig-fechan 97 K7
Grain 74 E4
Grainel 122 A4
Grains Bar 99 J2
Grainsby 103 F3
Grainthorpe 103 G3
Graizelound 101 K3
Grampound 53 G4
Grampound Road 53 G3
Granborough 81 J6
Granby 92 A2
Grand Pier, Teignmouth Devon TQ14 8BB 55 K3
Grandborough 81 F2
Grandes Rocques 53 J5
Grandtully 130 E5
Grange Cumb 110 D5
Grange EAyr 124 C7
Grange High 133 P7
Grange Med 74 D5
Grange Mersey 98 B4
Grange de Lings 102 C5
Grange Hill 73 H2
Grange Moor 100 E1
Grange of Lindores 130 H9
Grange Villa 112 C1
Grangemill 100 E7
Grangemouth 125 H2
Grange-over-Sands 105 H2
Grangeston 117 G4
Grangetown Cardiff 68 E4
Grangetown R&C 113 F4
Gransmoor 109 H4
Granston 66 B2
Grantchester 83 H3
Grantham 92 C2
Grantley 107 H2
Granton 126 A3
Granton House 119 F3
Grantown-on-Spey 134 E8
Grantsfield 78 E2
Grantshouse 127 G4
Grappenhall 99 F4
Grasby 102 D2
Grasmere 110 E6
Grass Green 84 B5
Grasscroft 99 J2
Grassendale 98 C4
Grassgarth 110 F7
Grassholme 111 L4
Grassington 107 F3
Grassmoor 101 G6
Grassthorpe 101 K6
Grateley 71 F7
Gratwich 90 C2
Gravel Hill 72 D2
Graveley Cambs 83 F2
Graveley Herts 83 F6
Gravelly Hill 90 D6
Gravels 88 C5
Graven 139 N5
Graveney 75 G5
Gravesend 74 C4
Grayingham 102 C3
Grayrigg 111 G7
Grays 74 C4
Grayshott 62 B3
Grayswood 62 C3
Grazeley 71 K5
Greasbrough 101 G3
Greasby 98 B4
Great Aberystwyth Camera Obscura Cere SY23 2DN 86 E7
Great Abington 83 J4
Great Addington 82 C1
Great Alne 80 C3
Great Altcar 98 C2
Great Amwell 83 G7
Great Asby 111 H5
Great Ashfield 84 D2
Great Ayton 113 F5
Great Baddow 74 D1
Great Bardfield 83 K5
Great Barford 82 E3
Great Barr 90 C6
Great Barrington 80 D7
Great Barrow 98 D6
Great Barton 84 C2
Great Barugh 108 D2
Great Bavington 120 E5
Great Bealings 85 G4
Great Bedwyn 71 F5
Great Bentley 85 F6
Great Bernera 138 G4
Great Billing 82 B2
Great Bircham 94 B2
Great Blakenham 85 F3
Great Bolas 89 F3
Great Bookham 72 E6
Great Bourton 81 F4
Great Bowden 92 A7
Great Bradley 83 K3
Great Braxted 84 C7
Great Bricett 84 E3
Great Brickhill 82 C5
Great Bridgeford 90 A3
Great Brington 81 H2
Great Bromley 84 E6
Great Broughton Cumb 110 B3
Great Broughton NYorks 113 F6
Great Buckland 74 C5
Great Budworth 99 F5
Great Burdon 112 D5
Great Burstead 74 C2
Great Busby 113 F6
Great Cambourne 83 G3
Great Canfield 83 J7
Great Canney 74 E1
Great Carlton 103 H4
Great Casterton 92 D5
Great Chalfield 70 B5
Great Chart 64 E3
Great Chatwell 89 G4
Great Chell 99 H7
Great Chesterford 83 J4
Great Cheverell 70 C6
Great Chishill 83 H5
Great Clacton 85 F7
Great Clifton 110 B4
Great Coates 103 F2
Great Comberton 79 J4
Great Corby 111 F1
Great Cornard 84 C4
Great Cowden 109 J5
Great Coxwell 71 F2
Great Crakehall 107 H1
Great Cransley 82 B1
Great Cressingham 94 C5
Great Crosby 98 C2
Great Crosthwaite 110 D4
Great Cubley 90 D2
Great Cumbrae 123 K5
Great Dalby 92 A4
Great Doddington 82 B2
Great Doward 78 E7
Great Dunham 94 C4
Great Dunmow 83 K6
Great Durnford 60 C1
Great Easton Essex 83 K6
Great Easton Leics 92 B6
Great Eccleston 105 H5
Great Edstone 108 D1
Great Ellingham 94 E6
Great Elm 70 A7
Great Eversden 83 G3
Great Fencote 112 C7
Great Finborough 84 E3
Great Fransham 94 C4
Great Gaddesden 82 D7
Great Gidding 92 E7
Great Givendale 108 E4
Great Glemham 85 H2
Great Glen 91 J6
Great Gonerby 92 B2
Great Gransden 83 F3
Great Green Cambs 83 F4
Great Green Norf 95 G7
Great Green Suff 84 D3
Great Green Suff 85 F1
Great Green Suff 84 E1
Great Habton 108 D2
Great Hale 92 E1
Great Hall Hants SO23 8UJ 49 Winchester
Great Hallingbury 83 J7
Great Hampden 72 B1
Great Harrowden 82 B1
Great Harwood 106 C6
Great Haseley 71 K1
Great Hatfield 109 H5
Great Haywood 90 C3
Great Heath 91 F7
Great Heck 108 B7
Great Henny 84 C5
Great Hinton 70 C6
Great Hockham 94 D6
Great Holland 85 G7
Great Horkesley 84 D5
Great Hormead 83 H5
Great Horton 107 G6
Great Horwood 81 J5
Great Houghton N'hants 81 J3
Great Houghton SYorks 101 G2
Great Hucklow 100 D5
Great Kelk 109 H4
Great Kimble 72 B1
Great Kingshill 72 B2
Great Langton 112 C7
Great Leighs 84 B7
Great Limber 102 E2
Great Linford 82 B4
Great Livermere 84 C1
Great Longstone 100 E5
Great Lumley 112 C2
Great Lyth 88 D5
Great Malvern 79 G4
Great Maplestead 84 C5
Great Marton 105 G6
Great Massingham 94 B3
Great Melton 95 F5
Great Milton 71 K1
Great Missenden 72 B1
Great Mitton 106 C6
Great Mongeham 65 J2
Great Moulton 95 F6
Great Munden 83 G6
Great Musgrave 111 J5
Great Ness 88 D4
Great Notley 84 B6
Great Nurcot 57 H2
Great Oak 69 G1
Great Oakley Essex 85 F6
Great Oakley N'hants 92 B7
Great Offley 82 E6
Great Orme Tramway Conwy LL30 2HG 97 F4
Great Ormside 111 J5
Great Orton 110 E1
Great Ouseburn 107 K3
Great Oxendon 92 A7
Great Oxney Green 74 C1
Great Palgrave 94 C4
Great Parndon 73 H1
Great Paxton 83 F2
Great Plumpton 105 G6
Great Plumstead 95 H5
Great Ponton 92 C2
Great Potheridge 56 D4
Great Preston 107 J7
Great Purston 81 G5
Great Raveley 93 F7
Great Rissington 80 C7
Great Rollright 80 E5
Great Ryburgh 94 D3
Great Ryle 121 F2
Great Ryton 88 D5
Great St. Mary's Church Cambs CB2 3PQ 35 Cambridge
Great Saling 84 B6
Great Salkeld 111 G3
Great Sampford 83 K5
Great Sankey 98 E4
Great Saredon 90 B5
Great Saxham 84 B2
Great Shefford 71 G4
Great Shelford 83 H3
Great Smeaton 112 D6
Great Snoring 94 D2
Great Somerford 70 C3
Great Stainton 112 D4
Great Stambridge 75 F2
Great Staughton 82 E2
Great Steeping 103 H6
Great Stonar 65 J2
Great Strickland 111 G4
Great Stukeley 83 F1
Great Sturton 103 F5
Great Sutton ChesW&C 98 C5
Great Sutton Shrop 88 E7
Great Swinburne 120 E6
Great Tew 80 E6
Great Tey 84 C6
Great Thorness 61 F5
Great Thurlow 83 K4
Great Torr 55 G6
Great Torrington 56 C4
Great Tosson 121 F3
Great Totham Essex 84 C7
Great Totham Essex 84 C7
Great Tows 103 F3
Great Urswick 105 F2
Great Wakering 75 F3
Great Waldingfield 84 D4
Great Walsingham 94 D2
Great Waltham 83 K7
Great Warley 73 J2
Great Washbourne 79 J5
Great Weeke 57 F7
Great Welnetham 84 C3
Great Wenham 84 E5
Great Whittington 121 F6
Great Wigborough 84 D7
Great Wigsell 64 C5
Great Wilbraham 83 J3
Great Wilne 91 G2
Great Wishford 60 B1
Great Witcombe 79 J7
Great Witley 79 G2
Great Wolford 80 D5
Great Wratting 83 K4
Great Wymondley 83 F6

Great Wyrley 90 B5
Great Wytheford 88 E4
Great Yarmouth 95 K5
Great Yeldham 84 B5
Greatford 92 D4
Greatgate 90 C1
Greatham Hants 61 J1
Greatham Hart 112 E4
Greatham WSuss 62 D5
Greatness 73 J6
Greatstone-on-Sea 65 F5
Greatworth 81 G4
Green 97 J6
Green Cross 62 B3
Green End Bed 82 E3
Green End Bucks 82 C5
Green End Cambs 83 H1
Green End Cambs 83 G1
Green End Herts 83 G6
Green End Herts 83 G5
Green End Warks 90 E7
Green Hammerton 107 K4
Green Hill 70 D3
Green Lane 80 B2
Green Moor 100 E3
Green Ore 69 J6
Green Quarter 111 F6
Green Street ESuss 64 C6
Green Street Herts 72 E2
Green Street Herts 83 H6
Green Street Worcs 79 H4
Green Street WSuss 62 E4
Green Street Green GtLon 73 H5
Green Street Green Kent 73 J4
Green Tye 83 H7
Greencroft 112 B2
Greendykes 121 F1
Greenend 80 E6
Greenfaulds 125 F3
Greenfield CenBeds 82 D5
Greenfield (Maes-Glas) Flints 97 K5
Greenfield GtMan 100 C2
Greenfield High 133 N10
Greenfield Lincs 103 H5
Greenfield Oxon 72 A2
Greenford 72 E3
Greengairs 125 F3
Greengates 107 G6
Greengill 110 C3
Greenhalgh 105 H6
Greenham 71 H5
Greenhaugh 120 C5
Greenhead 120 B7
Greenheys 99 G2
Greenhill GtLon 72 E3
Greenhill SYorks 101 F4
Greenhithe 73 J4
Greenholm 124 D7
Greenholme 111 G6
Greenhow Hill 107 G3
Greenigo 139 D7
Greenlands 72 A3
Greenlaw 127 F6
Greenloaning 130 D10
Greenmeadow 69 F2
Greenmoor Hill 71 K3
Greenmount 99 G1
Greenock 124 A3
Greenodd 105 G1
Greens Norton 81 H4
Greenside T&W 121 G7
Greenside WYorks 100 D1
Greenstead 84 E6
Greenstead Green 84 C6
Greensted 73 J1
Greensted Green 73 J1
Greenway Pembs 66 D2
Greenway Som 58 C2
Greenwell 111 G1
Greenwich 73 G4
Greenwood Forest Park, Y Felinheli Gwyn LL56 4QN 96 D6
Greet 80 B5
Greete 78 E1
Greetham Lincs 103 G5
Greetham Rut 92 C4
Greetland 107 F7
Gregson Lane 105 J7
Greinton 58 D1
Grenaby 104 B6
Grendon N'hants 82 B2
Grendon Warks 90 E6
Grendon Common 90 E6
Grendon Green 78 E3
Grendon Underwood 81 H6
Grenitote (Greinetobht) 138 C1
Grenofen 54 E3
Grenoside 101 F3
Greosabhagh 138 G8
Gresford 98 C7
Gresham 95 F2
Greshornish 132 D5
Gress (Griais) 138 K3
Gressenhall 94 D4
Gressingham 105 J3
Greta Bridge 112 A5
Gretna 119 J7
Gretna Green 119 J7
Gretton Glos 80 B5
Gretton N'hants 92 C6
Gretton Shrop 88 E6
Grewelthorpe 107 H2
Greygarth 107 G2
Greylake 58 C1
Greys Green 72 A3
Greysouthen 110 B4
Greystead 120 C5
Greystoke 110 F3
Greystone 106 D5
Greystones 101 F4
Greywell 72 A6
Gribthorpe 108 D6
Gribton 118 E5
Griff 91 F7
Griffithstown 69 F2
Grigghall 111 F7
Grimeford Village 99 F1
Grimesthorpe 101 F3
Grimethorpe 101 G2
Griminish (Griminis) 138 B3
Grimister 139 N3
Grimley 79 H2
Grimmet 117 H2
Grimoldby 103 G4
Grimpo 88 C3
Grimsargh 105 J6
Grimsay (Griomsaigh) 138 C3
Grimsbury 81 F4
Grimsby 103 F2
Grimscote 81 H3
Grimscott 56 A5
Grimshader (Griomsiadar) 138 K5
Grimsthorpe 92 D3
Grimston ERid 109 J6
Grimston Leics 91 J3
Grimston Norf 94 B3
Grimstone 59 F5
Grimstone End 84 D2
Grindale 109 H2
Grindiscol 139 N9
Grindle 89 G5
Grindleford 100 E5
Grindleton 106 C5
Grindley 90 C3
Grindley Brook 88 E1
Grindlow 100 D5
Grindon N'umb 127 H6
Grindon Staffs 100 C7
Grindon Stock 112 D4
Grindon T&W 112 D1
Gringley on the Hill 101 K3
Grinsdale 110 E1
Grinshill 88 E3
Grinton 112 A7
Grisdale 111 J7
Gristhorpe 109 G1
Griston 94 D6
Gritley 139 E7
Grittenham 70 D3
Grittleton 70 B4
Grizebeck 105 F1
Grizedale 110 E7
Grizedale Forest Park Cumb LA22 0QJ 110 E7
Grobister 139 F5
Groby 91 H5
Groes 97 J6
Groes-faen 68 D3
Groesffordd 86 B2
Groesffordd Marli 97 J5
Groeslon Gwyn 96 C7
Groeslon Gwyn 96 D6
Groes-lwyd 88 B4
Groes-wen 68 E3
Grogport 123 G6
Groigearraidh 138 B5
Gromford 85 H3
Gronant 97 J4
Groombridge 63 J3
Groombridge Place Gardens Kent TN3 9QG 63 J3
Grosmont Mon 78 D6
Grosmont NYorks 113 J6
Groton 84 D4
Groundistone Heights 119 K2
Grouville 53 K7
Grove Bucks 82 C6
Grove Dorset 59 F7
Grove Kent 75 J5
Grove Notts 101 K5
Grove Oxon 71 H2
Grove End 74 E5
Grove Green 64 C2
Grove Park 73 H4
Grove Town 107 K7
Grovehill 72 D1
Grovesend SGlos 69 K3
Grovesend Swan 67 J5
Gruids 136 H9
Gruline 128 G6
Grumbla 52 B6
Grundisburgh 85 G3
Gruting 139 L8
Grutness 139 N11
Gualachulain 129 N6
Guardbridge 131 K9
Guarlford 79 H4
Gubbergill 110 B7
Gubblecote 82 C7
Guernsey 53 J5
Guernsey Airport 53 H6
Guestling Green 64 D6
Guestling Thorn 64 D6
Guestwick 94 E3
Guestwick Green 94 E3
Guide 106 C7
Guide Post 121 H5
Guilden Down 88 C7
Guilden Morden 83 F4
Guilden Sutton 98 D6
Guildford 72 C7
Guildford House Gallery Surr GU1 3AJ 40 Guildford
Guildtown 130 G7
Guilsborough 81 H1
Guilsfield (Cegidfa) 88 B4
Guilthwaite 101 G4
Guisborough 113 G5
Guiseley 107 G5
Guist 94 E3
Guith 139 E4
Guiting Power 80 B6
Gulberwick 139 N9
Gullane 126 C2
Gullane Bents ELoth EH31 2AZ 126 C2
Gulval 52 B5
Gulworthy 54 E3
Gumfreston 66 E5
Gumley 91 J6
Gunby Lincs 92 C3
Gunby Lincs 103 H6
Gundleton 61 H1
Gunn 56 E2
Gunnersbury 72 E4
Gunnerside 111 L7
Gunnerton 120 E6
Gunness 102 B1
Gunnislake 54 E3
Gunnista 139 N8
Gunstone 90 A5
Gunter's Bridge 62 C4
Gunthorpe Norf 94 E2
Gunthorpe Notts 91 J1
Gunthorpe Rut 92 B5
Gunville 61 F6
Gunwalloe 52 D6
Gupworthy 57 H2
Gurnard 61 F5
Gurnett 99 J5
Gurney Slade 69 K7
Gurnos MTyd 68 D1
Gurnos Powys 68 A1
Gushmere 65 F2
Gussage All Saints 60 B3
Gussage St. Andrew 59 J3
Gussage St. Michael 59 J3
Guston 65 J3
Gutcher 139 P3
Guthram Gowt 92 E3
Guthrie 131 L5
Guyhirn 93 G5
Guy's Head 93 H3
Guy's Marsh 59 H2
Guyzance 121 H3
Gwaelod-y-garth 68 E3
Gwaenysgor 97 J4
Gwaithla 78 B3
Gwalchmai 96 B5
Gwastad 66 D3
Gwastadnant 96 E7
Gwaun-Cae-Gurwen 77 G7
Gwaynynog 97 J6
Gwbert 66 E1
Gweek 52 E6
Gwehelog 69 G1
Gwenddwr 77 K4
Gwennap 52 E4
Gwenter 52 E7
Gwernaffield 98 B6
Gwernesney 69 H1
Gwernogle 67 J2
Gwernymynydd 98 B6
Gwern-y-Steeple 68 D4
Gwersyllt 98 C7
Gwespyr 97 K4
Gwinear 52 C5
Gwithian 52 C4
Gwredog 96 C4
Gwrhay 68 E2
Gwyddelwern 87 K1
Gwyddgrug 67 H2
Gwynfryn 98 B7
Gwystre 77 K2
Gwytherin 97 G6
Gyfelia 88 C1
Gyre 139 C7
Gyrn Goch 86 D1

H

Habberley 88 C5
Habin 62 B4
Habrough 102 E1
Haccombe 55 J3
Hacconby 92 E3
Haceby 92 D2
Hacheston 85 H3
Hackbridge 73 F5
Hackenthorpe 101 G4
Hackford 94 E5
Hackforth 112 C7
Hackleton 82 B3
Hacklinge 65 J2
Hackness 113 K7
Hackney 73 G3
Hackthorn 102 C4
Hackthorpe 111 G4
Hacton 73 J3
Hadden 127 F7
Haddenham Bucks 72 A1
Haddenham Cambs 83 H1
Haddington ELoth 126 D3
Haddington Lincs 102 C6
Haddiscoe 95 J6
Haddo Country Park Aber AB41 7EQ 135 N7
Haddon 92 E6
Hade Edge 100 D2
Hademore 90 D5
Hadfield 100 C3
Hadham Cross 83 H7
Hadham Ford 83 H6
Hadleigh Essex 74 E3
Hadleigh Suff 84 E4
Hadleigh Castle Country Park Essex SS7 2PP 74 E3
Hadleigh Heath 84 D4
Hadley Tel&W 89 F4
Hadley Worcs 79 H2
Hadley End 90 D3
Hadley Wood 73 F2
Hadlow 73 K7
Hadlow Down 63 J4
Hadnall 88 E3
Hadspen 59 F1
Hadstock 83 J4
Hadston 121 H4
Hadzor 79 J2
Haffenden Quarter 64 D3
Hafod Bridge 67 K2
Hafod-Dinbych 97 G7
Hafodunos 97 G6
Hafodyrynys 69 F2
Haggate 106 D6
Haggbeck 119 K6
Haggersta 139 M8
Haggerston GtLon 73 G3
Haggerston N'umb 127 J6
Haggrister 139 M5
Haggs 125 F3
Hagley Here 78 E4
Hagley Worcs 90 B7
Hagnaby Lincs 103 G6
Hagnaby Lincs 103 H5
Hague Bar 99 J4
Hagworthingham 103 G6
Haigh 99 F2
Haigh Hall Country Park GtMan WN2 1PE 98 E2
Haighton Green 105 J6
Hail Weston 82 E2
Haile 110 B6
Hailes 80 B5
Hailey Herts 83 G7
Hailey Oxon 71 K3
Hailey Oxon 80 E7
Hailsham 63 J6
Hainault 73 H2
Hainault Forest Country Park Essex IG7 4QN 12 G2
Haine 75 K5
Hainford 95 G4
Hainton 102 E4
Haisthorpe 109 H3
Hakin 66 B5
Halam 101 J7
Halbeath 125 K2
Halberton 57 J4
Halcro 137 Q3
Hale Cumb 105 J2
Hale GtMan 99 G4
Hale Halton 98 D4
Hale Hants 60 C3
Hale Surr 72 B7
Hale Bank 98 D4
Hale Barns 99 G4
Hale Nook 105 G5
Hale Street 73 K7
Hales Norf 95 H6
Hales Staffs 89 G2
Hales Green 90 D1
Hales Place 65 G2
Halesgate 93 G3
Halesowen 90 B7
Halesworth 85 H1
Halewood 98 D4
Half Way Inn 57 J6
Halford Devon 55 J3
Halford Shrop 88 D7
Halford Warks 80 D4
Halfpenny 105 J1
Halfpenny Green 90 A6
Halfway Carmar 67 K2
Halfway Carmar 67 J5
Halfway Powys 77 H5
Halfway SYorks 101 G4
Halfway WBerks 71 H5
Halfway Bridge 62 C4
Halfway House 88 C4
Halfway Houses Kent 75 F4
Halfway Houses Lincs 102 B6
Halghton Mill 88 D1
Halifax 107 F7
Halistra 132 C5
Halket 124 C5
Halkirk 137 P4
Halkyn 98 B5
Hall 124 C5
Hall Cross 105 H7
Hall Dunnerdale 110 D7
Hall Green ChesE 99 H7
Hall Green Lancs 105 H7
Hall Green WMid 90 D7
Hall Grove 83 F7
Hall of the Forest 88 B7
Halland 63 J5
Hallaton 92 A6
Hallatrow 69 K6
Hallbankgate 111 G1
Hallen 69 J3
Hallfield Gate 101 F7
Hallglen 125 G3
Hallin 132 C5
Halling 74 D5
Hallington Lincs 103 G4
Hallington N'umb 120 E6
Halliwell 99 F1
Halloughton 101 J7
Hallow 79 H3
Hallow Heath 79 H3
Hallrule 120 A2
Halls 126 E3
Halls Green Essex 73 H1
Hall's Green Herts 83 F6
Hallsands 55 J7
Hallthwaites 104 E1
Hallwood Green 79 F5
Hallworthy 54 B2
Hallyne 125 K6
Halmer End 89 G1
Halmond's Frome 79 F4
Halmore 69 K1
Halmyre Mains 125 K6
Halnaker 62 C6
Halsall 98 C1
Halse N'hants 81 G4
Halse Som 57 K3
Halsetown 52 C5
Halsham 109 J7
Halsinger 56 D2
Halstead Essex 84 C5
Halstead Kent 73 H5
Halstead Leics 92 A5
Halstock 58 E4
Halsway 57 K2
Haltemprice Farm 109 G6
Haltham 103 F6
Haltoft End 93 G1
Halton Bucks 82 B7
Halton Halton 98 E4
Halton Lancs 105 J3
Halton N'umb 120 E7
Halton Wrex 88 C2
Halton East 107 F4
Halton Gill 106 D2
Halton Green 105 J3
Halton Holegate 103 H6
Halton Lea Gate 111 H1
Halton Park 105 J3
Halton West 106 D4
Haltwhistle 120 C7
Halvergate 95 J5
Halwell 55 H5
Halwill 56 C6
Halwill Junction 56 C6
Ham Devon 58 B4
Ham Glos 69 K2
Ham Glos 79 J6
Ham GtLon 72 E4
Ham High 137 Q2
Ham Kent 65 J2
Ham Plym 54 E5
Ham Shet 139 H9
Ham Som 58 B2
Ham Som 58 B3
Ham Wilts 71 G5
Ham Common 59 H2
Ham Green Here 79 G4
Ham Green Kent 74 E5
Ham Green Kent 64 D5
Ham Green NSom 69 J4
Ham Green Worcs 80 B2
Ham Hill 74 C5
Ham Hill Country Park Som TA14 6RW 58 D3
Ham Street 58 E1
Hambleden 72 A3
Hambledon Hants 61 H3
Hambledon Surr 62 C3
Hamble-le-Rice 61 F4
Hambleton Lancs 105 G5
Hambleton NYorks 108 B6
Hambridge 58 C2
Hambrook SGlos 69 K4
Hambrook WSuss 61 J4
Hameringham 103 G6
Hamerton 82 E1
Hamilton 125 F5
Hamlet Devon 57 K6
Hamlet Dorset 58 E4
Hammer 62 B3
Hammerpot 62 D6
Hammersmith 73 F4
Hammersmith Apollo GtLon W6 9QH 11 F8
Hammerwich 90 C5
Hammerwood 63 H3
Hammond Street 73 G1
Hammoon 59 H3
Hamnavoe Shet 139 M9
Hamnavoe Shet 139 N4
Hamnavoe Shet 139 N5
Hamnish Clifford 78 E3
Hamp 58 B1
Hampden Park 63 K6
Hampden Park Stadium Glas G42 9BA 30 E6
Hamperden End 83 J5
Hampnett 80 C7
Hampole 101 H2
Hampreston 60 B5
Hampstead 73 F3
Hampstead Norreys 71 J4
Hampsthwaite 107 H4
Hampton Devon 58 B5
Hampton GtLon 72 E5
Hampton Kent 75 H5
Hampton Peter 92 E6
Hampton Shrop 89 G7
Hampton Swin 70 E2
Hampton Worcs 80 B4
Hampton Bishop 78 E5
Hampton Court Palace & Garden GtLon KT8 9AU 11 D11
Hampton Fields 70 B2
Hampton Heath 88 D1
Hampton in Arden 90 E7
Hampton Loade 89 G7
Hampton Lovett 79 H2
Hampton Lucy 80 D3
Hampton on the Hill 80 D2
Hampton Poyle 81 G7
Hampton Wick 72 E5
Hamptworth 60 D3
Hamsey 63 H5
Hamstall Ridware 90 D4
Hamstead 60 E5
Hamstead Marshall 71 H5
Hamsteels 112 B2
Hamsterley Dur 112 B3
Hamsterley Dur 112 B1
Hamsterley Forest Dur DL13 3NL 112 A4
Hamstreet 65 F4
Hamworthy 59 J5
Hanbury Staffs 90 D3
Hanbury Worcs 79 J2
Hanbury Woodend 90 D3
Hanby 92 D2
Hanchurch 90 A1
Handa Island 136 D5
Handale 113 H5
Handbridge 98 D6
Handcross 63 F3
Handforth 99 H4
Handley ChesW&C 98 D7
Handley Derbys 101 F6
Handley Green 74 C1
Handsacre 90 C4
Handside 83 F7
Handsworth SYorks 101 G4
Handsworth WMid 90 C6
Handwoodbank 88 D4
Handy Cross 72 B2
Hanford Dorset 59 H3
Hanford Stoke 90 A1
Hanging Bridge 90 D1
Hanging Houghton 81 J1
Hanging Langford 60 B1
Hangingshaw 119 G5
Hanham 69 K4
Hankelow 89 F1
Hankerton 70 C2
Hankham 63 K6
Hanley 90 A1
Hanley Castle 79 H4
Hanley Child 79 F2
Hanley Swan 79 H4
Hanley William 79 F2
Hanlith 106 E3
Hanmer 88 D2
Hannah 103 H5
Hannington Hants 71 J6
Hannington N'hants 82 B1
Hannington Swin 70 E2
Hannington Wick 70 E2
Hanslope 82 B4
Hanthorpe 92 D3
Hanwell GtLon 72 E3
Hanwell Oxon 81 F4
Hanwood 88 D5
Hanworth GtLon 72 E4
Hanworth Norf 95 F2
Happisburgh 95 H2
Happisburgh Common 95 H3
Hapsford 98 D5
Hapton Lancs 106 C6
Hapton Norf 95 F6
Harberton 55 H5
Harbertonford 55 H5
Harbledown 65 G2
Harborne 90 C7
Harborough Magna 81 F1
Harbost (Tabost) 138 L1
Harbottle 120 E3
Harbour Park Amusements, Littlehampton WSuss BN17 5LL 62 D6
Harbourneford 55 H4
Harbridge 60 C3
Harbridge Green 60 C3
Harburn 125 J4
Harbury 80 E3
Harby Leics 92 A2
Harby Notts 102 B5
Harcombe 57 K6
Harcombe Bottom 58 C5
Harden WMid 90 C5
Harden WYorks 107 F6
Hardendale 111 G5
Hardenhuish 70 C4
Hardgate Aber 135 M10
Hardgate NYorks 107 H3
Hardham 62 D5
Hardhorn 105 G6
Hardingham 94 E5
Hardingstone 81 J3
Hardington 70 A6
Hardington Mandeville 58 E3
Hardington Marsh 58 E4
Hardington Moor 58 E3
Hardley 61 F4
Hardley Street 95 H5
Hardmead 82 C4
Hardraw 111 K7
Hardstoft 101 G6
Hardway Hants 61 H4
Hardway Som 59 G1
Hardwick Bucks 82 B7
Hardwick Cambs 83 G3
Hardwick Lincs 102 B5
Hardwick N'hants 82 B2
Hardwick Norf 95 G6
Hardwick Oxon 71 G1
Hardwick Oxon 81 G6
Hardwick SYorks 101 G4
Hardwick WMid 90 C6
Hardwick Hall Derbys S44 5QJ 101 G6
Hardwick Hall Country Park, Sedgefield Dur TS21 2EH 112 D4
Hardwick Village 101 J5
Hardwicke Glos 79 J6
Hardwicke Glos 79 J7
Hardwicke Here 78 B4
Hardy's Green 84 D6
Hare Green 84 E6
Hare Hatch 72 B4
Hare Street Herts 83 G6
Hare Street Herts 83 G6
Hareby 103 G6
Hareden 106 B4
Harefield 72 D2
Harehill 90 D2
Harehills 107 J6
Harehope 121 F1
Harelaw 125 H6
Hareplain 64 D4
Haresceugh 111 H2
Harescombe 79 H7
Haresfield 79 H7
Hareshaw NLan 125 G4
Hareshaw SLan 124 E6
Harestock 61 F1
Harewood 107 J5
Harewood End 78 E6
Harewood House WYorks LS17 9LG 107 J5
Harford Devon 55 G5
Harford Devon 57 G6
Hargate 95 F6
Hargatewall 100 D5
Hargrave ChesW&C 98 D6
Hargrave N'hants 82 D1
Hargrave Suff 84 B3
Hargrave Green 84 B3
Harker 119 J7
Harkstead 85 F5
Harlaston 90 E4
Harlaxton 92 B2
Harle Syke 106 D6
Harlech 86 E2
Harlech Castle Gwyn LL46 2YH 86 E2
Harlequin 91 J2
Harlescott 88 E4
Harlesden 73 F3
Harleston Devon 55 H6
Harleston Norf 95 G7
Harleston Suff 84 E2
Harlestone 81 J2
Harley Shrop 88 E5
Harley SYorks 101 F3
Harleyholm 125 H7
Harlington CenBeds 82 D5
Harlington GtLon 72 D4
Harlosh 132 C6
Harlow 73 H1
Harlow Hill 121 F7
Harlthorpe 108 D6
Harlton 83 G3
Harlyn 53 F1
Harman's Cross 59 J6
Harmby 107 G1
Harmer Green 83 F7
Harmer Hill 88 D3
Harmondsworth 72 D4
Harmston 102 C6
Harnage 88 E5
Harnham 60 C2
Harnhill 70 D1
Harold Hill 73 J2
Harold Park 73 J2
Harold Wood 73 J2
Haroldston West 66 B4
Haroldswick 139 Q1
Harome 108 C1
Harpenden 82 E7
Harpford 57 J6
Harpham 109 G3
Harpley Norf 94 B3
Harpley Worcs 79 F2
Harpole 81 H2
Harprigg 106 B1
Harpsden 72 A3
Harpswell 102 C4
Harpur Hill 100 C5
Harpurhey 99 H2
Harracott 56 D3
Harrietfield 130 E8
Harrietsham 64 D2
Harringay 73 G3
Harrington Cumb 110 A4
Harrington Lincs 103 G5
Harrington N'hants 81 J1
Harringworth 92 C6
Harris 132 D11
Harris Green 95 G6
Harris Museum & Art Gallery, Preston Lancs PR1 2PP 105 J7
Harriseahead 99 H7
Harriston 110 C2
Harrogate 107 J4
Harrogate International Centre NYorks HG1 5LA 40 Harrogate
Harrold 82 C3
Harrold-Odell Country Park Bed MK43 7DS 82 C3
Harrop Fold 106 C5
Harrow 72 E3
Harrow Green 84 C3
Harrow Museum GtLon HA2 6PX 10 C4
Harrow on the Hill 72 E3
Harrow Weald 72 E2
Harrowbarrow 54 E3
Harrowden 82 D4
Harrowgate Hill 112 C5
Harry Stoke 69 K4
Harston Cambs 83 H3
Harston Leics 92 B2
Harswell 108 E5
Hart 112 E3
Hartburn 121 F5
Hartest 84 C3
Hartfield 63 H3
Hartford Cambs 83 F1
Hartford ChesW&C 99 F5
Hartford Som 57 H3
Hartford End 83 K7
Hartfordbridge 72 A6
Hartforth 112 B6
Hartgrove 59 H3
Harthill ChesW&C 98 E7
Harthill NLan 125 H4
Harthill SYorks 101 G4
Hartington 100 D6
Hartington Hall 121 F5
Hartland 56 A3
Hartland Quay 56 A3
Hartlebury 79 H1
Hartlepool 113 F3
Hartlepool's Maritime Experience Hart TS24 0XZ 113 F3
Hartley Cumb 111 J6
Hartley Kent 74 C5
Hartley Kent 64 C4
Hartley N'umb 121 J6
Hartley Green 90 B3
Hartley Mauditt 61 J1
Hartley Wespall 71 K6
Hartley Wintney 72 A6
Hartlington 107 F3
Hartlip 74 E5
Hartoft End 113 H7
Harton NYorks 108 D3
Harton Shrop 88 D7
Harton T&W 121 J7
Hartpury 79 H6
Hartrigge 120 B1
Hartshead 107 G7
Hartshill 91 F6
Hartsholme Country Park Lincs LN6 0EY 102 C6
Hartshorne 91 F3
Hartsop 110 F5
Hartwell Bucks 81 J7
Hartwell ESuss 63 H3
Hartwell N'hants 81 J3
Hartwith 107 H3
Hartwood 125 G5
Harvel 74 C5
Harvington Worcs 80 B4
Harvington Worcs 79 H1
Harwell Notts 101 J3
Harwell Oxon 71 H3
Harwich 85 G5
Harwood Dur 111 K3
Harwood GtMan 99 G1
Harwood N'umb 121 F4
Harwood Dale 113 K7
Harwood on Teviot 119 K3
Harworth 101 J3
Hasbury 90 B7
Hascombe 72 D7
Haselbech 81 J1
Haselbury Plucknett 58 D3
Haseley 80 D2
Haseley Knob 80 D1
Haselor 80 C3
Hasfield 79 H6
Hasguard 66 B5
Haskayne 98 C2
Hasketon 85 G3
Hasland 101 F6
Hasland Green 101 F6
Haslemere 62 C3
Haslingden 106 C7
Haslingden Grane 106 C7
Haslingfield 83 H3
Haslington 99 G7
Hassall 99 G7
Hassall Green 99 G7
Hassell Street 65 F3
Hassendean 120 A1
Hassingham 95 H5
Hassocks 63 G5
Hassop 100 E5
Hasthorpe 103 H6
Hastigrow 137 Q3
Hastingleigh 65 F3
Hastings ESuss 64 D7
Hastings Som 58 C3
Hastings Fishermen's Museum ESuss TN34 3DW 40 Hastings
Hastingwood 73 H1
Hastoe 72 C1
Haswell 112 D2
Haswell Plough 112 D2
Hatch CenBeds 82 E4
Hatch Hants 71 K6
Hatch Beauchamp 58 C2
Hatch End 72 E2
Hatch Green 58 C3
Hatching Green 82 E7
Hatchmere 98 E5
Hatcliffe 103 F2
Hatfield Here 78 E3
Hatfield Herts 73 F1
Hatfield SYorks 101 J2
Hatfield Broad Oak 83 J7
Hatfield Heath 83 J7
Hatfield House Herts AL9 5NF 73 F1
Hatfield Peverel 84 B7
Hatfield Woodhouse 101 J2
Hatford 71 G2
Hatherden 71 G6
Hatherleigh 56 D5
Hathern 91 G3
Hatherop 70 E1
Hathersage 100 E4
Hathersage Booths 100 E4
Hathershaw 99 J2
Hatherton ChesE 89 F1
Hatherton Staffs 90 B4
Hatley St. George 83 F3
Hatt 54 D4
Hattingley 61 H1
Hatton Aber 135 Q7
Hatton Derbys 90 E3
Hatton GtLon 72 E4
Hatton Lincs 102 E5
Hatton Shrop 88 D6
Hatton Warks 80 D2
Hatton Warr 98 E4
Hatton Country World Warks CV35 8XA 80 D2
Hatton Heath 98 D6
Hatton of Fintray 135 N9
Haugh 103 H5
Haugh Head 121 F1
Haugh of Glass 135 J7
Haugh of Urr 115 J4
Haugham 103 G4
Haughhead 124 E3
Haughley 84 E2
Haughley Green 84 E2
Haughley New Street 84 E2
Haughton ChesE 98 E7
Haughton Notts 101 J5
Haughton Powys 88 C4
Haughton Shrop 89 F6
Haughton Shrop 88 E4
Haughton Shrop 88 C3
Haughton Staffs 90 A3
Haughton Green 99 J3
Haughton Le Skerne 112 D5
Haultwick 83 G6
Haunton 90 E4
Hauxton 83 H3
Havannah 99 H6
Havant 61 J4
Haven 78 D3
Havenstreet 61 G5
Havercroft 101 F1
Haverfordwest (Hwlffordd) 66 C4
Haverhill 83 K4
Haverigg 104 E2
Havering Park 73 H2
Havering-atte-Bower 73 J2
Haversham 82 B4
Haverthwaite 105 G1
Haverton Hill 112 E4
Haviker Street 64 C3
Havyat 58 E1
Hawarden (Penarlâg) 98 C6
Hawbridge 79 J4
Hawbush Green 84 B6
Hawcoat 105 F2
Hawes 106 D1
Hawe's Green 95 G6
Hawick 120 A2
Hawkchurch 58 C4
Hawkedon 84 B3
Hawkenbury Kent 63 J3
Hawkenbury Kent 64 D3
Hawkeridge 70 B6
Hawkerland 57 J7
Hawkes End 90 E7
Hawkesbury 70 A3
Hawkesbury Upton 70 A3
Hawkhill 121 H2
Hawkhurst 64 C4
Hawkinge 65 H3
Hawkley 61 J2
Hawkridge 57 G2
Hawkshead 110 E7
Hawkshead Hill 110 E7
Hawksheads 105 H3
Hawksland 125 G6
Hawkswick 106 E2
Hawksworth Notts 92 A1
Hawksworth WYorks 107 G5
Hawksworth WYorks 107 H6
Hawkwell Essex 74 E2
Hawkwell N'umb 121 F6
Hawley Hants 72 B6
Hawley Kent 73 J4
Hawley's Corner 73 H6
Hawling 80 B6
Hawnby 108 B1
Haworth 107 F6
Hawstead 84 C3
Hawstead Green 84 C3
Hawthorn Dur 112 E2
Hawthorn RCT 68 D3
Hawthorn Wilts 70 B5
Hawthorn Hill BrackF 72 B4
Hawthorn Hill Lincs 103 F7
Hawthorpe 92 D3
Hawton 101 K7
Haxby 108 C4
Haxey 101 K2
Haxted 73 H7
Haxton 70 E7
Hay Green 93 J4
Hay Mills 90 D7
Hay Street 83 G6
Haydock 98 E3
Haydon Dorset 59 F3
Haydon Swin 70 E3
Haydon Bridge 120 D7
Haydon Wick 70 E3
Hayes GtLon 72 D3
Hayes GtLon 73 H5
Hayes End 72 D3
Hayfield Derbys 100 C4
Hayfield Fife 126 A1
Haygrove 58 B1
Hayhillock 131 L6
Hayle 52 C5
Hayling Island 61 J4
Haymoor Green 99 F7
Hayne 57 H4
Haynes 82 E4
Haynes Church End 82 D4
Haynes West End 82 D4
Hay-on-Wye (Y Gelli Gandryll) 78 B4
Hayscastle 66 B3
Hayscastle Cross 66 C3
Hayton Cumb 111 G1
Hayton Cumb 110 C2
Hayton ERid 108 E5
Hayton Notts 101 K4
Hayton's Bent 88 E7
Haytor Vale 55 H3
Haytown 56 B4
Hayward Gallery GtLon SE1 8XZ 44 F4
Haywards Heath 63 G4
Haywood Oaks 101 J7
Hazel End 83 H6
Hazel Grove 99 J4
Hazel Street 63 K3
Hazelbank 125 G6
Hazelbury Bryan 59 G4
Hazeleigh 74 E1
Hazeley 72 A6
Hazelhurst 99 G1
Hazelside 118 D1
Hazelslack 105 H2
Hazelslade 90 C4
Hazelwood Derbys 91 F1
Hazelwood GtLon 73 H5
Hazlefield 115 H6
Hazlehead Aberdeen 135 N10
Hazlehead SYorks 100 D2
Hazlemere 72 B2
Hazlerigg 121 H6
Hazleton 80 B7
Hazon 121 G3
Heacham 94 A2
Head Bridge 56 E4
Headbourne Worthy 61 F1
Headcorn 64 D3
Headingley 107 H6
Headington 71 J1
Headlam 112 B5
Headless Cross 80 B2
Headley Hants 62 B3
Headley Hants 71 J5
Headley Surr 73 F6
Headley Down 62 B3
Headley Heath 80 B1
Headon 101 K5
Heads Nook 111 F1
Heady Hill 99 H1
Heage 101 F7
Healaugh NYorks 112 A7
Healaugh NYorks 108 B5
Heald Green 99 H4
Heale Devon 56 E1
Heale Som 58 C2
Healey Lancs 99 H1
Healey N'umb 112 A1
Healey NYorks 107 G1
Healey WYorks 107 H7
Healeyfield 112 A2
Healey's Cornish Cyder Farm Corn TR4 9LW 52 E3
Healing 103 F1
Heamoor 52 B5
Heaning 110 F7
Heanor 91 G1
Heanton Punchardon 56 D2
Heanton Satchville 56 D4
Heap Bridge 99 H1
Heapey 106 B7
Heapham 102 B4
Hearn 62 B3
Heart of the Country Centre Staffs WS14 9QR 90 D5
Hearthstane 119 G1
Heasley Mill 57 F2
Heast 132 G9
Heath Cardiff 68 E3
Heath Derbys 101 G6
Heath & Reach 82 C6
Heath End Derbys 91 F3
Heath End Hants 71 J5
Heath End Hants 71 H5
Heath End Surr 72 B7
Heath Hayes 90 C4
Heath Hill 89 G4
Heath House 69 H7
Heath Town 90 B6
Heathbrook 89 F3
Heathcote Derbys 100 D6
Heathcote Shrop 89 F3
Heathencote 81 J4
Heather 91 F4
Heatherton Activity Park Pembs SA70 8RJ 66 D5
Heathfield Devon 55 J3
Heathfield ESuss 63 J4
Heathfield NYorks 107 G3
Heathfield Som 57 K3
Heathrow Airport 72 D4
Heathton 90 A6
Heatley 99 G4
Heaton Lancs 105 H3
Heaton Staffs 99 J6
Heaton T&W 121 H7
Heaton WYorks 107 G6
Heaton Moor 99 H3
Heaton Park GtMan M25 2SW 25 G2
Heaton's Bridge 98 D1
Heaverham 73 J6
Heaviley 99 J4
Heavitree 57 H6
Hebburn 121 J7
Hebden 107 F3
Hebden Bridge 106 E7
Hebden Green 99 F6
Hebing End 83 G6
Hebron Carmar 66 E3
Hebron N'umb 121 G5
Heck 119 F5
Heckfield 72 A5
Heckfield Green 85 F1
Heckfordbridge 84 D6
Heckingham 95 H6
Heckington 92 E1
Heckmondwike 107 H7
Heddington 70 C5
Heddon-on-the-Wall 121 G7
Hedenham 95 H6
Hedge End 61 F3
Hedgerley 72 C3
Hedging 58 C2
Hedley on the Hill 112 A1
Hednesford 90 C4
Hedon 109 H7
Hedsor 72 C3
Heeley 101 F4
Heighington Darl 112 C4
Heighington Lincs 102 D6
Heightington 79 G1
Heights of Brae 133 R4
Heilam 136 G4
Heisker Islands (Monach Islands) 138 A2
Heithat 119 G5
Heiton 127 F7
Hele Devon 56 D1
Hele Devon 57 H5
Hele Devon 56 B6
Hele Devon 55 H3
Hele Som 57 K3
Hele Torbay 55 K4
Hele Bridge 56 D5
Hele Lane 57 F4
Helebridge 56 A5
Helensburgh 124 A2
Helford 52 E6
Helhoughton 94 C3
Helions Bumpstead 83 K4
Hell Corner 71 G5
Hellaby 101 H3
Helland Corn 54 A3
Helland Som 58 C2
Hellandbridge 54 A3
Hellesdon 95 G4
Hellidon 81 G3
Hellifield 106 D4
Hellingly 63 J5
Hellington 95 H5
Helmdon 81 G4
Helmingham 85 F3
Helmington Row 112 B3
Helmsdale 137 N8
Helmshore 106 C7
Helmsley 108 C1
Helperby 107 K3
Helperthorpe 109 F2
Helpringham 92 E1
Helpston 92 E5
Helsby 98 D5
Helsey 103 J5
Helston 52 D6
Helstone 54 A2
Helton 111 G4
Helwith 112 A6
Helwith Bridge 106 D3
Hem 88 B5
Hemborough Post 55 J5
Hemel Hempstead 72 D1
Hemerdon 55 F5
Hemingbrough 108 C6
Hemingby 103 F5
Hemingfield 101 F2
Hemingford Abbots 83 F1
Hemingford Grey 83 F1
Hemingstone 85 F3
Hemington Leics 91 G3
Hemington N'hants 92 D7
Hemington Som 70 A6
Hemley 85 G4
Hemlington 113 F5
Hemp Green 85 H2
Hempholme 109 G4
Hempnall 95 G6
Hempnall Green 95 G6
Hempstead Essex 83 K5
Hempstead Med 74 D5
Hempstead Norf 95 J3
Hempstead Norf 95 F2
Hempsted 79 H7
Hempton Norf 94 D3
Hempton Oxon 81 F5
Hemsby 95 J4
Hemswell 102 C3
Hemswell Cliff 102 C4
Hemsworth 101 G1
Hemyock 57 K4
Henbury Bristol 69 J4
Henbury ChesE 99 H5
Henderland 115 J3
Hendersyde Park 127 F7
Hendham 55 H5
Hendon GtLon 73 F3
Hendon T&W 112 D1
Hendraburnick 54 B2
Hendre Bridgend 68 C3
Hendre Gwyn 86 C2
Hendreforgan 68 C3
Hendy 67 J5
Heneglwys 96 C5
Henfield SGlos 69 K4
Henfield WSuss 63 F5
Henford 56 B6
Henghurst 64 E4
Hengoed Caerp 68 E2
Hengoed Powys 78 B3
Hengoed Shrop 88 B2
Hengrave 84 C2
Henham 83 J6
Heniarth 88 A5
Henlade 58 B2
Henley Dorset 59 F4
Henley Shrop 78 E1
Henley Som 58 D1
Henley Som 58 D4
Henley Suff 85 F3
Henley WSuss 62 B4
Henley Corner 58 D1
Henley Park 72 C6
Henley-in-Arden 80 C2
Henley-on-Thames 72 A3
Henley's Down 64 C6
Henllan Carmar 67 G1
Henllan Denb 97 J6
Henllan Amgoed 66 E3
Henllys 69 F2
Henlow 82 E5
Hennock 57 G7
Henny Street 84 C5
Henryd 97 F5
Henry's Moat 66 D3
Hensall 108 B7
Henshaw 120 C7
Hensingham 110 A5
Henstead 95 J7
Hensting 61 F2
Henstridge 59 G3
Henstridge Ash 59 G3
Henstridge Bowden 59 F2
Henstridge Marsh 59 G2
Henton Oxon 72 A1
Henton Som 69 H7
Henwood 54 C3
Heogan 139 N8
Heol Senni 77 J6
Heolgerrig 68 D1
Heol-y-Cyw 68 C3
Hepburn 121 F1
Hepburn Bell 121 F1
Hepple 120 E3
Hepscott 121 H5
Hepthorne Lane 101 G6
Heptonstall 106 E7
Hepworth Suff 84 D1
Hepworth WYorks 100 D2
Hepworth South Common 84 D1
Herbrandston 66 B5
Hereford 78 E4
Hereford Cathedral Here HR1 2NG 40 Hereford
Heriot 126 B5
Heritage Motor Centre, Gaydon Warks CV35 0BJ 80 E3
Herm 53 K5
Hermiston 125 K3
Hermitage D&G 115 H4
Hermitage Dorset 59 F4
Hermitage ScBord 120 A4
Hermitage WBerks 71 J4
Hermitage WSuss 61 J4
Hermitage Green 99 F3
Hermon Carmar 67 G2
Hermon IoA 96 B6
Hermon Pembs 67 F2
Herne 75 H5
Herne Bay 75 H5
Herne Common 75 H5
Herne Pound 73 K6
Herner 56 D3
Hernhill 75 G5
Herodsfoot 54 C4
Herongate 74 C2
Heron's Ghyll 63 H4
Heronsgate 72 D2
Herriard 71 K7
Herringfleet 95 J6
Herring's Green 82 D4
Herringswell 84 B2
Herringthorpe 101 G3
Hersden 75 H5
Hersham Corn 56 A5
Hersham Surr 72 E5
Herstmonceux 63 K5
Herston 139 D8
Hertford 83 G7
Hertford Heath 83 G7
Hertingfordbury 83 G7
Hesket Newmarket 110 E3
Hesketh Bank 105 H7
Hesketh Lane 106 B5
Heskin Green 98 E1
Hesleden 112 E3
Hesleyside 120 D5
Heslington 108 C4
Hessay 108 B4
Hessenford 54 D5
Hessett 84 D2
Hessle 109 G7
Hest Bank 105 H3
Hester's Way 79 J6
Hestley Green 85 F2
Heston 72 E4
Heswall 98 B4
Hethe 81 G6
Hethelpit Cross 79 G6
Hetherington 120 D6
Hethersett 95 F5
Hethersgill 119 K7
Hethpool 120 D1
Hett 112 C3
Hetton 106 E4
Hetton-le-Hole 112 D2
Heugh 121 F6
Heugh-head 134 H9
Heveningham 85 H1
Hever 73 H7
Hever Castle & Gardens Kent TN8 7NG 73 H7
Heversham 105 H1
Hevingham 95 F3
Hewas Water 53 G4
Hewell Grange 80 B2
Hewell Lane 80 B2
Hewelsfield 69 J1
Hewelsfield Common 69 J1
Hewish NSom 69 H5
Hewish Som 58 D4
Hewood 58 C4
Heworth 108 C4
Hewton 56 E6
Hexham 120 E7
Hexham Abbey N'umb NE46 3NB 120 E7
Hextable 73 J4
Hexthorpe 101 H2
Hexton 82 E5
Hexworthy 55 G3
Hey 106 D5
Hey Houses 105 G7
Heybridge Essex 74 C2
Heybridge Essex 74 E1
Heybridge Basin 74 E1
Heybrook Bay 54 E6
Heydon Cambs 83 H4
Heydon Norf 95 F3
Heydour 92 D2
Heyop 78 B1
Heysham 105 H3
Heyshaw 107 G3
Heyshott 62 B5

Joy's Green **79** F7
Jumpers Common **60** C5
Juniper Green **125** K4
Juniper Hill **81** G5
Jura **122** D2
Jura House **122** C4
Jurby East **104** C4
Jurby West **104** C4

K

Kaber **111** J5
Kaimes **126** A4
Kames *A&B* **123** H3
Kames *EAyr* **118** B1
Kathellan *Fife* KY4 0JR **125** K1
Kea **53** F4
Keadby **102** B1
Keal Cotes **103** G6
Kearsley **99** G2
Kearstwick **106** B2
Kearton **112** A7
Keasden **106** C3
Keckwick **98** E4
Keddington **103** G4
Keddington Corner **103** G4
Kedington **84** B4
Kedleston **91** F1
Keelby **102** E1
Keele **90** A1
Keeley Green **82** D4
Keelham **107** F6
Keenthorne **58** B1
Keeres Green **83** J7
Keeston **66** B4
Keevil **70** C6
Kegworth **91** G3
Kehelland **52** D4
Keighley **107** F5
Keighley & Worth Valley Railway *WYorks* BD22 8NJ **107** F5
Keil **116** A3
Keilhill **135** M5
Keillmore **122** E2
Keills **122** C4
Keils **122** D4
Keinton Mandeville **58** E1
Keir House **125** F1
Keir Mill **118** D4
Keisby **92** D3
Keisley **111** J4
Keiss **137** R3
Keith **135** J5
Kelbrook **106** E5
Kelby **92** D1
Keld *Cumb* **111** G5
Keld *NYorks* **111** K6
Keldholme **108** D1
Keldy Castle **113** H7
Kelfield *NLincs* **102** B2
Kelfield *NYorks* **108** B6
Kelham **101** K7
Kella **104** C4
Kellacott **56** C7
Kellan **128** G6
Kellas *Angus* **131** K7
Kellas *Moray* **134** F5
Kellaton **55** H7
Kellaways **70** C4
Kelleth **111** H6
Kelleythorpe **109** G4
Kelling **94** E1
Kellington **108** B7
Kelloe **112** D3
Kelloholm **118** C2
Kelly *Corn* **54** A3
Kelly *Devon* **56** B7
Kelly Bray **54** D3
Kelmarsh **81** J1
Kelmscott **71** F2
Kelsale **85** H2
Kelsall **98** E6
Kelsay **122** A5
Kelshall **83** G5
Kelsick **110** D1
Kelso **127** F7
Kelstedge **101** F6
Kelstern **103** F3
Kelston **70** A5
Kelton **115** K3
Kelton Hill (Rhonehouse) **115** H5
Kelty **125** K1
Kelvedon **84** C7
Kelvedon Hatch **73** J2
Kelvingrove Art Gallery & Museum *Glas* G3 8AG **39** B2
Kelvinside **124** D4
Kelynack **52** A6
Kemacott **56** E1
Kemback **131** K9
Kemberton **89** G5
Kemble **70** C2
Kemerton **79** J5
Kemeys Commander **69** G1
Kemeys Inferior **69** G2
Kemnay **135** M9
Kemp Town **63** G6
Kempe's Corner **65** F3
Kempley **79** F6
Kempley Green **79** F6
Kemps Green **80** C1
Kempsey **79** H4
Kempsford **70** E2
Kempshott **71** J7
Kempston **82** D4
Kempston Hardwick **82** D4
Kempston West End **82** C4
Kempton **88** C7
Kemsing **73** J6
Kemsley **75** F5
Kenardington **64** E4
Kenchester **78** D4
Kencot **71** F1
Kendal **111** G7
Kenderchurch **78** D6
Kendleshire **69** K4
Kenfig **68** A3
Kenfig Hill **68** B3
Kenidjack **52** A5
Kenilworth **80** D1
Kenilworth Castle *Warks* CV8 1NE **16** A6
Kenknock **129** R7
Kenley *GtLon* **73** G5
Kenley *Shrop* **88** E5
Kenmore *High* **132** H5
Kenmore *P&K* **130** C6
Kenn *Devon* **57** H7
Kenn *NSom* **69** H5
Kennacraig **123** G4
Kennards House **54** C2
Kennavay **138** H8
Kenneggy Downs **52** C6
Kennerleigh **57** G5
Kennet **125** H1
Kennethmont **135** K8
Kennett **83** K2
Kennford **57** H7
Kenninghall **94** E7
Kennington *Kent* **65** F3
Kennington *Oxon* **71** J1
Kennoway **131** J10
Kenny **58** C3
Kennyhill **83** K1
Kennythorpe **108** D3
Kenovay **128** A6
Kensaleyre **132** E5
Kensington **73** F3
Kensington Palace *GtLon* W8 4PX **11** G7
Kenstone **88** E3
Kensworth **82** D7
Kent & East Sussex Railway *Kent* TN30 6HE **64** D5
Kent International Airport **75** K5
Kent Street *ESuss* **64** C6
Kent Street *Kent* **73** K6
Kentallen (Ceann an t-Sàilein) **129** M5
Kentchurch **78** D6
Kentford **84** B2
Kentisbeare **57** J5
Kentisbury **56** E1
Kentisbury Ford **56** E1
Kentish Town **73** F3
Kentmere **111** F6
Kenton *Devon* **57** H7
Kenton *Suff* **85** F2
Kenton *T&W* **121** H7
Kenton Corner **85** G2
Kentra **128** H4
Kents Bank **105** G2
Kent's Green **79** G6
Kent's Oak **60** E2
Kenwick **88** D2
Kenwood House *GtLon* NW3 7JR **10** H4
Kenwyn **53** F4
Kenyon **99** F3
Keoldale **136** F3
Keose (Ceòs) **138** J5
Keppoch *A&B* **124** B3
Keppoch *High* **133** J8
Keprigan **116** A2
Kepwick **112** E7
Keresley **91** F7
Kernborough **55** H6
Kerrera **129** K8
Kerridge **99** J5
Kerris **52** B6
Kerry (Ceri) **88** A6
Kerrycroy **123** K4
Kerry's Gate **78** C5
Kerrysdale **133** J3
Kersall **101** K6
Kersey **84** E4
Kersey Vale **84** E4
Kershopefoot **119** K5
Kerswell **57** J5
Kerswell Green **79** H4
Kerthen Wood **52** C5
Kesgrave **85** G4
Kessingland **95** K7
Kessingland Beach **95** K7
Kestle **53** G4
Kestle Mill **53** F3
Keston **73** H5
Keswick *Cumb* **110** D4
Keswick *Norf* **95** G5
Keswick *Norf* **95** H2
Ketley Bank **89** F4
Ketsby **103** G5
Kettering **82** B1
Ketteringham **95** F5
Kettins **130** H7
Kettle Corner **64** C2
Kettlebaston **84** D3
Kettlebrook **90** E5
Kettleburgh **85** G2
Kettlehill **131** J10
Kettleholm **119** G6
Kettleness **113** J5
Kettleshulme **99** J5
Kettlesing **107** H4
Kettlesing Bottom **107** H4
Kettlesing Head **107** H4
Kettlestone **94** D2
Kettlethorpe **102** B5
Kettletoft **139** F4
Kettlewell **106** E2
Ketton **92** C5
Kevingtown **73** H5
Kew **72** E4
Kewstoke **69** G5
Kexbrough **101** F2
Kexby *Lincs* **102** B4
Kexby *York* **108** D4
Key Green **99** H6
Keyham **91** J5
Keyhaven **60** E5
Keyingham **109** J7
Keymer **63** G5
Keynsham **69** K5
Key's Toft **103** H7
Keysoe **82** D2
Keysoe Row **82** D2
Keyston **82** D1
Keyworth **91** J2
Kibblesworth **112** C1
Kibworth Beauchamp **91** J6
Kibworth Harcourt **91** J6
Kidbrooke **73** H4
Kiddemore Green **90** A5
Kidderminster **79** H1
Kiddington **81** F6
Kidlington **81** F7
Kidmore End **71** K4
Kidnal **88** D1
Kidsdale **114** E7
Kidsgrove **99** H7
Kidstones **106** E1
Kidwelly (Cydweli) **67** H5
Kielder **120** B4
Kielder Forest *N'umb* NE48 1ER **120** B4
Kielder Water *N'umb* NE48 1BX **120** C5
Kilbarchan **124** C4
Kilberry **123** F4
Kilbirnie **124** B5
Kilbride *A&B* **129** K8
Kilbride *A&B* **123** J4
Kilbride Farm **123** H4
Kilbridemore **123** J1
Kilburn *Derbys* **91** F1
Kilburn *GtLon* **73** F3
Kilburn *NYorks* **108** B2
Kilby **91** J6
Kilchattan Bay **123** K5
Kilchenzie **116** A1
Kilcheran **129** K7
Kilchiaran **122** A4
Kilchoan *A&B* **129** J9
Kilchoan *High* **128** F4
Kilchoman **122** A4
Kilchrenan (Cill Chrèanain) **129** M8
Kilchrist **116** A2
Kilconquhar **131** K10
Kilcot **79** F6
Kilcoy **133** R5
Kilcreggan **124** A2
Kildale **113** G6
Kildary **134** B3
Kildavie **116** B2
Kildonan **116** E1
Kildonan Lodge **137** M7
Kildonnan **128** F2
Kildrochet House **114** A5
Kildrummy **135** J9
Kildwick **107** F5
Kilfinan **123** H3
Kilfinnan **133** N11
Kilgetty **66** E5
Kilgwrrwg Common **69** H2
Kilham *ERid* **109** G3
Kilham *N'umb* **127** G7
Kilkenneth **128** A6
Kilkenny **80** B7
Kilkerran *A&B* **116** B2
Kilkerran *SAyr* **117** H3
Kilkhampton **56** A4
Killamarsh **101** G4
Killay **67** K6
Killean **122** E6
Killearn **124** D2
Killellan **116** A2
Killen **134** A5
Killerby **112** B4
Killerton **57** H5
Killerton *Devon* EX5 3LE **57** H5
Killichonan **130** A5
Killiechonate **129** P2
Killiechronan **128** G6
Killiecrankie **130** E4
Killilan **133** K7
Killimster **137** R4
Killin **130** A7
Killinallan **122** B3
Killinghall **107** H4
Killington *Cumb* **106** B1
Killington *Devon* **56** E1
Killingworth **121** H6
Killochyett **126** C6
Killocraw **122** E7
Killundine **128** G6
Kilmacolm **124** B4
Kilmahog **130** B10
Kilmalieu **129** K5
Kilmaluag **132** E3
Kilmany **131** J8
Kilmarie **132** F9
Kilmarnock **124** C7
Kilmartin **123** G1
Kilmaurs **124** C6
Kilmelford **129** K9
Kilmeny **122** B4
Kilmersdon **69** K6
Kilmeston **61** G2
Kilmichael **116** A1
Kilmichael Glassary **123** G1
Kilmichael of Inverlussa **123** F2
Kilmington *Devon* **58** B5
Kilmington *Wilts* **59** G1
Kilmington Common **59** G1
Kilmorack **133** Q6
Kilmore (A' Chille Mhòr) *A&B* **129** K8
Kilmore *High* **132** G10
Kilmory *A&B* **123** F2
Kilmory *A&B* **123** F3
Kilmory *High* **132** D10
Kilmory *High* **128** G3
Kilmory *NAyr* **116** D1
Kilmuir *High* **134** A6
Kilmuir *High* **134** B3
Kilmun **123** K2
Kiln Green *Here* **79** F7
Kiln Green *W'ham* **72** B4
Kiln Pit Hill **112** A1
Kilnave **122** A3
Kilncadzow **125** G6
Kilndown **64** C4
Kilnhurst **101** G3
Kilninian **128** F6
Kilninver **129** K8
Kilnsea **103** H1
Kilnsey **106** E3
Kilnwick **109** F5
Kilnwick Percy **108** E4
Kiloran **122** B1
Kilpatrick **116** D1
Kilpeck **78** D5
Kilphedir **137** M8
Kilpin **108** D7
Kilpin Pike **108** D7
Kilrenny **131** L10
Kilsby **81** G1
Kilspindie **130** H8
Kilstay **114** B7
Kilsyth **125** F3
Kiltarlity **133** R6
Kilton *Notts* **101** H5
Kilton *R&C* **113** G5
Kilton *Som* **57** K1
Kilton Thorpe **113** G5
Kiltyrie **130** B7
Kilvaxter **132** D4
Kilve **57** K1
Kilverstone **94** C7
Kilvington **92** B1
Kilwinning **124** B6
Kimberley *Norf* **94** E5
Kimberley *Notts* **91** H1
Kimberworth **101** G3
Kimble Wick **72** B1
Kimblesworth **112** C2
Kimbolton *Cambs* **82** D2
Kimbolton *Here* **78** E2
Kimbridge **60** E1
Kimcote **91** H7
Kimmeridge **59** J7
Kimmerston **127** H7
Kimpton *Hants* **71** F7
Kimpton *Herts* **82** E7
Kinbrace **137** L6
Kinbuck **130** C10
Kincaple **131** K9
Kincardine *Fife* **125** H2
Kincardine *High* **134** A2
Kincardine O'Neil **135** K11
Kinclaven **130** G7
Kincorth **135** P10
Kincraig **134** C10
Kindallachan **130** E5
Kineton *Glos* **80** B6
Kineton *Warks* **80** E3
Kineton Green **90** D7
Kinfauns **130** G8
King Sterndale **100** C5
Kingarth **123** J5
Kingcoed **69** H1
Kingerby **102** D3
Kingham **80** D6
Kingholm Quay **115** K3
Kinghorn **126** A2
Kinglassie **126** A1
Kingoodie **131** J8
King's Acre **78** D4
King's Bank **64** D5
King's Bromley **90** D4
Kings Caple **78** E6
King's Cliffe **92** D6
King's College Chapel, Cambridge *Cambs* CB2 1ST **83** H3
King's Coughton **80** B3
King's Green **79** G5
King's Heath **90** C7
Kings Hill *Kent* **73** K6
King's Hill *Warks* **80** E1
King's Hill *WMid* **90** B6
Kings Langley **72** D1
King's Lynn **94** A3
King's Meaburn **111** H4
Kings Mills **53** H5
King's Moss **98** E2
Kings Muir **126** A7
King's Newnham **81** F1
King's Newton **91** F3
King's Norton *Leics* **91** J5
King's Norton *WMid* **80** B1
Kings Nympton **56** E4
King's Pyon **78** D3
Kings Ripton **83** F1
King's Somborne **60** E1
King's Stag **59** G3
King's Stanley **70** B1
King's Sutton **81** F5
King's Tamerton **54** E5
King's Walden **82** E6
Kings Worthy **61** F1
Kingsand **54** E5
Kingsbarns **131** L9
Kingsbridge *Devon* **55** H6
Kingsbridge *Som* **57** H2
Kingsburgh **132** D5
Kingsbury *GtLon* **72** E3
Kingsbury *Warks* **90** E6
Kingsbury Episcopi **58** D2
Kingsbury Water Park *Warks* B76 0DY **90** E6
Kingscavil **125** J3
Kingsclere **71** J6
Kingscote **70** B2
Kingscott **56** D4
Kingscross **116** E1
Kingsdon **58** E2
Kingsdown *Kent* **65** J3
Kingsdown *Swin* **70** E3
Kingsdown *Wilts* **70** B5
Kingseat **125** K1
Kingsey **72** A1
Kingsfold *Pembs* **66** C6
Kingsfold *WSuss* **62** E3
Kingsford *Aberdeen* **135** N10
Kingsford *EAyr* **124** C6
Kingsford *Worcs* **90** A7
Kingsgate **75** K4
Kingshall Street **84** D2
Kingsheanton **56** D2
Kingshouse **130** A8
Kingshouse Hotel **129** P5
Kingshurst **90** D7
Kingskerswell **55** J4
Kingskettle **131** J10
Kingsland *Here* **78** D2
Kingsland *IoA* **96** A4
Kingsley *ChesW&C* **98** E5
Kingsley *Hants* **61** J1
Kingsley *Staffs* **90** C1
Kingsley Green **62** B3
Kingsley Holt **90** C1
Kingslow **89** G6
Kingsmoor **73** H1
Kingsmuir *Angus* **131** K6
Kingsmuir *Fife* **131** L10
Kingsnorth **65** F4
Kingsnorth Power Station **74** E4
Kingstanding **90** C6
Kingsteignton **55** J3
Kingsthorne **78** D5
Kingsthorpe **81** J2
Kingston *Cambs* **83** G3
Kingston *Corn* **54** D3
Kingston *Devon* **55** G6
Kingston *Devon* **57** J7
Kingston *Dorset* **59** G4
Kingston *Dorset* **59** J7
Kingston *ELoth* **126** D2
Kingston *GtMan* **99** J3
Kingston *Hants* **60** C4
Kingston *IoW* **61** F6
Kingston *Kent* **65** G2
Kingston *MK* **82** C5
Kingston *Moray* **134** H4
Kingston *WSuss* **62** D6
Kingston Bagpuize **71** H2
Kingston Blount **72** A2
Kingston by Sea **63** F6
Kingston Deverill **59** H1
Kingston Gorse **62** D6
Kingston Lacy *Dorset* BH21 4EA **3** A2
Kingston Lisle **71** G3
Kingston Maurward **59** G5
Kingston near Lewes **63** G6
Kingston on Soar **91** H3
Kingston Russell **58** E5
Kingston St. Mary **58** B2
Kingston Seymour **69** H5
Kingston Stert **72** A1
Kingston upon Hull **109** H7
Kingston upon Thames **72** E5
Kingston Warren **71** G3
Kingstone *Here* **78** D5
Kingstone *Here* **79** F6
Kingstone *Som* **58** C3
Kingstone *Staffs* **90** C3
Kingstone Winslow **71** F3
Kingstown **110** E1
Kingswear **55** J5
Kingswell **124** D6
Kingswinford **90** A7
Kingswood *Bucks* **81** H7
Kingswood *Glos* **70** A2
Kingswood *Here* **78** B3
Kingswood *Kent* **64** D2
Kingswood *Powys* **88** B5
Kingswood *SGlos* **69** K4
Kingswood *Som* **57** K2
Kingswood *Surr* **73** F6
Kingswood *Warks* **80** C1
Kingthorpe **102** E5
Kington *Here* **78** B3
Kington *Worcs* **79** J3
Kington Langley **70** C4
Kington Magna **59** G2
Kington St. Michael **70** C4
Kingussie **134** B10
Kingweston **58** E1
Kinharvie **115** K4
Kinkell **124** E3
Kinlet **89** G7
Kinloch *High* **136** F6
Kinloch *High* **132** E11
Kinloch *P&K* **130** G6
Kinloch Hourn (Ceann Loch Shubhairne) **133** K10
Kinloch Laggan **130** A2
Kinloch Rannoch **130** B5
Kinlochard **129** R10
Kinlochbervie **136** E4
Kinlocheil **129** L3
Kinlochewe **133** L4
Kinlochleven (Ceann Loch Liobhann) **129** N4
Kinlochmoidart **129** J3
Kinlochmore **129** N4
Kinloss **134** E4
Kinmel Bay (Bae Cinmel) **97** H4
Kinmuck **135** N9
Kinnaber **131** N4
Kinnadie **135** P6
Kinnaird **130** H8
Kinneff **131** P3
Kinnelhead **119** F3
Kinnell **131** M5
Kinnerley **88** C3
Kinnersley *Here* **78** C4
Kinnersley *Worcs* **79** H4
Kinnerton **78** B2
Kinnerton Green **98** C6
Kinnesswood **130** G10
Kinnettles **131** K6
Kinninvie **112** A4
Kinnordy **131** J5
Kinoulton **91** J2
Kinross **130** G10
Kinrossie **130** G7
Kinsbourne Green **82** E7
Kinsham *Here* **78** C2
Kinsham *Worcs* **79** J5
Kinsley **101** G1
Kinson **60** B5
Kintbury **71** G5
Kintessack **134** D4
Kintillo **130** G9
Kintocher **135** K10
Kinton *Here* **78** D1
Kinton *Shrop* **88** C4
Kintore **135** M9
Kintour **122** C5
Kintra *A&B* **122** B6
Kintra *A&B* **128** E8
Kinuachdrachd **123** F1
Kinveachy **134** D9
Kinver **90** A7
Kinwarton **80** C3
Kiplaw Croft **135** Q7
Kippax **107** K6
Kippen **124** E1
Kippford (Scaur) **115** J5
Kipping's Cross **73** K7
Kippington **73** J6
Kirbister **139** C7
Kirbuster **139** B5
Kirby Bedon **95** G5
Kirby Bellars **92** A4
Kirby Cane **95** H6
Kirby Corner **80** D1
Kirby Cross **85** G6
Kirby Fields **91** H5
Kirby Green **95** H6
Kirby Grindalythe **109** F3
Kirby Hill *NYorks* **112** B6
Kirby Hill *NYorks* **107** J3
Kirby Knowle **107** K1
Kirby le Soken **85** G6
Kirby Misperton **108** D2
Kirby Muxloe **91** H5
Kirby Row **95** H6
Kirby Sigston **112** E7
Kirby Underdale **108** E4
Kirby Wiske **107** J1
Kirdford **62** D4
Kirk **137** Q4
Kirk Bramwith **101** J1
Kirk Deighton **107** J4
Kirk Ella **109** G7
Kirk Hallam **91** G1
Kirk Hammerton **107** K4
Kirk Ireton **100** E7
Kirk Langley **90** E2
Kirk Merrington **112** C3
Kirk Michael **104** C4
Kirk of Shotts **125** G4
Kirk Sandall **101** J2
Kirk Smeaton **101** H1
Kirk Yetholm **120** D1
Kirkabister **139** N9
Kirkandrews **115** G6
Kirkandrews-upon-Eden **110** E1
Kirkbampton **110** E1
Kirkbean **115** K5
Kirkbride **110** D1
Kirkbuddo **131** L6
Kirkburn *ERid* **109** F4
Kirkburn *ScBord* **126** A7
Kirkburton **100** D1
Kirkby *Lincs* **102** D3
Kirkby *Mersey* **98** D3
Kirkby *NYorks* **113** F6
Kirkby Fleetham **112** C7
Kirkby Green **102** D7
Kirkby in Ashfield **101** G7
Kirkby la Thorpe **92** D1
Kirkby Lonsdale **106** B2
Kirkby Malham **106** D3
Kirkby Mallory **91** G5
Kirkby Malzeard **107** H2
Kirkby on Bain **103** F6
Kirkby Overblow **107** J5
Kirkby Stephen **111** J6
Kirkby Thore **111** H4
Kirkby Underwood **92** D3
Kirkby Wharfe **108** B5
Kirkby Woodhouse **101** G7
Kirkby-in-Furness **105** F1
Kirkbymoorside **108** C1
Kirkcaldy **126** A1
Kirkcambeck **120** A7
Kirkcolm **114** A4
Kirkconnel **118** C2
Kirkconnell **115** K4
Kirkcowan **114** D4
Kirkcudbright **115** G5
Kirkdale House **115** F5
Kirkdean **125** K6
Kirkfieldbank **125** G6
Kirkgunzeon **115** J4
Kirkham *Lancs* **105** H6
Kirkham *NYorks* **108** D3
Kirkhamgate **107** J7
Kirkharle **121** F5
Kirkhaugh **111** H2
Kirkheaton *N'umb* **121** F6
Kirkheaton *WYorks* **100** D1
Kirkhill **133** R6
Kirkhope **119** J1
Kirkibost (Circebost) **138** G4
Kirkinner **114** E5
Kirkintilloch **124** E3
Kirkland *Cumb* **111** H3
Kirkland *Cumb* **110** B5
Kirkland *D&G* **118** D4
Kirkland *D&G* **118** C2
Kirkland *D&G* **119** F5
Kirkland of Longcastle **114** D6
Kirkleatham **113** F4
Kirklevington **112** E5
Kirkley **95** K6
Kirklington *Notts* **101** J7
Kirklington *NYorks* **107** J1
Kirklinton **119** K7
Kirkliston **125** K3
Kirkmaiden **114** B7
Kirkmichael *P&K* **130** F4
Kirkmichael *SAyr* **117** H3
Kirkmuirhill **125** F6
Kirknewton *N'umb* **127** H7
Kirknewton *WLoth* **125** K4
Kirkney **135** K7
Kirkoswald *Cumb* **111** G2
Kirkoswald *SAyr* **117** G3
Kirkpatrick Durham **115** H3
Kirkpatrick-Fleming **119** H6
Kirksanton **104** E1
Kirkstall **107** H6
Kirkstead **102** E6
Kirkstile **119** J4
Kirkstyle **137** R2
Kirkthorpe **107** J7
Kirkton *Aber* **135** L8
Kirkton *Aber* **135** L5
Kirkton *Angus* **131** K6
Kirkton *D&G* **118** E5
Kirkton *High* **134** B1
Kirkton *High* **133** J8
Kirkton *ScBord* **120** A2
Kirkton Manor **126** A7
Kirkton of Auchterhouse **131** J7
Kirkton of Bourtie **135** N8
Kirkton of Craig **131** N5
Kirkton of Culsalmond **135** L7
Kirkton of Durris **135** M11
Kirkton of Glenbuchat **134** H9
Kirkton of Glenisla **130** H4
Kirkton of Kingoldrum **131** J5
Kirkton of Lethendy **130** G6
Kirkton of Logie Buchan **135** P8
Kirkton of Maryculter **135** N11
Kirkton of Menmuir **131** L4
Kirkton of Rayne **135** L7
Kirkton of Skene **135** N10
Kirkton of Tealing **131** K7
Kirktonhill **124** B3
Kirktown **135** Q5
Kirktown of Alvah **135** L4
Kirktown of Auchterless **135** M6
Kirktown of Deskford **135** K4
Kirktown of Fetteresso **131** P2
Kirktown of Slains **135** Q8
Kirkwall **139** D6
Kirkwall Airport **139** D7
Kirkwhelpington **120** E5
Kirmington **102** E1
Kirmond le Mire **102** E3
Kirn **123** K3
Kirriemuir **131** J5
Kirstead Green **95** G6
Kirtlebridge **119** H6
Kirtleton **119** H5
Kirtling **83** K3
Kirtling Green **83** K3
Kirtlington **81** G7
Kirtomy **137** K3
Kirton *Lincs* **93** G2
Kirton *Notts* **101** J6
Kirton *Suff* **85** G5
Kirton End **93** F1
Kirton Holme **93** F1
Kirton in Lindsey **102** C3
Kiscadale **116** E1
Kislingbury **81** H3
Kismeldon Bridge **56** B4
Kit Hill Country Park *Corn* PL17 8AX **54** D3
Kites Hardwick **81** F2
Kitley **55** F5
Kittisford **57** J3
Kittisford Barton **57** J3
Kittle **67** J7
Kitt's End **73** F2
Kitt's Green **90** D7
Kitwood **61** H1
Kivernoll **78** D5
Kiveton Park **101** G4
Klibreck **136** H6
Knaith **102** B4
Knaith Park **102** B4
Knap Corner **59** H2
Knaphill **72** C6
Knaplock **57** G2
Knapp *P&K* **130** H7
Knapp *Som* **58** C2
Knapthorpe **101** K7
Knaptoft **91** J7
Knapton *Norf* **95** H2
Knapton *York* **108** B4
Knapton Green **78** D3
Knapwell **83** G2
Knaresborough **107** J4
Knarsdale **111** H1
Knayton **107** K1
Knebworth **83** F6
Knebworth House *Herts* SG3 6PY **83** F6
Knedlington **108** D7
Kneesall **101** K6
Kneesworth **83** G4
Kneeton **92** A1
Knelston **67** H7
Knenhall **90** B2
Knettishall **94** D7
Knettishall Heath Country Park *Suff* IP22 2TQ **94** D7
Knightacott **56** E2
Knightcote **81** F3
Knightley **90** A3
Knightley Dale **90** A3
Knighton *Devon* **55** F6
Knighton *Dorset* **59** F3
Knighton *Leic* **91** H5
Knighton *Poole* **60** B5
Knighton (Tref-y-clawdd) *Powys* **78** B1
Knighton *Som* **57** K1
Knighton *Staffs* **89** G3
Knighton *Staffs* **89** G1
Knighton *Wilts* **71** F4
Knighton on Teme **79** F1
Knightswood **124** D4
Knightwick **79** G3
Knill **78** B2
Knipton **92** B2
Knitsley **112** B2
Kniveton **100** E7
Knock *A&B* **128** G7
Knock *Cumb* **111** H4
Knock *Moray* **135** K5
Knockalava **123** H1
Knockally **137** P7
Knockaloe Moar **104** B5
Knockan **136** E8
Knockandhu **134** G8
Knockarthur **137** K9
Knockbain **134** A5
Knockban **133** N4
Knockbrex **115** F6
Knockdee **137** P3
Knockdow **123** K3
Knockdown **70** B3
Knockenkelly **116** E1
Knockentiber **124** B7
Knockgray **117** K4
Knockholt **73** H6
Knockholt Pound **73** H6
Knockin **88** C3
Knockinlaw **124** C7
Knockintorran (Cnoc an Torrain) **138** B2
Knocklearn **115** H3
Knockmill **73** J5
Knocknaha **116** A2
Knocknain **116** D7
Knocknalling **117** K5
Knockrome **122** D3
Knocksharry **104** B5
Knockville **114** D3
Knodishall **85** J2
Knodishall Common **85** J2
Knodishall Green **85** J2
Knole **58** D2
Knolls Green **99** H5
Knolton **88** C2
Knook **70** C7
Knossington **92** B5
Knott End-on-Sea **105** G5
Knotting **82** D2
Knotting Green **82** D2
Knottingley **108** B7
Knotts **106** C4
Knotty Green **72** C2
Knowbury **78** E1
Knowe **114** D3
Knowesgate **120** E5
Knoweside **117** G2
Knowetownhead **120** A2
Knowl Green **84** B4
Knowl Hill **72** B4
Knowl Wall **90** A2
Knowle *Bristol* **69** K4
Knowle *Devon* **57** F5
Knowle *Devon* **56** C2
Knowle *Devon* **57** J7
Knowle *Shrop* **78** E1
Knowle *Som* **57** H1
Knowle *WMid* **80** C1
Knowle Cross **57** J6
Knowle Green **106** B6
Knowle Hall **69** G7
Knowle St. Giles **58** C3
Knowlton *Dorset* **60** B3
Knowlton *Kent* **65** H2
Knowsley **98** D3
Knowsley Safari Park *Mersey* L34 4AN **23** G3
Knowstone **57** G3
Knox Bridge **64** C3
Knucklas (Cnwclas) **78** B1
Knutsford **99** G5
Knypersley **99** H7
Krumlin **100** C1
Kuggar **52** E7
Kyle of Lochalsh (Caol Loch Aillse) **132** H8
Kyleakin (Caol Acain) **132** H8
Kylerhea (Ceol Reatha) **132** H8
Kyles Scalpay (Caolas Scalpaigh) **138** H8
Kylesku **136** E6
Kylesmorar **133** J11
Kylestrome **136** E6
Kynaston **88** C3
Kynnersley **89** F4
Kyre Park **79** F2

L

Labost **138** H3
Lacasaigh **138** J5
Lace Market Centre NG1 1HF **46** Nottingham
Laceby **103** F2
Lacey Green **72** B1
Lach Dennis **99** G5
Lackford **84** B1
Lacklee (Leac a' Li) **138** G8
Lacock **70** C5
Ladbroke **81** F3
Laddingford **73** K7
Lade Bank **103** G7
Ladies Hill **105** H5
Ladock **53** F3
Lady Hall **104** E1
Lady Lever Art Gallery *Mersey* CH62 5EQ **22** B6
Ladybank **131** J9
Ladycross **56** B7
Ladykirk **127** G6
Ladysford **135** P4
Ladywood **79** H2
Lagavulin **122** C6
Lagg *A&B* **122** D3
Lagg *NAyr* **116** D1
Lagg *SAyr* **117** G2
Laggan *A&B* **122** A5
Laggan (An Lagan) *High* **133** N11
Laggan *High* **134** A11
Laggan *Moray* **134** H7
Lagganulva **128** F6
Lagrae **118** C2
Laide **133** K1
Laig **128** F2
Laight **118** B2
Laindon **74** C3
Laing Art Gallery *T&W* NE1 8AG **41** Newcastle upon Tyne
Lairg **136** H9
Lairigmor **129** N4
Laisterdyke **107** G6
Laithes **111** F3
Lake *Devon* **56** D2
Lake *Devon* **55** F4
Lake *IoW* **61** G6
Lake *Wilts* **60** C1
Lake District Visitor Centre at Brockhole *Cumb* LA23 1LJ **110** E6
Lakenham **95** G5
Lakenheath **94** B7
Lakes Aquarium *Cumb* LA12 8AS **105** G1
Lakes End **93** J6
Lakes Glass Centre, Ulverston *Cumb* LA12 7LY **105** F2
Lakeside *Cumb* **105** G1
Lakeside *Thur* **73** J4
Lakeside & Haverthwaite Railway *Cumb* LA12 8AL **105** G1
Laleham **72** D5
Laleston **68** B4
Lamancha **126** A5
Lamarsh **84** C5
Lamas **95** G3
Lamb Corner **84** E5
Lamb Roe **106** C6
Lambden **127** F6
Lamberhurst **63** K3
Lamberhurst Quarter **63** K3
Lamberton **127** H5
Lambfell Moar **104** B5
Lambley *N'umb* **111** H1
Lambley *Notts* **91** J1
Lambourn **71** G4
Lambourn Woodlands **71** G4
Lambourne End **73** H2
Lambs Green **63** F3
Lambston **66** C4
Lambton **112** C1
Lamellion **54** C4
Lamerton **54** E3
Lamesley **112** C1
Lamington **125** H7
Lamlash **123** J7
Lamloch **117** K4
Lamonby **110** F3
Lamorna **52** B6
Lamorran **53** F4
Lampert **120** B6
Lampeter (Llanbedr Pont Steffan) **67** J1
Lampeter Velfrey **66** E4
Lamphey **66** D5
Lamplugh **110** B4
Lamport **81** J1
Lamyatt **59** F1
Lana *Devon* **56** B6
Lana *Devon* **56** B5
Lanark **125** G6
Lanarth **52** E6
Lancaster **105** H3
Lancaster Leisure Park *Lancs* LA1 3LA **105** H3
Lancaster Priory *Lancs* LA1 1YZ **105** H3
Lanchester **112** B2
Lancing **62** E6
Landbeach **83** H2
Landcross **56** C3
Landerberry **135** M10
Landewednack **52** E7
Landford **60** D3
Landican **98** B4
Landimore **67** H6
Landkey **56** D2
Landmoth **112** E7
Landore **67** K6
Landrake **54** D4
Land's End *Corn* TR19 7AA **52** A6
Land's End Airport **52** A6
Landscove **55** H4
Landshipping **66** D4
Landulph **54** E4
Landwade **83** K2
Landywood **90** B5
Lane Bottom **106** D6
Lane End *Bucks* **72** B2
Lane End *Cumb* **110** C7
Lane End *Derbys* **101** G6
Lane End *Dorset* **59** H5
Lane End *Hants* **61** G2
Lane End *Here* **79** F7
Lane End *Kent* **73** J4
Lane End *Wilts* **70** B7
Lane Ends *Derbys* **90** E2
Lane Ends *GtMan* **99** J3
Lane Ends *Lancs* **106** C6
Lane Ends *NYorks* **106** E5
Lane Green **90** A5
Lane Head *Dur* **112** B5
Lane Head *Dur* **112** A4
Lane Head *GtMan* **99** F3
Lane Head *WYorks* **100** D2
Lane Heads **105** H6
Lane Side **106** C7
Laneast **54** C2
Lane-end **54** A4
Laneham **102** B5
Lanehead *Dur* **111** K2
Lanehead *N'umb* **120** C5
Lanesend **66** D5
Lanesfield **90** B6
Laneshawbridge **106** E5
Langar **92** A2
Langbank **124** B3
Langbar **107** F4
Langbaurgh **113** F5
Langcliffe **106** D3
Langdale End **113** K7
Langdon *Corn* **54** C1
Langdon *Corn* **56** B7
Langdon Beck **111** K3
Langdon Hills **74** C3
Langdon Hills Country Park *Essex* SS17 9NH **74** C3
Langdon House **55** K3
Langford *CenBeds* **82** E4
Langford *Essex* **74** E1
Langford *Notts* **102** B7
Langford *Oxon* **71** F1
Langford Budville **57** K3
Langham *Essex* **84** E5
Langham *Norf* **94** E1
Langham *Rut* **92** B4
Langham *Suff* **84** D2
Langham Moor **84** E5
Langho **106** B6
Langholm **119** J5
Langland **67** K7
Langlands **115** G5
Langlee **120** B2
Langleeford **120** E1
Langley *ChesE* **99** J5
Langley *Derbys* **91** G1
Langley *Essex* **83** H5
Langley *Glos* **80** B6
Langley *GtMan* **99** H2
Langley *Hants* **61** F4
Langley *Herts* **83** F6
Langley *Kent* **64** C2
Langley *N'umb* **120** D7
Langley *Oxon* **80** E7
Langley *Slo* **72** D4
Langley *Som* **57** J3
Langley *Warks* **80** C2
Langley *WSuss* **62** B4
Langley Burrell **70** C4
Langley Corner **72** D3
Langley Green *Derbys* **90** E2
Langley Green *Warks* **80** D2
Langley Green *WSuss* **63** F3
Langley Heath **64** D2
Langley Marsh **57** J3
Langley Mill **91** G1
Langley Moor **112** C2
Langley Park **112** C2
Langley Park *Bucks* SL3 6DW **72** D3
Langley Street **95** H5
Langney **63** K6
Langold **101** H4
Langore **54** C2
Langport **58** D2
Langrick **93** F1
Langrick Bridge **93** F1
Langridge *B&NESom* **70** A5
Langridge *Devon* **56** D3
Langridgeford **56** D3
Langrigg **110** C2
Langrish **61** J2
Langsett **100** E2
Langshaw **126** D7
Langshawburn **119** H3
Langside **124** D4
Langstone *Hants* **61** J4
Langstone *Newport* **69** G2
Langthorne **112** C7
Langthorpe **107** J3
Langthwaite **112** A6
Langtoft *ERid* **109** G3
Langtoft *Lincs* **92** E4
Langton *Dur* **112** B5
Langton *Lincs* **103** G5
Langton *Lincs* **103** F6
Langton *NYorks* **108** D3
Langton by Wragby **102** E5
Langton Green *Kent* **63** J3
Langton Green *Suff* **85** F1
Langton Herring **59** F6
Langton Long Blandford **59** H4
Langton Matravers **59** J7
Langtree **56** C4
Langtree Week **56** C4
Langwathby **111** G3
Langwell House **137** P7
Langwith **101** H5
Langworth **102** D5
Lanhydrock *Corn* PL30 5AD **54** A4
Lanivet **54** A4
Lank **54** A3
Lanlivery **54** A5
Lanner **52** E4
Lanoy **54** C3
Lanreath **54** B5
Lansallos **54** B5
Lansdown **70** A5
Lanteglos **54** A2
Lanteglos Highway **54** B5
Lanton *N'umb* **127** H7
Lanton *ScBord* **120** B1
Lanvean **53** F2
Lapford **57** F5
Laphroaig **122** B6
Lapley **90** A4
Lapworth **80** C1
Larach na Gaibhre **123** F3
Larachbeg **128** H6
Larbert **125** G2
Larbreck **105** H5
Larden Green **98** E7
Larg **114** D3
Largie **135** L7
Largiemore **123** H2
Largoward **131** K10
Largs **124** A5
Largybaan **116** A2
Largybeg **116** E1
Largymore **116** E1
Lark Hall **83** J3
Larkfield **124** A3
Larkhall **125** F5
Larkhill **70** E7
Larklands **91** G1
Larling **94** D7
Larriston **120** A4
Lartington **112** A5
Lasborough **70** B2
Lasham **71** K7
Lashbrook **56** C5
Lashenden **64** D3
Lassington **79** G6
Lassintullich **130** C5
Lassodie **125** K1
Lasswade **126** B4
Lastingham **113** H7
Latchford **99** F4
Latchingdon **74** E1
Latchley **54** E3
Lately Common **99** F3
Lathbury **82** B4
Latheron **137** P6
Latheronwheel **137** P6
Latimer **72** D2
Latteridge **69** K3
Lattiford **59** F2
Latton **70** D2
Lauchentyre **115** F5
Lauder **126** D6
Laugharne (Lacharn) **67** G4
Laughterton **102** B5
Laughton *ESuss* **63** J5
Laughton *Leics* **91** J7
Laughton *Lincs* **102** B3
Laughton *Lincs* **92** D2
Laughton en le Morthen **101** H4
Launcells **56** A5
Launcells Cross **56** A5
Launceston **56** B7
Launde Abbey **92** A5
Launton **81** H6
Laurencekirk **131** N3
Laurieston *D&G* **115** G4
Laurieston *Falk* **125** H3
Lavendon **82** C3
Lavenham **84** D4
Laverhay **119** G4
Lavernock **68** E5
Laversdale **119** K7
Laverstock **60** C1
Laverstoke **71** H7
Laverton *Glos* **80** B5
Laverton *NYorks* **107** H2
Laverton *Som* **70** A6
Lavister **98** C7
Law **125** G5
Lawers **130** B7
Lawford *Essex* **84** E5
Lawford *Som* **57** K2
Lawhitton **56** B7
Lawkland **106** C3
Lawkland Green **106** C3
Lawley **89** F5
Lawnhead **90** A3
Lawrence Weston **69** J4
Lawrenny **66** D5
Lawshall **84** C3
Lawshall Green **84** C3
Lawton **78** D3
Laxdale (Lacasdal) **138** K4
Laxey **104** D5
Laxfield **85** G1
Laxford Bridge **136** E5
Laxo **139** N6
Laxton *ERid* **108** D7
Laxton *N'hants* **92** C6
Laxton *Notts* **101** K6
Laycock **107** F5
Layer Breton **84** D7
Layer de la Haye **84** D7
Layer Marney **84** D7
Layham **84** E4
Laymore **58** C4
Layter's Green **72** C2
Laytham **108** D6
Layton **105** G6
Lazenby **113** F4
Lazonby **111** G3
Lea *Derbys* **101** F7
Lea *Here* **79** F6
Lea *Lincs* **102** B4
Lea *Shrop* **88** C7
Lea *Shrop* **88** D5
Lea *Wilts* **70** C3
Lea Bridge **101** F7
Lea Green **79** F2
Lea Marston **90** E6
Lea Town **105** H6
Lea Yeat **106** C1
Leachd **123** J1
Leachkin (An Leacainn) **134** A6
Leadburn **126** A5
Leaden Roding **83** J7
Leadenham **102** C7
Leaderfoot **126** D7
Leadgate *Cumb* **111** J2
Leadgate *Dur* **112** B1
Leadgate *N'umb* **112** B1
Leadhills **118** D2
Leadingcross Green **64** D2
Leafield **80** E7
Leagrave **82** D6
Leake Commonside **103** G7
Leake Hurn's End **93** H1
Lealands **63** J5
Lealholm **113** H6
Lealt *A&B* **122** E1
Lealt *High* **132** F4
Leam **100** E5
Leamington Hastings **81** F2
Leamington Spa **80** E2
Leamington Spa Art Gallery & Museum *Warks* CV32 4AA **16** C8
Leamoor Common **88** D7
Leanach **123** J1
Leargybreck **122** D3
Leasgill **105** H1
Leasingham **92** D1
Leason **67** H6
Leasowe **98** B3
Leat **56** B7
Leatherhead **72** E6
Leathley **107** H5
Leaton *Shrop* **88** D4
Leaton *Tel&W* **89** F4
Leaveland **65** F2
Leavenheath **84** D5
Leavening **108** D3
Leaves Green **73** H5
Leavesden Green **72** E1
Lebberston **109** G1
Lechlade-on-Thames **71** F2
Leck **106** B2
Leckford **60** E1
Leckfurin **137** K4
Leckgruinart **122** A4
Leckhampstead *Bucks* **81** J5
Leckhampstead *WBerks* **71** H4
Leckhampstead Thicket **71** H4
Leckhampton **79** J7
Leckie **124** E1
Leckmelm (Leac Mailm) **133** M2
Leckuary **123** G1
Leckwith **68** E4
Leconfield **109** G5
Ledaig (Leideag) **129** L7
Ledburn **82** B6
Ledbury **79** G5
Ledgemoor **78** D3
Ledicot **78** D2
Ledmore **136** E8
Ledsham *ChesW&C* **98** C5
Ledsham *WYorks* **107** K7
Ledston **107** K7
Ledstone **55** H6
Ledwell **81** F6
Lee *A&B* **128** F8
Lee *Devon* **56** C1
Lee *Hants* **60** E3
Lee *Lancs* **105** J4
Lee *Shrop* **88** D2
Lee Brockhurst **88** E3
Lee Chapel **74** C3
Lee Clump **72** C1
Lee Mill Bridge **55** F5
Lee Moor **55** F4
Lee Valley Park *Essex* EN9 1XQ **73** G1
Leebotten **139** N10
Leebotwood **88** D6
Leece **105** F3
Leeds *Kent* **64** D2
Leeds *WYorks* **107** H6
Leeds Art Gallery *WYorks* LS1 3AA **42** E3
Leeds Bradford International Airport **107** H5
Leeds Castle & Gardens *Kent* ME17 1PL **64** D2
Leedstown **52** D5
Leegomery **89** F4
Leek **99** J7
Leek Wootton **80** D2
Leekbrook **99** J7
Leeming *NYorks* **107** H1
Leeming *WYorks* **107** F6
Leeming Bar **107** H1
Lee-on-the-Solent **61** G4
Lees *Derbys* **90** E2
Lees *GtMan* **99** J2
Leeswood **98** B7
Leftwich **99** F5
Legars **127** F6
Legbourne **103** G4
Legerwood **126** D6
Legoland Windsor *W&M* SL4 4AY **72** C4
Legsby **102** E4
Leicester **91** H5
Leicester Forest East **91** H5
Leigh *Dorset* **59** F4
Leigh *Dorset* **60** B5
Leigh *GtMan* **99** F2

153

Milton Abbot 54 E3
Milton Bridge 126 A4
Milton Bryan 82 C5
Milton Clevedon 59 F1
Milton Combe 54 E4
Milton Country Park Cambs CB24 6AZ 83 H2
Milton Damerel 56 B4
Milton End 79 G7
Milton Ernest 82 D3
Milton Green 98 D7
Milton Hill 71 H2
Milton Keynes 82 B5
Milton Keynes Village 82 B5
Milton Lilbourne 70 E5
Milton Malsor 81 J3
Milton of Auchinhove 135 K10
Milton of Balgonie 131 J10
Milton of Buchanan 124 C1
Milton of Cairnborrow 135 J6
Milton of Campfield 135 L10
Milton of Campsie 124 E3
Milton of Cullerlie 135 M10
Milton of Cushnie 135 K9
Milton of Tullich 134 H11
Milton on Stour 59 G2
Milton Regis 74 E5
Milton Street 63 J6
Miltonduff 134 F4
Miltonise 114 B3
Milton-Lockhart 125 G6
Milton-under-Wychwood 80 D7
Milverton Som 57 K3
Milverton Warks 80 E2
Milwich 90 B2
Mimbridge 72 C5
Minack Theatre Corn TR19 6JU 52 A6
Minard 123 H1
Minard Castle 123 H1
Minchington 59 J3
Minchinhampton 70 B1
Mindrum 127 G7
Mindrummill 127 G7
Minehead 57 H1
Minera 98 F7
Minety 70 D2
Minety Lower Moor 70 D2
Minffordd Gwyn 87 G4
Minffordd Gwyn 86 E2
Minffordd Gwyn 96 D5
Miningsby 103 G6
Minions 54 C3
Minishant 117 H2
Minley Manor 72 B6
Minllyn 87 H4
Minngearraidh 138 B6
Minnigaff 114 E4
Minskip 107 J3
Minstead 60 D3
Minsted 62 B4
Minster Kent 75 F4
Minster Kent 75 K5
Minster Lovell 80 E7
Minsteracres 112 A1
Minsterley 88 C5
Minsterworth 79 G7
Minterne Magna 59 F4
Minterne Parva 59 F4
Minting 102 E5
Mintlaw 135 Q6
Minto 120 A1
Minton 88 D6
Minwear 66 D4
Minworth 90 D6
Mirehouse 110 A5
Mireland 137 R3
Mirfield 107 H7
Miserden 70 C1
Miskin RCT 68 D3
Miskin RCT 68 D6
Misselfore 60 B2
Misson 101 J3
Misterton Leics 91 H7
Misterton Notts 101 K3
Misterton Som 58 D4
Mistley 85 F5
Mitcham 73 F5
Mitchel Troy 78 D7
Mitcheldean 79 F7
Mitchell 53 F3
Mitchelland 110 F7
Mitcheltroy Common 69 H1
Mitford 121 G5
Mithian 52 E3
Mitton 90 A4
Mixbury 81 H5
Mixenden 107 F7
Moat 119 K6
Moats Tye 84 E3
Mobberley ChesE 99 G5
Mobberley Staffs 90 C1
Moccas 78 C4
Mochdre Conwy 97 G5
Mochdre Powys 87 K7
Mochrum 114 D6
Mockbeggar Hants 60 C4
Mockbeggar Kent 64 C3
Mockerkin 110 B4
Modbury 55 G5
Moddershall 90 B2
Modern Art Oxford Oxon OX1 1BP 46 Oxford
Moel Famau Country Park Denb LL15 1US 97 K6
Moelfre IoA 96 D4
Moelfre Powys 88 A3
Moffat 119 F3
Mogerhanger 82 E4
Moin'a'choire 122 B4
Moine House 136 H4
Moira 91 F4
Molash 65 F2
Mol-chlach 132 E9
Mold (Yr Wyddgrug) 98 B6
Molehill Green Essex 83 J6
Molehill Green Essex 84 B6
Molescroft 109 G5
Molesden 121 G5
Molesworth 82 D1
Mollance 115 H4
Molland 57 G3
Mollington ChesW&C 98 C5
Mollington Oxon 81 F4
Mollinsburn 125 F3
Monach Islands (Heisker Islands) 138 A2
Monachty 76 E2
Monewden 85 G3
Moneyrow Green 72 B4
Moniaive 118 C4
Monifieth 131 L7
Monikie 131 L7
Monikie Country Park Angus DD5 3QN 131 K7
Monimail 130 H9
Monington 66 E1
Monk Bretton 101 F2
Monk Fryston 108 B7
Monk Hesleden 112 E3
Monk Sherborne 71 K6
Monk Soham 85 G2
Monk Soham Green 85 G2
Monk Street 83 K6
Monken Hadley 73 F2
Monkerton 57 H6
Monkey Mates W'ham RG41 1JA 72 A4
Monkey World, Wareham Dorset BH20 6HH 59 H6
Monkhide 79 F4
Monkhill 110 E1
Monkhopton 89 F6
Monkland 78 D3
Monkleigh 56 C3
Monknash 68 C4
Monkokehampton 56 D5
Monks Eleigh 84 D4
Monks Eleigh Tye 84 D4
Monk's Gate 63 F4
Monks' Heath 99 H5
Monk's Hill 64 D3
Monks Kirby 91 G7
Monks Risborough 72 B1
Monkscross 54 D3
Monkseaton 121 J6
Monksilver 57 J2
Monkstadt 132 D4
Monkswood 69 G1
Monkton Devon 57 K5
Monkton Kent 75 J5
Monkton Pembs 66 C5
Monkton SAyr 117 H1
Monkton T&W 121 J7
Monkton VGlam 68 C4
Monkton Combe 70 A5
Monkton Deverill 59 H1
Monkton Farleigh 70 B5
Monkton Heathfield 58 B2
Monkton Up Wimborne 60 B3
Monkton Wyld 58 C5
Monkwearmouth 112 D1
Monkwood 61 H1
Monmouth (Trefynwy) 78 E7
Monnington Court 78 C5
Monnington on Wye 78 C4
Monreith 114 D6
Montacute 58 E3
Montacute House Som TA15 6XP 58 E3
Montford 88 D4
Montford Bridge 88 D4
Montgarrie 135 K9
Montgomery (Trefaldwyn) 88 B6
Montgreenan 124 B6
Montpellier Gallery Warks CV37 6EP 48 Stratford-upon-Avon
Montrave 131 J10
Montrose 131 N5
Monxton 71 G7
Monyash 100 D6
Monymusk 135 L9
Monzie 130 D8
Moodiesburn 124 E3
Moons Moat North 80 B2
Moor Allerton 107 J6
Moor Cock 106 B3
Moor Crichel 59 J4
Moor End Bed 82 D3
Moor End CenBeds 82 C6
Moor End Cumb 105 J2
Moor End ERid 108 E6
Moor End Lancs 105 G5
Moor End NYorks 108 B6
Moor End WYorks 107 F7
Moor Green Wilts 70 B5
Moor Green WMid 90 C7
Moor Head 107 G6
Moor Monkton 108 B4
Moor Row 110 B5
Moor Side Cumb 105 F2
Moor Side Lancs 105 H6
Moor Side Lancs 105 H6
Moor Side Lincs 103 F7
Moor Street 74 E5
Moorby 103 F6
Moorcot 78 C3
Moordown 60 B5
Moore 98 E4
Moorend 110 E1
Moorends 101 J1
Moorfield 100 C3
Moorgreen 91 G1
Moorhall 101 F5
Moorhampton 78 C4
Moorhouse Cumb 110 E1
Moorhouse Notts 101 K6
Moorland (Northmoor Green) 58 C1
Moorlinch 58 C1
Moors Centre, Danby NYorks YO21 2NB 113 H6
Moors Valley Country Park Dorset BH24 2ET 3 E1
Moors Valley Railway Dorset BH24 2ET 3 E1
Moorsholm 113 G5
Moorside Dorset 59 G3
Moorside GtMan 99 J2
Moorside WYorks 107 H6
Moorthorpe 101 G1
Moortown IoW 61 F6
Moortown Lincs 102 D3
Moortown Tel&W 89 F4
Morar 132 G11
Morborne 92 E6
Morchard Bishop 57 F5
Morcombelake 58 D5
Morcott 92 C5
Morda 88 B3
Morden Dorset 59 J5
Morden GtLon 73 F5
Morden Hall Park GtLon SM4 5JD 11 G11
Morden Park 73 F5
Mordiford 78 E5
Mordington Holdings 127 H5
Mordon 112 D4
More 88 C6
Morebath 57 H3
Morebattle 120 C1
Morecambe 105 H3
Morefield 133 M1
Moreleigh 55 H5
Morenish 130 B7
Moresby Parks 110 A5
Morestead 61 G2
Moreton Dorset 59 H6
Moreton Essex 73 J1
Moreton Here 78 E2
Moreton Mersey 98 B4
Moreton Oxon 71 K1
Moreton Staffs 90 D2
Moreton Staffs 89 G4
Moreton Corbet 88 E3
Moreton Jeffries 79 F4
Moreton Mill 88 E3
Moreton Morrell 80 E3
Moreton on Lugg 78 E4
Moreton Paddox 80 E3
Moreton Pinkney 81 G4
Moreton Say 89 F2
Moreton Valence 70 A1
Moretonhampstead 57 F7
Moreton-in-Marsh 80 D5
Morfa Carmar 67 J4
Morfa Cere 76 C3
Morfa Bychan 86 E2
Morfa Glas 68 B1
Morfa Nefyn 86 B1
Morgan's Vale 60 C2
Morganstown 68 E3
Mork 69 J1
Morland 111 G4
Morley Derbys 91 F1
Morley Dur 112 B4
Morley WYorks 107 H7
Morley Green 99 H4
Morley St. Botolph 94 E6
Mornick 54 D3
Morningside Edin 126 A3
Morningside NLan 125 G5
Morningthorpe 95 G6
Morpeth 121 H5
Morrey 90 D4
Morridge Side 100 C7
Morrilow Heath 90 B2
Morriston SAyr 117 G3
Morriston Swan 67 K6
Morristown 68 E4
Morston 94 E1
Mortehoe 56 C1
Morthen 101 G4
Mortimer 71 K5
Mortimer West End 71 K5
Mortimer's Cross 78 D2
Mortlake 73 F4
Morton Derbys 101 G6
Morton Lincs 92 D3
Morton Lincs 102 B3
Morton Lincs 102 B6
Morton Notts 101 K7
Morton SGlos 69 K2
Morton Shrop 88 B3
Morton Bagot 80 C2
Morton on the Hill 95 F4
Morton Tinmouth 112 B4
Morton-on-Swale 112 D7
Morvah 52 B5
Morval 54 C5
Morvich (A'Mhormhaich) High 133 K8
Morvich High 137 K9
Morvil 66 D2
Morville 89 F6
Morwellham 54 E4
Morwellham Quay Museum Devon PL19 8JL 54 E3
Morwenstow 56 A4
Morwick Hall 121 H3
Mosborough 101 G4
Moscow 124 C6
Mosedale 110 E3
Moselden Height 100 C1
Moseley WMid 90 B6
Moseley Worcs 79 H3
Moses Gate 99 G2
Moss SYorks 101 H1
Moss Wrex 98 C7
Moss Bank 98 E3
Moss Houses 99 H5
Moss Nook 99 H4
Moss Side GtMan 99 H3
Moss Side Lancs 105 G6
Moss Side Mersey 98 C2
Mossat 135 J9
Mossbank 139 N5
Mossblown 117 J1
Mossburnford 120 B2
Mossdale 115 G3
Mossend 125 F4
Mosser 110 C4
Mossgiel 117 J1
Mossley ChesE 99 H6
Mossley GtMan 99 J2
Mossley Hill 98 C4
Mosspaul Hotel 119 J4
Moss-side 134 C5
Mosstodloch 134 H4
Mossy Lea 98 E1
Mosterton 58 D4
Moston GtMan 99 H2
Moston Shrop 88 E3
Moston Green 99 G6
Mostyn 97 K4
Motcombe 59 H2
Mothecombe 55 G6
Mother Shipton's Cave NYorks HG5 8DD 107 J4
Motherby 110 F4
Motherwell 125 F5
Mottingham 73 H4
Mottisfont 60 E2
Mottisfont Abbey Hants SO51 0LP 60 E2
Mottistone 61 F6
Mottram in Longdendale 99 J3
Mottram St. Andrew 99 H5
Mouldsworth 98 E5
Moulin 130 E5
Moulsecoomb 63 G6
Moulsford 71 J3
Moulsham 74 D1
Moulsoe 82 C4
Moulton ChesW&C 99 F6
Moulton Lincs 93 G3
Moulton N'hants 81 J2
Moulton NYorks 112 C6
Moulton Suff 83 K2
Moulton VGlam 68 D4
Moulton Chapel 93 F4
Moulton St. Mary 95 J5
Moulton Seas End 93 G3
Mount Corn 52 E3
Mount Corn 54 B4
Mount Kent 65 G3
Mount WYorks 100 D1
Mount Ambrose 52 E4
Mount Bures 84 D5
Mount Charles 54 A5
Mount Edgcumbe Country Park Corn PL10 1HZ 2 B4
Mount Hawke 52 E4
Mount Manisty 98 C5
Mount Oliphant 117 H2
Mount Pleasant ChesE 99 H7
Mount Pleasant Derbys 91 F1
Mount Pleasant Derbys 90 E4
Mount Pleasant ESuss 63 H5
Mount Pleasant Flints 98 B5
Mount Pleasant GtLon 72 D2
Mount Pleasant Hants 60 E5
Mount Pleasant Norf 94 D6
Mount Pleasant Suff 84 B4
Mount Sorrel 60 B2
Mount Tabor 107 F7
Mountain 107 F6
Mountain Ash (Aberpennar) 68 D2
Mountain Cross 125 K6
Mountain Water 66 C3
Mountbenger 119 J1
Mountblow 124 C3
Mountfield 64 C5
Mountgerald 133 R4
Mountjoy 53 F2
Mountnessing 74 C2
Mounton 69 J2
Mountsorrel 91 H4
Mousa 139 N10
Mousehole 52 B6
Mouswald 119 F6
Mow Cop 99 H7
Mowden 112 C5
Mowhaugh 120 D1
Mowsley 91 J7
Mowtie 131 P2
Moxley 90 B6
Moy High 129 R2
Moy High 134 B7
Moylgrove 66 E1
Muasdale 122 E6
Much Birch 78 E5
Much Cowarne 79 F4
Much Dewchurch 78 D5
Much Hadham 83 H7
Much Hoole 105 H7
Much Hoole Town 105 H7
Much Marcle 79 F5
Much Wenlock 89 F5
Muchalls 135 P11
Muchelney 58 D2
Muchelney Ham 58 D2
Muchlarnick 54 C5
Muchra 119 H2
Muchrachd 133 N7
Muck 128 D3
Mucking 74 C3
Muckle Roe 139 M6
Muckleford 59 F5
Mucklestone 89 G2
Muckleton 88 E3
Muckletown 135 K8
Muckley 89 F6
Muckley Corner 90 C5
Muckton 103 G4
Mudale 136 H6
Muddiford 56 D2
Muddles Green 63 J5
Muddleswood 63 F5
Mudeford 60 C5
Mudford 58 E3
Mudgley 69 H7
Mugdock 124 D3
Mugdock Country Park Stir G62 8EL 30 D1
Mugeary 132 E7
Mugginton 90 E1
Muggintonlane End 90 E1
Muggleswick 112 A2
Mugswell 73 F6
Muie 137 J9
Muir of Fowlis 135 K9
Muir of Ord (Am Blàr Dubh) 133 R5
Muiravonside Country Park Falk EH49 6LW 125 H3
Muirdrum 131 L7
Muiredge 126 B1
Muirhead 124 E4
Muirhouses 125 J2
Muirkirk 118 B1
Muirmill 125 F2
Muirton 130 G8
Muirton of Ardblair 130 G6
Muker 111 L7
Mulbarton 95 F5
Mulben 134 H5
Mull 128 G7
Mullacott Cross 56 D1
Mullion 52 D7
Mullion Cove 52 D7
Mumby 103 J5
Munderfield Row 79 F3
Munderfield Stocks 79 F3
Mundesley 95 H2
Mundford 94 C6
Mundham 95 H6
Mundon 74 E1
Munerigie 133 N10
Mungasdale 133 K1
Mungoswells 126 C3
Mungrisdale 110 E3
Munlochy 134 A5
Munnoch 124 A6
Munsley 79 F4
Munslow 88 E7
Murchington 56 E7
Murcott Oxon 81 G7
Murcott Wilts 70 C2
Murdostoun 125 G5
Murieston 125 J4
Murkle 137 P3
Murlaggan 133 L11
Murrell Green 72 A6
Murrow 93 G5
Mursley 82 B6
Murston 75 F5
Murthly 130 F7
Murton Cumb 111 J4
Murton Dur 112 D2
Murton N'umb 127 H6
Murton Swan 67 J7
Murton York 108 C4
Musbury 58 B5
Muscliff 60 B5
Museum in Docklands GtLon E14 4AL 13 C7
Museum of Childhood Edin EH1 1TG 38 G4
Museum of Childhood GtLon E2 9PA 12 C6
Museum of Flight ELoth EH39 5LF 126 D3
Museum of Garden History, London GtLon SE1 7LB 44 F6
Museum of London GtLon EC2Y 5HN 44 J1
Museum of Science & Industry, Manchester GtMan M3 4FP 45 C4
Museum of Transport Glas G3 8DP 39 A2
Musselburgh 126 B3
Mustard Hyrn 95 J4
Mustard Shop Norf NR2 1NQ 46 Norwich
Muston Leics 92 B2
Muston NYorks 109 G2
Mustow Green 79 H1
Mutford 95 J7
Muthill 130 D9
Mutley 54 E5
Mutterton 57 J5
Muxton 89 G4
M.V. Princess Pocahontas Kent DA11 0BS 74 C4
Mybster 137 P4
Myddfai 77 G5
Myddle 88 D3
Myddlewood 88 D3
Mydroilyn 76 D3
Myerscough College 105 H6
Myerscough Smithy 106 B6
Mylor 53 F5
Mylor Bridge 53 F5
Mynachdy 68 E4
Mynachlog-ddu 66 E2
Myndtown 88 C7
Mynydd Llandygai 96 E6
Mynydd Mechell 96 B4
Mynydd-bach Mon 69 H2
Mynydd-bach Swan 67 K6
Mynyddygarreg 67 H5
Mynytho 86 C2
Mytchett 72 B6
Mytholm 106 E7
Mytholmroyd 107 F7
Mythop 105 G6
Myton-on-Swale 107 K3
Mytton 88 D4

N

Naast 133 J2
Nab's Head 106 B7
Na-Buirgh 138 F8
Naburn 108 B5
Nackington 65 G2
Nacton 85 G4
Nadderwater 57 G6
Nafferton 109 G4
Nailbridge 79 F7
Nailsbourne 58 B2
Nailsea 69 H4
Nailstone 91 G5
Nailsworth 70 B2
Nairn 134 C5
Nancegollan 52 D5
Nancekuke 52 D4
Nancledra 52 B5
Nanhoron 86 B2
Nannau 87 G3
Nannerch 97 K6
Nanpantan 91 H4
Nanpean 53 G3
Nanstallon 54 A4
Nant Peris 96 E7
Nant-ddu 77 K7
Nanternis 76 C3
Nantgaredig 67 H3
Nantgarw 68 E3
Nant-glas 77 J2
Nantglyn 97 J6
Nantgwyn 77 J1
Nantlle 96 D7
Nantmawr 88 B3
Nantmel 77 K2
Nantmor 87 F1
Nantwich 99 F7
Nantycaws 67 H4
Nant-y-derry 69 G1
Nant-y-dugoed 87 J4
Nantyffyllon 68 B2
Nantyglo 78 A7
Nant-y-Gollen 88 B3
Nant-y-groes 77 K2
Nant-y-moel 68 C2
Nant-y-Pandy 96 E5
Naphill 72 B2
Napley Heath 89 G2
Nappa 106 D4
Napton on the Hill 81 F2
Narberth (Arberth) 66 E4
Narborough Leics 91 H6
Narborough Norf 94 B4
Narkurs 54 D5
Nasareth 86 D1
Naseby 81 H1
Nash Bucks 81 J5
Nash Here 78 C2
Nash Newport 69 G3
Nash Shrop 79 F1
Nash VGlam 68 C4
Nash Street 74 C5
Nassington 92 D6
Nasty 83 G6
Nateby Cumb 111 J6
Nateby Lancs 105 H5
Nately Scures 72 A6
National Agricultural Centre, Stoneleigh Warks CV8 2LZ 16 C6
National Army Museum GtLon SW3 4HT 11 H8
National Botanic Garden of Wales Carmar SA32 8HG 67 J4
National Coal Mining Museum for England WYorks WF4 4RH 27 H8
National Exhibition Centre WMid B40 1NT 15 M6
National Fishing Heritage Centre, Grimsby NELincs DN31 1UZ 103 F2
National Gallery GtLon WC2N 5DN 44 D3
National Gallery of Scotland Edin EH2 2EL 38 F4
National Indoor Arena, Birmingham WMid B1 2AA 34 D3
National Marine Aquarium PL4 0LF 46 Plymouth
National Maritime Museum Cornwall Corn TR11 3QY 53 F5
National Maritime Museum, Greenwich GtLon SE10 9NF 13 D8
National Media Museum WYorks BD1 1NQ 35 Bradford
National Memorial Arboretum, Alrewas Staffs DE13 7AR 90 D4
National Motorcycle Museum, Solihull WMid B92 0EJ 15 M6
National Museum Cardiff CF10 3NP 36 Cardiff
National Museum of Scotland Edin EH1 1JF 38 G5
National Portrait Gallery GtLon WC2H 0HE 44 D3
National Railway Museum YO26 4XJ 49 York
National Sea Life Centre, Birmingham WMid B1 2JB 34 D3
National Seal Sanctuary Corn TR12 6UG 52 E6
National Slate Museum, Llanberis Gwyn LL55 4TY 96 D7
National Space Centre Leic LE4 5NS 17 D5
National Wallace Monument Stir FK9 5LF 125 G1
National War Museum Edin EH1 2NG 38 E4
National Waterfront Museum SA1 3RD 48 Swansea
National Wildflower Centre, Liverpool Mersey L16 3NA 22 E4
Natland 105 J1
Natural History Museum at Tring Herts HP23 6AP 82 C7
Natural History Museum, London GtLon SW7 5BD 11 G7
Natureland Seal Sanctuary Lincs PE25 1DB 103 J6
Naughton 84 E4
Naunton Glos 80 C6
Naunton Worcs 79 H5
Naunton Beauchamp 79 J3
Navenby 102 C7
Navestock 73 J2
Navestock Side 73 J2
Navidale 137 N8
Nawton 108 C1
Nayland 84 D5
Nazeing 73 H1
Neacroft 60 C5
Neal's Green 91 F7
Neap House 102 B1
Near Sawrey 110 E7
Nearton End 82 B6
Neasden 73 F3
Neasham 112 D5
Neat Enstone 80 E6
Neath (Castell-nedd) 68 A2
Neatham 72 A7
Neatishead 95 H3
Nebo Cere 76 E2
Nebo Conwy 97 G7
Nebo Gwyn 96 D7
Nebo IoA 96 C3
Necton 94 C5
Nedd 136 D6
Nedderton 121 H5
Nedging 84 D4
Nedging Tye 84 E4
Needham 95 G7
Needham Lake Suff IP6 8NU 84 E3
Needham Market 84 E3
Needham Street 84 B2
Needingworth 83 G1
Needles Pleasure Park IoW PO39 0JD 60 E6
Needwood 90 D3
Neen Savage 79 F1
Neen Sollars 79 F1
Neenton 89 F7
Nefyn 86 C1
Neighbourne 69 K7
Neilston 124 C5
Neithrop 81 F4
Nelson Caerp 68 E2
Nelson Lancs 106 D6
Nelson Village 121 H6
Nemphlar 125 G6
Nempnett Thrubwell 69 J5
Nenthall 111 J2
Nenthead 111 J2
Nenthorn 126 E7
Neopardy 57 F6
Nerabus 122 A5
Nercwys 98 B6
Neriby 122 B4
Nerston 124 E5
Nesbit 127 H7
Nesfield 107 F5
Ness 98 C5
Ness Botanic Gardens ChesW&C CH64 4AY 22 A8
Nesscliffe 88 C4
Neston ChesW&C 98 B5
Neston Wilts 70 B5
Nether Alderley 99 H5
Nether Auchendrane 117 H2
Nether Barr 114 E4
Nether Blainslie 126 D6
Nether Broughton 91 J3
Nether Burrow 106 B2
Nether Cerne 59 F5
Nether Compton 58 E3
Nether Dalgliesh 119 H3
Nether Dallachy 134 H4
Nether Edge 101 F4
Nether End 100 E5
Nether Exe 57 H6
Nether Glasslaw 135 N5
Nether Haugh 101 G3
Nether Heage 101 F7
Nether Heselden 106 D2
Nether Heyford 81 H3
Nether Kellet 105 J3
Nether Kinmundy 135 Q6
Nether Langwith 101 H5
Nether Loads 101 F6
Nether Moor 101 F6
Nether Padley 100 E5
Nether Poppleton 108 B4
Nether Silton 112 E7
Nether Skyborry 78 B1
Nether Stowey 57 K2
Nether Wallop 60 E1
Nether Wasdale 110 C6
Nether Wellwood 118 B1
Nether Welton 110 E2
Nether Westcote 80 D6
Nether Whitacre 90 E6
Nether Winchendon (Lower Winchendon) 81 J7
Nether Worton 81 F6
Netheravon 70 E7
Netherburn 125 G6
Netherbury 58 D5
Netherby Cumb 119 J6
Netherby NYorks 107 J5
Nethercott 81 F6
Netherend 69 J1
Netherfield ESuss 64 C6
Netherfield Notts 91 J1
Netherfield SLan 125 F6
Netherhall 124 A4
Netherhampton 60 C2
Netherhay 58 D4
Netherland Green 90 D2
Netherley 135 N11
Nethermill 119 F5
Netherseal 90 E4
Nethershield 117 K1
Netherstreet 70 C5
Netherthird D&G 115 H5
Netherthird EAyr 117 K2
Netherthong 100 D2
Netherthorpe 101 H4
Netherton Angus 131 L5
Netherton ChesW&C 98 E5
Netherton Devon 55 J3
Netherton Hants 71 G6
Netherton Mersey 98 C2
Netherton N'umb 120 E3
Netherton NLan 125 F5
Netherton Oxon 71 H1
Netherton P&K 130 G5
Netherton SLan 125 H5
Netherton WMid 90 B7
Netherton Worcs 79 J4
Netherton WYorks 100 E1
Netherton WYorks 100 D1
Netherton Burnfoot 120 E3
Netherton Northside 120 E3
Nethertown Cumb 110 A6
Nethertown Staffs 90 D4
Netherwitton 121 G4
Netherwood D&G 115 K3
Netherwood EAyr 118 B1
Nethy Bridge 134 E8
Netley Abbey 61 F4
Netley Marsh 60 E3
Nettlebed 71 K3
Nettlebridge 69 K7
Nettlecombe Dorset 58 E5
Nettlecombe IoW 61 G7
Nettlecombe Som 57 J2
Nettleden 82 D7
Nettleham 102 D5
Nettlestead Kent 73 K6
Nettlestead Suff 84 E4
Nettlestead Green 73 K6
Nettlestone 61 H5
Nettlesworth 112 C2
Nettleton Lincs 102 E2
Nettleton Wilts 70 B4
Nettleton Hill 100 C1
Netton Devon 55 F6
Netton Wilts 60 C1
Neuadd Cere 76 D3
Neuadd IoA 96 B3
Neuadd Powys 77 J4
Nevendon 74 D2
Nevern 66 E1
Nevill Holt 92 B6
New Abbey 115 K4
New Aberdour 135 N4
New Addington 73 G5
New Alresford 61 G1
New Alyth 130 H6
New Arley 90 E6
New Arram 109 G5
New Ash Green 74 C5
New Balderton 102 B7
New Barn 74 C5
New Belses 120 A1
New Bewick 121 F1
New Bolingbroke 103 G7
New Boultham 102 C5
New Bradwell 82 B4
New Brancepeth 112 C2
New Bridge D&G 115 K3
New Bridge Devon 55 H3
New Brighton Flints 98 B6
New Brighton Hants 61 J4
New Brighton Mersey 98 C3
New Brighton Wrex 98 B7
New Brighton WYorks 107 H7
New Brinsley 101 G7
New Broughton 98 C7
New Buckenham 94 E6
New Byth 135 N5
New Cheriton 61 G2
New Cross Cere 77 F1
New Cross GtLon 73 G4
New Cumnock 118 B2
New Deer 135 N6
New Duston 81 J2
New Earswick 108 C4
New Edlington 101 H3
New Elgin 134 G4
New Ellerby 109 H6
New Eltham 73 H4
New End 80 B2
New England 92 E5
New Farnley 107 H6
New Ferry 98 C4
New Galloway 115 G3
New Gilston 131 K10
New Greens 72 E1
New Grimsby 52 B1
New Hartley 121 J6
New Haw 72 D5
New Heaton 127 G7
New Hedges 66 E5
New Herrington 112 D1
New Hinksey 71 J1
New Holland 109 G7
New Houghton Derbys 101 H6
New Houghton Norf 94 B3
New Houses 106 D2
New Hunwick 112 B3
New Hutton 111 G7
New Hythe 64 C2
New Inn Carmar 67 H2
New Inn Mon 69 H1
New Inn Torfaen 69 F2
New Invention Shrop 78 B1
New Invention WMid 90 B5
New Lanark 125 G6
New Lanark World Heritage Site SLan ML11 9DB 125 G6
New Lane 98 D1
New Lane End 99 F3
New Leake 103 H7
New Leeds 135 P5
New Lodge 101 F2
New Longton 105 J7
New Luce 114 B4
New Mains 125 G7
New Malden 73 F5
New Marske 113 G4
New Marton 88 C2
New Mill Corn 52 B5
New Mill Herts 82 C7
New Mill WYorks 100 D2
New Mill End 82 E7
New Mills Corn 53 F3
New Mills Derbys 100 C4
New Mills Glos 69 K1
New Mills Mon 69 J1
New Mills (Y Felin Newydd) Powys 87 K5
New Milton 60 D5
New Mistley 85 F5
New Moat 66 D3
New Ollerton 101 J6
New Orleans 116 B2
New Oscott 90 C6
New Palace & Adventureland, New Brighton Mersey CH45 2JX 22 A2
New Park Corn 54 B2
New Park NYorks 107 H4
New Pitsligo 135 N5
New Polzeath 53 G1
New Quay (Ceinewydd) 76 C2
New Rackheath 95 G4
New Radnor (Maesyfed) 78 B2
New Rent 111 F3
New Ridley 121 F7
New Road Side 106 E5
New Romney 65 F5
New Rossington 101 J3
New Row Cere 77 G1
New Row Lancs 106 B6
New Sawley 91 G2
New Shoreston 127 K7
New Silksworth 112 D1
New Stevenston 125 F5
New Swannington 91 G4
New Totley 101 F5
New Town CenBeds 82 E4
New Town Cere 66 E1
New Town Dorset 59 J3
New Town Dorset 59 J4
New Town ELoth 126 C3
New Town ESuss 63 H4
New Town Glos 80 B5
New Tredegar 68 E1
New Tupton 101 F6
New Ulva 123 F2
New Valley 138 K4
New Village 101 H2
New Walk Museum & Art Gallery LE1 7EA 41 Leicester
New Walsoken 93 H5
New Waltham 103 F2
New Walton Pier Essex CO14 8ES 85 G6
New Winton 126 C3
New World 93 G6
New Yatt 80 E7
New York Lincs 103 F7
New York T&W 121 J6
Newall 107 H5
Newark Ork 139 G3
Newark Peter 93 F5
Newark Castle, Newark-on-Trent Notts NG24 1BG 101 K7
Newark-on-Trent 102 B7
Newarthill 125 F5
Newball 102 D5
Newbarn 65 G4
Newbarns 104 E2
Newbattle 126 B4
Newbiggin Cumb 111 F4
Newbiggin Cumb 111 H4
Newbiggin Cumb 111 G2
Newbiggin Cumb 105 F3
Newbiggin Cumb 110 B7
Newbiggin Dur 111 L4
Newbiggin N'umb 120 E7
Newbiggin NYorks 107 F1
Newbiggin NYorks 111 L7
Newbiggin-by-the-Sea 121 J5
Newbigging Angus 131 K7
Newbigging SLan 125 J6
Newbiggin-on-Lune 111 J6
Newbold Derbys 101 F5
Newbold Leics 91 G4
Newbold on Avon 81 F1
Newbold on Stour 80 D4
Newbold Pacey 80 D3
Newbold Verdon 91 G5
Newborough (Niwbwrch) IoA 96 C6
Newborough Peter 93 F5
Newborough Staffs 90 D3
Newbottle N'hants 81 G5
Newbottle T&W 112 D1
Newbourne 85 G4
Newbridge (Cefn Bychan) Caerp 69 F2
Newbridge Corn 52 B5
Newbridge Corn 54 D4
Newbridge Edin 125 K3
Newbridge ESuss 63 H3
Newbridge Hants 60 D3
Newbridge IoW 61 F6
Newbridge NYorks 108 E1
Newbridge Oxon 71 H1
Newbridge Pembs 66 C2
Newbridge Wrex 88 B1
Newbridge Green 79 H5
Newbridge on Wye 77 K3
Newbridge-on-Usk 69 G2
Newbrough 120 D7
Newbuildings 57 F5
Newburgh Aber 135 P8
Newburgh Fife 130 H9
Newburgh Lancs 98 D1
Newburgh ScBord 119 J1
Newburn 121 G7
Newbury Som 69 K6
Newbury WBerks 71 H5
Newbury Wilts 70 B7
Newbury Park 73 H3
Newby Cumb 111 G4
Newby Lancs 106 D5
Newby NYorks 113 F5
Newby NYorks 106 C3
Newby NYorks 109 G1
Newby Bridge 105 G1
Newby Cote 106 C2
Newby Cross 110 E1
Newby East 111 F1
Newby Hall NYorks HG4 5AE 107 J3
Newby West 110 E1
Newby Wiske 107 J1
Newcastle Bridgend 68 B4
Newcastle Mon 78 D7
Newcastle Shrop 88 B7
Newcastle Emlyn (Castell Newydd Emlyn) 67 G1
Newcastle International Airport 121 G6
Newcastle upon Tyne 121 H7
Newcastleton 119 K5
Newcastle-under-Lyme 90 A1
Newchapel Pembs 67 F2
Newchapel Staffs 99 H7
Newchapel Surr 73 G7
Newchurch Carmar 67 G3
Newchurch IoW 61 G6
Newchurch Kent 65 F4
Newchurch Lancs 106 D7
Newchurch Lancs 106 D6
Newchurch Mon 69 H2
Newchurch Powys 78 B3
Newchurch Staffs 90 D3
Newcott 58 B4
Newcraighall 126 B3
Newdigate 72 E7
Newell Green 72 B4
Newenden 64 D5
Newent 79 G6
Newerne 69 K1
Newfield Dur 112 C3
Newfield Dur 112 C1
Newfound 71 J6
Newgale 66 B3
Newgate 94 E1
Newgate Street 73 G1
Newhall ChesE 89 F1
Newhall Derbys 90 E3
Newham 121 G1
Newham Hall 121 G1
Newhaven 63 H6
Newhey 99 J1
Newholm 113 J5
Newhouse 125 F4
Newick 63 H4
Newingreen 65 G4
Newington Edin 126 A3
Newington Kent 65 G4
Newington Kent 74 E5
Newington Notts 101 J3
Newington Oxon 71 K2
Newington Bagpath 70 B2
Newland Cumb 105 G2
Newland Glos 69 J1
Newland Hull 109 G6
Newland NYorks 108 C7
Newland Oxon 80 E7
Newland Worcs 79 G4
Newlandrig 126 B4
Newlands Cumb 110 E3
Newlands Essex 74 E3
Newlands N'umb 112 A1
Newlands ScBord 120 A4
Newland's Corner 72 D7
Newlands of Geise 137 N3
Newlyn 52 B6
Newmachar 135 N9
Newmains 125 G5
Newman's End 83 J7
Newman's Green 84 C4
Newmarket Suff 83 K2
Newmarket ESiar 138 K4
Newmill Aber 131 N2
Newmill Moray 135 J5
Newmill ScBord 119 K2
Newmillerdam 101 F1
Newmillerdam Country Park WYorks WF2 6QP 27 L8
Newmiln 130 G7
Newmilns 124 D7
Newney Green 74 C1
Newnham Glos 79 F7
Newnham Hants 72 A6
Newnham Herts 83 F5
Newnham Kent 64 E2
Newnham N'hants 81 G3
Newnham Bridge 79 F2
Newnham Paddox 91 G7
Newport Corn 56 B7
Newport ERid 108 E6
Newport Essex 83 J5
Newport Glos 69 K2
Newport High 137 P7
Newport IoW 61 G6
Newport (Casnewydd) Newport 69 G3
Newport Norf 95 K4
Newport (Trefdraeth) Pembs 66 D2
Newport Som 58 C2
Newport Tel&W 89 G4
Newport Pagnell 82 B4
Newport-on-Tay 131 K8
Newpound Common 62 D4
Newquay 53 F2
Newquay Cornwall International Airport 53 F2
Newquay Zoo Corn TR7 2LZ 53 F2
Newsbank 99 H6
Newseat 135 M7
Newsells 83 G5
Newsham Lancs 105 J6
Newsham N'umb 121 H6
Newsham NYorks 112 B5
Newsham NYorks 107 J1
Newsholme ERid 108 D7
Newsholme Lancs 106 D4
Newsome 100 D1
Newstead N'umb 121 G1
Newstead Notts 101 H7
Newstead ScBord 126 D7
Newstead Abbey Notts NG15 8NA 101 H7
Newthorpe Notts 91 G1
Newthorpe NYorks 107 K6
Newtoft 102 D4
Newton A&B 123 J1
Newton Bridgend 68 B4
Newton Cambs 93 H4
Newton Cambs 83 H4
Newton Cardiff 69 F4
Newton ChesW&C 98 E7
Newton ChesW&C 98 E5
Newton Cumb 105 F2
Newton D&G 119 G4
Newton Derbys 101 G7
Newton GtMan 99 J3
Newton Here 78 C2
Newton Here 78 E3
Newton Here 78 C5
Newton High 134 B6
Newton High 133 R5
Newton High 134 B4
Newton Lancs 106 B4
Newton Lancs 105 J2
Newton Lancs 105 G6
Newton Lincs 92 D2
Newton N'hants 92 B7
Newton N'umb 121 F7
Newton N'umb 120 E3
Newton NAyr 123 H5
Newton Norf 94 C4
Newton Notts 91 J1
Newton Pembs 66 B3
Newton Pembs 66 C5
Newton ScBord 120 B1
Newton SGlos 69 K2
Newton Shrop 88 D2
Newton SLan 125 H7
Newton Som 57 K2
Newton Staffs 90 C3
Newton Suff 84 D4
Newton Swan 67 K7
Newton Warks 81 G1
Newton Wilts 60 D2
Newton WLoth 125 J3
Newton WYorks 107 K7
Newton Abbot 55 J3
Newton Arlosh 110 D1
Newton Aycliffe 112 C4
Newton Bewley 112 E4
Newton Blossomville 82 C3
Newton Bromswold 82 C2
Newton Burgoland 91 F5
Newton by Toft 102 D4
Newton Ferrers 55 F6
Newton Flotman 95 G6
Newton Green 69 J2
Newton Harcourt 91 J6
Newton Kyme 107 K5
Newton Longville 82 B5
Newton Mearns 124 D5
Newton Morrell NYorks 112 C6
Newton Morrell Oxon 81 H6
Newton Mountain 66 C5
Newton Mulgrave 113 H5
Newton of Leys 134 A7
Newton on the Hill 88 D3
Newton on Trent 102 B5
Newton Poppleford 57 J7
Newton Purcell 81 H5
Newton Regis 90 E5
Newton Reigny 111 F3
Newton St. Cyres 57 G6
Newton St. Faith 95 G4
Newton St. Loe 70 A5
Newton St. Petrock 56 C4
Newton Solney 90 E3
Newton Stacey 71 H7
Newton Stewart 114 E4
Newton Tony 71 F7
Newton Tracey 56 D3
Newton under Roseberry 113 F5
Newton Underwood 121 G5
Newton upon Derwent 108 D5
Newton Valence 61 J1
Newton with Scales 105 H6
Newtonairds 118 D5
Newtongrange 126 B4
Newtonhill 135 P11
Newton-le-Willows Mersey 98 E3
Newton-le-Willows NYorks 107 H1
Newtonmore (Baile Ùr an t-Slèibh) 134 B11
Newton-on-Ouse 108 B4
Newton-on-Rawcliffe 113 J7
Newton-on-the-Moor 121 G3
Newtown Bucks 72 C1
Newtown ChesW&C 98 E7
Newtown Corn 54 C3
Newtown Corn 52 C6
Newtown Cumb 120 A7
Newtown Derbys 99 J4
Newtown Devon 57 F3
Newtown Devon 57 J6
Newtown Dorset 58 D4
Newtown Glos 69 K1
Newtown GtMan 98 E2
Newtown GtMan 99 G2
Newtown Hants 61 H3
Newtown Hants 71 H5
Newtown Hants 60 E2
Newtown Hants 60 D3
Newtown Here 79 F4
Newtown Here 78 D3
Newtown High 133 P10
Newtown IoM 104 C6
Newtown IoW 61 F5
Newtown N'umb 121 F3
Newtown N'umb 121 F1
Newtown Oxon 72 A3
Newtown (Y Drenewydd) Powys 88 A6
Newtown RCT 68 D2
Newtown Shrop 88 D2
Newtown Som 58 B1
Newtown Som 58 B3
Newtown Staffs 99 J6
Newtown Staffs 100 C6
Newtown Staffs 90 B5
Newtown Wilts 59 J2
Newtown Wilts 71 G5
Newtown Linford 91 H5
Newtown St. Boswells 126 D7
Newtown Unthank 91 G5
Newtown-in-St-Martin 52 E6
Newtyle 130 H6
Newyears Green 72 D3
Neyland 66 C5
Nibley Glos 69 K1
Nibley SGlos 69 K3
Nibley Green 70 A2
Nicholashayne 57 K4
Nicholaston 67 J7
Nidd 107 J3
Nigg Aberdeen 135 P10
Nigg High 134 C3
Nightcott 57 G3

Scruton 112 D7
Sculthorpe 94 C2
Scunthorpe 102 B1
Scurlage 67 H7
Sea 58 C3
Sea Life Centre, Blackpool FY1 5AA 33 Blackpool
Sea Life Centre, Brighton B&H BN2 1TB 35 Brighton
Sea Life Centre, Great Yarmouth Norf NR30 3AH 95 K5
Sea Life Sanctuary, Hunstanton Norf PE36 5BH 94 A1
Sea Mills 69 J4
Sea Palling 95 J3
Seaborough 58 D4
Seaburn 121 K7
Seacombe 98 B3
Seacroft Lincs 103 J6
Seacroft WYorks 107 J6
Seadyke 93 G2
Seafield A&B 123 F2
Seafield SAyr 117 H1
Seafield WLoth 125 J4
Seaford 63 H7
Seaforth 98 C3
Seagrave 91 J4
Seagry Heath 70 C3
Seaham 112 E2
Seaham Grange 112 E1
Seahouses 127 K7
Seal 73 J6
Sealand 98 C6
Seale 72 B7
Sea-Life Adventure S'end SS1 2ER 74 E3
Sealyham 66 C3
Seamer NYorks 112 E5
Seamer NYorks 109 G1
Seamill 123 K6
SeaQuarium, Rhyl Denb LL18 3AF 97 J4
Searby 102 D2
Seasalter 75 G5
Seascale 110 B6
Seathorne 103 J6
Seathwaite Cumb 110 D5
Seathwaite Cumb 110 D7
Seatle 105 G1
Seatoller 110 D5
Seaton Corn 54 D5
Seaton Cumb 110 B3
Seaton Devon 58 B5
Seaton Dur 112 D1
Seaton ERid 109 H5
Seaton N'umb 121 J6
Seaton Rut 92 C6
Seaton Burn 121 H6
Seaton Carew 113 F4
Seaton Delaval 121 J6
Seaton Junction 58 B5
Seaton Ross 108 D5
Seaton Sluice 121 J6
Seaton Tramway Devon EX12 2NQ 58 B5
Seatown 58 D5
Seave Green 113 F6
Seaview 61 H5
Seaville 110 C1
Seavington St. Mary 58 D3
Seavington St. Michael 58 D3
Seawick 85 F7
Sebastopol 69 F2
Sebergham 110 E2
Seckington 90 E5
Second Coast 133 K1
Sedbergh 111 H7
Sedbury 69 J2
Sedbusk 111 K7
Seddington 82 E4
Sedgeberrow 80 B5
Sedgebrook 92 B2
Sedgefield 112 D4
Sedgeford 94 B2
Sedgehill 59 H2
Sedgemere 80 D1
Sedgley 90 B6
Sedgwick 105 J1
Sedlescombe 64 C6
Sedlescombe Street 64 C6
Seend 70 C5
Seend Cleeve 70 C5
Seer Green 72 C2
Seething 95 H6
Sefton 98 C2
Seghill 121 H6
Seifton 88 D7
Seighford 90 A3
Seil 129 J9
Seilebost 138 F8
Seion 96 D6
Seisdon 90 A6
Seisiadar 138 L4
Seized! Revenue & Customs Uncovered Mersey L3 4AQ 43 B5
Selattyn 88 B2
Selborne 61 J1
Selby 108 C6
Selham 62 C4
Selhurst 73 G5
Selkirk 119 K1
Sellack 78 E6
Sellafield 110 B6
Sellafield Visitors Centre Cumb CA20 1PG 110 B6
Sellafirth 139 P3
Sellindge 65 G4
Selling 65 F3
Sells Green 70 C5
Selly Oak 90 C7
Selmeston 63 J6
Selsdon 73 G5
Selsey 62 B7
Selsfield Common 63 G3
Selside Cumb 111 G7
Selside NYorks 106 C2
Selsley 70 B1
Selstead 65 H3
Selston 101 G7
Selworthy 57 H1
Semblister 139 M7
Semer 84 D4
Semington 70 B5
Semley 59 H2
Send 72 D6
Send Marsh 72 D6
Senghenydd 68 E2
Sennen 52 A6
Sennen Cove 52 A6
Sennybridge 77 J6
Senwick 115 G6
Sequer's Bridge 55 G5
Serlby 101 J4
Serpentine Gallery GtLon W2 3XA 11 G7
Serrington 60 B1
Sessay 107 K2
Setchey 94 A4
Setley 60 E4
Settiscarth 139 C6
Settle 106 D3
Settrington 108 E2
Seven Ash 57 K2
Seven Bridges 70 E2
Seven Kings 73 H3
Seven Sisters 68 B1
Seven Springs 79 J7
Sevenhampton Glos 80 B6
Sevenhampton Swin 71 F2
Sevenoaks 73 J6
Sevenoaks Weald 73 J6
Severn Beach 69 J3
Severn Stoke 79 H4
Severn Valley Railway Shrop DY12 1BG 79 H1
Sevick End 82 D3
Sevington 65 F3
Sewards End 83 J5
Sewardstone 73 G2
Sewerby 109 H3
Sewerby Hall & Gardens ERid YO15 1EA 109 J3
Seworgan 52 E5
Sewstern 92 B3
Seymour Villas 56 C1
Sezincote 80 C5
Sgarasta Mhòr 138 F8
Sgiogarstaigh 138 L1
Shabbington 71 K1
Shackerley 90 A5
Shackerstone 91 F5
Shackleford 72 C7
Shadfen 121 H5
Shadforth 112 D2
Shadingfield 95 J7
Shadoxhurst 64 E4
Shadsworth 106 C7
Shadwell Norf 94 D7
Shadwell WYorks 107 J5
Shaftenhoe End 83 H5
Shaftesbury 59 H2
Shafton 101 F1
Shakespeare's Birthplace Warks CV37 6QW 48 Stratford-upon-Avon
Shakespeare's Globe Theatre GtLon SE1 9DT 44 J3
Shalbourne 71 G5
Shalcombe 60 E6
Shalden 71 K7
Shalden Green 72 A7
Shaldon 55 K3
Shalfleet 61 F6
Shalford Essex 84 B6
Shalford Surr 72 D7
Shalford Green 84 B6
Shallowford Devon 57 F1
Shallowford Staffs 90 A3
Shalmsford Street 65 F2
Shalstone 81 H5
Shalunt 123 J3
Shambellie 115 K4
Shamley Green 72 D7
Shandon 124 A2
Shandwick 134 C3
Shangton 92 A6
Shankend 120 A3
Shankhouse 121 H6
Shanklin 61 G6
Shanklin Chine IoW PO37 6BW 61 G6
Shannochie 116 D1
Shantron 124 B2
Shap 111 G5
Shapinsay 139 E6
Shapwick Dorset 59 J4
Shapwick Som 58 D1
Sharcott 70 E6
Shard End 90 D7
Shardlow 91 G2
Shareshill 90 B5
Sharlston 101 F1
Sharlston Common 101 F1
Sharnal Street 74 D4
Sharnbrook 82 C3
Sharneyford 106 D7
Sharnford 91 G6
Sharnhill Green 59 G4
Sharow 107 J2
Sharp Street 95 H3
Sharpenhoe 82 D5
Sharperton 120 E3
Sharpham House 55 J5
Sharpness 69 K1
Sharpthorne 63 G3
Sharrington 94 E2
Shatterford 89 G7
Shatterling 65 H2
Shaugh Prior 55 F4
Shave Cross 58 D5
Shavington 99 G7
Shaw GtMan 99 J2
Shaw Swin 70 E3
Shaw WBerks 71 H5
Shaw Wilts 70 B5
Shaw Green Herts 83 F5
Shaw Green NYorks 107 H4
Shaw Mills 107 H3
Shaw Side 99 J2
Shawbost (Siabost) 138 H3
Shawbury 88 E3
Shawell 91 H7
Shawfield GtMan 99 H1
Shawfield Staffs 100 C6
Shawford 61 F2
Shawforth 106 D7
Shawhead 115 J3
Shawtonhill 124 E6
Sheanachie 116 B2
Shearington 119 F7
Shearsby 91 J6
Shebbear 56 C5
Shebdon 89 G3
Shebster 137 N3
Shedfield 61 G3
Sheen 100 D6
Sheepridge 100 D1
Sheepscombe 79 H7
Sheepstor 55 F4
Sheepwash Devon 56 C5
Sheepwash N'umb 121 H5
Sheepway 69 H4
Sheepy Magna 91 F5
Sheepy Parva 91 F5
Sheering 83 J7
Sheerness 75 F4
Sheet 61 J2
Sheffield 101 F4
Sheffield Botanic Gardens SYorks S10 2LN 21 B4
Sheffield Bottom 71 K5
Sheffield Green 63 H4
Sheffield Park Garden ESuss TN22 3QX 63 H4
Shefford 82 E5
Shefford Woodlands 71 G4
Sheigra 136 D3
Sheinton 89 F5
Shelderton 78 D1
Sheldon Derbys 100 D6
Sheldon Devon 57 K5
Sheldon WMid 90 D7
Sheldwich 65 F2
Sheldwich Lees 65 F2
Shelf Bridgend 68 C3
Shelf WYorks 107 G7
Shelfanger 95 F7
Shelfield Warks 80 C2
Shelfield WMid 90 C5
Shelfield Green 80 C2
Shelford 91 J1
Shellbrook 91 F4
Shellbrook Hill 88 C1
Shelley Essex 73 J1
Shelley Suff 84 E5
Shelley WYorks 100 E1
Shellingford 71 G2
Shellow Bowells 74 C1
Shelsley Beauchamp 79 G2
Shelsley Walsh 79 G2
Shelswell 81 H5
Shelthorpe 91 H4
Shelton Bed 82 D2
Shelton Norf 95 G6
Shelton Notts 92 A1
Shelton Shrop 88 D4
Shelve 88 C6
Shelwick 78 E4
Shelwick Green 78 E4
Shenfield 74 C2
Shenington 80 E4
Shenley 72 E1
Shenley Brook End 82 B5
Shenley Church End 82 B5
Shenleybury 72 E1
Shenmore 78 C5
Shennanton 114 D4
Shenstone Staffs 90 D5
Shenstone Worcs 79 H1
Shenstone Woodend 90 D5
Shenton 91 F5
Shenval 134 G8
Shepeau Stow 93 G4
Shephall 83 F6
Shepherd's Bush 73 F4
Shepherd's Green 72 A3
Shepherd's Patch 70 A1
Shepherdswell (Sibertswold) 65 H3
Shepley 100 D2
Shepperdine 69 K2
Shepperton 72 D5
Shepreth 83 G4
Shepreth Wildlife Park Cambs SG8 6PZ 83 G4
Shepshed 91 G4
Shepton Beauchamp 58 D3
Shepton Mallet 69 K7
Shepton Montague 59 F1
Shepway 64 C2
Sheraton 112 E3
Sherborne Dorset 59 F3
Sherborne Glos 80 C7
Sherborne St. John 71 K6
Sherbourne 80 D2
Sherbourne Street 84 D4
Sherburn Dur 112 D2
Sherburn NYorks 109 F2
Sherburn Hill 112 D2
Sherburn in Elmet 107 K6
Shere 72 D7
Shereford 94 C3
Sherfield English 60 D2
Sherfield on Loddon 71 K6
Sherford Devon 55 H6
Sherford Som 58 B2
Sheriff Hutton 108 C3
Sheriffhales 89 G4
Sheringham 95 F1
Sheringham Park Norf NR26 8TL 95 F1
Sherington 82 B4
Shernal Green 79 J2
Shernborne 94 B2
Sherramore 133 R11
Sherrington 59 J1
Sherston 70 B3
Sherwood 91 H1
Sherwood Forest Country Park Notts NG21 9HN 101 J6
Sherwood Forest Fun Park Notts NG21 9QA 101 J6
Sherwood Green 56 D3
Sherwood Pines Forest Park Notts NG21 9JL 101 J6
Shetland Islands 139 L7
Shevington 98 E2
Shevington Moor 98 E1
Sheviock 54 D5
Shide 61 G6
Shiel Bridge (Drochaid Sheile) 133 K9
Shieldaig High 133 J5
Shieldaig High 133 J3
Shieldhill 125 G3
Shielfoot 128 H3
Shifford 71 G1
Shifnal 89 G5
Shilbottle 121 G3
Shildon 112 C4
Shillingford Devon 57 H3
Shillingford Oxon 71 J2
Shillingford Abbot 57 H7
Shillingford St. George 57 H7
Shillingstone 59 H3
Shillington 82 E5
Shillmoor 120 D3
Shilstone 56 D5
Shilton Oxon 71 F1
Shilton Warks 91 G7
Shimpling Norf 95 F7
Shimpling Suff 84 C3
Shimpling Street 84 C3
Shincliffe 112 C2
Shiney Row 112 D1
Shinfield 72 A5
Shingay 83 G4
Shingham 94 B5
Shingle Street 85 H4
Shinness Lodge 136 H8
Shipbourne 73 J6
Shipbrookhill 99 F5
Shipdham 94 D5
Shipham 69 H6
Shiphay 55 J4
Shiplake 72 A4
Shiplake Row 72 A4
Shipley N'umb 121 G2
Shipley Shrop 90 A6
Shipley WSuss 62 E4
Shipley WYorks 107 G6
Shipley Bridge Devon 55 G4
Shipley Bridge Surr 73 G7
Shipley Common 91 G1
Shipley Country Park Derbys DE75 7GX 18 E2
Shipmeadow 95 H6
Shippea Hill 94 A7
Shippon 71 H2
Shipston on Stour 80 D4
Shipton Glos 80 B7
Shipton NYorks 108 B4
Shipton Shrop 88 E6
Shipton Bellinger 71 F7
Shipton Gorge 58 D5
Shipton Green 62 B6
Shipton Moyne 70 B3
Shipton Oliffe 80 B7
Shipton Solers 80 B7
Shipton-on-Cherwell 81 F7
Shiptonthorpe 108 E5
Shipton-under-Wychwood 80 D7
Shirburn 71 K2
Shirdley Hill 98 C1
Shire Hall Gallery, Stafford Staffs ST16 2LD 90 B3
Shire Oak 90 C5
Shirebrook 101 H6
Shirecliffe 101 F3
Shiregreen 101 F3
Shirehampton 69 J4
Shiremoor 121 J6
Shirenewton 69 H2
Shireoaks 101 H4
Shirl Heath 78 D3
Shirland 101 F7
Shirley Derbys 90 E1
Shirley GtLon 73 G5
Shirley Hants 60 C5
Shirley Soton 61 F3
Shirley WMid 80 C1
Shirley Heath 80 C1
Shirley Warren 60 E3
Shirleywich 90 B3
Shirrell Heath 61 G3
Shirwell 56 D2
Shirwell Cross 56 D2
Shiskine 116 D1
Shittlehope 112 A3
Shobdon 78 C2
Shobley 60 C4
Shobrooke 57 G5
Shocklach 88 D1
Shocklach Green 88 D1
Shoeburyness 75 F3
Sholden 65 J2
Sholing 61 F3
Shoot Hill 88 D4
Shooter's Hill 73 H4
Shop Corn 53 F3
Shop Corn 56 A4
Shop Corner 85 G5
Shopnoller 57 K2
Shore 99 J1
Shoreditch 73 G3
Shoreham 73 J5
Shoreham Airport 62 E6
Shoreham-by-Sea 63 F6
Shoresdean 127 H6
Shoreswood 127 H6
Shorley 61 G2
Shorncote 70 D2
Shorne 74 C4
Shorne Ridgeway 74 C4
Short Cross 88 B5
Short Green 94 E7
Short Heath Derbys 91 F4
Short Heath WMid 90 C6
Shortacombe 56 D7
Shortbridge 63 H4
Shortfield Common 72 B7
Shortgate 63 H5
Shortgrove 83 J5
Shorthampton 80 E6
Shortlands 73 G5
Shortlanesend 53 F4
Shorton 55 J4
Shorwell 61 F6
Shoscombe 70 A6
Shotatton 88 C3
Shotesham 95 G6
Shotgate 74 D2
Shotley N'hants 92 C6
Shotley Suff 85 G5
Shotley Bridge 112 A1
Shotley Gate 85 G5
Shotleyfield 112 A1
Shottenden 65 F2
Shottermill 62 B3
Shottery 80 C3
Shotteswell 81 F4
Shottisham 85 H4
Shottle 101 F7
Shottlegate 91 F1
Shotton Dur 112 E3
Shotton Dur 112 D4
Shotton Flints 98 C6
Shotton N'umb 121 H6
Shotton Colliery 112 D2
Shotts 125 G4
Shotwick 98 C5
Shouldham 94 A5
Shouldham Thorpe 94 A5
Shoulton 79 H3
Shover's Green 63 K3
Shrawardine 88 C4
Shrawley 79 H2
Shreding Green 72 D3
Shrewley 80 D2
Shrewsbury 88 D4
Shrewton 70 D7
Shri Venkateswara (Balaji) Temple of the United Kingdom WMid B69 3DU 14 E3
Shrine of Our Lady of Walsingham (Anglican) Norf NR22 6EF 94 D2
Shripney 62 C6
Shrivenham 71 F3
Shropham 94 D6
Shroton (Iwerne Courtney) 59 H3
Shrub End 84 D6
Shucknall 78 E4
Shudy Camps 83 K4
Shugborough Estate Staffs ST17 0XB 90 B3
Shurdington 79 J7
Shurlock Row 72 B4
Shurnock 80 B2
Shurton 69 F7
Shustoke 90 E6
Shut Heath 90 A3
Shute Devon 58 B5
Shute Devon 57 G5
Shutford 80 E4
Shuthonger 79 H5
Shutlanger 81 J4
Shutt Green 90 A5
Shuttington 90 E5
Shuttlewood 101 G5
Shuttleworth 99 J1
Siadar Iarach 138 J2
Sibbaldbie 119 G5
Sibbertoft 91 J7
Sibdon Carwood 88 D7
Sibertswold (Shepherdswell) 65 H3
Sibford Ferris 80 E5
Sibford Gower 80 E5
Sible Hedingham 84 B5
Sibley's Green 83 K6
Sibsey 103 G7
Sibson Cambs 92 D6
Sibson Leics 91 F5
Sibster 137 R4
Sibthorpe 92 A1
Sibton 85 H2
Sibton Green 85 H1
Sicklesmere 84 C2
Sicklinghall 107 J5
Sidbury Devon 57 K6
Sidbury Shrop 89 F7
Sidcot 69 H6
Sidcup 73 H4
Siddal 107 G7
Siddington ChesE 99 H5
Siddington Glos 70 D2
Sidemoor 79 J1
Sidestrand 95 G2
Sidford 57 K6
Sidlesham 62 B7
Sidley 64 C7
Sidlow 73 F7
Sidmouth 57 K7
Sigford 55 H3
Sigglesthorne 109 H5
Sigingstone 68 C4
Signet 80 D7
Silchester 71 K5
Sileby 91 J4
Silecroft 104 E1
Silfield 95 F6
Silian 76 E3
Silk Willoughby 92 D1
Silkstead 61 F2
Silkstone 100 E2
Silkstone Common 100 E2
Sill Field 105 J1
Silloth 110 C1
Sills 120 D3
Silpho 113 K7
Silsden 107 F5
Silsoe 82 D5
Silver End CenBeds 82 E4
Silver End Essex 84 C6
Silver Green 95 G6
Silver Street Kent 74 E5
Silver Street Som 58 E1
Silverburn 126 A4
Silvercraigs 123 G2
Silverdale Lancs 105 H2
Silverdale Staffs 90 A1
Silvergate 95 F3
Silverhill 64 C6
Silverlace Green 85 H3
Silverley's Green 85 G1
Silverstone 81 H4
Silverton 57 H5
Silvington 79 F1
Simister 99 H2
Simmondley 100 C3
Simonburn 120 D6
Simonsbath 57 F2
Simonside 121 J7
Simonstone Bridgend 68 C3
Simonstone Lancs 106 C6
Simprim 127 G6
Simpson 82 B5
Sinclair's Hill 127 G5
Sinclairston 117 J2
Sinderby 107 J1
Sinderhope 111 K1
Sindlesham 72 A5
Sinfin 91 F2
Singdean 120 A3
Singleton Lancs 105 G6
Singleton WSuss 62 B5
Singlewell 74 C4
Singret 98 C7
Sinkhurst Green 64 D3
Sinnahard 135 J9
Sinnington 108 D1
Sinton Green 79 H2
Sipson 72 D4
Sirhowy 78 A7
Sirhowy Valley Country Park Caerp NP11 7BD 7 C1
Sisland 95 H6
Sissinghurst 64 C4
Sissinghurst Castle Garden Kent TN17 2AB 64 D4
Siston 69 K4
Sithney 52 D6
Sittingbourne 75 F5
Siulaisiadar 138 L4
Six Ashes 89 G7
Six Hills 91 J3
Six Mile Bottom 83 J3
Six Roads End 90 D3
Sixhills 102 E4
Sixmile 65 G3
Sixpenny Handley 60 B3
Sizewell 85 J2
Skail 137 K5
Skaill Ork 139 B6
Skaill Ork 139 E7
Skares Aber 135 L7
Skares EAyr 117 K2
Skateraw 127 F3
Skeabost 132 E6
Skeeby 112 C6
Skeffington 92 A5
Skeffling 103 G1
Skegby 101 H6
Skegness 103 J6
Skegness Water Leisure Park Lincs PE25 1JF 103 J6
Skelberry 139 N6
Skelbo 134 B1
Skelbo Street 134 B1
Skelbrooke 101 H1
Skeld (Easter Skeld) 139 M8
Skeldon 117 H2
Skeldyke 93 G2
Skellingthorpe 102 C5
Skellister 139 N7
Skellow 101 H1
Skelmanthorpe 100 E1
Skelmersdale 98 D2
Skelmorlie 123 K4
Skelpick 137 K4
Skelton Cumb 110 F3
Skelton ERid 108 D7
Skelton NYorks 112 A6
Skelton (Skelton-in-Cleveland) R&C 113 G5
Skelton York 108 B4
Skelton-in-Cleveland (Skelton) 113 G5
Skelwick 139 D3
Skelwith Bridge 110 E6
Skendleby 103 H6
Skendleby Psalter 103 H5
Skenfrith 78 D6
Skerne 109 G4
Skeroblingarry 116 B1
Skerray 137 J3
Skerton 105 H3
Sketchley 91 G6
Sketty 67 K6
Skewen 68 A2
Skewsby 108 C2
Skeyton 95 G3
Skeyton Corner 95 G3
Skidbrooke 103 H3
Skidbrooke North End 103 H3
Skidby 109 G6
Skilgate 57 H3
Skillington 92 B3
Skinburness 110 C1
Skinflats 125 H2
Skinningrove 113 H5
Skipness 123 G5
Skippool 105 G5
Skipsea 109 H4
Skipsea Brough 109 H4
Skipton 106 E4
Skipton Castle NYorks BD23 1AW 106 E4
Skipton-on-Swale 107 J2
Skipwith 108 C6
Skirbeck 93 G1
Skirbeck Quarter 93 G1
Skirethorns 106 E3
Skirlaugh 109 H6
Skirling 125 J7
Skirmett 72 A3
Skirpenbeck 108 D4
Skirwith Cumb 111 H3
Skirwith NYorks 106 C2
Skirza 137 R3
Skittle Green 72 A1
Skomer Island 66 A5
Skullomie 137 J3
Skyborry Green 78 B1
Skye 132 E7
Skye Green 84 C6
Skyreholme 107 F3
Slack Derbys 101 F6
Slack WYorks 106 E7
Slackhall 100 C4
Slackhead 135 J4
Slad 70 B1
Slade Devon 56 D1
Slade Devon 57 K5
Slade Pembs 66 C4
Slade Swan 67 H7
Slade Green 73 J4
Slade Hooton 101 H4
Sladesbridge 54 A3
Slaggyford 111 H1
Slaidburn 106 C4
Slaithwaite 100 C1
Slaley 111 L1
Slamannan 125 G3
Slapton Bucks 82 C6
Slapton Devon 55 J6
Slapton N'hants 81 H4
Slatepit Dale 101 F6
Slattadale 133 J3
Slaugham 63 F4
Slaughden 85 J3
Slaughterford 70 B4
Slawston 92 A6
Sleaford Hants 62 B3
Sleaford Lincs 92 D1
Sleagill 111 G5
Sleap 88 D3
Sledge Green 79 H5
Sledmere 109 F3
Sleights 113 J6
Slepe 59 J5
Slerra 56 B3
Slickly 137 Q3
Sliddery 116 D1
Sligachan 132 E8
Slimbridge 70 A1
Slimbridge Wildfowl & Wetlands Trust Glos GL2 7BT 70 A1
Slindon Staffs 90 A2
Slindon WSuss 62 C6
Slinfold 62 E3
Sling 69 J1
Slingsby 108 C2
Slip End CenBeds 82 D7
Slip End Herts 83 F5
Slipper Chapel, Houghton St. Giles Norf NR22 6AL 94 D2
Slipton 82 C1
Slitting Mill 90 C4
Slochd 134 C8
Slockavullin 123 G1
Slogarie 115 G4
Sloley 95 G3
Slongaber 115 J3
Sloothby 103 H5
Slough 72 C3
Slough Green Som 58 B2
Slough Green WSuss 63 F4
Sluggan 134 C8
Slyne 105 H3
Smailholm 126 E7
Small Dole 63 E5
Small Hythe 64 D4
Smallbridge 99 J1
Smallbrook 57 G6
Smallburgh 95 H3
Smallburn 118 B1
Smalldale 100 C5
Smalley 91 G1
Smallfield 73 G7
Smallford 72 E1
Smallridge 58 B4
Smallthorne 99 H7
Smallworth 94 E7
Smannell 71 G7
Smardale 111 J6
Smarden 64 D3
Smaull 122 A4
Smeatharpe 57 K4
Smeeth 65 F4
Smeeton Westerby 91 J6
Smestow 90 A6
Smethwick 90 C7
Smethwick Green 99 H6
Smirisary 128 H3
Smisby 91 F4
Smith End Green 79 G3
Smithfield 119 K7
Smithies 101 F2
Smithincott 57 J4
Smith's End 83 G5
Smith's Green Essex 83 J6
Smith's Green Essex 83 K4
Smithton 134 B6
Smithy Green 99 G5
Smockington 91 G7
Smugglers Adventure ESuss TN34 3HY 40 Hastings
Smyrton 117 F5
Smythe's Green 84 D7
Snailbeach 88 C5
Snailwell 83 K2
Snainton 109 F1
Snaith 108 C7
Snape NYorks 107 H1
Snape Suff 85 H3
Snape Green 98 C1
Snape Watering 85 H3
Snarestone 91 F5
Snarford 102 D4
Snargate 64 E5
Snave 65 F5
Sneachill 79 J3
Snead 88 C6
Snead's Green 79 H2
Sneath Common 95 F7
Sneaton 113 J6
Sneatonthorpe 113 K6
Snelland 102 D4
Snellings 110 A6
Snelston 90 D1
Snetterton 94 D6
Snettisham 94 A2
Snipeshill 75 F5
Snitter 121 F3
Snitterby 102 C3
Snitterfield 80 D3
Snitterton 100 E6
Snittlegarth 110 D3
Snitton 78 E1
Snodhill 78 C4
Snodland 74 D5
Snow End 83 H5
Snow Street 94 E7
Snowden Hill 100 E2
Snowdon Mountain Railway Gwyn LL55 4TY 96 D7
Snowshill 80 B5
Snowshill Manor Glos WR12 7JU 80 B5
Soar Cardiff 68 D3
Soar Carmar 67 K3
Soar Devon 55 H7
Soay 132 E9
Soberton 61 H3
Soberton Heath 61 H3
Sockbridge 111 G4
Sockburn 112 D6
Sodom 97 J5
Sodylt Bank 88 C2
Softley 112 A4
Soham 83 J1
Soham Cotes 83 J1
Soldon 56 B4
Soldon Cross 56 B4
Soldridge 61 H1
Sole Street Kent 65 F3
Sole Street Kent 74 C5
Soleburn 114 A4
Solihull 80 C1
Solihull Lodge 80 B1
Sollas (Solas) 138 C1
Sollers Dilwyn 78 D3
Sollers Hope 79 F5
Sollom 98 D1
Solomon's Tump 79 G7
Solsgirth 125 H1
Solva 66 A3
Solwaybank 119 J6
Somerby Leics 92 A4
Somerby Lincs 102 D2
Somercotes 101 G7
Somerford 90 B5
Somerford Keynes 70 D2
Somerley 62 B7
Somerleyton 95 J6
Somersal Herbert 90 D2
Somersby 103 G5
Somerset House GtLon WC2R 1LA 44 F3
Somersham Cambs 83 G1
Somersham Suff 84 E4
Somerton Newport 69 G3
Somerton Oxon 81 F6
Somerton Som 58 D2
Somerton Suff 84 C3
Sompting 62 E6
Sompting Abbotts 62 E6
Sonning 72 A4
Sonning Common 72 A3
Sonning Eye 72 A4
Sontley 88 C1
Sookholme 101 H6
Sopley 60 C5
Sopworth 70 B3
Sorbie 114 E6
Sordale 137 P3
Sorisdale 128 D4
Sorn 117 K1
Sornhill 124 D7
Sortat 137 Q3
Sotby 103 F5
Sots Hole 102 E6
Sotterley 95 J7
Soudley 89 G3
Soughton 98 B6
Soulbury 82 B6
Soulby 111 J5
Souldern 81 G5
Souldrop 82 C2
Sound ChesE 89 F1
Sound Shet 139 N8
Sourhope 120 D1
Sourin 139 D4
Sourton 56 D6
Soutergate 105 F1
South Acre 94 C4
South Acton 72 E4
South Alkham 65 H3
South Allington 55 H7
South Alloa 125 G1
South Ambersham 62 C4
South Anston 101 H4
South Ascot 72 C5
South Baddesley 60 E5
South Balloch 117 H4
South Bank 113 F4
South Barrow 58 E2
South Bellsdyke 125 H2
South Benfleet 74 D3
South Bersted 62 C6
South Bockhampton 60 C5
South Bowood 58 D5
South Brent 55 G4
South Brentor 56 C7
South Brewham 59 G1
South Broomhill 121 H4
South Burlingham 95 H5
South Cadbury 59 F2
South Cairn 116 D7
South Carlton 102 C5
South Cave 109 F6
South Cerney 70 D2
South Chard 58 C4
South Charlton 121 G1
South Cheriton 59 F2
South Church 112 C4
South Cliffe 108 E6
South Clifton 102 B5
South Cockerington 103 G4
South Common 63 G5
South Cornelly 68 B3
South Corrielgills 123 J7
South Cove 95 J7
South Creake 94 C2
South Crosland 100 D1
South Croxton 91 J4
South Croydon 73 G5
South Dalton 109 F5
South Darenth 73 J5
South Dell (Dail Bho Dheas) 138 K1
South Duffield 108 C6
South Elkington 103 F4
South Elmsall 101 G1
South End Bucks 82 B6
South End Cumb 105 F3
South End Hants 60 C3
South End NLincs 109 H7
South Erradale 132 H3
South Fambridge 74 E2
South Fawley 71 G3
South Ferriby 109 F7
South Field 109 G7
South Godstone 73 G7
South Gorley 60 C3
South Green Essex 74 C2
South Green Essex 84 E7
South Green Norf 94 E4
South Green Suff 85 F1
South Gyle 125 K3
South Hall 123 J3
South Hanningfield 74 D2
South Harefield 72 D3
South Harting 61 J3
South Hayling 61 J5
South Hazelrigg 127 J7
South Heath 72 C1
South Heighton 63 H6
South Hetton 112 D2
South Hiendley 101 F1
South Hill 54 D3
South Hinksey 71 J1
South Hole 56 A4
South Holme 108 C2
South Holmwood 72 E7
South Hornchurch 73 J3
South Hourat 124 A5
South Huish 55 G6
South Hykeham 102 C6
South Hylton 112 D1
South Kelsey 102 D3
South Killingholme 102 E1
South Kilvington 107 K1
South Kilworth 91 J7
South Kirkby 101 G1
South Kirkton 135 M10
South Knighton 55 J3
South Kyme 92 E1
South Lakes Wild Animal Park Cumb LA15 8JR 105 F2
South Lancing 62 E6
South Leigh 71 G1
South Leverton 101 K4
South Littleton 80 B4
South Lopham 94 E7
South Luffenham 92 C5
South Malling 63 H5
South Marston 70 E3
South Middleton 120 E1
South Milford 107 K6
South Milton 55 H6
South Mimms 73 F1
South Molton 57 F3
South Moor 112 B1
South Moreton 71 J3
South Mundham 62 B6
South Muskham 101 K7
South Newbald 109 F6
South Newington 81 F5
South Newton 60 B1
South Normanton 101 G7
South Norwood 73 G5
South Nutfield 73 G7
South Ockendon 73 J3
South Ormsby 103 G5
South Ossett 100 E1
South Otterington 107 J1
South Owersby 102 D3
South Oxhey 72 E2
South Park 73 F7
South Perrott 58 D4
South Petherton 58 D3
South Petherwin 56 B7
South Pickenham 94 C5
South Pool 55 H6
South Queensferry (Queensferry) 125 K3
South Radworthy 57 F2
South Rauceby 92 D1
South Raynham 94 C3
South Reston 103 H4
South Ronaldsay 139 D9
South Ruislip 72 E3
South Runcton 94 A5
South Scarle 102 B6
South Shields 121 J7
South Shields Museum & Art Gallery T&W NE33 2JA 28 G3
South Somercotes 103 H3
South Somercotes Fen Houses 103 H3
South Stainley 107 J3
South Stoke B&NESom 70 A5
South Stoke Oxon 71 K3
South Stoke WSuss 62 D6
South Street ESuss 63 G5
South Street GtLon 73 H6
South Street Kent 74 C5
South Street Kent 75 H5
South Street Kent 74 E5
South Tawton 56 E6
South Thoresby 103 H5
South Tidworth 71 F7
South Tottenham 73 G3
South Town Devon 57 H7
South Town Hants 61 H1
South Uist (Uibhist a Deas) 138 B5
South View 71 K6
South Walsham 95 H4
South Warnborough 72 A7
South Weald 73 J2
South Weston 72 A2
South Wheatley Corn 54 C1
South Wheatley Notts 101 K4
South Wigston 91 H6
South Willingham 102 E4
South Wingfield 101 F7
South Witham 92 C4
South Wonston 61 F1
South Woodham Ferrers 74 E2
South Wootton 94 A3
South Wraxall 70 B5
South Yardle 90 D7
South Zeal 56 E6
Southall 72 E3
Southam Glos 79 J6
Southam Warks 81 F2
Southampton 61 F3
Southampton Airport 61 F3
Southbar 124 C4
Southborough GtLon 73 H5
Southborough Kent 73 J7
Southbourne Bourne 60 C5
Southbourne WSuss 61 J4
Southbrook 57 J6
Southburgh 94 E5
Southburn 109 F4
Southchurch 75 F3
Southcott Devon 56 D6
Southcott Wilts 70 E6
Southcourt 82 B7
Southdean 120 B3
Southdene 98 D3
Southease 63 H6
Southend A&B 116 A3
Southend Bucks 72 A3
Southend (Bradfield Southend) WBerks 71 J4
Southend Wilts 70 E4
Southend Airport 74 E3
Southend Pier S'end SS1 1EE 74 E3
Southend-on-Sea 74 E3
Southerfield 110 C2
Southerly 56 D7
Southern Green 83 G5
Southerndown 68 B4
Southerness 115 K5
Southery 94 A6
Southfield 126 A1
Southfields 73 F4
Southfleet 74 C4
Southgate Cere 86 E7
Southgate GtLon 73 G2
Southgate Norf 95 F3
Southgate Norf 94 A2
Southgate Swan 67 J7
Southill 82 E4
Southington 71 J7
Southleigh 58 B5
Southmarsh 59 G1
Southminster 75 F2
Southmoor 71 G2
Southoe 82 E2
Southolt 85 F2
Southorpe 92 D5
Southowram 107 G7
Southport 98 C1
Southport Pier Mersey PR8 1QX 98 C1
Southrepps 95 G2
Southrey 102 E6
Southrop 70 E1
Southrope 71 K7
Southsea Ports 61 H5
Southsea Wrex 98 B7
Southtown Norf 95 K5
Southtown Ork 139 D8
Southwaite Cumb 111 J6
Southwaite Cumb 111 F2
Southwark Cathedral GtLon SE1 9DA 13 B7
Southwater 62 E4
Southwater Street 62 E4
Southway 69 J7
Southwell Dorset 59 F7
Southwell Notts 101 J7
Southwell Minster Notts NG25 0HD 101 K7
Southwick D&G 115 K5
Southwick Hants 61 H4
Southwick N'hants 92 D6
Southwick Som 69 G7
Southwick T&W 112 D1
Southwick Wilts 70 B6
Southwick WSuss 63 F6
Southwold 85 K1
Southwood 58 E1
Sowden 57 H7
Sower Carr 105 G5
Sowerby NYorks 107 K1
Sowerby WYorks 107 F7
Sowerby Bridge 107 F7
Sowerby Row 110 E2
Sowerhill 57 G3
Sowley Green 84 B3
Sowood 100 C1
Sowton 57 H6
Spa Common 95 G2
Spa Complex NYorks YO11 2HD 47 Scarborough
Spadeadam 120 A6
Spalding 93 F3
Spaldington 108 D6
Spaldwick 82 E1
Spalford 102 B6
Spanby 92 D2
Sparham 94 E4
Spark Bridge 105 G1
Sparkford 59 F2
Sparkhill 90 C7
Sparkwell 55 F5
Sparrow Green 94 D4
Sparrowpit 100 C4
Sparrow's Green 63 K3
Sparsholt Hants 61 F1
Sparsholt Oxon 71 G3
Spartylea 111 K2
Spath 90 C2
Spaunton 108 D1
Spaxton 58 B1
Spean Bridge (Drochaid an Aonachain) 129 P2
Spean Bridge Woollen Mill High PH34 4EP 129 P2
Spear Hill 62 E5
Speddoch 118 D5
Speedwell 69 K4
Speen Bucks 72 B1
Speen WBerks 71 H5
Speeton 109 H2
Speke 98 D4
Speldhurst 73 J7
Spellbrook 83 H7
Spelsbury 80 E6
Spen Green 99 H6
Spencers Wood 72 A5
Spennithorne 107 G1
Spennymoor 112 C3
Spernall 80 B2
Spetchley 79 H3
Spetisbury 59 J4
Spexhall 95 H7
Spey Bay 134 H4
Spilsby 103 G6
Spindlestone 127 K7
Spinkhill 101 G5
Spinnaker Tower PO1 3TN 47 Portsmouth
Spinningdale 134 A2
Spirthill 70 C4
Spital High 137 P4
Spital W&M 72 C4
Spital in the Street 102 C3
Spitalbrook 73 G1
Spitfire & Hurricane Memorial, R.A.F. Manston Kent CT12 5DF 75 K5
Spithurst 63 H5
Spittal D&G 114 E4
Spittal D&G 114 D5
Spittal ELoth 126 C3
Spittal N'umb 127 J5
Spittal Pembs 66 C3
Spittal of Glenmuick 131 J2
Spittal of Glenshee 130 G4
Spittalfield 130 G6
Spixworth 95 G4
Splayne's Green 63 H4
Splott 69 F4
Spofforth 107 J4
Spondon 91 G2
Spooner Row 94 E6
Spoonley 89 F2
Sporle 94 C4
Sportsman's Arms 97 H7
Spott 126 E3
Spratton 81 J1
Spreakley 72 B7
Spreyton 56 E6
Spriddlestone 55 F5
Spridlington 102 D4
Spring Grove 72 E4
Spring Vale 61 H5
Springburn 124 E4
Springfield A&B 123 J3
Springfield D&G 119 J7
Springfield Fife 131 J9
Springfield Moray 134 E5
Springfield WMid 90 C7
Springhill Staffs 90 C5
Springhill Staffs 90 B5
Springholm 115 J4
Springkell 119 H6
Springside 124 B7
Springthorpe 102 B4
Springwell 112 C1
Sproatley 109 H6
Sproston Green 99 G6
Sprotbrough 101 H2
Sproughton 85 F4
Sprouston 127 F7
Sprowston 95 G4
Sproxton Leics 92 B3
Sproxton NYorks 108 C1
Sprytown 56 C7
Spurlands End 72 B2
Spurstow 98 E7
Spyway 58 E5
Square Point 115 H3
Squires Gate 105 G6
Srondoire 123 G3
Sronphadruig Lodge 130 C3
S.S. Great Britain Bristol BS1 6TY 8 C5
Stableford Shrop 89 G6
Stableford Staffs 90 A2
Stacey Bank 100 E3
Stackhouse 106 D3
Stackpole 66 C6
Stacksteads 106 D7
Staddiscombe 55 F5
Staddlethorpe 108 E7
Staden 100 C5
Stadhampton 71 K2
Staffield 111 G2
Staffin 132 E4
Stafford 90 B3
Stagden Cross 83 K7
Stagsden 82 C4
Stagshaw Bank 120 E7
Stainburn Cumb 110 B4
Stainburn NYorks 107 H5
Stainby 92 C3
Staincross 101 F1
Staindrop 112 B4
Staines 72 D4
Stainfield Lincs 92 D3
Stainfield Lincs 102 E5
Stainforth NYorks 106 D3
Stainforth SYorks 101 J1
Staining 105 G6
Stainland 100 C1
Stainsacre 113 K6
Stainsby Derbys 101 G6
Stainsby Lincs 103 G5
Stainton Cumb 105 J1
Stainton Cumb 111 F4
Stainton Dur 112 A5
Stainton Middl 112 E5
Stainton NYorks 112 B7
Stainton SYorks 101 H3
Stainton by Langworth 102 D5
Stainton le Vale 102 E3
Stainton with Adgarley 105 F2
Staintondale 113 K7
Stair Cumb 110 D4
Stair EAyr 117 J1
Stairfoot 101 F2
Staithes 113 H5
Stake Pool 105 H5
Stakeford 121 H5
Stakes 61 H4
Stalbridge 59 G3
Stalbridge Weston 59 G3
Stalham 95 H3
Stalham Green 95 H3
Stalisfield Green 64 E2
Stalling Busk 106 E1
Stallingborough 102 E1
Stallington 90 B2
Stalmine 105 G5
Stalybridge 99 J3
Stambourne 84 B5
Stamford Lincs 92 D5
Stamford N'umb 121 H2
Stamford Bridge ChesW&C 98 D6
Stamford Bridge ERid 108 D4
Stamfordham 121 F6
Stanah 105 G5
Stanborough 83 F7
Stanborough Park Herts AL8 6XF 83 F7
Stanbridge CenBeds 82 C6
Stanbridge Dorset 60 B4
Stanbridge Earls 60 E2
Stanbury 107 F6
Stand 125 F4
Standalone Farm, Letchworth Garden City Herts SG6 4JN 83 F5
Standburn 125 H3
Standedge Tunnel & Visitor Centre WYorks HD7 6NQ 100 C1
Standeford 90 B5
Standen 64 D4
Standen Street 64 D4
Standerwick 70 B6
Standford 62 B3
Standford Bridge 89 G3
Standish Glos 70 B1

Sta - The

Standish GtMan 98 E1
Standlake 71 G1
Standon Hants 61 F2
Standon Herts 83 G6
Standon Staffs 90 A2
Standon Green End 83 G7
Stane 125 G5
Stanecastle 124 B7
Stanfield 94 D3
Stanford CenBeds 82 E4
Stanford Kent 65 G4
Stanford Shrop 88 C4
Stanford Bishop 79 F3
Stanford Bridge 79 G2
Stanford Dingley 71 J4
Stanford End 72 A5
Stanford in the Vale 71 G2
Stanford on Avon 81 G1
Stanford on Soar 91 H3
Stanford on Teme 79 G2
Stanford Rivers 73 J1
Stanford-le-Hope 74 C3
Stanfree 101 G5
Stanghow 113 G5
Stanground 93 F6
Stanhoe 94 C2
Stanhope Dur 111 L3
Stanhope ScBord 119 G1
Stanion 92 C7
Stanklyn 79 H1
Stanley Derbys 91 G1
Stanley Dur 112 B1
Stanley Notts 101 G6
Stanley P&K 130 G7
Stanley Staffs 99 J7
Stanley Wilts 70 C4
Stanley WYorks 107 J7
Stanley Common 91 G1
Stanley Crook 112 B3
Stanley Gate 98 D2
Stanley Hill 79 F4
Stanleygreen 88 E2
Stanlow ChesW&C 98 D5
Stanlow Shrop 89 G6
Stanmer 63 G5
Stanmore GtLon 72 E2
Stanmore WBerks 71 H4
Stannersburn 120 C5
Stanningfield 84 C3
Stannington N'umb 121 H6
Stannington SYorks 101 F4
Stansbatch 78 C2
Stansfield 84 B3
Stanshope 100 D7
Stanstead 84 C4
Stanstead Abbotts 83 G7
Stansted 74 C5
Stansted Airport 83 J6
Stansted Mountfitchet 83 J6
Stanton Derbys 90 E4
Stanton Glos 80 B5
Stanton N'umb 121 G4
Stanton Staffs 90 D1
Stanton Suff 84 D1
Stanton by Bridge 91 F3
Stanton by Dale 91 G2
Stanton Drew 69 J5
Stanton Fitzwarren 70 E2
Stanton Harcourt 71 H1
Stanton Hill 101 G6
Stanton in Peak 100 E6
Stanton Lacy 78 D1
Stanton Lees 100 E6
Stanton Long 88 E6
Stanton Prior 69 K5
Stanton St. Bernard 70 D5
Stanton St. John 71 J1
Stanton St. Quintin 70 C4
Stanton Street 84 D2
Stanton under Bardon 91 G4
Stanton upon Hine Heath 88 E3
Stanton Wick 69 K5
Stanton-on-the-Wolds 91 J2
Stanwardine in the Fields 88 D3
Stanwardine in the Wood 88 D3
Stanway Essex 84 D6
Stanway Glos 80 B5
Stanway Green Essex 84 D6
Stanway Green Suff 85 G1
Stanwell 72 D4
Stanwell Moor 72 D4
Stanwick 82 C1
Stanwix 110 F1
Staoinebrig 138 B5
Stapeley 89 F1
Stapeley Water Gardens ChesE CW5 7LH 99 F7
Stapenhill 90 E3
Staple Kent 65 H2
Staple Som 57 K1
Staple Cross 57 J3
Staple Fitzpaine 58 B3
Staplecross 64 C5
Staplefield 63 F4
Stapleford Cambs 83 H3
Stapleford Herts 83 G7
Stapleford Leics 92 B4
Stapleford Lincs 102 B7
Stapleford Notts 91 G2
Stapleford Wilts 60 B1
Stapleford Abbotts 73 H2
Stapleford Tawney 73 J2
Staplegrove 58 B2
Staplehay 58 B2
Staplehurst 64 C3
Staplers 61 G6
Staplestreet 75 G5
Stapleton Cumb 120 A6
Stapleton Here 78 C2
Stapleton Leics 91 G6
Stapleton NYorks 112 C5
Stapleton Shrop 88 D5
Stapleton Som 58 D2
Stapley 57 K4
Staploe 82 E2
Staplow 79 F4
Star Pembs 67 F2
Star Som 69 H6
Starbotton 106 E2
Starcross 57 H7
Stareton 80 E1
Starkholmes 101 F7
Starling 99 G1
Starling's Green 83 H5
Starr 117 J4
Starston 95 G7
Startforth 112 A5
Startley 70 C3
Statham 99 F4
Stathe 58 C2
Stathern 92 A2
Station Town 112 E3
Staughton Green 82 E2
Staughton Highway 82 E2
Staunton Glos 78 E7
Staunton Glos 79 G6
Staunton Harold Hall 91 F3
Staunton Harold Reservoir Derbys DE73 8DN 91 F3
Staunton in the Vale 92 B1
Staunton on Arrow 78 C2
Staunton on Wye 78 C4
Staveley Cumb 111 F7
Staveley Derbys 101 G5
Staveley NYorks 107 J3
Staveley-in-Cartmel 105 G1
Staverton Devon 55 H4
Staverton Glos 79 H6
Staverton N'hants 81 G2
Staverton Wilts 70 B5
Staverton Bridge 79 H6
Stawell 58 C1
Stawley 57 J3
Staxigoe 137 R4
Staxton 109 G2
Staylittle (Penffordd-las) 87 H6
Staynall 105 G5
Staythorpe 101 K7
Stean 107 F2
Steane 81 G5
Stearsby 108 C2
Steart 69 F7
Stebbing 83 K6
Stebbing Green 83 K6
Stechford 90 D7
Stedham 62 B4
Steel Cross 63 J3
Steel Green 104 E2
Steele Road 120 A4
Steen's Bridge 78 E3
Steep 61 J2
Steep Marsh 61 J2
Steeple Dorset 59 J6
Steeple Essex 75 F1
Steeple Ashton 70 C6
Steeple Aston 81 F6
Steeple Barton 81 F6
Steeple Bumpstead 83 K4
Steeple Claydon 81 H6
Steeple Gidding 92 E7
Steeple Langford 60 B1
Steeple Morden 83 F4
Steeraway 89 F5
Steeton 107 F5
Stella 121 G7
Stelling Minnis 65 G3
Stembridge 58 D2
Stenalees 54 E5
Stenhill 57 J4
Stenhousemuir 125 G2
Stenigot 103 F4
Stenness 139 L5
Stenscholl 132 E4
Stenson 91 F3
Stenton 126 E3
Stepaside Pembs 66 E5
Stepaside Powys 87 K7
Stepney 73 G3
Steppingley 82 D5
Stepps 124 E4
Sternfield 85 H2
Sterridge 56 D1
Stert 70 D6
Stetchworth 83 K3
Stevenage 83 F6
Stevenston 124 A6
Steventon Hants 71 J7
Steventon Oxon 71 H2
Steventon End 83 K4
Stevington 82 C3
Stewart Park Middl TS7 8AR 29 D4
Stewartby 82 D4
Stewarton D&G 114 E6
Stewarton EAyr 124 C6
Stewkley 82 B6
Stewley 58 C3
Stewton 103 G4
Steyning 62 E5
Steynton 66 C5
Stibb 56 A4
Stibb Cross 56 C4
Stibb Green 71 F5
Stibbard 94 D3
Stibbington 92 D6
Stichill 127 F7
Sticker 53 G3
Stickford 103 G6
Sticklepath Devon 56 E6
Sticklepath Som 58 C3
Stickling Green 83 H5
Stickney 103 G7
Stiff Street 74 E5
Stiffkey 94 D1
Stifford's Bridge 79 G4
Stileway 69 H7
Stilligarry (Stadhlaigearraidh) 138 B5
Stillingfleet 108 B5
Stillington NYorks 108 B3
Stillington Stock 112 D4
Stilton 92 E7
Stinchcombe 70 A2
Stinsford 59 G5
Stirchley Tel&W 89 G5
Stirchley WMid 90 C7
Stirling (Sruighlea) 125 F1
Stirling Castle Stir FK8 1EJ 125 F1
Stirling Visitor Centre Stir FK8 1EH 125 F1
Stirton 106 E4
Stisted 84 C6
Stitchcombe 71 F5
Stithians 52 E5
Stivichall 80 E1
Stixwould 102 E6
Stoak 98 D5
Stobo 125 K7
Stoborough 59 J6
Stoborough Green 59 J6
Stobwood 125 H5
Stock 74 C2
Stock Green 79 J3
Stock Lane 71 F4
Stock Wood 80 B3
Stockbridge Hants 60 E1
Stockbridge WSuss 62 B6
Stockbury 74 E5
Stockcross 71 H5
Stockdale 52 E5
Stockdalewath 110 E2
Stockerston 92 B6
Stockgrove Country Park CenBeds LU7 0BA 82 C6
Stocking Green Essex 83 J5
Stocking Green MK 82 B4
Stocking Pelham 83 H6
Stockingford 91 F6
Stockland Cardiff 68 E4
Stockland Devon 58 B4
Stockland Bristol 69 F7
Stockleigh English 57 G5
Stockleigh Pomeroy 57 G5
Stockley 70 D5
Stocklinch 58 C3
Stockport 99 H3
Stocksbridge 100 E3
Stocksfield 121 F7
Stockton Here 78 E2
Stockton Norf 95 H6
Stockton Shrop 89 G6
Stockton Shrop 88 B5
Stockton Tel&W 89 G4
Stockton Warks 81 F2
Stockton Wilts 59 J1
Stockton Heath 99 F4
Stockton on Teme 79 G2
Stockton on the Forest 108 C4
Stockton-on-Tees 112 E5
Stockwell 79 J7
Stockwell Heath 90 C3
Stockwood Bristol 69 K5
Stockwood Dorset 58 E4
Stodday 105 H4
Stodmarsh 75 J5
Stody 94 E2
Stoer 136 C7
Stoford Som 58 E3
Stoford Wilts 60 B1
Stogumber 57 J2
Stogursey 69 F7
Stoke Devon 56 A3
Stoke Hants 71 H6
Stoke Hants 61 J4
Stoke Med 74 E4
Stoke Plym 54 E5
Stoke WMid 80 E1
Stoke Abbott 58 D4
Stoke Albany 92 B7
Stoke Ash 85 F1
Stoke Bardolph 91 J1
Stoke Bishop 69 J4
Stoke Bliss 79 F2
Stoke Bruerne 81 J3
Stoke by Clare 84 B4
Stoke Canon 57 H6
Stoke Charity 61 F1
Stoke Climsland 54 D3
Stoke D'Abernon 72 E6
Stoke Doyle 92 D7
Stoke Dry 92 B6
Stoke Edith 79 F4
Stoke Farthing 60 B2
Stoke Ferry 94 B6
Stoke Fleming 55 J6
Stoke Gabriel 55 J5
Stoke Gifford 69 K4
Stoke Golding 91 F6
Stoke Goldington 82 B4
Stoke Green 72 C3
Stoke Hammond 82 B6
Stoke Heath Shrop 89 F3
Stoke Heath Worcs 79 J2
Stoke Holy Cross 95 G5
Stoke Lacy 79 F4
Stoke Lyne 81 G6
Stoke Mandeville 82 B7
Stoke Newington 73 G3
Stoke on Tern 89 F3
Stoke Orchard 79 J6
Stoke Pero 57 G1
Stoke Poges 72 C3
Stoke Pound 79 J2
Stoke Prior Here 78 E3
Stoke Prior Worcs 79 J2
Stoke Rivers 56 E2
Stoke Rochford 92 C3
Stoke Row 71 K3
Stoke St. Gregory 58 C2
Stoke St. Mary 58 B2
Stoke St. Michael 69 K7
Stoke St. Milborough 88 E7
Stoke sub Hamdon 58 D3
Stoke Talmage 71 K2
Stoke Trister 59 G2
Stoke Villice 69 J5
Stoke Wake 59 G4
Stoke-by-Nayland 84 D5
Stokeford 59 H6
Stokeham 101 K5
Stokeinteignhead 55 K3
Stokenchurch 72 A2
Stokenham 55 J6
Stoke-on-Trent 90 A1
Stokesay 88 D7
Stokesby 95 J4
Stokesley 113 F6
Stolford 69 F7
Ston Easton 69 K6
Stonar Cut 75 K5
Stondon Massey 73 J1
Stone Bucks 81 J7
Stone Glos 69 K2
Stone Kent 73 J4
Stone Kent 64 E5
Stone Som 58 E1
Stone Staffs 90 B2
Stone SYorks 101 H4
Stone Worcs 79 H1
Stone Allerton 69 H6
Stone Cross Dur 112 A5
Stone Cross ESuss 63 K6
Stone Cross ESuss 63 J4
Stone Cross Kent 65 F4
Stone Cross Kent 63 J3
Stone House 106 C1
Stone Street Kent 73 J6
Stone Street Suff 95 H7
Stone Street Suff 84 D5
Stonea 93 H6
Stonebridge ESuss 63 J4
Stonebridge NSom 69 G6
Stonebridge WMid 90 E7
Stonebroom 101 G7
Stonecross Green 84 C3
Stonefield A&B 123 G3
Stonefield Staffs 90 B2
Stonegate ESuss 63 K4
Stonegate NYorks 113 H6
Stonegrave 108 C2
Stonehaugh 120 C6
Stonehaven 131 P2
Stonehenge Wilts SP4 7DE 70 E7
Stonehill 72 C5
Stonehouse ChesW&C 98 E5
Stonehouse D&G 115 J4
Stonehouse Glos 70 B1
Stonehouse N'umb 111 H1
Stonehouse Plym 54 E5
Stonehouse SLan 125 F6
Stoneleigh Surr 73 F5
Stoneleigh Warks 80 E1
Stoneley Green 99 F7
Stonely 82 E2
Stoner Hill 61 J2
Stones 106 E7
Stones Green 85 F6
Stonesby 92 B3
Stonesfield 80 E7
Stonestreet Green 65 F4
Stonethwaite 110 D5
Stoney Cross 60 D3
Stoney Middleton 100 E5
Stoney Stanton 91 G6
Stoney Stoke 59 G1
Stoney Stratton 59 F1
Stoney Stretton 88 C5
Stoneyburn 125 H4
Stoneyford 57 J7
Stoneygate 91 J5
Stoneyhills 75 F2
Stoneykirk 114 A5
Stoneywood 135 N9
Stonham Aspal 85 F3
Stonham Barns Suff IP14 6AT 85 F3
Stonnall 90 C5
Stonor 72 A3
Stonton Wyville 92 A6
Stony Houghton 101 G6
Stony Stratford 81 J4
Stonybreck 139 K10
Stoodleigh Devon 57 H4
Stoodleigh Devon 56 E2
Stopham 62 D5
Stopsley 82 E6
Stoptide 53 G1
Storeton 98 C4
Stormontfield 130 G8
Stornoway (Steornabhagh) 138 K4
Stornoway Airport 138 K4
Storridge 79 G4
Storrington 62 D5
Storrs 100 E4
Storth 105 H1
Storwood 108 D5
Storybook Glen Aber AB12 5FT 135 N11
Stotfold 83 F5
Stottesdon 89 F7
Stoughton Leics 91 J5
Stoughton Surr 72 C6
Stoughton WSuss 61 J3
Stoughton Cross 69 H7
Stoul 132 H11
Stoulton 79 J4
Stour Provost 59 G2
Stour Row 59 H2
Stourbridge 90 A7
Stourhead Wilts BA12 6QD 59 G1
Stourpaine 59 H4
Stourport-on-Severn 79 H1
Stourton Staffs 90 A7
Stourton Warks 80 D5
Stourton Wilts 59 G1
Stourton Caundle 59 G3
Stoven 95 J7
Stow Lincs 102 B4
Stow ScBord 126 C6
Stow Bardolph 94 A5
Stow Bedon 94 D6
Stow cum Quy 83 J2
Stow Longa 82 E1
Stow Maries 74 E2
Stow Pasture 102 B4
Stowbridge 93 J5
Stowe Glos 69 J1
Stowe Shrop 78 C1
Stowe Staffs 90 D4
Stowe Landscape Gardens Bucks MK18 5DQ 81 H5
Stowe-by-Chartley 90 C3
Stowehill 81 H3
Stowell Glos 80 B7
Stowell Som 59 F2
Stowey 69 J6
Stowford Devon 56 C7
Stowford Devon 56 E3
Stowford Devon 57 K7
Stowlangtoft 84 D2
Stowmarket 84 E3
Stow-on-the-Wold 80 C6
Stowting 65 G3
Stowupland 84 E3
Straad 123 J4
Strachan 131 M4
Strachur (Clachan Strachur) 129 M10
Stradbroke 85 G1
Stradishall 84 B3
Stradsett 94 A5
Stragglethorpe 102 C7
Straight Soley 71 G4
Straiton Edin 126 A4
Straiton SAyr 117 H3
Straloch 130 F4
Stramshall 90 C2
Strands 104 E1
Strang 104 C6
Strangford 78 E6
Strannda 138 F9
Stranraer 114 A4
Strata Florida 77 G2
Stratfield Mortimer 71 K5
Stratfield Saye 71 K5
Stratfield Turgis 71 K6
Stratford CenBeds 82 E4
Stratford Glos 79 H5
Stratford GtLon 73 G3
Stratford St. Andrew 85 H3
Stratford St. Mary 84 E5
Stratford sub Castle 60 C1
Stratford Tony 60 B2
Stratford-upon-Avon 80 D3
Stratford-upon-Avon Butterfly Farm Warks CV37 7LS 48 Stratford-upon-Avon
Strath 137 Q4
Strathan High 136 C7
Strathan High 133 K11
Strathaven 125 F6
Strathblane 124 D3
Strathcanaird 136 D9
Strathcarron 133 K8
Strathclyde Country Park NLan ML1 3ED 31 K6
Strathdon 134 H9
Strathkinness 131 K9
Strathmiglo 130 H9
Strathpeffer (Strath Pheofhair) 133 Q5
Strathtay 130 E5
Strathwhillan 123 J7
Strathy 137 L3
Strathyre 130 A9
Stratton Corn 56 A5
Stratton Dorset 59 F5
Stratton Glos 70 D1
Stratton Audley 81 H6
Stratton Hall 85 G5
Stratton St. Margaret 70 E3
Stratton St. Michael 95 G6
Stratton Strawless 95 G3
Stratton-on-the-Fosse 69 K6
Stravanan 123 J5
Strawberry Hill 72 E4
Stream 57 J2
Streat 63 G5
Streatham 73 F4
Streatham Vale 73 F4
Streatley CenBeds 82 D6
Streatley WBerks 71 J3
Street Devon 57 K7
Street Lancs 105 J4
Street NYorks 113 H6
Street Som 58 D1
Street Som 58 C4
Street Ashton 91 G7
Street Dinas 88 C2
Street End 62 B7
Street Gate 112 C1
Street Houses 108 B5
Street Lane 91 F1
Street on the Fosse 59 F1
Streethay 90 D4
Streethouse 107 J7
Streetlam 112 D7
Streetly 90 C6
Streetly End 83 K4
Strefford 88 D7
Strelley 91 H1
Strensall 108 C3
Strensham 79 J4
Stretcholt 69 F7
Strete 55 J6
Stretford GtMan 99 G3
Stretford Here 78 D3
Stretford Here 78 E3
Strethall 83 H5
Stretham 83 J1
Strettington 62 B6
Stretton ChesW&C 98 D7
Stretton Derbys 101 F6
Stretton Rut 92 C4
Stretton Staffs 90 A4
Stretton Staffs 90 E3
Stretton Warr 99 F4
Stretton en le Field 91 F4
Stretton Grandison 79 F4
Stretton Heath 88 C4
Stretton Sugwas 78 D4
Stretton under Fosse 91 G7
Stretton Westwood 88 E6
Stretton-on-Dunsmore 81 F1
Stretton-on-Fosse 80 D5
Stribers 105 G1
Strichen 135 P5
Strines 99 J4
Strinesdale Countryside Area GtMan OL4 2JJ 25 L1
Stringston 57 K1
Strixton 82 C2
Stroat 69 J2
Stromeferry 133 J7
Stromemore 133 J7
Stromness 139 B7
Stronaba 129 P2
Stronachlachar 129 R9
Strone A&B 123 K2
Strone High 133 R8
Strone High 129 N2
Stronlonag 123 K2
Stronmilchan (Sròn nam Mialchon) 129 N8
Stronsay 139 F5
Stronsay Airfield 139 F5
Strontian (Sròn an t-Sithein) 129 K4
Strood 74 D5
Strood Green Surr 73 F7
Strood Green WSuss 62 D4
Strood Green WSuss 62 E3
Stroquhan 118 D5
Stroud Glos 70 B1
Stroud Hants 61 J2
Stroud Common 72 D7
Stroud Green Essex 74 E2
Stroud Green Glos 70 B1
Stroude 72 D5
Stroul 124 A2
Stroxton 92 C2
Struan 130 C4
Strubby Lincs 103 H4
Strubby Lincs 102 E5
Strumpshaw 95 H5
Struy 133 Q7
Stryd y Facsen 96 B4
Stryt-cae-rhedyn 98 B6
Stryt-issa 88 B1
Stuart & Waterford Crystal Factory Shop, Crieff P&K PH7 4HQ 130 D8
Stuart Line Cruises, Exmouth Devon EX8 1EJ 57 J7
Stuartfield 135 P6
Stub Place 110 B7
Stubber's Green 90 C5
Stubbington 61 G4
Stubbins 99 G1
Stubbs Green 95 H6
Stubhampton 59 J3
Stubley 101 F5
Stubshaw Cross 98 E2
Stubton 92 B1
Stuck A&B 123 J4
Stuck A&B 123 K1
Stuckbeg 124 A1
Stuckreoch 123 J1
Stuckton 60 C3
Stud Green 72 B4
Studdon 111 K1
Studfold 106 D2
Studham 82 D7
Studholme 110 D1
Studland 60 B6
Studland & Godlingston Heath NNR Dorset BH19 3AX 60 B6
Studley Warks 80 B2
Studley Wilts 70 C4
Studley Common 80 B2
Studley Green 72 A2
Studley Roger 107 H2
Studley Royal Park & ruins of Fountains Abbey NYorks HG4 3DY 107 H3
Stuggadhoo 104 C6
Stump Cross Essex 83 J4
Stump Cross Lancs 105 J6
Stuntney 83 J1
Stunts Green 63 K5
Sturbridge 90 A2
Sturgate 102 B4
Sturmer 83 K4
Sturminster Common 59 G3
Sturminster Marshall 59 J4
Sturminster Newton 59 G3
Sturry 75 H5
Sturton by Stow 102 B4
Sturton le Steeple 101 K4
Stuston 85 F1
Stutton NYorks 107 K5
Stutton Suff 85 F5
Styal 99 H4
Styrrup 101 J3
Suardail 138 K4
Succoth 129 P10
Succothmore 129 N10
Suckley 79 G3
Suckley Green 79 G3
Suckley Knowl 79 G3
Sudborough 92 C7
Sudbourne 85 J3
Sudbrook Lincs 92 C1
Sudbrook Mon 69 J3
Sudbrooke 102 D5
Sudbury Derbys 90 D2
Sudbury GtLon 72 E3
Sudbury Suff 84 C4
Sudbury Hall Derbys DE6 5HT 90 D2
Sudden 99 H1
Sudgrove 70 C1
Suffield Norf 95 G2
Suffield NYorks 113 K7
Sugarloaf 64 E4
Sugnall 89 G2
Sugwas Pool 78 D4
Suie Lodge Hotel 129 R8
Sulby IoM 104 C4
Sulby IoM 104 C6
Sulgrave 81 G4
Sulham 71 K4
Sulhamstead 71 K5
Sullington 62 D5
Sullom 139 M5
Sullom Voe Oil Terminal 139 M5
Sully 68 E5
Sumburgh 139 M11
Sumburgh Airport 139 M11
Summer Bridge 107 H3
Summer Isles 136 B9
Summer Lodge 111 L7
Summercourt 53 F3
Summerfield Norf 94 B2
Summerfield Worcs 79 H1
Summerhill 98 C7
Summerhouse 112 C5
Summerlands 105 J1
Summerleaze 69 H3
Summertown 71 J1
Summit 99 J1
Sun Green 99 J3
Sunadale 123 G6
Sunbiggin 111 H6
Sunbury 72 E5
Sundaywell 118 D5
Sunderland Cumb 110 C3
Sunderland Lancs 105 H4
Sunderland T&W 112 D1
Sunderland Bridge 112 C3
Sunderland Museum & Winter Gardens T&W SR1 1PP 48 Sunderland
Sundhope 119 J1
Sundon Park 82 D6
Sundown Adventure Land Notts DN22 0HX 101 K5
Sundridge 73 H6
Sundrum Mains 117 J1
Sunhill 70 E1
Sunk Island 103 F1
Sunningdale 72 C5
Sunninghill 72 C5
Sunningwell 71 H1
Sunniside Dur 112 B3
Sunniside T&W 112 C1
Sunny Bank 110 D7
Sunny Brow 112 B3
Sunnylaw 125 F1
Sunnyside N'umb 120 E7
Sunnyside SYorks 101 G3
Sunnyside WSuss 63 G3
Sunton 71 F6
Sunwick 127 G5
Surbiton 72 E5
Surfleet 93 F3
Surfleet Seas End 93 F3
Surlingham 95 H5
Sustead 95 F2
Susworth 102 B2
Sutcombe 56 B4
Sutcombemill 56 B4
Suton 94 E6
Sutors of Cromarty 134 C4
Sutterby 103 G5
Sutterton 93 F2
Sutton Cambs 83 H1
Sutton CenBeds 83 F4
Sutton Devon 57 F5
Sutton Devon 55 H6
Sutton GtLon 73 F5
Sutton Kent 65 J3
Sutton Lincs 102 B7
Sutton Norf 95 H3
Sutton Notts 92 A2
Sutton Notts 101 J4
Sutton Oxon 71 H1
Sutton Pembs 66 C4
Sutton Peter 92 D6
Sutton Shrop 89 G7
Sutton Shrop 89 F2
Sutton Shrop 88 E4
Sutton Shrop 88 C3
Sutton Staffs 89 G3
Sutton Suff 85 H4
Sutton SYorks 101 H1
Sutton WSuss 62 C5
Sutton Abinger 72 E7
Sutton at Hone 73 J4
Sutton Bank National Park Centre NYorks YO7 2EH 108 B1
Sutton Bassett 92 A7
Sutton Benger 70 C4
Sutton Bingham 58 E3
Sutton Bonington 91 H3
Sutton Bridge 93 H3
Sutton Cheney 91 G5
Sutton Coldfield 90 D6
Sutton Courtenay 71 J2
Sutton Crosses 93 H3
Sutton Grange 107 H2
Sutton Green Oxon 71 H1
Sutton Green Surr 72 D6
Sutton Green Wrex 88 D1
Sutton Holms 60 B4
Sutton Howgrave 107 J2
Sutton in Ashfield 101 G7
Sutton in the Elms 91 H6
Sutton Ings 109 H6
Sutton Lane Ends 99 J5
Sutton le Marsh 103 J4
Sutton Leach 98 E3
Sutton Maddock 89 G5
Sutton Mallet 58 C1
Sutton Mandeville 59 J2
Sutton Montis 59 F2
Sutton on Sea 103 J4
Sutton on the Hill 90 E2
Sutton on Trent 101 K6
Sutton Poyntz 59 G6
Sutton St. Edmund 93 G4
Sutton St. James 93 H4
Sutton St. Nicholas 78 E4
Sutton Scarsdale 101 G6
Sutton Scotney 61 F1
Sutton upon Derwent 108 D5
Sutton Valence 64 D3
Sutton Veny 70 B7
Sutton Waldron 59 H3
Sutton Weaver 98 E5
Sutton Wick B&NESom 69 J6
Sutton Wick Oxon 71 H2
Sutton-in-Craven 107 F5
Sutton-on-Hull 109 H6
Sutton-on-the-Forest 108 B3
Sutton-under-Brailes 80 E5
Sutton-under-Whitestonecliffe 107 K1
Swaby 103 G5
Swadlincote 91 F4
Swaffham 94 C5
Swaffham Bulbeck 83 J2
Swaffham Prior 83 J2
Swafield 95 G2
Swainbost (Suainebost) 138 L1
Swainby 112 E6
Swainshill 78 D4
Swainsthorpe 95 G5
Swainswick 70 A5
Swalcliffe 80 E5
Swalecliffe 75 H5
Swallow 102 E2
Swallow Beck 102 C6
Swallow Falls Conwy LL24 0DW 97 F7
Swallowcliffe 59 J2
Swallowfield 72 A5
Swallows Cross 74 C2
Swampton 71 H6
Swan Green ChesW&C 99 G5
Swan Green Suff 85 G1
Swan Street 84 C6
Swanage 60 B7
Swanage Railway Dorset BH19 1HB 60 B7
Swanbach 89 F1
Swanbourne 82 B6
Swanbridge 68 E5
Swancote 89 G6
Swanland 109 F7
Swanlaws 120 C2
Swanley 73 J5
Swanley Village 73 J5
Swanmore Hants 61 G3
Swanmore IoW 61 G5
Swannington Leics 91 G4
Swannington Norf 95 F4
Swanscombe 74 C4
Swansea (Abertawe) 67 K6
Swansea Museum SA1 1SN 48 Swansea
Swanston 126 A4
Swanton Abbot 95 G3
Swanton Morley 94 E4
Swanton Novers 94 E2
Swanton Street 64 D2
Swanwick Derbys 101 G7
Swanwick Hants 61 G4
Swanwick Green 88 E1
Swarby 92 D1
Swardeston 95 G5
Swarkestone 91 F3
Swarland 121 G3
Swarraton 61 G1
Swarthmoor 105 F2
Swaton 92 E2
Swavesey 83 G2
Sway 60 D5
Swayfield 92 C3
Swaythling 61 F3
Swaythorpe 109 G3
Sweetham 57 G6
Sweethay 58 B2
Sweetshouse 54 A4
Sweffling 85 H2
Swell 58 C2
Swepstone 91 F4
Swerford 80 E5
Swettenham 99 H6
Swffryd 69 F2
Swift's Green 64 D3
Swiftsden 64 C5
Swilland 85 F3
Swillington 107 J6
Swimbridge 56 E3
Swimbridge Newland 56 D2
Swinbrook 80 D7
Swincliffe 107 H4
Swincombe 56 E1
Swinden 106 D4
Swinderby 102 B6
Swindon Staffs 90 A6
Swindon Swin 70 E3
Swindon Village 79 J6
Swine 109 H6
Swinefleet 108 D7
Swineford 69 K5
Swineshead Bed 82 D2
Swineshead Lincs 93 F1
Swineshead Bridge 93 F1
Swineside 107 F1
Swiney 137 Q6
Swinford Leics 81 G1
Swinford Oxon 71 H1
Swingate 91 H1
Swingfield Minnis 65 H3
Swingleton Green 84 D4
Swinhoe 121 H1
Swinhope 103 F3
Swinithwaite 107 F1
Swinscoe 90 D1
Swinside Hall 120 C2
Swinstead 92 D3
Swinton GtMan 99 G2
Swinton NYorks 108 D2
Swinton NYorks 107 H2
Swinton ScBord 127 G6
Swinton SYorks 101 G3
Swinton Quarter 127 G6
Swintonmill 127 G6
Swithland 91 H4
Swordale 133 R4
Swordland 132 H11
Swordly 137 K3
Sworton Heath 99 F4
Swyddffynnon 77 F2
Swyncombe 71 K2
Swynnerton 90 A2
Swyre 58 E6
Sychnant 77 J1
Syde 79 J7
Sydenham GtLon 73 G4
Sydenham Oxon 72 A1
Sydenham Damerel 54 E3
Syderstone 94 C2
Sydling St. Nicholas 59 F5
Sydmonton 71 H6
Sydney 99 G7
Syerston 92 A1
Sykehouse 101 J1
Sykes 106 B4
Sylen 67 J5
Symbister 139 P6
Symington SAyr 124 B7
Symington SLan 125 H7
Symonds Yat 78 E7
Symondsbury 58 D5
Synod Inn (Post-mawr) 76 D3
Syre 137 J5
Syreford 80 B6
Syresham 81 H4
Syston Leics 91 J4
Syston Lincs 92 C1
Sytchampton 79 H2
Sywell 82 B2
Sywell Country Park N'hants NN6 0QX 82 B2

T

Tableyhill 99 G5
Tachbrook Mallory 80 E2
Tackley 81 F6
Tacolneston 95 F6
Tadcaster 107 K5
Tadden 59 J4
Taddington Derbys 100 D5
Taddington Glos 80 B5
Taddiport 56 C4
Tadley 71 K5
Tadlow 83 F4
Tadmarton 80 E5
Tadpole Bridge 71 G1
Tadworth 73 F6
Tafarnaubach 78 A7
Tafarn-y-bwlch 66 D2
Tafarn-y-Gelyn 97 K6
Taff Merthyr Garden Village 68 E2
Taff's Well (Ffynnon Taf) 68 E3
Tafolwern 87 H5
Taibach NPT 68 A3
Tai-bach Powys 88 A3
Taicynhaeaf 87 F4
Tain 134 B2
Tai'n Lôn 86 D1
Tai'r Bull 77 J6
Tairgwaith 77 G7
Tai'r-heol 68 E2
Tairlaw 117 J3
Tai'r-ysgol 67 K6
Takeley 83 J6
Takeley Street 83 J6
Talachddu 77 K5
Talacre 97 K4
Talardd 87 H3
Talaton 57 J6
Talbenny 66 B4
Talbot Green 68 D3
Talbot Village 60 B5
Talerddig 87 J5
Talgarreg 76 D3
Talgarth 78 A5
Taliesin 87 F6
Talisker 132 D7
Talke Pits 99 H7
Talkin 111 G1
Talkin Tarn Country Park Cumb CA8 1HN 111 G1
Talla Linnfoots 119 G1
Talladale 133 K3
Talland 54 C5
Tallarn Green 88 D1
Tallentire 110 C3
Talley (Talyllychau) 67 K2
Tallington 92 D5
Talmine 136 H3
Talog 67 G3
Tal-sarn 76 E3
Talsarnau 87 F2
Talskiddy 53 G2
Talwrn IoA 96 C5
Talwrn Wrex 88 B1
Talwrn Wrex 88 C1
Talybont Cere 87 F7
Tal-y-bont Conwy 97 F6
Tal-y-bont Gwyn 86 E3
Tal-y-bont Gwyn 96 E5
Talybont-on-Usk 78 A6
Tal-y-Cae 96 E6
Tal-y-cafn 97 F5
Tal-y-coed 78 D7
Talygarn 68 D3
Tal-y-llyn Gwyn 87 G5
Talyllyn Powys 78 A6
Talysarn 96 C7
Tal-y-wern 87 H5
Tamavoid 124 D1
Tamerton Foliot 54 E4
Tamworth 90 E5
Tamworth Green 93 G1
Tan Office Green 84 B3
Tandem 100 D1
Tandridge 73 G6
Tanerdy 67 H3
Tanfield 112 B1
Tanfield Lea 112 B1
Tang 107 H4
Tang Hall 108 C4
Tangiers 66 C4
Tangley 71 G6
Tangmere 62 C6
Tangy 116 A1
Tank Museum, Bovington Dorset BH20 6JG 59 H6
Tankersley 101 F2
Tankerton 75 H5
Tan-lan 87 F1
Tannach 137 R5
Tannadice 131 K5
Tannington 85 G2
Tannochside 124 E4
Tansley 101 F7
Tansley Knoll 101 F7
Tansor 92 D6
Tantobie 112 B1
Tanton 113 F5
Tanworth in Arden 80 C1
Tan-y-fron 97 H6
Tan-y-graig 86 C2
Tanygrisiau 87 F1
Tan-y-groes 67 F1
Tan-y-pistyll 87 K3
Tan-yr-allt 97 G4
Taobh Siar 138 G7
Tapeley 56 C3
Taplow 72 C3
Tapton Grove 101 G5
Taransay (Tarasaigh) 138 F7
Tarbert A&B 123 G4
Tarbert A&B 122 E5
Tarbert A&B 122 E2
Tarbert (Tairbeart) ESiar 138 G7
Tarbet (An Tairbeart) A&B 129 Q10
Tarbet High 132 H11
Tarbet High 136 D5
Tarbock Green 98 D4
Tarbolton 117 J1
Tarbrax 125 J5
Tardebigge 79 J2
Tardy Gate 105 J7
Tarfside 131 K3
Tarland 135 J10
Tarleton 105 H7
Tarlscough 98 D1
Tarlton 70 C2
Tarnbrook 105 J4
Tarnock 69 G6
Tarporley 98 E6
Tarr 57 K2
Tarrant Crawford 59 J4
Tarrant Gunville 59 J3
Tarrant Hinton 59 J3
Tarrant Keyneston 59 J4
Tarrant Launceston 59 J4
Tarrant Monkton 59 J4
Tarrant Rawston 59 J4
Tarrant Rushton 59 J4
Tarrel 134 C2
Tarring Neville 63 H6
Tarrington 79 F4
Tarrnacraig 123 H7
Tarskavaig 132 F10
Tarves 135 N7
Tarvie (Tairbhidh) High 133 Q5
Tarvie P&K 130 F4
Tarvin 98 D6
Tarvin Sands 98 D6
Tasburgh 95 G6
Tasley 89 F6
Taston 80 E6
Tate Britain GtLon SW1P 4RG 13 A7
Tate Liverpool Mersey L3 4BB 43 B5
Tate Modern GtLon SE1 9TG 44 H4
Tate St. Ives Corn TR26 1TG 52 C4
Tatenhill 90 E3
Tathall End 82 B4
Tatham 106 B3
Tathwell 103 G4
Tatsfield 73 H6
Tattenhall 98 D7
Tattenhoe 82 B5
Tatterford 94 C3
Tattersett 94 C2
Tattershall 103 F7
Tattershall Bridge 102 E7
Tattershall Thorpe 103 F7
Tattingstone 85 F5
Tatton Park ChesE WA16 6QN 99 G4
Tatworth 58 C4
Tauchers 134 H6
Taunton 58 B2
Tavelty 135 M9
Taverham 95 F4
Tavernspite 66 E4
Tavistock 54 E3
Taw Bridge 56 E5
Taw Green 56 E6
Tawstock 56 D3
Taxal 100 C5
Tayburn 124 D6
Tayinloan 122 E6
Taylors Cross 56 A4
Taynish 123 F2
Taynton Glos 79 G6
Taynton Oxon 80 D7
Taynuilt (Taigh an Uillt) 129 M7
Tayock 131 M5
Tayovullin 122 A3
Tayport 131 K8
Tayvallich 123 F2
Tea Green 82 E6
Tealby 102 E3
Tealing 131 K7
Team Valley 121 H7
Teanamachar 138 B2
Teangue 132 G10
Tebay 111 H6
Tebworth 82 C6
Techniquest Cardiff CF10 5BW 7 C6
Tedburn St. Mary 57 G6
Teddington Glos 79 J5
Teddington GtLon 72 E4
Tedstone Delamere 79 F3
Tedstone Wafre 79 F3
Teeton 81 H1
Teffont Evias 59 J1
Teffont Magna 59 J1
Tegryn 67 F2
Tehidy Country Park Corn TR14 0HA 52 D4
Teigh 92 B4
Teign Village 57 G7
Teigngrace 55 J3
Teignmouth 55 K3
Telford 89 F5
Telford Wonderland Tel&W TF3 4AY 89 G5
Telham 64 C6
Tellisford 70 B6
Telscombe 63 H6
Telscombe Cliffs 63 H6
Templand 119 F5
Temple Corn 54 B3
Temple Midlo 126 B5
Temple Balsall 80 D1
Temple Bar 76 E3
Temple Cloud 69 K6
Temple End 83 K3
Temple Ewell 65 H3
Temple Grafton 80 C3
Temple Guiting 80 B6
Temple Herdewyke 80 E3
Temple Hirst 108 C7
Temple Newsam WYorks LS15 0AE 27 M3
Temple Normanton 101 G6
Temple Sowerby 111 H4
Templecombe 59 G2
Templeton Devon 57 G4
Templeton Pembs 66 E4
Templeton Bridge 57 G4
Tempsford 82 E3
Ten Mile Bank 94 A6
Tenbury Wells 78 E2
Tenby (Dinbych-y-pysgod) 66 E5
Tendring 85 F6
Tendring Green 85 F6
Tenterden 64 D4
Terally 114 B6
Terling 84 B7
Tern 89 F4
Ternhill 89 F2
Terregles 115 K3
Terriers 72 B2
Terrington 108 C2
Terrington St. Clement 93 J3
Terrington St. John 93 J4
Terry's Green 80 C1
Teston 64 C2
Testwood 60 E3
Tetbury 70 B2
Tetbury Upton 70 B2
Tetchill 88 C2
Tetcott 56 B6
Tetford 103 G5
Tetney 103 G2
Tetney Lock 103 G2
Tetsworth 71 K1
Tettenhall 90 A5
Tettenhall Wood 90 A6
Tetworth 83 F3
Teversal 101 G6
Teversham 83 H3
Teviot Water Gardens ScBord TD5 8LE 120 C1
Teviothead 119 K3
Tewin 83 F7
Tewkesbury 79 H5
Tewkesbury Abbey Glos GL20 5RZ 79 H5
Teynham 75 F5
Thackley 107 G6
Thainston 131 M3
Thakeham 62 E5
Thame 72 A1
Thames Ditton 72 E5
Thames Haven 74 D3
Thamesmead 73 H3
Thanington 65 G2
Thankerton 125 H7
Tharston 95 F6
Thatcham 71 J5
Thatto Heath 98 E3
Thaxted 83 J5
The Apes Hall 93 J6
The Bage 78 B4
The Balloch 130 D9
The Bar 62 E4
The Birks 135 M10
The Bog 88 C6
The Bourne 72 B7
The Bratch 90 A6
The Broad 78 D2
The Bryn 69 G1
The Burf 79 H2
The Butts 70 A7
The Camp 70 C1
The Chequer 88 D1
The City Bucks 72 A2
The City Suff 95 H7
The Common Wilts 60 D1
The Common Wilts 70 D3
The Craigs 133 Q1
The Cronk 104 C4
The Delves 90 C6
The Den 124 B5
The Dicker 63 J6
The Down 89 F6
The Drums 131 J4
The Eaves 69 K1
The Flatt 120 A6
The Folly 82 E7
The Forge 78 C3
The Forstal ESuss 63 J3
The Forstal Kent 65 F4
The Grange Lincs 103 J5
The Grange Shrop 88 C2
The Grange Surr 73 G7
The Green Cumb 104 E1
The Green Essex 84 B7
The Green Flints 98 B6
The Green Wilts 59 H1
The Grove 79 H4
The Haven 62 D3
The Headland 113 F3
The Heath 90 C2
The Herberts 68 C4
The Hermitage 73 F6
The Hill 104 E1
The Holme 107 H4
The Howe 104 A7
The Isle 88 D4
The Laurels 95 H6
The Leacon 64 E4
The Lee 72 B1
The Leigh 79 H6
The Lhen 104 C3
The Lodge 123 K1
The Marsh 88 C6
The Moor ESuss 64 D6
The Moor Kent 64 C5
The Mumbles 67 K7
The Murray 124 E5
The Mythe 79 H5
The Narth 69 J1
The Node 83 F7
The Oval 70 A5
The Quarter 64 D3
The Reddings 79 J6
The Rhos 66 D4
The Rookery 99 H7
The Rowe 90 A2
The Sale 90 D4
The Sands 72 B7
The Shoe 70 B4
The Slade 71 J4
The Smithies 89 F6
The Stocks 64 E5
The Swillett 72 D2
The Thrift 83 G5
The Vauld 78 E4
The Wern 98 B7
The Wyke 89 G5
Theakston 107 J1
Thealby 102 B1
Theale Som 69 H7
Theale WBerks 71 K4
Thearne 109 G6
Theberton 85 J2
Thedden Grange 61 H1
Theddingworth 91 J7
Theddlethorpe All Saints 103 H4
Theddlethorpe St. Helen 103 H4
Thelbridge Barton 57 F4
Thelbridge Cross 57 F4
Thelnetham 84 E1
Thelveton 95 F7
Thelwall 99 F4
Themelthorpe 94 E3
Thenford 81 G4
Therfield 83 G5
Thermae Bath Spa B&NESom BA1 1SJ 33 Bath

Whitbourne 79 G3
Whitburn T&W 121 K7
Whitburn WLoth 115 H4
Whitby ChesW&C 98 C5
Whitby NYorks 113 J5
Whitby Abbey NYorks YO22 4JT 113 K5
Whitby Lifeboat Museum NYorks YO21 3PU 113 J5
Whitbyheath 98 C5
Whitchurch B&NESom 69 K5
Whitchurch Bucks 82 B6
Whitchurch Cardiff 68 E3
Whitchurch Devon 54 E3
Whitchurch Hants 71 H7
Whitchurch Here 78 E7
Whitchurch Pembs 66 A3
Whitchurch Shrop 88 E1
Whitchurch Warks 80 D4
Whitchurch Canonicorum 58 C5
Whitchurch Hill 71 K4
Whitchurch-on-Thames 71 K4
Whitcombe 59 G6
Whitcott Keysett 88 B7
White Ball 57 J4
White Colne 84 C6
White Coppice 99 F1
White Cross Corn 53 F3
White Cross Devon 57 J6
White Cross Here 78 D4
White Cross Wilts 59 G1
White Cube GtLon N1 6PB 12 B6
White End 79 H6
White Hill 59 H1
White Houses 101 K5
White Kirkley 112 A3
White Lackington 59 G5
White Ladies Aston 79 J3
White Lund 105 H3
White Mill 67 H3
White Moor 91 F1
White Notley 84 B7
White Ox Mead 70 A6
White Pit 103 G5
White Post Farm Centre, Farnsfield Notts NG22 8HL 101 J7
White Rocks 78 D6
White Roding 83 J7
White Waltham 72 B4
Whiteash Green 84 B5
Whitebirk 106 C7
Whitebridge (An Drochaid Bhàn) 133 Q9
Whitebrook 69 J1
Whiteburn 126 D6
Whitecairn 114 C5
Whitecairns 135 P9
Whitecastle 125 J6
Whitechapel 105 J5
Whitechurch 66 E2
Whitecote 107 H6
Whitecraig 126 B3
Whitecroft 69 K1
Whitecrook 114 B5
Whitecross Corn 52 C5
Whitecross Corn 53 G1
Whitecross Dorset 58 D5
Whitecross Falk 125 H3
Whitefield Devon 57 F2
Whitefield Dorset 59 J5
Whitefield GtMan 99 H2
Whitegate 99 F6
Whitehall Devon 57 K4
Whitehall Hants 72 A6
Whitehall Ork 139 F5
Whitehall WSuss 62 E4
Whitehaven 110 A5
Whitehill Hants 61 J1
Whitehill Kent 64 E2
Whitehill Midlo 126 B4
Whitehill NAyr 124 A5
Whitehills 135 L4
Whitehouse A&B 123 G4
Whitehouse Aber 135 L9
Whitehouse Common 90 D6
Whitekirk 126 D2
Whitelackington 58 C3
Whitelaw 127 G5
Whitelees 124 B7
Whiteley 61 G4
Whiteley Bank 61 G6
Whiteley Green 99 J5
Whiteley Village 72 D5
Whiteleys 114 A5
Whitemans Green 63 G4
Whitemire 134 D5
Whitemoor 53 G3
Whiteness 139 M8
Whiteoak Green 80 E7
Whiteparish 60 D2
Whiterashes 135 N8
Whiteshill 70 B1
Whiteside N'umb 120 C7
Whiteside WLoth 125 H4
Whitesmith 63 J5
Whitestaunton 58 B3
Whitestone A&B 123 F7
Whitestone Devon 57 G6
Whitestreet Green 84 D5
Whiteway 79 J7
Whitewell Lancs 106 B5
Whitewell Wrex 88 D1
Whiteworks 55 G3
Whitewreath 134 G5
Whitfield Here 78 D5
Whitfield Kent 65 J3
Whitfield N'hants 81 H5
Whitfield N'umb 111 J1
Whitfield SGlos 69 K2
Whitford Devon 58 B5
Whitford (Chwitffordd) Flints 97 K5
Whitgift 108 E7
Whitgreave 90 A3
Whithorn 114 E6
Whiting Bay 116 E1
Whitkirk 107 J6
Whitland (Hendy-Gwyn) 67 F4
Whitland Abbey 67 F4
Whitleigh 54 E4
Whitletts 117 H1
Whitley NYorks 108 B7
Whitley Read 72 A5
Whitley Wilts 70 B5
Whitley WMid 80 E1
Whitley Bay 121 L6
Whitley Chapel 111 L1
Whitley Heath 90 A3
Whitley Lower 100 E1
Whitley Row 73 H6
Whitlock's End 80 C1
Whitminster 70 A1
Whitmore Dorset 60 B4
Whitmore Staffs 90 A1
Whitnage 57 J4
Whitnash 80 E2
Whitnell 69 F7
Whitney-on-Wye 78 B4
Whitrigg Cumb 110 D1
Whitrigg Cumb 110 D3
Whitsbury 60 C3
Whitsome 127 G5
Whitson 69 G3
Whitstable 75 H5
Whitstone 54 C1
Whittingham 121 F2
Whittingslow 88 D7
Whittington Derbys 101 F5
Whittington Glos 80 B6
Whittington Lancs 106 B2
Whittington Norf 94 B6
Whittington Shrop 88 C2
Whittington Staffs 90 A7
Whittington Staffs 90 D5
Whittington Worcs 79 H3
Whittlebury 81 H4
Whittle-le-Woods 105 J7
Whittlesey 93 F6
Whittlesford 83 H4
Whittlestone Head 99 G1
Whitton GtLon 72 E4
Whitton N'umb 121 F3
Whitton NLincs 109 F7
Whitton Powys 78 B2
Whitton Shrop 78 E1
Whitton Stock 112 D4
Whitton Suff 85 F4
Whittonditch 71 F4
Whittonstall 112 A1
Whitway 71 H6
Whitwell Derbys 101 H5
Whitwell Herts 82 E6
Whitwell IoW 61 G7
Whitwell NYorks 112 C7
Whitwell Rut 92 C5
Whitwell Street 95 F3
Whitwell-on-the-Hill 108 D3
Whitwick 91 G4
Whitwood 107 K7
Whitworth 99 H1
Whitworth Art Gallery, Manchester GtMan M15 6ER 25 H5
Whixall 88 E2
Whixley 107 K4
Whorlton Dur 112 B5
Whorlton NYorks 112 E6
Whygate 120 C6
Whyle 78 E2
Whyteleafe 73 G6
Wibdon 69 J2
Wibsey 107 G6
Wibtoft 91 G7
Wichenford 79 G2
Wichling 64 E2
Wick Bourne 60 C5
Wick Devon 57 K5
Wick (Inbhir Ùige) High 137 R4
Wick SGlos 70 A4
Wick Som 69 F7
Wick Som 58 E1
Wick VGlam 68 C4
Wick Wilts 60 C2
Wick Worcs 79 J4
Wick WSuss 62 D6
Wick Airport 137 R4
Wick Hill Kent 64 D3
Wick Hill W'ham 72 A5
Wick St. Lawrence 69 G5
Wicken Cambs 83 J1
Wicken N'hants 81 J5
Wicken Bonhunt 83 H5
Wickenby 102 D4
Wicker Street Green 84 D4
Wickerslack 111 H5
Wickersley 101 G3
Wicketwood Hill 91 J1
Wickford 74 D2
Wickham Hants 61 G3
Wickham WBerks 71 G4
Wickham Bishops 84 C7
Wickham Heath 71 H5
Wickham Market 85 H3
Wickham St. Paul 84 C5
Wickham Skeith 84 E2
Wickham Street Suff 84 B3
Wickham Street Suff 84 E2
Wickhambreaux 65 H2
Wickhambrook 84 B3
Wickhamford 80 B4
Wickhampton 95 J5
Wicklewood 94 E5
Wickmere 95 F2
Wicksteed Park N'hants NN15 6NJ 82 B1
Wickstreet 63 J6
Wickwar 70 A3
Widcombe 70 A5
Widdington 83 J5
Widdop 106 E6
Widdrington 121 H4
Widdrington Station 121 H4
Wide Open 121 H6
Widecombe in the Moor 55 H3
Widegates 54 C5
Widemouth Bay 56 A5
Widewall 139 D8
Widford Essex 74 C1
Widford Herts 83 H7
Widford Oxon 80 D7
Widgham Green 83 K3
Widmer End 72 B2
Widmerpool 91 J3
Widnes 98 E4
Widworthy 58 B5
Wigan 98 E2
Wigan Pier GtMan WN3 4EU 98 E2
Wiganthorpe 108 C2
Wigborough 58 D3
Wiggaton 57 K6
Wiggenhall St. Germans 93 J4
Wiggenhall St. Mary Magdalen 93 J4
Wiggenhall St. Mary the Virgin 93 J4
Wiggenhall St. Peter 94 A4
Wiggens Green 83 K4
Wigginton Herts 82 C7
Wigginton Oxon 80 E5
Wigginton Shrop 88 C2
Wigginton Staffs 90 E5
Wigginton York 108 C4
Wigglesworth 106 D4
Wiggonby 110 E1
Wiggonholt 62 D5
Wighill 107 K5
Wighton 94 D2
Wightwizzle 100 E3
Wigley 60 E3
Wigmore Here 78 D2
Wigmore Med 74 E5
Wigsley 102 B5
Wigsthorpe 92 D7
Wigston 91 J6
Wigston Parva 91 G7
Wigthorpe 101 H4
Wigtoft 93 F2
Wigton 110 D2
Wigtown 114 E5
Wike 107 J5
Wilbarston 92 B7
Wilberfoss 108 D4
Wilburton 83 H1
Wilby N'hants 82 B2
Wilby Norf 94 E6
Wilby Suff 85 G1
Wilcot 70 E5
Wilcott 88 C4
Wilcrick 69 H3
Wilday Green 101 F5
Wildboarclough 99 J6
Wilde Street 84 B1
Wilden Bed 82 D3
Wilden Worcs 79 H1
Wildhern 71 G6
Wildhill 73 F1
Wildmoor 79 J1
Wildsworth 102 B3
Wilford 91 H2
Wilkesley 89 F1
Wilkhaven 134 D2
Wilkieston 125 K4
Wilksby 103 F6
Willand Devon 57 J4
Willand Som 57 K4
Willaston ChesE 99 F7
Willaston ChesW&C 98 C5
Willaston Shrop 88 E2
Willen 82 B4
Willen Lakeside Park MK MK15 9HQ 9 E3
Willenhall WMid 90 B6
Willenhall WMid 80 E1
Willerby ERid 109 G7
Willerby NYorks 109 G2
Willersey 80 C5
Willersley 78 C4
Willesborough 65 F3
Willesborough Lees 65 F3
Willesden 73 F3
Willesleigh 56 D2
Willesley 70 B3
Willett 57 K2
Willey Shrop 89 F6
Willey Warks 91 G7
Willey Green 72 C6
William's Green 84 D4
Williamscot 81 F4
Williamson Park, Lancaster Lancs LA1 1UX 105 H3
Williamthorpe 101 G6
Willian 83 F5
Willimontswick 120 C7
Willingale 73 J1
Willingdon 63 J6
Willingham 83 H1
Willingham by Stow 102 B4
Willingham Green 83 K3
Willington Bed 82 E3
Willington Derbys 90 E3
Willington Dur 112 B3
Willington Kent 64 C2
Willington T&W 121 J7
Willington Warks 80 D5
Willington Corner 98 E6
Willisham 84 E3
Willitoft 108 D6
Williton 57 J1
Willoughbridge 89 G1
Willoughby Lincs 103 H5
Willoughby Warks 81 G2
Willoughby Waterleys 91 H6
Willoughby-on-the-Wolds 91 J3
Willoughton 102 C3
Willow Green 99 F5
Willows Farm Village Herts AL2 1BB 72 E1
Willows Green 84 B7
Willsbridge 69 K4
Willslock 90 C2
Willsworthy 56 D7
Willtown 58 C2
Wilmcote 80 C3
Wilmington B&NESom 69 K5
Wilmington Devon 58 B4
Wilmington ESuss 63 J6
Wilmington Kent 73 J4
Wilmslow 99 H4
Wilnecote 90 E5
Wilney Green 94 E7
Wilpshire 106 B6
Wilsden 107 F6
Wilsford Lincs 92 D1
Wilsford Wilts 60 C1
Wilsford Wilts 70 E6
Wilsham 57 F1
Wilshaw 100 D2
Wilsill 107 G3
Wilsley Green 64 C4
Wilsley Pound 64 C4
Wilson 91 G3
Wilstead 82 D4
Wilsthorpe ERid 109 H3
Wilsthorpe Lincs 92 D4
Wilstone 82 C7
Wilton Cumb 110 B5
Wilton Here 78 E6
Wilton NYorks 108 E1
Wilton R&C 113 F5
Wilton ScBord 119 K2
Wilton Wilts 71 F5
Wilton Wilts 60 B1
Wilton House Wilts SP2 0BJ 60 B1
Wiltown 57 K4
Wimbish 83 J5
Wimbish Green 83 K5
Wimblebury 90 C4
Wimbledon 73 F4
Wimbledon All England Lawn Tennis & Croquet Club GtLon SW19 5AG 11 G10
Wimblington 93 H6
Wimborne Minster 60 B4
Wimborne Minster Dorset BH21 1HT 3 B3
Wimborne St. Giles 60 B3
Wimbotsham 94 A5
Wimpole 83 G3
Wimpole Home Farm Cambs SG8 0BW 83 G4
Wimpole Lodge 83 G4
Wimpstone 80 D4
Wincanton 59 G2
Winceby 103 G6
Wincham 99 F5
Winchburgh 125 J3
Winchcombe 80 B6
Winchelsea 64 E6
Winchelsea Beach 64 E6
Winchester 61 F2
Winchester Cathedral Hants SO23 9LS 49 Winchester
Winchet Hill 64 C3
Winchfield 72 A6
Winchmore Hill Bucks 72 C2
Winchmore Hill GtLon 73 G2
Wincle 99 J6
Wincobank 101 F3
Windermere 110 F7
Windermere Lake Cruises Cumb LA12 8AS 110 E7
Winderton 80 E4
Windle Hill 98 C5
Windlehurst 99 J4
Windlesham 72 C5
Windley 91 F1
Windmill 100 D5
Windmill Hill ESuss 63 K5
Windmill Hill Som 58 C3
Windmill Hill Worcs 79 J4
Windrush 80 C7
Windsor 72 C4
Windsor Castle W&M SL4 1NJ 49 Windsor
Windsor Green 84 C3
Windy Nook 121 H7
Windygates 131 J10
Windy-Yett 124 C5
Wineham 63 F4
Winestead 109 J7
Winewall 106 E6
Winfarthing 95 F7
Winford IoW 61 G6
Winford NSom 69 J5
Winforton 78 B4
Winfrith Newburgh 59 H6
Wing Bucks 82 B6
Wing Rut 92 B5
Wingate 112 D3
Wingates GtMan 99 F2
Wingates N'umb 121 F4
Wingerworth 101 F6
Wingfield CenBeds 82 D6
Wingfield Suff 85 G1
Wingfield Wilts 70 B6
Wingfield Green 85 G1
Wingham 65 H2
Wingham Well 65 H2
Wingmore 65 G3
Wingrave 82 B7
Winkburn 101 K7
Winkfield 72 C4
Winkfield Row 72 B4
Winkhill 100 C7
Winkleigh 56 E5
Winksley 107 H2
Winkton 60 C5
Winlaton 121 G7
Winlaton Mill 121 G7
Winmarleigh 105 H5
Winnard's Perch 53 G2
Winnersh 72 A4
Winnington 99 F5
Winscombe 69 H6
Winsford ChesW&C 99 F6
Winsford Som 57 H2
Winsham Devon 56 C2
Winsham Som 58 C4
Winshill 90 E3
Winsh-wen 67 K6
Winskill 111 G3
Winslade 71 K7
Winsley 70 B5
Winslow 81 J6
Winson 70 D1
Winsor 60 E3
Winster Cumb 110 F7
Winster Derbys 100 E6
Winston Dur 112 B5
Winston Suff 85 F2
Winston Green 85 F2
Winstone 70 C1
Winswell 56 C4
Winter Gardens FY1 1HW 33 Blackpool
Winter Gardens NSom BS23 1AJ 49 Weston-super-Mare
Winterborne Came 59 G6
Winterborne Clenston 59 H4
Winterborne Herringston 59 F6
Winterborne Houghton 59 H4
Winterborne Kingston 59 H5
Winterborne Monkton 59 F6
Winterborne Stickland 59 H4
Winterborne Whitechurch 59 H4
Winterborne Zelston 59 H5
Winterbourne SGlos 69 K3
Winterbourne WBerks 71 H4
Winterbourne Abbas 59 F5
Winterbourne Bassett 70 E4
Winterbourne Dauntsey 60 C1
Winterbourne Earls 60 C1
Winterbourne Gunner 60 C1
Winterbourne Monkton 70 E4
Winterbourne Steepleton 59 F6
Winterbourne Stoke 70 D7
Winterbrook 71 K3
Winterburn 106 E4
Wintercleugh 118 E2
Winteringham 109 F7
Winterley 99 G7
Wintersett 101 F1
Wintershill 61 G3
Winterslow 60 D1
Winterton 102 C1
Winterton-on-Sea 95 J4
Winthorpe Lincs 103 J6
Winthorpe Notts 102 B7
Winton Bourne 60 B5
Winton Cumb 111 J5
Wintringham 108 E2
Winwick Cambs 92 E7
Winwick N'hants 81 H1
Winwick Warr 99 F3
Wirksworth 100 E7
Wirksworth Moor 101 F7
Wirral Country Park Mersey CH61 0HN 98 B4
Wirswall 88 E1
Wisbech 93 H5
Wisbech St. Mary 93 H5
Wisborough Green 62 D4
Wiseton 101 K4
Wishaw NLan 125 F5
Wishaw Warks 90 D6
Wisley 72 D6
Wispington 103 F5
Wissett 85 H1
Wissington 84 D5
Wistanstow 88 D7
Wistanswick 89 F3
Wistaston 99 F7
Wiston Pembs 66 D4
Wiston SLan 125 H7
Wiston WSuss 62 E5
Wistow Cambs 93 F7
Wistow NYorks 108 B6
Wiswell 106 C6
Witcham 83 H1
Witchampton 59 J4
Witchburn 116 B1
Witchford 83 J1
Witcombe 58 D2
Witham 84 C7
Witham Friary 70 A7
Witham on the Hill 92 D4
Withcall 103 F4
Withcote 92 A5
Withdean 63 G6
Witherenden Hill 63 K4
Witherhurst 63 K4
Witheridge 57 G4
Witherley 91 F6
Withern 103 H4
Withernsea 109 K7
Withernwick 109 H5
Withersdale Street 95 G7
Withersfield 83 K4
Witherslack 105 H1
Witherslack Hall 105 H1
Withiel 53 G2
Withiel Florey 57 H2
Withielgoose 54 A4
Withington Glos 80 B7
Withington GtMan 99 H3
Withington Here 78 E4
Withington Shrop 88 E4
Withington Staffs 90 C2
Withington Green 99 H5
Withington Marsh 78 E4
Withleigh 57 H4
Withnell 106 B7
Withnell Fold 106 B7
Withybrook Som 69 K7
Withybrook Warks 91 G7
Withycombe 57 J1
Withycombe Raleigh 57 J7
Withyham 63 H3
Withypool 57 G2
Witley 62 C3
Witnesham 85 F3
Witney 71 G1
Wittering 92 D5
Wittersham 64 D5
Witton Angus 131 L3
Witton Norf 95 H5
Witton Worcs 79 H2
Witton Bridge 95 H2
Witton Gilbert 112 C2
Witton Park 112 B3
Witton-le-Wear 112 B3
Wiveliscombe 57 J3
Wivelsfield 63 G4
Wivelsfield Green 63 G5
Wivenhoe 84 E6
Wiveton 94 E1
Wix 85 F6
Wixford 80 B3
Wixhill 88 E3
Wixoe 84 B4
Woburn 82 C5
Woburn Safari Park CenBeds MK17 9QN 9 H5
Woburn Sands 82 C5
Wokefield Park 71 K5
Woking 72 D6
Wokingham 72 B5
Wolborough 55 J3
Wold Newton ERid 109 G2
Wold Newton NELincs 103 F3
Woldingham 73 G6
Wolds Village, Bainton ERid YO25 9EF 109 F4
Wolfelee 120 A3
Wolferlow 79 F2
Wolferton 94 A3
Wolfhampcote 81 G2
Wolfhill 130 G7
Wolfpits 78 B3
Wolf's Castle 66 C3
Wolfsdale 66 C3
Woll 119 K1
Wollaston N'hants 82 C2
Wollaston Shrop 88 C4
Wollaston WMid 90 A7
Wollaton 91 H2
Wollerton 89 F3
Wollescote 90 B7
Wolsingham 112 A3
Wolston 81 F1
Wolsty 110 C1
Wolvercote 71 J1
Wolverhampton 90 B6
Wolverhampton Art Gallery WMid WV1 1DU 14 B1
Wolverley Shrop 88 D2
Wolverley Worcs 79 H1
Wolvers Hill 69 G5
Wolverton Hants 71 J6
Wolverton MK 82 B4
Wolverton Warks 80 D2
Wolverton Wilts 59 G1
Wolverton Common 71 J6
Wolvesnewton 69 H2
Wolvey 91 G7
Wolvey Heath 91 G7
Wolviston 112 E4
Womaston 78 B2
Wombleton 108 C1
Wombourne 90 A6
Wombwell 101 F2
Womenswold 65 H2
Womersley 101 H1
Wonastow 78 D7
Wonersh 72 D7
Wonford 57 H6
Wonson 56 E7
Wonston 61 F1
Wooburn 72 C3
Wooburn Green 72 C3
Wood Bevington 80 B3
Wood Burcote 81 H4
Wood Dalling 94 E3
Wood Eaton 90 A4
Wood End Bed 82 D4
Wood End Bed 82 D2
Wood End Bucks 81 J5
Wood End Herts 83 G6
Wood End Warks 90 E6
Wood End Warks 80 C1
Wood End Warks 90 E7
Wood End WMid 90 B5
Wood Enderby 103 F6
Wood Green GtLon 73 G2
Wood Green Norf 95 G6
Wood Green Animal Shelter, Godmanchester Cambs PE29 2NH 83 F2
Wood Lane 88 D2
Wood Norton 94 E3
Wood Seats 101 F3
Wood Stanway 80 B5
Wood Street 95 H3
Wood Street Village 72 C6
Woodacott 56 B5
Woodale 107 F2
Woodall 101 G4
Woodbastwick 95 H4
Woodbeck 101 K5
Woodborough Notts 91 J1
Woodborough Wilts 70 E6
Woodbridge Devon 57 K6
Woodbridge Dorset 59 G3
Woodbridge Suff 85 G4
Woodbury Devon 57 J7
Woodbury Som 69 J7
Woodbury Salterton 57 J7
Woodchester 70 B1
Woodchurch Kent 64 E4
Woodchurch Mersey 98 B4
Woodcombe 57 H1
Woodcote Oxon 71 K3
Woodcote Tel&W 89 G4
Woodcote Green 79 J1
Woodcott 71 H6
Woodcroft 69 J2
Woodcutts 59 J3
Woodditton 83 K3
Woodeaton 81 G7
Woodend Cumb 110 C7
Woodend N'hants 81 H4
Woodend WSuss 62 B6
Woodend Green 83 J6
Woodfalls 60 C2
Woodfield Oxon 81 G6
Woodfield SAyr 117 H1
Woodfoot 111 H5
Woodford Corn 56 A4
Woodford Devon 55 H5
Woodford Glos 69 K2
Woodford GtLon 73 H2
Woodford GtMan 99 H4
Woodford N'hants 82 C1
Woodford Som 57 J2
Woodford Bridge 73 H2
Woodford Green 73 H2
Woodford Halse 81 G3
Woodgate Devon 57 K4
Woodgate Norf 94 E4
Woodgate WMid 90 B7
Woodgate Worcs 79 J2
Woodgate WSuss 62 C6
Woodgreen 60 C3
Woodhall Invcly 124 B3
Woodhall NYorks 111 L7
Woodhall Hills 107 G6
Woodhall Spa 102 E6
Woodham Bucks 81 H7
Woodham Dur 112 C4
Woodham Surr 72 D5
Woodham Ferrers 74 D2
Woodham Mortimer 74 E1
Woodham Walter 74 E1
Woodhaven 131 K8
Woodhead Aber 135 M7
Woodhead Staffs 90 C1
Woodhey 98 C4
Woodhey Green 98 E7
Woodhill Shrop 89 G7
Woodhill Som 58 C2
Woodhorn 121 H5
Woodhouse Cumb 105 J1
Woodhouse Leics 91 H4
Woodhouse SYorks 101 G4
Woodhouse WYorks 107 H6
Woodhouse WYorks 107 J7
Woodhouse WYorks 107 G7
Woodhouse Down 69 K3
Woodhouse Eaves 91 H4
Woodhouse Green 99 J6
Woodhouses GtMan 99 H2
Woodhouses Staffs 90 D4
Woodhouses Staffs 90 C5
Woodhuish 55 K5
Woodhurst 83 G1
Woodingdean 63 G6
Woodington 60 E2
Woodland Devon 55 H4
Woodland Dur 112 A4
Woodland Kent 65 G3
Woodland Head 57 F6
Woodlands Dorset 60 B4
Woodlands Hants 60 E3
Woodlands NYorks 107 J4
Woodlands Shrop 89 G7
Woodlands Som 57 K1
Woodlands Leisure Park, Dartmouth Devon TQ9 7DQ 55 J5
Woodlands Park 72 B4
Woodlands St. Mary 71 G4
Woodlane 90 D3
Woodleigh 55 H6
Woodlesford 107 J7
Woodley GtMan 99 J3
Woodley W'ham 72 A4
Woodmancote Glos 70 D1
Woodmancote Glos 79 J6
Woodmancote Glos 70 A2
Woodmancote WSuss 63 F5
Woodmancote WSuss 61 J4
Woodmancott 71 J7
Woodmansey 109 G6
Woodmansterne 73 F6
Woodmanton 57 J7
Woodmill 90 D3
Woodminton 60 B2
Woodmoor 88 B5
Woodnesborough 65 J2
Woodnewton 92 D6
Woodperry 81 G7
Woodplumpton 105 J6
Woodrising 94 D5
Woodrow 59 G3
Wood's Corner 63 K5
Woods Eaves 78 B4
Wood's Green 63 K3
Woodseaves Shrop 89 F2
Woodseaves Staffs 89 G3
Woodsend 71 F4
Woodsetts 101 H4
Woodsford 59 G5
Woodside BrackF 72 C4
Woodside CenBeds 82 D7
Woodside Cumb 110 B3
Woodside D&G 119 F6
Woodside GtLon 73 G5
Woodside Hants 60 E5
Woodside Herts 73 F1
Woodside NAyr 124 B5
Woodside P&K 130 G7
Woodside Shrop 88 C7
Woodside WMid 90 B7
Woodside Animal Farm & Leisure Park CenBeds LU1 4DG 82 D7
Woodside Green 64 E2
Woodstock Oxon 81 F7
Woodstock Pembs 66 D3
Woodthorpe Derbys 101 G5
Woodthorpe Leics 91 H4
Woodthorpe Lincs 103 H4
Woodthorpe SYorks 101 F4
Woodthorpe York 108 B5
Woodton 95 G6
Woodtown 56 C3
Woodvale 98 C1
Woodville 91 F4
Woodwall Green 89 G2
Woodwalton 93 F7
Woodwick 139 C5
Woodworth Green 98 E7
Woodyates 60 B3
Woofferton 78 E2
Wookey 69 J7
Wookey Hole 69 J7
Wookey Hole Caves & Papermill Som BA5 1BB 69 J7
Wool 59 H6
Woolacombe 56 C1
Woolage Green 65 H3
Woolage Village 65 H3
Woolaston 69 J2
Woolaston Slade 69 J1
Woolavington 69 G7
Woolbeding 62 B4
Woolcotts 57 H2
Wooldale 100 D2
Wooler 120 E1
Woolfardisworthy Devon 57 G5
Woolfardisworthy Devon 56 B3
Woolfold 99 G1
Woolfords Cottages 125 J5
Woolgarston 59 J6
Woolgreaves 101 F1
Woolhampton 71 J5
Woolhope 79 F5
Woolland 59 G4
Woollard 69 K5
Woollaton 56 C4
Woollensbrook 73 G1
Woolley B&NESom 70 A5
Woolley Cambs 82 E1
Woolley Corn 56 A4
Woolley Derbys 101 F6
Woolley WYorks 101 F1
Woolley Green W&M 72 B4
Woolley Green Wilts 70 B5
Woolmer Green 83 F7
Woolmere Green 79 J2
Woolmersdon 58 B1
Woolpit 84 D2
Woolpit Green 84 D2
Woolscott 81 F2
Woolsgrove 57 F5
Woolstaston 88 D6
Woolsthorpe 92 B2
Woolsthorpe by Colsterworth 92 C3
Woolston Devon 55 H6
Woolston Shrop 88 C3
Woolston Shrop 88 D7
Woolston Soton 61 F3
Woolston Warr 99 F4
Woolston Green 55 H4
Woolstone Glos 79 J5
Woolstone MK 82 B5
Woolstone Oxon 71 F3
Woolton 98 D4
Woolton Hill 71 H5
Woolverstone 85 F5
Woolverton 70 A6
Woolwich 73 H4
Woonton 78 C3
Wooperton 121 F2
Woore 89 G1
Wootten Green 85 G1
Wootton Bed 82 D4
Wootton Hants 60 D5
Wootton IoW 61 G5
Wootton Kent 65 H3
Wootton N'hants 81 J3
Wootton NLincs 102 D1
Wootton Oxon 81 F7
Wootton Oxon 71 H1
Wootton Shrop 78 D1
Wootton Shrop 88 C3
Wootton Staffs 90 A3
Wootton Staffs 90 D1
Wootton Bassett 70 D3
Wootton Bridge 61 G5
Wootton Common 61 G5
Wootton Courtenay 57 H1
Wootton Fitzpaine 58 C5
Wootton Green 82 D4
Wootton Rivers 70 E5
Wootton St. Lawrence 71 J6
Wootton Wawen 80 C2
Worcester 79 H3
Worcester Cathedral Worcs WR1 2LH 49 Worcester
Worcester Park 73 F5
Worcester Woods Country Park Worcs WR5 2LG 79 H3
Wordsley 90 A7
Wordwell 84 C1
Worfield 89 G6
Worgret 59 J6
Workhouse End 82 E3
Workington 110 B4
Worksop 101 H5
Worlaby Lincs 103 G5
Worlaby NLincs 102 D1
World Museum Liverpool Mersey L3 8EN 43 D3
World of Beatrix Potter Attraction Cumb LA23 3BX 110 F7
World of James Herriot, Thirsk NYorks YO7 1PL 107 K1
World's End Bucks 72 B1
Worlds End Hants 61 H3
World's End WBerks 71 H4
Worlds End WMid 90 D7
Worle 69 G5
Worleston 99 F7
Worlingham 95 J7
Worlington 83 K1
Worlingworth 85 G2
Wormald Green 107 J3
Wormbridge 78 D5
Wormegay 94 A4
Wormelow Tump 78 D5
Wormhill 100 D5
Wormingford 84 D5
Worminghall 71 K1
Wormington 80 B5
Worminster 69 J7
Wormit 131 J8
Wormleighton 81 F3
Wormley Herts 73 G1
Wormley Surr 62 C3
Wormley West End 73 G1
Wormshill 64 D2
Wormsley 78 D4
Worplesdon 72 C6
Worrall 101 F3
Worsbrough 101 F2
Worsley 99 G2
Worstead 95 H3
Worsted Lodge 83 J3
Worsthorne 106 D6
Worston 106 C5
Worswell 55 F6
Worth Kent 65 J2
Worth WSuss 63 F3
Worth Matravers 59 J7
Wortham 84 E1
Worthen 88 C5
Worthenbury 88 D1
Worthing Norf 94 D4
Worthing WSuss 62 E6
Worthington 91 G3
Wortley Glos 70 A2
Wortley SYorks 101 F3
Wortley WYorks 107 H6
Worton NYorks 106 E1
Worton Wilts 70 C6
Wortwell 95 G7
Wothersome 107 K5
Wotherton 88 B5
Wotter 55 F4
Wotton 72 E7
Wotton Underwood 81 H7
Wotton-under-Edge 70 A2
Woughton on the Green 82 B5
Wouldham 74 D5
W.R. Outhwaite & Son Ropemakers NYorks DL8 3NT 106 D1
Wrabness 85 F5
Wrafton 56 C2
Wragby 102 E5
Wragholme 103 G3
Wramplingham 95 F5
Wrangaton 55 G5
Wrangle 103 H7
Wrangle Lowgate 103 H7
Wrangway 57 K4
Wrantage 58 C2
Wrawby 102 D2
Wraxall NSom 69 H4
Wraxall Som 59 F1
Wray 106 B3
Wray Castle 110 E6
Wrays 73 F7
Wraysbury 72 D4
Wrayton 106 B2
Wrea Green 105 G6
Wreay Cumb 110 F4
Wreay Cumb 110 F2
Wrecclesham 72 B7
Wrekenton 112 C1
Wrelton 108 D1
Wrenbury 88 E1
Wrench Green 109 F1
Wreningham 95 F6
Wrentham 95 J7
Wrenthorpe 107 J7
Wrentnall 88 D5
Wressle ERid 108 D6
Wressle NLincs 102 C2
Wrestlingworth 83 F4
Wretham 94 D6
Wretton 94 A5
Wrexham (Wrecsam) 88 C1
Wrexham Arts Centre Wrex LL11 1AU 98 C7
Wrexham Industrial Estate 88 C1
Wribbenhall 79 G1
Wrightington Bar 98 E1
Wrightpark 124 E1
Wright's Green 83 J7
Wrinehill 89 G1
Wrington 69 H5
Writhlington 69 K6
Writtle 74 C1
Wrockwardine 89 F4
Wroot 101 K2
Wrose 107 G6
Wrotham 73 K6
Wrotham Heath 73 K6
Wrotham Hill Park 74 C5
Wrotesley 90 A5
Wroughton 70 E3
Wroxall IoW 61 G7
Wroxall Warks 80 D1
Wroxeter 88 E5
Wroxham 95 H4
Wroxham Barns Norf NR12 8QU 95 H3
Wroxton 81 F4
Wstrws 67 G1
Wyaston 90 D1
Wyberton 93 G1
Wyboston 82 E3
Wybunbury 89 F1
Wych Cross 63 H3
Wychbold 79 J2
Wychnor 90 D4
Wychnor Bridges 90 D4
Wyck 61 J1
Wyck Rissington 80 C6
Wycliffe 112 B5
Wycoller 106 E6
Wycoller Country Park Lancs BB8 8SY 106 E6
Wycomb 92 A3
Wycombe Marsh 72 B2
Wyddial 83 G5
Wye 65 F3
Wyesham 78 E7
Wyfordby 92 A4
Wyke Devon 57 G6
Wyke Dorset 59 G2
Wyke Shrop 89 F5
Wyke Surr 72 C6
Wyke WYorks 107 G7
Wyke Champflower 59 F1
Wyke Regis 59 F7
Wykeham NYorks 109 F1
Wykeham NYorks 108 E2
Wyken Shrop 89 G6
Wyken WMid 91 F7
Wykey 88 C3
Wylam 121 G7
Wylde Green 90 D6
Wyllie 68 E2
Wylye 60 B1
Wymering 61 H4
Wymeswold 91 J3
Wymington 82 C2
Wymondham Leics 92 B4
Wymondham Norf 95 F5
Wyndham 68 C2
Wynford Eagle 58 E5
Wynnstay Park 88 C1
Wynyard 112 E4
Wynyard Woodland Park Stock TS21 3JG 112 D4
Wyre Forest Worcs DY14 9XQ 79 G1
Wyre Piddle 79 J4
Wyresdale Tower 106 B4
Wysall 91 J3
Wyson 78 E2
Wythall 80 B1
Wytham 71 H1
Wythburn 110 E5
Wythenshawe 99 H4
Wyton Cambs 83 F1
Wyton ERid 109 H6
Wyverstone 84 E2
Wyverstone Street 84 E2
Wyville 92 B3

X

Xscape Castleford WYorks WF10 4DA 107 K7

Y

Y Bryn 87 H3
Y Fan 87 J7
Y Felinheli 96 D6
Y Ffôr 86 C2
Y Fron (Upper Llandwrog) 96 D7
Yaddlethorpe 102 B2
Yafford 61 F6
Yafforth 112 D7
Yalberton 55 J5
Yalding 73 K7
Yanley 69 J5
Yanwath 111 G4
Yanworth 80 B7
Yapham 108 D4
Yapton 62 C6
Yarburgh 103 G3
Yarcombe 58 B4
Yardley 90 D7
Yardley Gobion 81 J4
Yardley Hastings 82 B3
Yardro 78 B3
Yarford 58 B2
Yarkhill 79 F4
Yarlet 90 B3
Yarley 69 J7
Yarlington 59 F2
Yarm 112 E5
Yarmouth 60 E6
Yarnacott 56 E2
Yarnbrook 70 B6
Yarnfield 90 A2
Yarnscombe 56 D3
Yarnton 81 F7
Yarpole 78 D2
Yarrow ScBord 119 J1
Yarrow Som 69 G7
Yarrow Feus 119 J1
Yarrowford 119 K1
Yarsop 78 D4
Yarwell 92 D6
Yate 70 A3
Yatehouse Green 99 G6
Yateley 72 B5
Yatesbury 70 D4
Yattendon 71 J4
Yatton Here 78 D2
Yatton NSom 69 H5
Yatton Keynell 70 B4
Yaverland 61 H6
Yawl 58 C5
Yaxham 94 E4
Yaxley Cambs 92 E6
Yaxley Suff 85 F1
Yazor 78 D4
Ye Olde Pork Pie Shoppe, Melton Mowbray Leics LE13 1NW 92 A4
Yeabridge 58 D3
Yeading 72 E3
Yeadon 107 H5
Yealand Conyers 105 J2
Yealand Redmayne 105 J2
Yealand Storrs 105 J2
Yealmbridge 55 F5
Yealmpton 55 F5
Yearby 113 G4
Yearsley 108 B2
Yeaton 88 D4
Yeaveley 90 D1
Yeavering 127 H7
Yedingham 108 E2
Yelford 71 G1
Yell 139 N4
Yelland Devon 56 C2
Yelland Devon 56 D6
Yelling 83 F2
Yellowcraig ELoth EH39 5DS 126 D2
Yelvertoft 81 G1
Yelverton Devon 55 F4
Yelverton Norf 95 G5
Yenston 59 G2
Yeo Mill 57 G3
Yeo Vale 56 C3
Yeoford 57 F6
Yeolmbridge 56 B7
Yeomadon 56 B5
Yeovil 58 E3
Yeovil Country Park Som BA20 1QZ 58 E3
Yeovil Marsh 58 E3
Yeovilton 58 E2
Yerbeston 66 D5
Yesnaby 139 B6
Yesterday's World, Battle ESuss TN33 0AQ 64 C6
Yetholm Mains 120 D1
Yetlington 121 F2
Yetminster 58 E3
Yettington 57 J7
Yetts o'Muckhart 130 F10
Yew Green 80 D2
Yielden 82 D2
Yieldshields 125 G5
Ynys 86 E2
Ynys Tachwedd 87 F6
Ynysboeth 68 D2
Ynysddu 68 E2
Ynyshir 68 D2
Ynyslas 87 F6
Ynysmaerdy 68 D3
Ynysmeudwy 68 A1
Ynystawe 67 K5
Ynyswen 68 C1
Ynysybwl 68 D2
Yockenthwaite 106 E2
Yockleton 88 C4
Yokefleet 108 E7
Yoker 124 D4
York 108 C4
York Castle Museum YO1 9SA 49 York
York Dungeon YO1 9RD 49 York
York Minster YO1 7HH 49 York
Yorkletts 75 G5
Yorkley 69 K1
Yorkshire Museum YO1 7FR 49 York
Yorkshire Sculpture Park WYorks WF4 4LG 100 E1
Yorton 88 E3
Yorton Heath 88 E3
Youldon 56 B5
Youldonmoor Cross 56 B5
Youlgreave 100 E6
Youlthorpe 108 D4
Youlton 107 K3
Young's End 84 B7
Yoxall 90 D4
Yoxford 85 H2
Ysbyty Cynfyn 77 G1
Ysbyty Ifan 87 H1
Ysbyty Ystwyth 77 G1
Ysceifiog 97 K5
Ysgubor-y-coed 87 F6
Ystalyfera 68 A1
Ystrad 68 C2
Ystrad Aeron 76 E3
Ystrad Meurig 77 G2
Ystrad Mynach 68 E2
Ystradfellte 77 J7
Ystradffin 77 G4
Ystradgynlais 77 G7
Ystradowen Carmar 77 G7
Ystradowen VGlam 68 D4
Ystumtuen 77 G1
Ythanwells 135 L7
Ythsie 135 N7

Z

Zeal Monachorum 57 F5
Zeals 59 G1
Zelah 53 F3
Zennor 52 B5
Zouch 91 H3

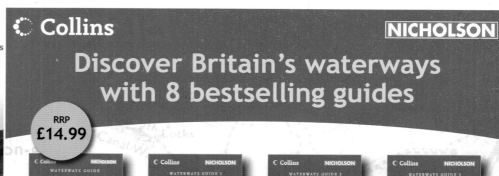

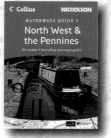

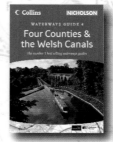
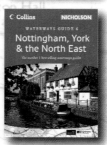
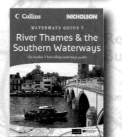

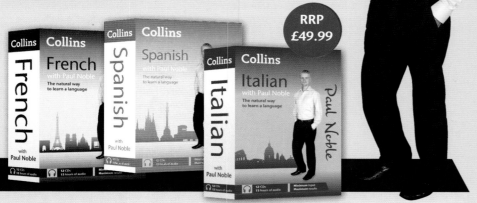

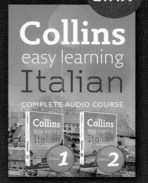
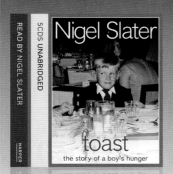

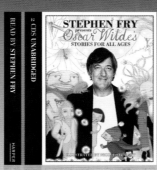
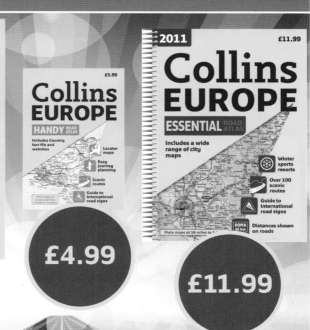